Tom Masters

St Petersburg

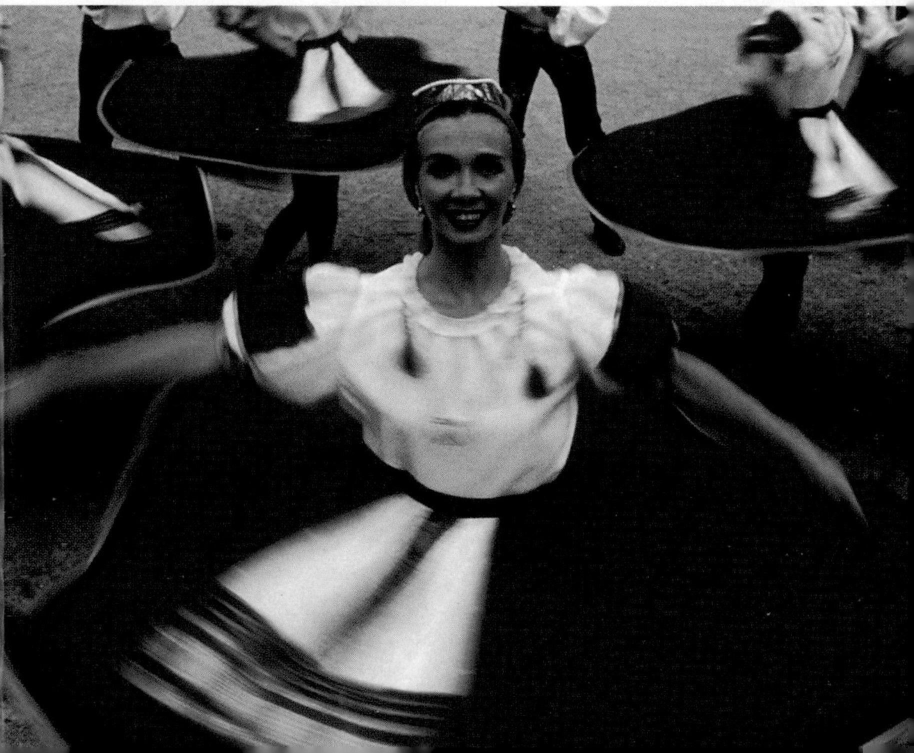

The Top Five

1 Sumptuous Art

Explore the Hermitage's unrivalled collection (p67)

2 Museum of Anthropology and Ethnography (Kunstkamera)

Don't miss this ghoulish place (p109)

3 Cruising the Canals

Take a pleasure ride or see the city by water bus (p206)

4 Church on Spilled Blood

Marvel at this spectacular church (p91)

5 Peter and Paul Fortress

Soak in the city's history (p114)

4

Contents

Published by Lonely Planet Publications Pty Ltd
ABN 36 005 607 983

Australia Head Office, Locked Bag 1, Footscray, Victoria 3011, ☎ 03 8379 8000, fax 03 8379 8111, talk2us@lonelyplanet.com.au

USA 150 Linden St, Oakland, CA 94607, ☎ 510 893 8555, toll free 800 275 8555, fax 510 893 8572, info@lonelyplanet.com

UK 72–82 Rosebery Ave, Clerkenwell, London, EC1R 4RW, ☎ 020 7841 9000, fax 020 7841 9001, go@lonelyplanet.co.uk

© Lonely Planet 2005
Photographs © Jonathan Smith and as listed (p226), 2005
All rights reserved. No part of this publication may be copied, stored in a retrieval system, or transmitted in any form by any means, electronic, mechanical, recording or otherwise, except brief extracts for the purpose of review, and no part of this publication may be sold or hired, without the written permission of the publisher.

Printed by SNP Security Printing Pte Ltd, Singapore

Lonely Planet and the Lonely Planet logo are trademarks of Lonely Planet and are registered in the US Patent and Trademark Office and in other countries.

Lonely Planet does not allow its name or logo to be appropriated by commercial establishments, such as retailers, restaurants or hotels. Please let us know of any misuses: www.lonelyplanet.com/ip.

Although the authors and Lonely Planet have taken all reasonable care in preparing this book, we make no warranty about the accuracy or completeness of its content and, to the maximum extent permitted, disclaim all liability arising from its use.

The Author

TOM MASTERS

Tom first came to St Petersburg as a student in 1996 after three months spent in the wilds of provincial Russia learning the intricacies of the Russian language. Despite initially preferring Moscow, St Petersburg slowly weaved its Gogolian magic and after completing his degree at the University of London's School of Slavonic and East European Studies, Tom moved to St Petersburg to work at the *St Petersburg Times* in 2000. During this time his assignments included travelling around the Baltic Sea with Greenpeace, finding a homeless man to write a newspaper column and visiting as many of the city's bars and clubs as possible, all selflessly in the name of research. While now living back in London, where he works as a travel writer and journalist, he goes back for work and pleasure as much as he can.

PHOTOGRAPHER

Jonathan Smith

Raised in the Scottish Highlands, Jon graduated from St Andrews University in 1994 with an MA in German. Unsure of what to do with his life, he took a flight to Vilnius and spent the next four years travelling around the former USSR. Having tried everything from language teaching to translating Lithuanian cookery books into English, Jon resolved to seek his fortune as a freelance travel photographer. Since then Jon's byline has appeared in over 50 Lonely Planet titles – recent commissions have included *Edinburgh, Stockholm, Paris* and *Best of Dublin*. This is Jon's fourth assignment in St Petersburg, a city which he says has always felt like home. But with more interesting weather.

Lonely Planet books provide independent advice. Lonely Planet does not accept advertising in guidebooks, nor do we accept payment in exchange for listing or endorsing any place or business. Lonely Planet writers do not accept discounts or payments in exchange for positive coverage of any sort.

Introducing St Petersburg

Peter the Great's incredible contribution to world heritage glimmers enticingly on the Neva Delta, its 44 islands and 300 bridges – one for every year of its existence – resplendent with sublime architectural fusion. Russia's former imperial capital has retained its original splendour despite the 20th century's cruelty and today visitors flock to discover the simple truth: St Petersburg is one of the most beautiful cities on earth.

In fact, you could say that if beauty is a commodity, then St Petersburg must be one of the wealthiest cities on the planet. If you ever had any doubts about how good a mosquito-infested swamp on the Baltic could look after three centuries of relentless home improvement, they will be assuaged once you spend a few days in this magical place. From overwhelming architectural ensembles (try standing on the Troitsky Bridge looking downriver to the Winter Palace without your jaw dropping) to magnificent cultural life (yes, in just 300 years St Petersburg has given the world Shostakovich, Nabokov, Mendeleev, Malevich, Kandinsky, Prokofiev, Rachmaninoff, Brodsky, Mandelshtam, Akhmatova, Ustinov and Stravinsky to name but a few), St Petersburg's stock in trade is awing anyone lucky enough to visit.

Whether watching world-class ballet at the Mariinsky Theatre, comparing Picasso and Poussin in the vast Hermitage Museum or just absorbing the enormous array of baroque, neoclassical, Art Nouveau and constructivist buildings, themselves a living lesson in history, be warned that you may come away aesthetically drunk and your home town may look a little dull by comparison.

But it's not all about art and beauty. Did someone say hedonism? St Petersburg could teach most people a few things about

Lowdown

Population 4.7 million

Time zone GMT/UTC + 3 hours

Average comfortable hotel room Around €100

Metro ticket R8 (about €0.20)

Take-away blin (pancake) R50 (about €1.50)

Cup of coffee R40 (about €1.10)

Marshrutka ride R14 (about €0.40)

Remember In summer months the bridges rise at night, so don't get trapped on the wrong side of the river or you'll be waiting until dawn to get home

Don't say 'I like St Petersburg but Moscow is nicer' (you'd be mad anyway)

Do say 'Davay yesho' ('let's have another')

Essential St Petersburg

- **The Hermitage** (p67)
- **Church on Spilled Blood** (p90)
- **Cruising the canals by water taxi** (p206)
- **Nevsky Prospekt** (p98)
- **Alexander Nevsky Monastery** (p102)

it. With its carefree, sultry White Nights in midsummer and its Prozac-necessitating winters when the sun rises at 10am and sets in the mid-afternoon, it's no surprise that partying is the activity of choice at both times of year and to a healthy degree in between as well. After all, where else can you buy a pint of draught lager while doing grocery shopping and find a museum devoted to the joys of vodka?

But St Petersburg has its unsung charms as well. For one, the people are a rich lesson in what-you-see-may-not-be-what-you-get: the sour-faced ticket-selling babushka who breaks out in a huge smile when you stumble over a few words of Russian, or the gruff taxi driver who after a five-minute conversation insists on giving you a glass of his home-made firewater and drinking to world peace, are both typical characters you may well meet.

Another delight that few expect from these northern latitudes is the warmth and light of the summer months. From May to September, the city is wonderful – usually balmy and sunny but rarely too hot. Visiting in midwinter is another treat, when bright skies, snow and ice make for a magically timeless setting. Eating out has never been so good either – gone are the days of Soviet service and mass stodge-fest communal dining served with a sneer. Today St Petersburg's fashionable residents move nonchalantly between sushi and tapas bars, discuss the merits of Indonesian over Lebanese cuisine and enjoy more than a few world-class dining options.

St Petersburg's 300th birthday in 2003 brought a new confidence (not to mention vast investment) to a city that has been relentlessly downgraded throughout the course of the 20th century. Nicholas II changed the city's name to Petrograd in 1914, Lenin moved the capital to Moscow in 1918, Stalin renamed the city Leningrad and concentrated his terror here, and finally Hitler arrived, determined to wipe the city out. Yet St Petersburg is a fighter and is making a convincing comeback today. With local-boy-done-good Vladimir Putin now tsar of the new Russia and spending as much time in the 'northern capital' as possible, things have never looked more positive.

Indeed, it's hard to imagine that the city has seen so much blood and fear – its brightly painted buildings seem to shout out optimism even if they are crumbling after centuries of neglect. This is one of St Petersburg's most enduring features and extends to its citizens too – they are survivors, 300 years and counting on marshy, inhospitable land on the Gulf of Finland; and nothing, be it Nazism, Stalinism, capitalism or those damn mosquitoes, is going to budge them now.

TOM'S TOP ST PETERSBURG DAY

Any day in St Petersburg usually begins with a slight hangover, best dealt with by means of a vodka shot at my favourite breakfast spot a short distance from St Isaac's Sq (if this sounds dangerously alcoholic to you, you've obviously never been to Russia before). In the company of a few friends, I take this useful opportunity to forensically reconstruct the events of the night before over strong coffee and bliny with jam.

Emerging refreshed into the sunshine I head off down the canal, wandering from the beaten path through gorgeously crumbling streets of brightly painted mansions. No matter how many times I come here, there always seem to be new streets to explore and new, strange and dilapidated buildings to marvel at. After lunch outside in the sun, I head for a museum, perhaps one of the palaces taken over by the Russian Museum to see temporary exhibits from the huge collections that have remained under wraps for years, or maybe just to see some old favourites (and *still* discover an entire wing I've never been in) in the Hermitage. A late afternoon trip to the *banya* will sort me out for the evening, which is spent wandering the banks of the gloriously wide Neva with some more friends, drinking cold Baltika in the midsummer warmth, losing track of time and taking a midnight boat ride in the grey light that hangs about all night.

City Life

City Life

ST PETERSBURG TODAY

The northern capital is riding high. As famous today for producing Russia's current president as it used to be for producing the revolution that completely changed world history, the recently 300-year-old city is enjoying a boom that it hasn't seen since Moscow snatched back the coveted title of capital in 1918.

The palaces may still be crumbling and the once-brightly painted buildings still largely peeling, flaking and generally disintegrating, but St Petersburg, once again confident of its place in world history and European culture, knows that it's going to be saved. Having sponsors in very high places (and in Russia you can't get much higher up than the Kremlin) means that the city stands to receive vast amounts of new investment and St Petersburg has even been developing a slight swagger as a result.

Not only did it enjoy the world's attention in May 2003 for its enormous tricentennial celebrations, but the restoration and refurbishment of many of the city's major attractions has meant that since then St Petersburg's tourist industry has boomed. The slew of hotels, hostels and guesthouses that opened for 2003 are having no problems finding guests to fill their beds well after the event, and the buzzing restaurants, bars and clubs are similarly full.

In 2004 plans were announced to sell off many of the crumbling 18th- and 19th-century palaces to private investors who, in exchange for ownership, would then be obliged to oversee their restoration. This is contentious as inevitably many properties will go to the city's new rich, whose fortunes were often acquired dubiously, but most reluctantly agree that this is perhaps the only way the essential maintenance and restoration of these great

Marshrutka on Nevsky Prospekt

creations can be ensured: the city budget is not large enough for the local authorities to undertake all the reconstruction work themselves.

That said, the government, both federal and local, has itself unveiled some remarkable successes in landmark restoration in the past few years, and the pace of change from imperious ruin to imperial splendour is incredible. Massive ongoing schemes such as the restoration of the city's oldest shopping arcade, Gostiny Dvor, and Rastrelli's magnificent Smolny Cathedral look set to impress when they are eventually completed.

The Mariinsky Theatre, the centre of St Petersburg's cultural life, has also enjoyed a good few years. Along with the continued critical acclaim of Valery Gergiev, the man who has put the former Kirov Theatre on the map and created a world-famous brand, the Mariinsky has finalised plans for the building of an incredibly innovative second theatre behind its current premises. This is inevitably the subject of some controversy in a city whose centre even the Soviets didn't overburden with modern architecture. There are two schools of thought on the matter – those that revel in the prestige of a state-of-the-art ballet and opera theatre in the city centre, believing that it will become something equivalent to the Sydney Opera House or the various Guggenheim Museums around the world; and those who believe it will be a costly disaster, contributing nothing and detracting enormously from the present classical ensemble of the square. Construction is under way, with the new theatre scheduled to open in 2008.

Political currents, always quick to change in St Petersburg, have yet again been reversed with former St Petersburg deputy mayor Vladimir Putin now president of Russia and keen to settle scores in his home town. In 2003, he managed to lure city governor and political enemy Vladimir Yakovlev out of his office at the Smolny and into Federal Government, and – lo and behold! – saw his political ally Valentina Matvienko quickly take over the empty post. Roundly seen as Kremlin stooge, Matvienko was duly elected with a strong majority of the vote. Her popularity (when in evidence) is usually due to her good connections, rather than any real popular love for this most archetypal, cold and aloof Soviet technocrat. Most locals will have nothing positive to say about politics here and it's hard not to see their point; Matvienko's victory was seriously marred by widespread accusations of unfair campaigning methods and intimidation.

However, the economic boom looks set to continue. Matvienko has brought with her Kremlin patronage (read: money) and St Petersburg, as a Kremlin-friendly city, looks set to benefit from ever greater federal spending on its infrastructure, transport and heritage.

The city still has a long way to go to compensate for the neglect of the 20th century, the mess in which the Soviets left the local economy and the environmental problems it has itself created with its post-war heavy industry, but things have not looked this good for St Petersburg for an entire century.

Hot Conversation Topics

- 'What's she done now?' The perceived sycophantic acts of Putinophile local governor Valentina Matvienko do not impress the fiercely independent city residents, who feel that their governor was chosen for them in Moscow (even though she did get over 60% of the vote in St Petersburg).
- 'Are they really going to build that second Mariinsky?' People have seen the elaborate plans for the golden glass envelope design for the new Mariinsky Theatre, but few can actually believe that such a modern and original design will be built in this most classical of European cities.
- 'Will they ever open the Admiralteyskaya metro station?' The whole of St Petersburg has been waiting for years for a metro station to open by the Admiralty and relieve them of walking everywhere from Nevsky pr. Apparently the station is complete, but the escalators and exit still need to be built and money shortages are perennial.
- 'Where is the new place for the local *tusovka* (in crowd) to hang out?' Relentlessly fashionable, St Petersburg's golden youth are on a permanent quest to find the newest and most glamorous nightspots in town.
- 'What network are you on?' Petersburgers are charged even to receive calls from mobile phones that aren't on their own network, making this one of the most common refrains in town.

CITY CALENDAR

Petersburgers, even more than their famously festive fellow countrymen, love a good knees-up. Whether it be through the carnival atmosphere of those endless summer nights or merrymaking during the freezing, dark winter days, rarely more than a week or two passes without special events taking place.

Most celebrated are the legendary 'white nights' during the last 10 days of June, when due to the city's northern latitude the sun never properly sets. Many Petersburgers stay out all night celebrating White Nights (particularly on weekends), with festivities focussed around the Neva Embankment. The other major events tend to reflect the city's main passions: music and dance, with world-class festivals such as the Mariinsky's Stars of the White Nights Festival.

Less tourist-oriented are the Christmas Musical Meetings in Northern Palmyra, a classical music festival held before Christmas. More recently, the Early Music Festival has revived a period in Russia's musical heritage to international acclaim.

Religion in Russia is of course no longer taboo as it was under the Soviets, and there are many Orthodox celebrations as well as Protestant, Catholic, Muslim, Jewish and Buddhist festivals throughout the year.

See the Directory (p213) for a list of public holidays.

Top Five St Petersburg Holidays & Events

- **White Nights** Join the crowds, wander the spooky midnight riverbank and lose all sense of time.
- **Victory Day** Excitement throughout the city, fireworks over the Neva and a great night out for all.
- **Sergei Kuryokhin International Festival** The best contemporary music festival in the city draws a very hip crowd of locals and visitors from abroad.
- **Orthodox Easter** Visit a church for midnight mass on Easter eve for an unforgettable atmosphere of excitement and good will.
- **Arts Square Festival** One of St Petersburg's best classical music and opera events draws the crowds to the Philharmonic.

JANUARY

NEW YEAR'S DAY

Like most other places, 1 January is a day for nursing hangovers from the previous night's excesses. The Soviet classic film *Ironiya Sudby* (The Irony of Fate) plays on TV and Russians over 30 reminisce about the 'good old days'.

RUSSIAN ORTHODOX CHRISTMAS (ROZHDESTVO)

Traditional Russian Christmas is on 7 January. Beginning with midnight church services, it is usually celebrated at home in family groups with a large meal.

FEBRUARY

MARIINSKY BALLET FESTIVAL

www.mariinsky.ru

The city's principal dance theatre hosts a week-long international festival, usually in mid- to late February, where the talents of the cream of Russian ballet dancers and many international stars are showcased.

DEFENDERS OF THE MOTHERLAND DAY

A new holiday since 1996 to celebrate the anniversary of the founding of the Red Army on 23 February. Wreaths are laid at war memorials throughout the city. Commonly referred to as 'Men's Day'.

GOODBYE RUSSIAN WINTER

Often feeling a bit premature as there's still snow and ice on the ground, these feel-good festivities, held late February to early March, take place outside of the city, with troika rides and folk shows as a curtain-raiser for spring.

MASLENITSA

Russia's only surviving pagan festival is *maslenitsa,* similar in origins to Italian *carnevale*, held in late February or early March. Locals gorge themselves on bliny (pancakes), caviar and cakes in the week before Lent *(Velikaya Posta)*. The festival culminates in Forgiveness Day, in which people traditionally ask their family and friends for forgiveness for wrongdoings in the past year.

MARCH

MONOCLE INTERNATIONAL THEATRE FESTIVAL OF ONE-MAN SHOWS

This festival usually runs throughout March and is hosted by the Baltiisky Dom Theatre on the Petrograd Side. It aims to bring together the very best one-man shows from northern and Eastern Europe.

INTERNATIONAL FESTIVAL OF JAZZ DANCE & MUSIC

Since 1999, this festival in early March has been aimed at developing contemporary jazz dance in St Petersburg. Choreographers from Europe and the US are often invited to town to give master classes at the Canon Dance School, and beginners are made to feel welcome.

INTERNATIONAL WOMEN'S DAY

St Petersburg shuts down and all women walk around with flowers on 8 March. Men will be thought of as most ungentlemanly if they do not give chocolates and a bouquet to at least one lady. This holiday gives rise to the popular Russian joke that one day a year is set aside for women, while the other 364 are for men.

APRIL & MAY

SERGEI KURYOKHIN INTERNATIONAL FESTIVAL (SKIF)

www.kuryokhin.com

A three-day avant-garde festival in late April bringing together a stunning array of international figures of alternative modern music and performance. Named after the eclectic Russian musician Sergei Kuryokhin, a key part of the Leningrad rock and jazz underground of the 1970s who died in 1996.

INTERNATIONAL LABOUR DAY/ SPRING FESTIVAL

Once a sort of ersatz communist Christmas, Labour Day (Den Truda) was under the Soviets marked by vast parades on Palace Sq and an electric party atmosphere. More subdued now, 1–2 May is still a time for (ever smaller) communist demonstrations and merrymaking.

EASTER (PASKHA)

2006: 23 April; 2007: 8 April; 2008: 27 April; 2009: 19 April

The main festival of the Orthodox Church year, the dates of Russian Easter differ from those of Catholic and Protestant Easter, although they coincide every now and again. Banners declaring 'Khristos Vosskres' (Christ has risen) are hung outside churches and all churches swarm with worshippers at midnight mass on Easter eve. It's a fascinating cultural experience for anyone lucky enough to be visiting at the time.

VICTORY (1945) DAY

The national and international importance of this 9 May celebration is felt even more acutely in St Petersburg, where it's also a day of celebration for the breaking of the Nazi blockade. Crowds assemble at Piskaryovskoe Cemetery in the north of the city and there's also a victory parade on Nevsky pr, culminating in crowd-pleasing soldiers marching on Palace Sq and fireworks over the Neva in the evening.

CITY DAY

Mass celebrations and merrymaking are held throughout the city centre on 27 May. Brass bands, folk dancing and mass drunkenness are the salient features of this perennial favourite, which marks the day when Peter the Great made a cross on Zayachy Island and announced 'Here will be a city'.

JUNE

RUSSIAN INDEPENDENCE DAY

Independence from what, you may well ask... despite creating the Soviet Union, the Russians still make a point of celebrating its demise and the return of their statehood. Held 12 June.

KLEZFEST

A music festival celebrating Klezmer, or Eastern European Jewish folk music. The mid-June festival has a busy programme of concerts, walking tours about Jewish history and lectures.

BEER FESTIVAL

This has fast become one of the city's best-attended festivals, for unsurprising reasons. Held annually in mid-June in the Peter and Paul Fortress, this rather messy but much fun summer excuse for public inebriation is well worth a visit.

MESSAGE TO MAN

www.message-to-man.spb.ru

A well-respected festival of short, animated and documentary films, *Poslaniye k Cheloveku* is held annually in mid-June in the neighbouring Dom Kino and Rodina cinemas.

FESTIVAL OF FESTIVALS

www.filmfest.ru

St Petersburg's annual international film festival is held during the White Nights in late June and is a non-competitive showcase of the best Russian and world cinema.

ST PETERSBURG WHITE NIGHTS
General merrymaking and staying out late (or early, depending on how you look at it) during the last 10 days of June – when the sun never properly sets. Crowds gather on the Neva Embankment and the Strelka, and drink through the night watching the raising of the bridges.

STARS OF THE WHITE NIGHTS FESTIVAL
www.mariinsky.ru

Held at the Mariinsky, the Conservatoire and the Hermitage Theatre, this festival from late May until July has become a huge draw and now lasts far longer than the White Nights after which it is named. Premieres, international stars attend and special tributes to St Petersburg's operatic and balletic past are held, culminating in a fabulous ball at Tsarskoe Selo to draw the event to a close.

AUGUST
SAILING WEEK
Hundreds of sportsmen and yachts from the northern capital and some other cities take part in a regatta founded by the sailing union of the city on the Neva in 1898. Competitors compete on a 150km race from Vyborg to St Petersburg in late August.

SEPTEMBER & OCTOBER
EARLY MUSIC FESTIVAL
www.earlymusic.ru

Ground-breaking musical festival that seeks to bring back to the stage forgotten masterpieces from the age of Catherine the Great, including operas and performances from the Catherine the Great opera. The festival is held from mid-September until early October.

NOVEMBER
DAY OF RECONCILIATION & ACCORD
The former Great October Socialist Revolution Anniversary on 7 November is a good time to see demonstrations and parades of communist old-timers, although it's officially a day for reflection upon and forgiveness for the atrocities of communism!

DECEMBER
CHRISTMAS MUSICAL MEETINGS IN NORTHERN PALMYRA
A classical music festival that runs for three weeks leading up to Russian Orthodox Christmas. Main venues are the Bolshoy Zal and Maly Zal of the Philharmonic.

RUSSIAN WINTER FESTIVAL
Tourist-oriented troika rides, folklore shows, games held outside of the city, much like the Goodbye Russian Winter Festival. Held 25 December to 5 January.

WESTERN CHRISTMAS
While many of the Orthodox disapprove, 25 December is increasingly marked (mainly by retailers), and some Russians now enjoy a little pre-Christmas celebration, although the emphasis is still of course on Russian Christmas two weeks later.

ARTS SQUARE WINTER FESTIVAL
www.artsquarewinterfest.ru

Held at the Philharmonic (which sits on pl Iskusstv, or Arts Square) and presided over by conductor Yuri Temirkanov, this is one of St Petersburg's annual musical highlights, taking different themes each year, and staging both classical and contemporary opera and orchestral works. Held late December to early January.

SYLVESTR & NEW YEAR
The main winter and gift-giving festival is 31 December to 1 January. Gifts are put under the traditional *yolka* (fir tree). See out the old year with vodka and welcome the new one with champagne while listening to the Kremlin chimes on radio and TV.

CULTURE
IDENTITY
Locals arguably define themselves far less in terms of what they are than what they are not – and they are certainly *not* Muscovites. St Petersburg residents tend to believe (against all evidence) that it's Moscow's population who are gruff, rude and materially obsessional, while Petersburgers universally walk the streets declaiming Pushkin and opening doors for

people. The rivalry between the two cities has always existed, and while the middle-class youth of both cities flit between the two without batting an eyelid, many older people still take the rivalry seriously, viewing the other with unabashed suspicion. You can rest assured that on your first meeting with a Russian of any age here you'll be asked which city you prefer: try to come armed with a crowd-pleasing answer.

With its imperial legacy it comes as no surprise that St Petersburg produces the biggest snobs in Russia as well. Those with aristocratic heritage and relatives of grand writers or composers are never shy of telling you about their background, even if they're telling you from a tiny Formica kitchen table in a ramshackle communal apartment. This is not to say that the Peterburzhtsi are in any way serious about snobbery – but there's always the consciousness of being from the old capital, the cultural heart of Russia.

The population – some 4.6 million according to Russia's 2002 census – is increasing despite the overall decline in Russia's national population. It's also remarkably homogenous, Russians making up over 92% of that number and the ethnically very similar Ukrainians a further 3%. Jews (counted as a distinct ethnic group in Russia, despite most being entirely Russian), Central Asians, Caucasians, Belarusians and Tatars make up the other 5% of the population.

Orthodox Christianity is the religion of the vast majority of the city's residents, at least superficially. While there's been a vogue for the church since the end of communism, few people who claim to be Orthodox actually attend services regularly or allow the church's less progressive ideas to infringe on their social lives. There's a healthy religious tolerance however, and the city has a large number of churches and temples from a variety of world religions, including the world's most northerly Buddhist *datsan* (temple).

One final thing that holds the city together like invisible glue is the memory (real or inherited) of the Nazi blockade during WWII. Even though this occurred over 60 years ago, its psychological impact, passed down from generation to generation, remains as strong as ever. Most young people in the city will still be able to cite family members who died fighting the Germans or from starvation caused by the siege, and for this reason celebrations such as Victory Day (9 May) remain important for people of all ages.

LIFESTYLE

Like all of Russia, St Petersburg is inconvenient, inhumanly large and exhausting. Thankfully, the pace and general stress of life that has been adopted in Moscow is unlikely ever to truly catch on here, as witnessed by the vast number of people who amble rather than walk with a great deal of purpose.

After 48 hours in the city, you'd be forgiven for thinking that the staple of St Petersburg life is the daily trudge up and down Nevsky, deftly slipping between unsmiling crowds of babushki, pickpockets, off-duty soldiers and teenage drinkers. Indeed, an experienced resident of the city will often try to avoid the thankless walk down the city's vast central avenue by hopping on a trolleybus or *marshrutka,* stopping a car to help them get about, or taking the infinitely more scenic route through the back streets.

One kink peculiar to St Petersburg is that during the months of navigation on the Neva (May to November), all the bridges

Motorbike in Palace Sq (p88)

Metro Etiquette

Entering a metro station, ensure you allow the door to swing back towards the person behind you hard enough to deprive them of their teeth. Holding doors open for people is a sign of weakness. Likewise, always enter a station with your hand in front of you to retain your teeth. On the escalators stand (or sit as many do due to the vast depth of the stations) on the right and eye up people on the escalator going the other way. This is a St Petersburg tradition. On the platform position yourself on the exact spot from which you can begin pushing your way into the carriage as soon as the doors open. Allowing people to leave the carriage first is a sign of weakness. In the train fight for a seat – draw blood if necessary (it's perfectly OK for men to compete with women or children). Babushki (if sufficiently decrepit) get preferential treatment, however, and about six people get up to allow one to sit down. Don't forget your trashy detective novel with its brightly coloured cover featuring a naked woman and a gun for inter-station reading. When getting out at the other end push and swear at the people who refuse to let you out of the carriage first. What *is* their problem?

over the river are raised at night to allow boats to pass between the Baltic and central Russia. This leads to lines of cars by the bridges and quite a festival atmosphere (many are lowered again midway through the night to allow people home before dawn).

The ethnic homogeneity of the city is in marked contrast to the economic diversity here. While perhaps not as pronounced as in the mid-1990s, the contrast between the haves and have nots is stark – grandmothers beg in the streets and homeless children roam the city while the wealthy move about in the latest Landcruiser or BMW spending vast amounts at the city's high-end shops and fashionable restaurants.

Unemployment is not a particular problem, but finding a good job certainly is. The average wage in the city is impossible to determine, as so many people earn money on the 'shadow' economy by force of circumstance. Many, for example, will do a day's work in the office before working the evening as an unofficial taxi driver, or set up their own makeshift market stall at the weekends. In real terms wages have decreased since the end of the Soviet Union as price rises have far outstripped salary increases.

Housing is another sore point in St Petersburg. While many people continue to live in their Soviet-era apartments at low rents, the middle classes are more and more buying up their own flats. All new residential construction is aimed squarely at the middle and upper classes – the poor having to make do with the far-flung Soviet *mikrorayoni* (micro regions), the soulless landscapes of Soviet mass housing projects.

Under the Soviets larger flats from imperial times were divided up into *kommunalki* (communal flats) housing several families, where the kitchen and bathroom are shared. In recent years these have become the only affordable accommodation for many young Russians, living with old alcoholics in dirty, run-down flats where theft and domestic violence are never far away.

Drinking arguably unifies certain elements in the city – come Friday lunch time you can already see drunk men falling down on the street, while by Saturday night the city begins to resemble Sodom and/or Gomorrah. While these excesses appear to confirm many a Western stereotype of Russian alcoholism, most Russians are more comfortable going *v gosti,* or as guests to their friends' houses to socialise, rather than heading out on the town. This has changed among the younger generation in St Petersburg now, but many people who grew up in the far more conservative environment of the Soviet Union will feel slightly uncomfortable visiting bars or nightclubs; and if you really want a taste of Russian hospitality you should leap at a chance to go *v gosti* yourself.

Russians have a fairly traditional approach to family life. It's common for men and women to marry before they are 25 and the housing problems mean that they'll usually cohabit with either the bride or groom's family. However, until marriage (and in many cases even afterwards) sexual mores remain fairly fluid, both men and women often enjoying multiple sexual partners. Like most Slavic peoples, Russians don't associate sex with shame, but see it as a natural and enjoyable pastime. Indeed, as many have joked, during the stagnation at the tail end of the Soviet era there was little else to do. This has of course given rise to the unfortunate stereotypes about Russian women abroad. 'Natashas' (the

Turkish term for a Russian prostitute) are common – from the girls that hang about on Staronevsky pr in the evenings to the girls who work in hotels and nightclubs, single men are likely to be propositioned if drinking alone.

Given these harsh realities why do so many Russians want to live in St Petersburg? The answer is that St Petersburg is a uniquely non-Russian city, and for much of its population it represents the furthest one can get from provincial, traditional Russia where all the above problems are multiplied several times over. The city attracts the educated, the cultured and, to a degree, social misfits who are embraced by St Petersburg's enlightened ecumenical atmosphere. Whoever you are and whatever you are looking for, St Petersburg will usually be able to deliver what it is you seek.

FOOD & DRINK

More realistically, this section might be called Drink & Food, as many people (including coachloads of Finns in search of cheap alcohol) come to St Petersburg for liquid refreshments and far fewer do so for fine dining. With expectations generally low (black bread, cabbage and herring anyone?) the reality is nearly always a pleasant surprise. Russian food has undergone a mini-revolution of its own since the end of Soviet rule and suddenly the bliny are tastier, the *smetana* (sour cream) creamier and the caviar more plentiful…

St Petersburg Cuisine

Russian cuisine tends to include few regional specialities and there are only a small number of dishes that are particular to St Petersburg. More than anything, this is due to the city's relative youth and the enormous amount of foreign influence to which it has always been exposed.

A local speciality is *koryushki* (freshwater smelt), the delicious fish that appears in the Neva shortly after the ice melts in the spring (usually early May). The regularity of the arrival of *koryushki* in a city as historically tumultuous as St Petersburg, not to mention the arrival marking the end of the long dark winter, has given the fish a special place in the hearts and palates of locals, and there's even an annual *koryushki* festival in the Peter and Paul Fortress. It is served fried across the city's restaurants as well as in private homes and is delicious.

Beef Stroganov (beef cooked in sour cream and mushroom sauce) was famously invented by the chef of the Stroganov family, whose palace remains one of the finest in the city on the corner of Nevsky pr and the Moyka River. It's a local staple and you'll find it on the menu of most Russian restaurants.

All potential diners should be warned that herbs are still used minimally in much Russian cooking. When they are used, it's usually a blanket covering of chopped dill sprinkled on anything. Unless you are a huge dill fan, it's often a safe bet to pre-empt the cook and ask for *vsyo bez ukropa* (everything without dill).

Snacks

Whether as the preamble to a meal or something to nibble on between shots of vodka, *zakuski* (snacks) are a big feature of Russian cuisine. They range from olives (in Russia these are very rarely fresh), to bliny with mushrooms, *tvorog* (cheese curd) or caviar, freshly baked black bread and delicious salads. Nearly all restaurants will serve *stolichny salat* (chicken, mayonnaise and sweet corn), as well as *salat olivye* (black olives chopped up in mayonnaise with cheese and vegetables). Another more Russian staple is *grenki* (black bread fried in garlic) – a delicious beer snack.

Soups

No Russian meal is truly a meal without a soup. In a proper sit-down meal in a Russian home, soup will precede the main meat dish. Most famous is of course borsch, a wonderful soup made from a base of beetroot, originally from Ukraine, but synonymous throughout the world with Russia. If you don't try anything else during your stay, make sure you try

Menu Decoder

This glossary is a brief guide to some basics.

Breakfast

блины (bli-*ny*) – leavened buckwheat pancakes; also eaten as an appetiser or dessert
блинчики (*blin*-chi-ki) – bliny rolled around meat or cheese and browned
каша (*ka*-sha) – Russian-style buckwheat porridge
кефир (ki-*feer*) – buttermilk, served as a drink
омлет (ahm-*lyet*) – omelette
творог (tva-*rok*) – cottage cheese
яйцо (yai-*tso*) – egg
яичница (ya-*ish*-ni-tsa) – fried egg

Lunch & Dinner

закуски (za-*ku*-ski) – appetisers
первые блюда (*per*-vi-ye bl*yu*-da) – first courses (usually soups)
вторые блюда (*fta*-ryye bl*yu*-da) – second courses or 'main' dishes
горячие блюда (gar-*ya*-chi-ye bl*yu*-da) – hot courses or 'main' dishes
сладкие блюда (*slat*-ki-ye bl*yu*-da) – sweet courses or desserts

Appetisers

икра (i-*kra*) – black (sturgeon) caviar
икра красная (i-*kra kras*-na-ya) – red (salmon) caviar
грибы в сметане (gri-*by* fsme-*ta*-ne) – mushrooms baked in sour cream; also called жульен из грибов (zhul-*yen* iz gri-*bov*)
салат (sa-*lat*) – salad
из помидоров (iz pa-mi-*dor*-ov) – tomato salad
салат столичный (sa-*lat* sta-*lich*-nyy) – salad of vegetable, beef, potato and egg in sour cream and mayonnaise

Soup

борщ (borshch) – beetroot soup with vegetables and sometimes meat
лапша (lap-*sha*) – chicken noodle soup
окрошка (a-*krosh*-ka) – cold or hot soup made from cucumbers, sour cream, potatoes, eggs, meat and kvas
рассольник (ra-*ssol'*-nik) – cucumber and kidney soup
солянка (sal-*yan*-ka) – thick meat or fish soup
уха (u-*kha*) – fish soup with potatoes and vegetables
харчо (khar-*choh*) – traditional Georgian soup made of lamb and spices
щи (shchi) – cabbage or sauerkraut soup

Fish

осетрина (a-se-*tri*-na) – sturgeon
отварная (at-*var*-na-yah) – poached sturgeon
осетрина с грибами (a-se-*tri*-na zgri-*ba*-mi) – sturgeon with mushrooms
рыба (*ry*-ba) – fish
судак (su-*dak*) – pike perch
форель (far-*yel'*) – trout

this. Borsch can be served hot or cold and usually with *smetana* poured on top of it. Some borsch is vegetarian (ask for *postny* borsch), although most is made with beef stock.

The Russian national soup, *solyanka,* is a sometimes rather bland concoction of pickled vegetables and potato that used to be the staple winter food for the peasantry. Other commonly served soups worth trying include *ukha* (fish soup), *shchee* (cabbage soup) and *okroshka* (cold vegetable soup).

Main Courses

Russian cuisine is very meaty and quite heavy. Staples include *zharkoye* (hot pot) – a meat stew served up piping hot in a little jug, *kotleta po kievsky* (better known as Chicken Kiev) and *shashlyk* (meat kebab), all of which will usually be found on any restaurant menu.

Lower brow establishments will sell *pelmeni,* Russian beef ravioli served in sour cream, which can be dismissed by many snobbier restaurants as 'workers' food'. Variations such as salmon or mushroom *pelmeni* are becoming popular on more chic menus, however. *Bifshtek* (steak) can be a hit-and-miss adventure in St Petersburg. If you are at a decent contemporary establishment, it's likely to be very good, but you are best off avoiding it on the menus of less swanky restaurants, where it'll most likely be served tough and flavourless.

Fish is extremely popular and freshly caught in St Petersburg, either from the Baltic or from Lake Ladoga, Europe's largest lake, which is to the northeast of the city. The range is enormous, but common staples include *osyetrina* (sturgeon), *shchuka* (pike), *losos/syomga* (salmon) and *treska* (chub).

Poultry & Meat Dishes

антрекот (an-tri-*kot*) – entrecote – boned sirloin steak
бефстроганов (bef-*stro*-ga-nov) – beef stroganov – beef slices in a rich sauce
бифштекс (bif-*shteks*) – 'steak', usually a glorified hamburger filling
говядина (gav-*ya*-di-na) – beef
голубцы (ga-lup-*tsy*) – cabbage rolls stuffed with meat
жаркое по домашнему (zhar-*koy*-e pa da-*mash*-ni-mu) – meat stewed in a clay pot 'home-style', with mushrooms, potatoes and vegetables
жаркое из птицы (zhar-*koy*-e iz *pti*-tsa) – poultry stewed in a clay pot
котлета (kat-*le*-ta) – usually a croquette of ground meat
котлета по киевски (kat-*le*-ta pa *ki*-ev-ski) – chicken Kiev; fried chicken breast stuffed with garlic butter
котлета по пожарски (kat-*le*-ta pa pa-*zhar*-ski) – croquette of minced chicken
мясные (*mya*-sni-ye) – meat
пельмени (pil'-*men*-i) – meat dumplings
плов (plov) – pilaf, rice with mutton bits
свинина (sfi-*ni*-na) – pork
шашлык (shashlyk) – skewered and grilled mutton or other meat

Vegetables

гарниры (gar-*ni*-ry) – any vegetable garnish
горох (ga-*rokh*) – peas
грибы (*gri*-by) – wild mushrooms
капуста (ka-*pus*-ta) – cabbage
картошка/картофель (kar-*tosh*-ka/kar-*to*-fil') – potato
морковь (mar-*kof'*) – carrots
зелень (*zye*-lin') – greens
овощи (*o*-va-shchi) – vegetables
огурец (a-gur-*yets*) – cucumber
помидор (pa-mi-*dor*) – tomato

Fruit

абрикос (a-bri-*kos*) – apricot
апельсин (a-pel'-*sin*) – orange
вишня (*vish*-ni-ya) – cherry
банан (ba-*nan*) – banana
виноград (vi-na-*grad*) – grapes
груша (*gru*-sha) – pear
фрукты (*fruk*-ty) – fruits
яблоко (*ya*-bla-ko) – apple

Other Foods

масло (*mas*-la) – butter
перец (*pyer*-its) – pepper
рис (ris) – rice
сахар (*sa*-khar) – sugar
соль (sol') – salt
сыр (syr) – cheese
хлеб (khlep) – bread

Desserts

мороженое (ma-ro-zhi-ne-ya) – ice cream
кисель (ki-*sel'*) – fruit jelly/jello
компот (kam-*pot*) – fruit in syrup
пирожное (pi-*rozh*-na-ye) – pastries

Russian cuisine borrows enormously from neighbouring countries, most obviously from the Caucasus, from where *shashlyk* originated. Georgian food is the most common Caucasian cuisine in St Petersburg, and even nominally Russian restaurants may serve traditional Georgian dishes such as *baklazhan s orekhami* (aubergines with walnut paste), *lobio* (stewed bean paste) and *khachapuri* (cheese pie).

Desserts

The Russian sweet tooth is seriously sweet. *Morozhenoye* (ice cream) is very good, and usually included on the dessert menu, as are a range of *torty* (cakes). *Pecheniye* (pastries) are not usually served as dessert but eaten at tea-time in the traditional English style and are available at any *bulochnaya* (bakery).

Drinking

Russians are certainly not shy of alcohol and planning to make a trip here without sampling vodka would be rather naive, however much you may be convinced you hate it.

What surprises many is that it's actually *pivo* (beer) that is the most popular alcoholic beverage in the city by far – at any time of day or night you'll see men and women wandering the streets swigging it from glass bottles – and the range is indeed fine. The local standard is Baltika, a decent St Petersburg brew that comes in 12 standard varieties, including No 3 and 7, the most popular standard lagers, a wheat beer (No 8), dark beers (No 4 and 6)

Vodka Etiquette

Few traditions in Russia are as sacrosanct as that involving the drinking of 'little water' or vodka. Forget any foreign notions of drinking vodka mixed with tonic or orange juice – this is anathema to your average Russian, most of whom like to have a mixer in a separate glass that they then use to chase the taste. Vodka should always be served chilled.

One person makes a toast, then everyone clinks glasses and knocks it back in one go. Women can usually get away with sipping at it, while men will be viewed as *nenormalny* (unusual) if they don't at least knock the first one back.

Never place an empty bottle of vodka on the table – it must be placed on the floor. Most importantly of all, snack between shots; Russians swear that by doing this you'll *never* get drunk...

and 'strong beer' (No 9) which at 8% proof is extremely popular. Other leading Russian beers are Bochkarev, Nevskoye, Stepan Razin and Tri Medvedi. While Russian beer is good, many smarter restaurants insist on serving (usually mediocre) Western European beers, which are obviously more expensive and usually not much better.

Wine is also a popular accompaniment to meals. It used to be almost impossible to buy good red or white wine unless you spent a fortune, but over the past five years the situation has been reversed, and while you'll still pay a little more for a good Bordeaux or Chianti here, you'll have no trouble finding them. Russians largely prefer Georgian wines, although people with a Western palate may find these quite sweet and lacking any subtlety. Try a red Saperavi if you are curious.

Vodka, of course, is king. It's usually brought out on special occasions (although certainly not exclusively) and drunk rather ceremonially. Russky Standard and Stolichnaya are the two best varieties commonly available, although it's very rare to get bad vodka in any restaurant, so don't worry if you are unfamiliar with the brand – the variety is vast. In shops it's a different story, though, so always buy vodka from a respectable-looking store (avoid street kiosks if possible) and always check for an unbroken seal, as some St Petersburg urban myths include people being sold antifreeze and being too drunk to notice.

There's the usual array of soft drinks available everywhere – *voda* (bottled water) comes both *s gazom* (sparkling) and *bez gaza* (still). All Western brands of soft drink can be found, although those wanting to try something different should order some *kvas* (or better still, buy it on the street where it is dispensed to thirsty workers). This unique Russian drink is a juice distilled from fermented beets and is a delicious, very mildly alcoholic tipple.

FASHION

Russian fashion? Yes, actually, the citizens of St Petersburg take clothing very seriously. While the days when fashion meant spending hundreds of dollars on foreign-produced designer threads have passed to a degree (although there's an entire stratum of the highest society that believes in this), many visitors to St Petersburg notice how faultlessly attired locals are and can often feel scruffy by comparison. Do bring a smart outfit if you are planning to eat out in style or go to the ballet or theatre, where trainers and T-shirts will make you stick out like a sore thumb.

St Petersburg has seen local design houses slowly develop their reputations. Most famous are couturiers such as Tatyana Parfionova, who set up the first couture house in the city back in the 1990s. There's a smattering of international fashion houses in the city too – while Western brand names such as Versace, Hugo Boss and Comme des Garçons have their own boutiques here, other labels are sold in various upmarket shopping salons.

Of all items of clothing, Russians take shoes the most seriously. In a country where there's snow or slush on the ground for at least six months a year, having clean, well polished shoes is a sign of prestige at all levels of society. Even rebellious teenagers will pause a minute before leaving the house to scour their shoes of any detritus before setting out onto the street. While trainers are trendy here, they are somewhat impractical outside the summer months, and during winter, spring and autumn black leather shoes or boots are the universal norm. If you want people to think of you as cultured and stylish, make sure that your shoes are immaculate. Obviously outside May to September they'll become filthy as soon as you go outside, but wiping them down as soon as you get inside will give you an undeniable aura of prestige.

In a city where winter temperatures frequently drop to –20°C, fur is unsurprisingly popular. There's little understanding of why this might offend some people and St Petersburg women are often at pains to show off their luxurious garments. Try to look at this in cultural context – making comments or actively displaying your disdain is likely to make people think you are mentally unhinged. If fur offends, avoid the smart shopping arcades where a huge selection of fur is on sale year round.

There are certain idiosyncrasies to St Petersburg street fashion that you are bound to notice. Most obvious is the pan-Russian phenomenon of wearing your sunglasses over the back of your neck (hanging backwards off your ears, as if you have eyes at the base of your neck). This is *the* way to carry your shades when not actually wearing them. Rather humorously, the gentleman's handbag is still an accessory that appeals to many of the most macho types who strut about in gold chains and leather jackets. Women are encouraged to combine white knee-high boots and jeans. Hair dye is a *sine qua non* of the elite, as is bling bling jewellery that would make Mary J Blige blush.

SPORT

The two sports that enthral the northern capital are ice hockey and soccer. Few others get a look in, in fact, and a trip to see one of the big teams play is a great way to see another side to a city that can often appear to be entirely devoted to high culture.

The main local soccer side is Zenith, founded in 1930 (and known until 1940 as Stalinets). The team plays at the Petrovsky Stadium on the Petrograd Side. You'll know when there's a match on as exuberant supporters in Zenith's blue strip crowd the streets drinking, whatever the result.

Next door to the Petrovsky Stadium is the Yubileyny Palace of Sport where the local ice hockey team SKA (an acronym meaning 'the Army Sports Club') play during the season (September to June).

St Petersburg's maritime location makes sailing and various other water sports popular – the Sailing Festival in August attracts a large number of yachting enthusiasts from all over the Baltics and beyond.

For details on St Petersburg's sporting facilities, see p162.

MEDIA

The Russian media has long been in a fairly sorry state. While no longer under central control as in the days of *Pravda*, the mass media is today a battleground where the Kremlin fights the oligarchs and other big business interests for control of the so-called free press. Many commentators have argued that the Russian press is now self-censoring rather than censored at government level and there is doubtless some truth to this. Newspapers and TV stations critical of the Kremlin have been silenced over the past few years in a manner of ways that have created concern in the West, and you are unlikely to read or see much that is critical of the government anywhere in the Russian media today.

The more serious Russian newspapers are *Kommersant*, *Vedomosti* (affiliated with the *Financial Times* and the *Wall Street Journal*) and *Izvestia*, all of which are entirely incomprehensible to the non-Russian speaker, of course. Local news media in English is dominated by the semi-weekly *St Petersburg Times*, available at hotels, restaurants and clubs throughout the city.

A public hungry for tawdry gossip has crowned the tabloid king of print media and trashy women's magazines the heir apparent. This is obvious whenever you see a *gazetny kiosk* (newsstand) overloaded with scandal rags and celebrity tat. If this is your thing, you'll love *Komsomolskaya Pravda*, *Zhizn* ('Life' – shamelessly plagiarising its entire layout and worldview from Britain's *Sun* tabloid) and the bizarrely named *SPID Info* (AIDS information).

The grand and undeniably positive Soviet tradition of pasting newspapers up on public notice boards continues today in the city. Unfortunately, they are usually the dullest of the local offerings, although you'll still see babushki catching up on the news this way as they wait for the bus.

Most of St Petersburg's popular radio stations play a mix of trashy Euro pop and its even more over-the-top Russian variant. Still, their play lists are often unexpectedly eclectic. Some of the more popular FM stations include Eldoradio (101.4 MHz), Radio Modern (104 MHz), the grating Europa Plus (100.5 MHz) and the more diversified Radio Nostalgie (105.3 MHz). More Russian content can be heard on Kanal Melodia (91.1 MHz), Russky Shanson (100.9 MHz) and Russkoe Radio (104.4 MHz). Two stations focus almost exclusively on St Petersburg-related news, music and features: Eko Peterburga (91.5 MHz) and Severnaya Stolitsa (105.9 MHz).

Television has had even less luck with freedom of expression than the beleaguered print media in Russia. Soon after his election as president, Putin set his sights on NTV, Russia's first professionally run, editorially independent national TV station. Almost from his first day in office, Putin began putting pressure on the errant station, deciding at last to hound Vladimir Gusinsky, the multimillionaire owner of the station, for tax evasion and other charges of corruption. This led Gusinsky to flee to Spain, where he was placed under arrest but not extradited to face criminal prosecution in Russia.

Few commentators regarded Gusinsky as any more corrupt than any other oligarch (or high-level politician for that matter), but why he was being singled out seemed a clear signal that Putin's new government wished to control, if not silence, voices of dissent and encourage pro-government reporting. A surprise buy-out of a controlling portion of NTV shares by the state gas giant Gazprom in April 2001 brought tens of thousands of protesters out in the streets of Moscow, demanding that NTV be left alone. Dozens of reporters quit the station, and its programming and acerbic tone were changed overnight.

Despite these machinations against serious news coverage, most Russian TV is an appalling mix of South American soap operas dubbed into Russian, Soviet films, straight-to-video Hollywood pap and endless musical concerts. The few highlights have been controversial and satirical programming such as *Kukly* (Puppets – a carbon copy of Britain's *Spitting Image*) and *Namedni* (Lately) – all of which have been taken off air due to (explicit or implicit) pressure from the Kremlin.

LANGUAGE

Russian, one of the world's richest and most beautiful languages, appears to many to be as impenetrable and mysterious as Russia itself, both due to its Cyrillic alphabet (which has only five letters in common with the Latin alphabet) and its cryptic rules and regulations – eight grammatical cases in which all nouns and adjectives potentially decline.

In fact, Russian is an exceptionally logical language and has none of the chaotic unpredictability of English. Words are nearly all spelled phonetically, you can determine a noun's gender by the way it ends and there's only one irregular verb (*byt*, to be). It has fundamental similarities with English, being an Indo-European language, and learning a few basic phrases in Russian is no harder than learning them in French or German.

While Russians in St Petersburg often claim to speak the purest form of Russian, there are really so few variations of standard Russian as to make this claim fanciful at best. There are few accents detectable in Russian but there are certainly registers. The well educated in St Petersburg (the majority) genuinely speak Russian beautifully, although *muzhiki* (a slang term for gruff men's men who always have a filterless cigarette in their hands and for whom coughing up phlegm is a competitive sporting event) have created their own fascinating dialect of Russian peppered with expletives, particularly *blyad* (whore) – which is usually rendered as simply *blya* – and plays an equivalent role to 'fucking' in English for those who use it as a verbal stutter.

Russians are exceptionally proud of *russky mat* (Russian swearing). The complexities of the system take years to understand and foreigners are unlikely ever to master it. Russian swearing allows for enormous chains of swearwords strung together, almost like poetry. Listening to someone fully in control of their swearing is a linguistic feast. Be aware, however, that the social gulf between those who swear and those who don't is vast and entirely unbridgeable, unlike in modern English. Don't try to impress your educated Russian friends by recounting swearwords taught to you by cab drivers – 'cultured' Russians don't swear at all, and at best they'll look slightly embarrassed for you and think of you as *nekulturny* (literally 'uncultured'), about as damning an adjective as any you could apply to someone in St Petersburg.

Inevitably, Anglicisms have been entering into Russian in enormous volume since the 1990s. *Biznesmeni* will have *biznes lanch,* people shop at *second hend* stores and clubs execute policies of *face kontrol* (ie allowing only the rich or beautiful to enter their premises). While some people look at these borrowings with horror, this is certainly not a first for the Russian language, which absorbed a huge number of French words during the 18th and 19th centuries.

At the city's fruit and vegetable markets you'll hear a cacophony of Caucasian and Central Asian languages – mainly Azeri, Uzbek and Tajik. The city's most visible ethnic minority groups hail from these one-time Soviet Republics, and there are large Azeri, Armenian, Georgian, Uzbek and Tajik Diasporas still living in St Petersburg.

See the language chapter (p219) for useful phrases.

RELIGION

The Russian Federation officially recognises four faiths: Orthodoxy, Judaism, Buddhism and Islam. All other churches must apply to be officially registered in order to operate missions in Russia. This attempt to limit the number of sects in the country has not prevented the appearance of numerous minority religious groups. In 2001, the Salvation Army was denied official registration in Moscow (despite the fact that it was already registered and operating in five other Russian cities); courts judged that they 'pose a national security threat'.

Russian Orthodox Church

During the Soviet regime, hundreds of churches were torn down, gutted, and turned into swimming pools, skating rinks, factories and warehouses, or used for military target practice. Believers faced victimisation, deportation and execution. But despite all of this, belief was never stamped out. Since the 1990s, the Russian Orthodox Church (Russkaya Pravoslavnaya Tserkov) has enjoyed a big revival. The Church is an intimate part of many Russians' notions of Russia and 'Russianness', despite recriminations over its infiltration by the KGB during the Sovietera – three metropolitans (senior bishops) were accused in 1992 of having been KGB agents. President Putin has shown himself to be a believer, has held public meetings with the Moscow Patriarch Alexei II and has even mentioned God in speeches.

Many people nonetheless decry a hypocrisy among a number of churchgoers, accusing them of merely following a trend (check out an Easter church service and try to spot all the 'repentant' Mafia bosses and bandits). The Orthodox Church now comprises over 17,000 full-time priests and bishops, and has 462 operational monasteries throughout Russia.

Prince Vladimir of Kyiv effectively founded the Russian Orthodox Church in 988 by adopting Christianity from Constantinople. The church's headquarters stayed in Kyiv until 1300, when it moved north to Vladimir and then in the 1320s to Moscow.

Patriarch Alexy II of Moscow and All Russia is head of the Russian Orthodox Church; Metropolitan (Senior Bishop) Vladimir is the spiritial leader for St Petersburg and Ladoga and has a residence in the Alexander Nevsky Lavra (a *lavra* is a monastery of the highest rank). The Russian Orthodox Church is one of the main fellowship of 15 autocephalous (self-headed) orthodox churches, in which Constantinople is a kind of first among equals.

BELIEFS & PRACTICE

Russian Orthodoxy is highly traditional and the atmosphere inside a church is formal and solemn. Priests dress in an imposing fashion, the smell of candles and incense permeates the air, and elderly women bustle about the church sweeping and polishing. However, to Catholic and Protestant visitors who are accustomed to the rituals of standing, kneeling and praying on command, things can look a tad chaotic during a service: there are no seats so people move freely about the church, seemingly engaged in their own affairs,

Church Names

In Russian, *sobor* means cathedral; *tserkov* and *khram* mean church. Common church names include:

Blagoveshchenskaya	Annunciation
Nikolskaya	St Nicholas
Petropavlovskaya	SS Peter and Paul
Pokrovskaya	Intercession of the Virgin
Preobrazhenskaya	Transfiguration
Rozhdestvenskaya	Nativity
Troitskaya	Trinity
Uspenskaya	Assumption or Dormition
Vladimirskaya	St Vladimir
Voskresenskaya	Resurrection
Voznesenskaya	Ascension
Znamenskaya	Holy Sign

kissing or kneeling before icons and such, while priests engage in a series of complex and mysterious motions no-one fully seems to follow. As a rule, working churches are open to one and all but, as a visitor, take care not to disturb any devotions or otherwise offend sensibilities.

The Virgin Mary (Bogomater; Mother of God) is greatly honoured. The language of the liturgy is 'Church Slavonic', the old Bulgarian dialect into which the Bible was first translated for Slavs. Easter (Paskha) is the focus of the Church year, with festive midnight services to launch Easter Day. Christmas Day (Rozhdestvo) falls on 7 January because the Church still uses the Julian calendar that the Soviet state abandoned in 1918.

In most churches, Bozhestvennaya Liturgia (Divine Liturgy), lasting about two hours, is at 8am, 9am or 10am Monday to Saturday, and usually at 7am and 10am on Sunday and festival days. Most churches also hold services at 5pm or 6pm daily. Some of these include an *akathistos (akafist)*, a series of chants to the Virgin or saints.

OLD BELIEVERS

The Russian Church was split in 1666 by the reforms of Patriarch Nikon, who thought it had departed from its roots. He insisted, among other things, that the translation of the Bible be altered to conform with the Greek original and that the sign of the cross be made with three fingers, not two. Those who wouldn't accept these changes became known as Starovery (Old Believers), some of Russia's earliest social dissidents. Escaping official persecution, they fled west to the border of Estonia or east to the Siberian forests and remote parts of Central Asia. Only in the periods 1771–1827 and 1905–18, and again recently have Old Believers had real freedom of worship. They probably number over a million but in 1917 there were as many as 20 million. Old Believers have two churches in St Petersburg, returned to them in 1988.

SS Peter and Paul Cathedral in Peter and Paul Fortress (p114)

Other Christian Churches

Russia has small numbers of Roman Catholics and Lutheran and Baptist Protestants, mostly among the German and other non-Russian ethnic groups. Other groups, including the Jehovah's Witnesses, Seventh Day Adventists, Mormons and the Salvation Army, are sending missionaries into the fertile ground of a country where God officially didn't exist for 70 years.

Islam

Islam has, like Christianity, enjoyed growth since the mid-1980s. Though it has been some Muslim peoples – notably the Chechens and Tatars among Russian minorities – who have most resisted being brought within the Russian national fold since the fall of the Soviet Union in 1991, nationalism has played at least as big a part as religion in this.

Islam in Russia is fairly secularised, eg women are not veiled and the Friday Sabbath is not a commercial holiday. St Petersburg's working Sunni-Muslim mosque (p111) is closed to women and often to non-Muslim men, though men may occasionally be invited in.

Judaism

Many of Russia's 700,000 or so Jews have been assimilated into Russian culture and do not seriously practise Judaism. However, there were approximately 30 synagogues in Russia by 1991. Jews have long been the target of prejudice and even pogroms – ethnic cleansing – in Russia. Since the time of *glasnost,* hundreds of thousands of Jews have emigrated to Israel and other countries to escape the state-sponsored anti-Semitism that existed under the former government and which is still subtly felt today. St Petersburg has two working synagogues and a Jewish cemetery. A sign of the times is a new trend of Russian Jews returning to Russia's economic and political stability from the miserable cycle of terrorism in Israel.

Buddhism

The members of St Petersburg's Buddhist *datsan* (p116) belong to the Gelugpa or 'Yellow-Hat' sect of Tibetan Buddhism, whose spiritual leader is the Dalai Lama. However, a battle for ownership of the *datsan* between two rival Buddhist groups still occasionally flares up. Buddhism was tolerated by the Soviet state until Stalin nearly wiped it out in the 1930s.

ECONOMY & COSTS

While Russia's economy has been in overdrive (it ended 2003 with its fifth straight year of growth, averaging 6.5% annually since the financial crisis of 1998), St Petersburg is still experiencing the fallout from Lenin's decision to move the Russian capital back to Moscow in 1918. That's not to say that it's not experiencing economic growth, but it's still very much playing second fiddle to big brother Moscow, Russia's economic powerhouse.

St Petersburg is a major industrial centre, producing 3% of all Russian manufactured goods. Second only to Moscow in industrial output, a quarter of the city's residents are employed in local industry. The city authorities were very cautious about instituting reforms to attract investment in the years immediately after *perestroika* and most foreign companies chose Moscow as their base in Russia. Even the region around St Petersburg, the Leningradskaya Oblast, has been more successful at attracting foreign investment than the city proper, although in the past few years this has begun to change.

Despite this, the city remains an industrial and commercial centre largely from Soviet days. Some big local plants include the Leningrad Metal Works, LOMO (best known for their multi-lens cameras that have a cult following around the world), the Baltika Brewery (producing 10% of Russian beer) and the Kirov, Izhorsk and Lomonosov plants. There are also several big shipbuilding yards in the city's sprawling docklands, producing both military and civilian vessels from nuclear icebreakers to cruise ships. Other major local industries include fishing, textiles, furniture, tobacco, petro-chemicals and food processing.

Tourism is a growth industry, and with the expansion of mid- and top-end accommodation in the city for the 2003 tercentenary celebrations, one that looks set to continue its expansion.

After Moscow, St Petersburg is the most expensive city in Russia. While it's quite possible to live here fairly frugally, anyone wanting to enjoy an equivalent lifestyle to that in their home country – *yevroremont* (Western-standard) accommodation, good restaurants and comfortable transport options – will not save a huge amount here, although the city is still without doubt far cheaper than most Western European capitals. A traveller can expect to pay around €100 to €200 per day for two- to four-star accommodation and food.

GOVERNMENT & POLITICS

Politics in St Petersburg has never been a particularly harmonious affair. In fact, it's perfectly possible to read the political failures of the city since the end of communism as a microcosm of those on a national scale. The lack of transparency, the corruption, the use of violence and blackmail in political discourse, the cronyism and the prostitution of various parts of the media to big business, gangsters and political clans – all of which are realities in local politics in St Petersburg – are mirrored on a national level in Moscow.

As the late reformer Anatoly Sobchak, St Petersburg's first post-communist mayor, remarked ruefully in his last years, 'We have not achieved a democratic, but rather a police state over the past 10 years'. He was right to be negative – politics here is a pretty depressing business and what's most striking when you talk to locals is their apparent lack of inclination to do (or believe that they can do) anything about it, preferring instead to fall back on such hackneyed axioms as 'Russia needs a strong pair of hands' (ie 'bring back Stalin, he did an all right job') or 'Russia isn't ready for democracy'.

One of Putin's first acts as president was to divide up Russia into seven vast 'superregions'. The city of St Petersburg makes up one part of the Northwest Region of Russia, which includes the autonomous republics of Karelia and Komi, much of Western Arctic Russia and the enclave of Kaliningrad. There are therefore three separate power strata – the local governor, the regional presidential envoy and the national government.

The local governor works in tandem with the St Petersburg legislative assembly to run the city, although the main seat of power in the city is the governor's office at Smolny, currently occupied by Valentina Matvienko, a Putin loyalist parachuted in by the Kremlin to put an end to dissent from the northern capital once and for all. President Vladimir Putin has always paid close attention to the local political scene ever since he worked as deputy to Mayor Anatoly Sobchak in the early 1990s. He worked side by side with another deputy, Vladimir Yakovlev, who – in the eyes of Putin at least – betrayed Mayor Sobchak by announcing his own candidature for the mayor's seat in 1996 and surprised everyone by winning.

Yakovlev's first act as mayor was to change the title to the more impressive sounding *gubernator* (governor) and his time at Smolny was marked by attempts to balance the city's budget by doubling the rents paid by locals for housing. Despite the measure's inevitable unpopularity, it did

Exterior of Mariinsky Theatre (p105)

How Much?

Admission to the Hermitage R350

Ticket to the Mariinsky R800 to R3000

Good mid-range meal R350

Public toilet R10

Taxi journey within historic centre R50 to R100

Baltika beer R25

Bottle of Sovietskaya Champagne R90

Matryoshka (nesting doll) R300 to R500

allow him to balance the city budget, which in turn entitled St Petersburg to raise US$300 million from a Eurobond issue that was then invested into the city's ailing infrastructure. Despite this success, his governorship was overshadowed by consistent accusations of corruption, connections to the city's notorious mafia clans and his close association with legislative assembly deputy Yury Shutov, who was later indicted for ordering seven contract killings.

During the 1990s St Petersburg gained a not entirely unfair image as a centre for banditry. This inevitably extended into the sphere of politics and resulted in two very high-profile local assassinations that sent shock waves through Russia. First there was the shock execution of Vladimir Yakovlev's vice governor, Mikhail Manevich, by an unknown assassin as he was driven to work in broad daylight on Nevsky pr in August 1997. A year later came the assassination of Galina Starovoitova, a liberal member of the State Duma representing a district of St Petersburg. Starovoitova's death was pure tragedy for the fragile Russian democracy – she had been a vociferous critic of the communists and corruption, and a leading human rights advocate. These politically motivated murders are just the tip of the iceberg in a city where criminal elements still wield an enormous amount of power and political scores are often settled through threats, blackmail and eventually bullets.

Putin's rise to power meant Yakovlev's position was inevitably in trouble. While on the surface they paid lip service to being friends, Putin was determined to remove Yakovlev from Smolny. Ironically he eventually did this by promoting the governor to the federal government where he made him a deputy prime minister and later a presidential envoy to the south of Russia in the turbulent region that includes Chechnya.

An election followed in October 2003 and the Presidential Envoy to the Northwest Region (ie Putin's favoured candidate) Valentina Matvienko was duly elected amid accusations of abuse of power (rival candidates had their campaigning disrupted by the police and other local authorities).

Matvienko's governorship has worrying implications for Russian democracy. Even if the campaign was totally fair (very unlikely), it seems to be the case that most people supported her not for her abilities, but simply for her connections to the Kremlin, which they (correctly) assume will lead to more federal spending in the city.

ENVIRONMENT

THE LAND

St Petersburg is on the delta of the Neva River (Europe's youngest major river, emerging only around 4000 years ago) on low-lying, marshy lands that are extremely vulnerable to flooding. You'll occasionally see plaques around the city marking water levels from the great floods of the past (the 1824 flood killed some 10,000 people and inspired Pushkin's brooding masterpiece *The Bronze Horseman*).

The St Petersburg flood defences have been under construction since 1979 and remain incomplete, due first to fears that they would too significantly alter the water quality in the Neva, and then due to the collapse of the Soviet Union. The *damba* (as the defences are known to city residents) are finally on course to be finished by 2008 after the European Bank of Reconstruction and Development approved a US$245 million loan in 2002. The *damba* is crucial to the structural survival of the city, which has experienced over 270 floods in the three centuries of its existence. Indeed, stand back from any unrenovated buildings in the city centre and you'll usually see marks from years of floods.

ENVIRONMENTAL ISSUES

Most environmentally aware people will be mildly horrified when visiting St Petersburg. Despite a nascent green movement in the country, most people have little respect for their surroundings, as the sad sight of endless tides of rubbish thrown into the canals will more than attest. Moreover, traffic fumes can be overwhelming, especially as much of the city still gets about with pre-catalytic converter Soviet cars using leaded petrol and belching exhaust everywhere.

Greenpeace opened an office in Moscow in 1992, but the movement has had constant problems with its status within Russia and on numerous occasions has been subject to police harassment. Major environmental worries in St Petersburg include toxic waste being dumped into the Baltic Sea and the consequent effects on the civilian population.

A major environmental disaster occurred at the Sosnovy Bor power station, some 80km west of St Petersburg, in 1992, when a cloud of radioactive waste was released into the atmosphere during a routine shutdown of one of the plant's four Chornobyl-type reactors.

GREEN ST PETERSBURG

St Petersburg has some pleasant green spaces, although if you are looking for greenery rather than manicured gardens in the French style (such as the Summer Garden or the Alexandrinsky Garden), your best bets are some way from the historic heart. By far the best place to enjoy greenery in the city is by taking a walk on car-less Yelagin Island (p116). There are also endless possibilities around the city, from the parklands of tsarist palaces to the beaches along the Gulf of Finland.

Other pleasant parks include the Seaside Park of Victory (p116), the Tauride Gardens (p101) and the Alexandrovsky Park (p111) behind the Peter and Paul Fortress.

URBAN PLANNING & DEVELOPMENT

St Petersburg has had more than its fair share of urban planners – Peter the Great is the obvious one, of course, followed by Empress Anna and Catherine the Great, all of whom sought to imprint their vision onto the city.

Peter changed his mind constantly about how the city should develop. First he concentrated on the Petrograd Side, then Admiralty Island (around the present-day Admiralty) before settling on Vasilevsky Island to be the city centre. It wasn't until later on in the century that a formal plan for the whole city was instituted under Anna.

But even Peter's despotism couldn't overcome the city residents' pragmatism – as going to any of the islands meant taking a boat, commerce and house-building naturally thrived on the city's left bank (ie mainland Russia), where it remains today.

Stalin never liked St Petersburg – to him the palaces, churches and canals were all symbols of utmost bourgeois decadence and quite unfit for a city bearing the name of Lenin. Unlike Hitler, who planned to simply wipe the city off the face of the earth, Stalin's plan was to create a new city centre to the south of the historic heart. Anyone interested in Stalinist town planning will enjoy visiting the city's Moskovsky Rayon (Moscow Region) – an impressively grandiose neighbourhood featuring some bombastic high-Stalinist treats, although ultimately it never developed into the heart of the city and the whole plan was dropped after Stalin's death in 1953.

Under Soviet rule, particularly following WWII, the city expanded over a vast area as *mikrorayoni* spread over the outskirts of the old city – to Avtovo and Pulkovo in the south and Ozerki and Udelnaya in the north – served by metro lines that connected these far-flung housing estates to the city centre in minutes.

In the absence of Soviet central planning, modern development has been limited, although haphazard where it has occurred. The building effort that is not going into restoration has been poured into building new houses and buildings in the city centre, as well as large modern *dachas* in the surrounding countryside for the new rich of the city.

Luckily, the city authorities have not granted planning permission for any tall buildings in the historic centre (like Paris, skyscrapers have been relegated to suburbs) and St Isaac's Cathedral remains the historic heart's highest building.

Arts & Architecture

Arts & Architecture

There are few cities in the world more culturally and aesthetically oriented than St Petersburg. When Peter the Great set his sword down in the marshlands here to create a new capital, he also laid the foundations for a city that would rank next to Paris, Florence, Rome and Vienna in terms of its cultural significance to the world. Cradle of the nation's art, home to its greatest poet (Pushkin) and novelist (Dostoevsky), the place where the avant-garde exploded at the end of the 19th century, and with an architectural heritage richer than nearly any other city on earth – St Petersburg is heaven for aesthetes.

LITERATURE

Russian literature is even younger than St Petersburg, but a slow start has been more than amply compensated for in the past two centuries, and a huge number of Russia's most famous writers lived and worked here, both inspired and oppressed by the city in a number of magical ways.

19TH-CENTURY LITERATURE

National bard Alexander Pushkin lived all over town, although most famously at his last address on the Moyka River which is now a suitably hagiographic museum to him, its interior preserved exactly as it was at the moment of his death in 1837.

His epic poem *Yevgeny Onegin* is set in part among the foppish aristocratic society of the imperial capital that he ridicules savagely, despite being a fairly consistent fixture of it himself for most of his adult life. The wonderful short story *The Queen of Spades* is set in the house of a countess in the city (she lived on Nevsky pr) and charts the weird supernatural story of a man who uncovers her Mephistophelian gambling trick.

Pushkin's most famous work, published posthumously in 1841, is *The Bronze Horseman,* depicting the great flood of 1824. In it, the hopes and wishes of the people – represented here by the lowly clerk Yevgeny, who has lost his beloved in the flood – take on the conquering, empire-building spirit of Peter the Great, represented by the animation of the bronze statue of him installed by Catherine the Great.

Unclassifiably brilliant is the writing of Nikolai Gogol (1809–52) whose troubled genius created some of Russian literature's most memorable characters, including Akaki Akakievich, the tragi-comic hero of *The Overcoat*, and the brilliant Major Kovalyev, who chases his errant nose around St Petersburg when it makes a break for it in the absurdist short story *The Nose.* Gogol came to the city from his native Ukraine in 1829, and wrote and lived here for a decade before spending his final years abroad, mainly in Italy. Under-awed by the legendary capital (in a letter to his mother he described it as a place where 'people seem more dead than alive' and complained endlessly about the air pressure, which he believed caused illness), Gogol was nevertheless inspired by St Petersburg to write a number of absurdist stories, collectively known as *The Petersburg Tales* and generally recognised as being the zenith of his creativity.

Leo Tolstoy, an inveterate Muscovite, nevertheless set much of *Anna Karenina* in the city and Ivan Turgenev wrote *Notes of a Hunter,* a work of huge social importance due to its criticism of serfdom, while living in his house on Bolshaya Konyushennaya ul.

Fyodor Dostoevsky (1821–81) is perhaps the most famous writer that St Petersburg has nursed. Despite being a Muscovite, Dostoevsky moved to the imperial capital in 1838, aged just 16, and began his literary and journalistic career here.

Despite a decade's exile in Siberia, Dostoevsky set *Crime and Punishment, The Idiot, White Nights* and *The Devils* in the city. *Crime and Punishment* is perhaps the most evocative of the lives of the poor living in and around the 19th-century Haymarket (Sennaya pl)

Dostoevsky

No other figure in world literature is more closely connected with Russia – and St Petersburg – than Fyodor Dostoevsky. He was among the first writers to navigate the murky, uninvestigated waters of the human subconscious, blending powerful prose with psychology, philosophy and spirituality.

He, like most intellectuals, had deep but mixed feelings about his home country, calling it a 'sublime, universal, ordered chaos' and Russians themselves 'half-saint, half-savage'. Increasingly religious as he grew older, he quoted two inspirations for his life views: the New Testament and the Russian people. He felt Russians have an unrealised Christ-like harmony that could redeem humanity if acknowledged. Yet he all too clearly saw, and depicted, the squalid reality around him, framed by a society that stifled individuality.

His first novel, *Poor Folk,* written when he was 24 years old, was immediately seen as the work of a genius, though his next offerings, *The Double* and *White Nights,* disappointed the other literary figures of the time, namely Nekrasov and Belinsky, who had championed him as the best writer in Russia since Gogol.

His career was halted – but ultimately shaped – by his casual involvement with a group of young free-thinkers who would meet weekly at the home of an eccentric socialist, Mikhail Petrashevsky, and free-associate liberal ideas. Nicholas I decided to make an example of the harmless group to any burgeoning revolutionaries and had 34 of their members arrested and sentenced to death, including Dostoevsky. After spending a few months in the Peter and Paul Fortress prison, he, along with 20 others, were marched out to Semyonovskaya pl (today's Pionerskaya pl) on 22 December 1849 for the execution which, as the guns were aimed and ready to fire, was suddenly called off, commuted to a sentence of hard labour. The mock execution was Nicholas I's idea of a good, sick joke.

In a labour camp in Omsk, Siberia, Dostoevsky witnessed incredible suffering at the hands of wicked brutality, yet also limitless courage and acts of unforgettable kindness. After he was pardoned by Alexander II and allowed to return to St Petersburg, he wrote *Notes from the House of the Dead* (1861), a vivid recounting of his prison sojourn. His life was marred by personal tragedy in the following years, with the deaths of his wife and beloved brother in 1864 plunging him into grief. Addicted to gambling, he was also always in debt.

The ultimate St Petersburg novel and a classic of literature is his *Crime and Punishment* (1866), which depicts in great detail the squalor of anti-hero Raskolnikov's surroundings. As well as being a tale of frustrated individuality and redemption, it also acknowledged the 'other side' of the regal, pretty capital that was now becoming industrialised, gritty and spawning shifty, unsavoury characters.

In his later works, *The Idiot, The Possessed* and *The Brothers Karamazov,* his emerging criticism of the revolutionary movement as morally bankrupt was expressed, as was his belief that only by following Christ's ideal could humanity be saved. His writing also reflected a compassionate understanding of man's strengths, weaknesses and motivations.

While for many his writing is merely gloomy (he apparently had a light, happy side that is rarely made mention of), he remains one of history's most insightful writers. His depiction of St Petersburg also captured the city's essence and shaped audiences' impressions of it the world over.

at the time. Despite living here most of his life, Dostoevsky eventually turned against the city and the Europeanisation that it represented. A deep Russophilia and suspicion of all Western imports characterised Dostoevsky's life, and he took personally against the city he lived in during his last years.

THE SILVER AGE

The late 19th century saw the rise of the symbolist movement in the Russian arts world. The outstanding figures of this time were the novelists Vladimir Solovyov (1853–1900), Andrei Bely (1880–1934) and Alexander Blok (1880–1921) as well as the poets Sergei Yesenin, Lev Gumilev and Anna Akhmatova. The Stray Dog, an underground bar on Arts Sq that has been reopened in recent years, was the meeting place where poets would read aloud from their work and writers, musicians and artists would exchange ideas over plenty of alcohol.

Alexander Blok took over where Dostoevsky left off, writing of prostitutes, drunks, Roma and other characters marginalised by society. Blok's sympathies with the revolutions of 1905 and 1917 were held up by the Bolsheviks – as was the work of Vladimir Mayakovsky – as an example of an established writer who had seen the light; Blok's *The Twelve,* published in 1918, is pretty much a love letter to Lenin. However, he soon grew deeply disenchanted with the revolution, consequently fell out of favour and died a sad, lonely poet. In one of his last letters, he wrote, 'She did devour me, lousy, snuffling dear Mother Russia, like a sow devouring her piglet'. The flat where he spent the last eight years of his life is now a museum.

REVOLUTIONARY LITERATURE

The immediate aftermath of 1917 saw a huge creative upswing in Russia – writers inspired by the revolution produced work of unprecedented brilliance. However, this was very temporary, the Bolsheviks being no connoisseurs of culture and not appreciating literature unless it was directly supporting the communist movement. While some brilliant writers such as Mayakovsky managed to write within the system, penning some excellent poetry and plays in the 1920s, most writers found little success in the prevailing climate of Philistinism and art 'serving the people'.

Under Stalin, who made Lenin look like a cultured renaissance man, Maxim Gorky, one of the less talented writers of his generation, was promoted to unofficial laureate of the revolution, with Mayakovsky bringing up the rear.

At the same time superbly talented contemporaries such as Boris Pilnyak, Yury Olesha, Yevgeny Zamyatin and Osip Mandelshtam found themselves faced with silence, exile or death, refusing as they did to produce the kind of work that Stalin demanded of Soviet writers. Stalin announced that writers were 'engineers of the human soul' and as such had a responsibility to write in a partisan direction. Ultimately Stalin's ceaseless demands for propaganda got too much for some – Mayakovsky shot himself in 1930.

The clampdown on diverse literary styles culminated in the late 1930s with the creation of socialist realism, a literary form created by communist functionaries to promote the needs of the state, praise industrialisation and demonise social misfits and anyone else deemed unsupportive of the revolution. The long-established tradition of underground writing flourished under the communists, and while Stalin's propaganda machine was churning out novels with titles such as *How the Steel Was Tempered* and *Cement,* St Petersburg's writing community were secretly writing about life under the great tyrant.

No literary figure, though, is as inextricably linked to the fate of St Petersburg-Petrograd-Leningrad as Anna Akhmatova (1889–1966), the long-suffering poet whose work contains bittersweet depictions of the city she so loved. Akhmatova's life was filled with sorrow and loss – her family was imprisoned and killed, her friends exiled, tortured and arrested, her colleagues were constantly hounded – but she refused to leave her beloved city and died there in 1966. Her work depicts the city with realism and monumentalism, painted with Russian as well as personal history. Her major work is *Poem Without a Hero.* While the Communist Party's condemnation of her work (in a denunciation in August 1946) as 'the poetry of a crazed lady, chasing back and forth between boudoir and chapel' may not have been fair, her love for her city was unconditional but unblinking: 'The capital on the Neva; Having forgotten its greatness; Like a drunken whore; Did not know who was taking her'.

Top Five St Petersburg Books

- *The Bronze Horseman* (Alexander Pushkin) – Pushkin's great poetic epic sees the sculpture of Peter the Great coming to life after a ruinous flood that all but wipes out the city.
- *Nevsky Prospekt* (Nikolai Gogol) – Gogol's superb evocation of the city's vast main avenue and the amusing characters that haunt it will usually draw any first-time readers to discover Gogol's other St Petersburg tales.
- *Crime and Punishment* (Fyodor Dostoevsky) – The quintessential St Petersburg novel. Poor student Raskolnikov decides to take control of his destiny by killing an old money lender who is a blight on society. If only it were all that simple…
- *Petersburg* (Andrei Bely) – A modernist novel that either baffles or thrills, often both: the city as it was in 1905 is evoked through interweaved stories and glimpses into peoples' lives.
- *Pushkin House* (Andrei Bitov) – A search for personal identity in a country where individualism is all but proscribed, Bitov's 1960s masterpiece is considered to be one of the greatest Soviet novels.

POST-WAR LITERATURE

Akhmatova, partly as a reward for her cooperation in the war effort, was allowed to publish again after the war and remained the great name in St Petersburg letters. More cautious this time after the misery of her son's constant arrest and imprisonment during the 1930s, Akhmatova worked mainly in secret on her masterpieces *Requiem* and *Poem Without a Hero*. After Stalin's death and the Khrushchev thaw slowly began to set in, a group of young poets in the city started to meet at Akhmatova's apartment regularly. Soon known as 'Akhmatova's Orphans', the star of the group was the fiercely talented Joseph Brodsky.

Brodsky was a true original. Despite growing up in the Soviet Union he seemed to have no fear of the consequences that writing your mind in the USSR might bring. He was heading for disaster from a very young age. In 1964, he was tried for 'social parasitism' and exiled to the north of Russia for five years, although after concerted international protests led by Jean-Paul Sartre, his sentence was shortened to time served and he returned to Leningrad in 1965, only to continue being a thorn in the side of the authorities immediately.

During Brodksy's absence, Khrushchev had been overthrown and the conservative Brezhnev took over the reins of power, reversing most of his predecessor's liberal decisions. It was Brezhnev who came up with another plan to silence Soviet writers and sending the troublemakers into foreign exile began soon after. Brodsky was put on a plane to Germany in 1972 and Alexander Solzhenitsyn was deported to the United States in 1974, having been awarded the Nobel Prize for his *Gulag Archipelago*. Both writers became world famous overnight, their freedom to speak the truth about life in the Soviet Union being used as the ultimate anti-Soviet propaganda.

The literature of St Petersburg thereafter was less eventful, the fall of communism leading to a huge round of printing as the banned works of the Soviet period, both foreign and Russian, flooded the market. While Russia has produced several important writers since the end of communism including Viktor Pelevin, Boris Akunin, Ludmilla Petrushevskaya and Vladimir Sorokin, St Petersburg itself is still waiting to find its 21st-century voice.

DANCE

First brought to Russia under Tsar Alexis Mikhailovich in the 17th century, ballet in Russia evolved as an offshoot of French dance combined with Russian folk and peasant dance techniques. It stunned Western Europeans when it was first taken on tour during the 19th century.

The 'official' beginnings of Russian ballet date to 1738 and the establishment by French dance master Jean Baptiste Lande of a school of dance in the Winter Palace, the precursor to the famed Vaganova School of Choreography. Catherine the Great created the Bolshoy Theatre to develop opera and ballet in 1765, and imported foreign composers and teachers.

Marius Petipa (1819–1910) is considered to be the father of Russian ballet. The French dancer and choreographer acted first as principal dancer, then Premier Ballet Master of the Imperial Theatre. All told he produced more than 60 full ballets (including Tchaikovsky's *Sleeping Beauty* and *Swan Lake*).

At the turn of the 20th century, the heyday of Russian ballet, St Petersburg's Imperial School of Ballet rose to world prominence, producing superstar after superstar. Names such as Vaslav Nijinsky, Anna Pavlova, Mathilda Kshesinskaya, George Balanchine, Michel Fokine and Olga Spessivtzeva turned the Mariinsky Theatre into the world's most dynamic display of the art of dance. Sergei Diaghilev's Ballets Russes took Europe by storm. The stage décor was unlike anything seen before. Painted by artists (like Alexander Benois) and not stagehands, it suspended disbelief and shattered the audience's sense of illusion.

Under the Soviets ballet was treated as a natural resource. It enjoyed highly privileged status, which allowed schools like the Vaganova and companies like the Kirov to maintain a level of lavish production and no-expense-spared star-searches. Still, the story of 20th-century Russian ballet is connected with the West, to where so many of its brightest stars emigrated or defected. Pavlova, Nijinsky, Rudolf Nureyev, Mikhail Baryshnikov, Balanchine, Kshesinskaya, Natalia Makarova, to name a few, all found fame in Western Europe or America.

Monarchs of the Ballet World

In the West, most people associate Russian ballet with the male stars whose notoriety and well-documented flights from the Soviet Union made them household names: Nureyev, Nijinsky, Baryshnikov. But to Petersburgers, the true magic of their rich ballet lore is tied to two women – Anna Pavlova and Mathilda Kshesinskaya.

Pavlova, born just outside St Petersburg in 1881, first danced at the Mariinsky in 1899. Within a decade she and Nijinsky were dancing together in some of the most excitingly choreographed productions the world had seen, mainly by Michel Fokine. In 1909, when Diaghilev's Ballets Russes in Paris produced Fokine's *Les Sylphides* (*Chopiana* in Russia), audiences were rapturous. Pavlova's light-as-air grace was an instant sensation.

In 1912 she emigrated to form her own ballet company in the West. Her ambassadorial skills (representing ballet, that is) remain unmatched – in an age without seat sales and air-mile points, she travelled some 500,000km across the globe in 15 years. A dessert was even named after her in Australia! She is largely credited for bringing ballet to the US. Her most remembered role is in Fokine's *The Dying Swan,* written especially for her.

She died in a hotel room in The Hague in 1931 and was cremated close to her London home. Over the years there were many attempts to bring her ashes back to Russia for a proper burial, but these were always marred by bureaucracy and indecisiveness on the Russian side, which at one point called the proposition 'of highly dubious legality'. Problems were settled and Pavlova's ashes were finally sent to Moscow for a September 2001 burial.

Mathilda Kshesinskaya, born in 1872 near Petrodvorets, graduated from the Imperial Ballet School and instantly became its star. She was the first Russian dancer to master 32 consecutive *fouettés en tournant* (spins done in place on one leg), considered then the ultimate achievement in ballet. She was also the subject of curiosity and admiration for her private life – she was the lover of Nicholas II in his pre-tsar days and later married his cousin, the Grand Duke André. She hosted glamorous balls in her mansion that were attended by the elite of St Petersburg society.

She emigrated to France in 1920, where she lived and taught ballet until she died in 1971. She is revered as a heroine of her times – for her outspokenness, her professional mastery and for the debonair way she controlled her own affairs (only men were supposed to do all that!).

Her old mansion now houses the **Museum of Political History** (p113), but there's a wonderful exhibit on the ballerina inside and the ladies working inside will be happy to fill you in on details of Kshesinskaya's life.

The Kirov, whose home is the Mariinsky Theatre (the company is sometimes referred to as the Mariinsky Opera and Ballet), has been rejuvenated under the fervent directorship of Valery Gergiev, a charismatic Ossetian who has made the Mariinsky once again one of the top companies in the world. Not afraid to take chances, he has revived with great success some lesser-known operas by his personal favourite Prokofiev, such as *War and Peace* (the premiere of which was attended by Putin and guest Tony Blair). In 1998 he also opened the Academy of Young Singers at the Mariinsky, now one of the only major theatres in the world to cast young, fresh talent in some of opera's juiciest roles. While the Mariinsky's calling card has always been its flawless classical ballet, recent names to have worked on St Petersburg's premier stage have included William Forsythe and John Neumeier, bringing modern ballet choreography to an establishment not traditionally associated with innovation. The Mariinsky's credibility on the world stage is set to soar further in 2008 on completion of its controversial new theatre being built adjacent to the old one on the Kryukov Canal.

Valery Mikhailovsky's fantastic St Petersburg Male Ballet company (www.maleballet.spb.ru), formed in 1992, has also made an international name for itself, dressing world-class male dancers in tutus and staging innovative, emotional productions of classical and modern ballets.

MUSIC

CLASSICAL

The roots of Russian music lie in folk song and dance and Orthodox Church chants. *Byliny,* epic folk songs of Russia's peasantry, preserved folk culture and lore through celebration of particular events such as great battles or harvests. More formal music slowly reached acceptance in Russian society, first as a religious aid, then for military and other ceremonial use, and eventually for entertainment.

The defining period of Russian music was from the 1860s to 1900. As Russian composers (and painters and writers) struggled to find a national identity, several influential schools formed, from which some of Russia's most famous composers and finest music emerged. The Group of Five – Mussorgsky, Rimsky-Korsakov, Borodin, Kui and Balakirev – believed that a radical departure was necessary, and they looked to *byliny* and folk music for themes. Their main opponent was Anton Rubinshteyn's conservatively rooted Russian Musical Society, which became the St Petersburg Conservatory in 1861, the first in Russia.

The middle ground was, it seems, discovered by Pyotr Tchaikovsky (1840–93), a student of the conservatory, who embraced Russian folklore and music as well as the disciplines of the Western European composers. Tchaikovsky is widely regarded as the father of Russian national composers.

Far from the middle ground was composer Dmitri Shostakovich (1906–75), who wrote alternately brooding, bizarrely dissonant works, as well as accessible traditional classical works. His belief that music and ideology went hand in hand meant that his career would be alternately praised and condemned by the Soviet government; after official condemnation by Stalin, Shostakovich's 7th Symphony – the Leningrad – brought him honour and international standing when it was performed by the Leningrad Philharmonic during the Siege of Leningrad. The authorities changed their mind again and banned his anti-Soviet music in 1948, then 'rehabilitated' him after Stalin's death.

Igor Stravinsky spent some 30 years in America but in his memoirs credits his childhood in St Petersburg as having had major effects on his music, such as *Petrouchka*. The official Soviet line was that he was a 'political and ideological renegade', but after visiting the USSR in 1962 and being received by Khrushchev himself, he was rehabilitated.

OPERA

When Peter the Great began throwing Western culture at his fledgling capital, the music of Western European composers was one of the chief weapons in his arsenal. He held weekly concerts of music by composers from the West – Vivaldi was a favourite. Catherine the Great further encouraged Western music and it gained popularity. St Petersburg was the birthplace of Russian opera when Mikhail Glinka's *A Life for the Tsar,* which merged traditional and Western influence, was performed on 9 December 1836. It told the story of peasant Ivan Susanin, who sacrifices himself to save Mikhail Romanov. Another pivotal moment was the

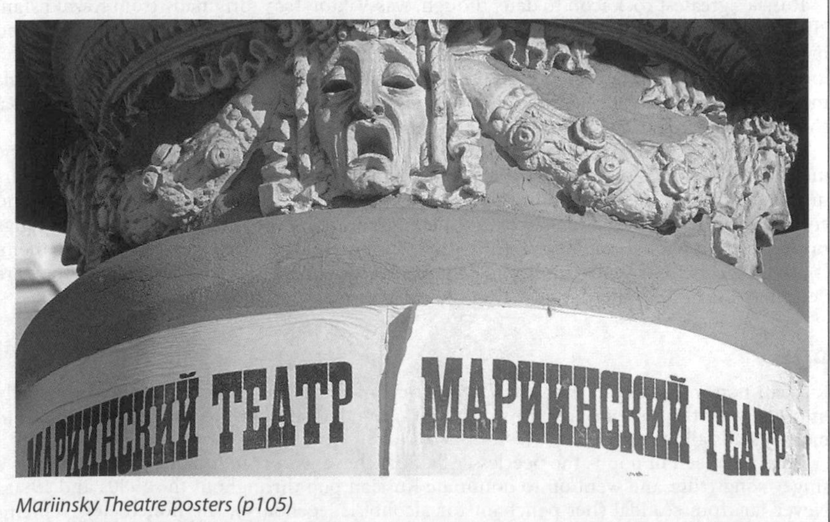

Mariinsky Theatre posters (p105)

5 December 1890 premiere of Tchaikovsky's *Queen of Spades* at the Mariinsky. His adaptation of the famous Pushkin tale surprised and invigorated the artistic community at the time as Tchaikovsky's deviations from the original text – infusing it with more cynicism and a brooding sense of doom – tied the piece to contemporary St Petersburg itself, and to its future. Tchaikovsky had successfully merged opera with topical social comment.

Classical opera was performed regularly in the Soviet period, though audiences went mad for the occasional foreign tour, to see something new and different, like a series of Benjamin Britten operas in 1964 performed at the Mariinsky. Valery Gergiev has revitalised the **Mariinsky** (p105), and operas are as popular as ever. Recent triumphs have included the ambitious production of Shostakovich's *The Nose* (based on Gogol's surreal story set in St Petersburg) in 2004 and the staging of Wagner's entire *Ring Cycle* in 2003.

ROCK

While subversive poetry and *samizdat* (underground) literature fascinated the intelligentsia during the years of stagnation, rock became an entire generation's tool of dissent, having the popular appeal to create a mass movement on such a scale as to worry the Kremlin.

It was the Beatles that first stunned St Petersburg's youth when they first filtered through (future Nobel laureate Joseph Brodsky's translation of *Yellow Submarine* was widely circulated). Rock developed underground, starved of decent equipment and the chance to record or perform to big audiences, but it gathered a huge following among the disaffected, distrustful youth of the 1970s (the Soviet hippy era) and 1980s. Vladimir Rekshan, leader of the band Sankt Peterburg, became one of the first rock stars in Russia.

Bands in the 1970s started by imitating Western counterparts but eventually home-grown music emerged. In the early 1980s, many influential bands sprung up in Leningrad. Mitki was a band of artists, poets and musicians who self-styled a Russian variation of hippiedom, donning sailor gear, drinking fantastic amounts of alcohol and putting a Russian accent on the term Bohemian. Boris Grebenshikov and his band Akvarium (Aquarium) caused sensations wherever they performed; his folk rock and introspective lyrics became the emotional cry of a generation. Yury Shevchuk and his band DDT, also from Leningrad and penning very strong lyrics, emerged as the country's main rock band. At first, all of their music was circulated by illegal tapes known as *magizdat,* passed from listener to listener; concerts were held, if at all, in remote halls in city suburbs and even to attend them could be risky. All three bands continue to record to this day.

Russia's greatest rock icon to date, though, was Viktor Tsoy, originally from Kazakhstan. His group Kino was the stuff of legends. A few appearances in kung fu–type flicks helped make Tsoy the King of Cool and his early death in a 1990 car crash ensured the legend a long life. To this day, fans gather on the anniversary of his death (15 August) and play his music. His grave, at the Bogoslovskogo Cemetery in St Petersburg, has been turned into a shrine not dissimilar to Jim Morrison's in Paris.

St Petersburg is responsible for producing the highly unlikely rock-gods that are the members of Leningrad, particularly its charismatic lead singer Sergei Shnurov. The swearing in their lyrics as well as Shnurov's propensity for on-stage nudity has outraged and enthralled in equal measure. Currently, Leningrad are banned from performing big gigs in the Russian capital due to the antipathy Moscow Mayor Yury Luzhkov has for them. If anything, this has vastly multiplied the band's popularity and notoriety, and they are definitely the hottest alternative act on the Russian market today.

POP

Russian pop music began with the *Estrada* acts of the 1970s, which developed gradually into *popsy,* or the heinous creations of synthesizers that still blast from metro stations and market stalls all over the city.

Russia's queen of pop is the peerless Alla Pugacheva who rose to fame in the 1960s as a singer/songwriter and went on to dominate Russian pop throughout the 1980s and 1990s. Never far from scandal (her penchant for alcohol is legendary), she nonetheless remains popular and is still making music in her 50s. She is married to Bulgarian singer Fillip

Kirkorov, a bug-eyed showman many years her junior who has been called the Russian George Michael, although the comparison is hugely flattering.

Pugacheva's daughter Kristina Orbakayte is also a pop star. Other big stars include tATu, the Moscow-based pseudo-lesbian duo whose 2003 smash hit *All the Things She Said* was number one throughout Europe, Boris Moiseev (Russia's first openly gay singer), and Shura, a flamboyant purveyor of pop tunes who famously has no front teeth. In 2003, an unknown girl group called Poyushiye Vmestye (Singing Together) made themselves famous overnight with a pop-ode to presidential heart-throb Vladimir Putin, *Takogo kak Putin* (Just Like Putin), roundly dismissed as a misfired attempt by the Kremlin to make the president appeal to the country's youth, despite furious denials by the administration.

For information on music venues, see p153.

VISUAL ARTS

PEREDVIZHNIKI

In the 18th century, when Peter the Great encouraged Western trends in Russian art, Dmitry Levitsky's portraits were outstanding. The major artistic force of the 19th century was the Peredvizhniki (Wanderers) movement, a group formed by 14 artists who broke away from the conventions of the powerful but conservative Academy of Arts, and who saw art as a force for national awareness and social change. Their name refers to their idea of travelling around the country with yearly exhibits, so that not only Petersburgers would have access to art. They became very famous in their time and counted Alexander III as one of their main patrons.

Its members included Vasily Surikov, who painted vivid Russian historical scenes, Nicholas Ghe (biblical and historical scenes), Arkhip Kuindzhi (moonlit Crimean landscapes) and Ilya Repin, perhaps the best loved of all Russian artists, whose works ranged from social criticism *(Barge Haulers on the Volga)* through history *(Zaporozhie Cossacks Writing a Letter to the Turkish Sultan)* to portraits of the famous.

Isaak Levitan, who revealed the beauty of the Russian landscape, was one of many others associated with the Peredvizhniki. The end-of-century genius Mikhail Vrubel, inspired by sparkling Byzantine and Venetian mosaics, showed early traces of Western influence.

FUTURISM

Around the turn of the 20th century the Mir Iskusstva (World of Art) movement (and art magazine) in St Petersburg, led by Alexander Benois and Sergei Diaghilev under the motto 'art pure and unfettered', opened Russia up to Western innovations like impressionism, Art Nouveau and symbolism. They also wished their movement to be the linchpin for broad cultural change. From about 1905 Russian art became a maelstrom of groups and isms as it absorbed decades of European change in a few years before giving birth to its own avant-garde futurist movements, which in turn helped Western art go head over heels.

Natalia Goncharova and Mikhail Larionov were at the centre of the Jack of Diamonds group (a Cézanne-influenced group with which Vasily Kandinsky was associated) before developing neo-primitivism, based on popular arts and primitive icons.

In 1915 Kazimir Malevich announced the arrival of suprematism, declaring that his utterly abstract geometrical shapes, with the black square representing the ultimate 'zero form', finally freed art from having to depict the material world and made it a doorway to higher realities. Another famed futurist, who managed to escape subordinate isms, was acclaimed poet Vladimir Mayakovsky.

THE SOVIET ERA

It was the futurists who with mixed enthusiasm supplied the revolution with posters, banners and education. They now had a chance to act on their theories of how art shapes society. Even by the early 1920s, formalist art fell sharply out of official favour. Workers felt dispassionate and vaguely confused at the sight of abstract, cubist shapes and coloured panels draping bridges, buildings and posters. The Party wanted socialist realism. Striving workers, heroic soldiers and inspiring leaders took over; Malevich ended up painting penetrating portraits of workers and doing designs for Red Sq parades; Mayakovsky committed suicide.

After Stalin, an avant-garde 'conceptualist' underground was allowed to surface. Ilya Kabakov painted, or sometimes just arranged, the debris of everyday life to show the gap between the promises and realities of Soviet existence. Erik Bulatov's 'Sotsart' pointed to the devaluation of language by ironically reproducing Soviet slogans or depicting words disappearing over the horizon. In 1962 the authorities set up a show of such 'unofficial' art at the Moscow Manezh; Khrushchev called it 'dog shit' and sent it back underground.

Eventually a thaw set in and the avant-garde became international big business.

NEO-ACADEMISM

The main wave in Russian art in the post-Soviet period is undoubtedly neo-academism, founded by St Petersburg artist Timur Novikov in the early 1990s as an antidote to 'the barbarism of modernism'. The neo-academism movement sprung from a short-lived wave of so-called Necro-Realists, who focused on decay as a symbol of a dying social system.

Novikov was a leader of the St Petersburg and Russian arts scenes for over a decade. Until his death in 2002, he continued to work and exhibit despite being blind. In 1982 his theory of 'Zero Object' acted as one of the foundations of Russian conceptual art, and his work with some of Russia's best artists and musicians in the 1980s and 1990s culminated in his Museum of the New Academy of Fine Arts, otherwise known as its address, Pushkinskaya 10, established in 1993. Neo-academic artists, including co-founder Bella Matveeva, Oleg Maslov and Viktor Kuznetzov, and digital artist Olga Tobreluts, once prided themselves on – and even advertised – their propensity towards drugs and alcohol while turning out works that pay homage to classicism (some even dress ominously in Victorian clothes) though infusing it with a street-level, almost junk-shop feel. One common thread that binds them is a hatred for modernism, which they feel killed contemporary art. Their works – not only paintings, but photographs, sculptures, collages, videos, set and graphic designs, and music – have been shown throughout the world.

ARCHITECTURE

St Petersburg provides a fascinating showcase of 18th- and 19th-century architectural styles in its central districts, one of the handsomest of any city in the world and described by one commentator as 'an architecture student's wet dream'. Beginning with Peter and ending with Nicholas I in the mid-19th century, each monarch favoured a distinct architectural style – usually one broadly in keeping with the political philosophy they espoused.

PETRINE BAROQUE

The first major building in the city was the **Peter and Paul Fortress** (p114), completed in 1704 and still intact today. To oversee this and other early projects, Peter recruited Domenico Trezzini from Switzerland and his team of engineers in 1704. It was Trezzini more than any other architect who created the style known as Petrine Baroque – heavily influenced by Dutch architecture at the time, of which, like everything else from Holland, Peter was enamoured. Buildings created by Trezzini and his team included the **Alexander Nevsky Monastery** (p102), the **SS Peter and Paul Cathedral** (p114) within the fortress and the **Twelve Colleges** (p111) on Vasilevsky Island. Trezzini was given the title of 'chief architect' and his office planned and executed all major civic buildings in the city. Despite this, the poor of St Petersburg were quickly creating their own very un-Petrine architecture in the form of log huts that crowded the city, creating fast-expanding suburbs that were a constant cause of fire. The state coffers, emptied by the war against Sweden, initially meant that there simply wasn't enough money to create the European-style city that Peter dreamed of. Once Russia's victory was secured by success at Poltava in 1709, the city really began to see feverish development.

In 1711 the Grand Perspective, later becoming **Nevsky Prospekt** (p99), began to be laid out, initially as a road connecting the city to Russia's interior and along which building supplies could be transported. Its kink on today's pl Vosstaniya is attributed to a miscalculation by builders constructing the road from Novgorod – it was intended to be a perfectly straight avenue.

Peter's second trip abroad in 1716–17 would fill him with a far wider appreciation of European architecture than that he had acquired during his Grand Embassy of 1697–98. Returning to the city in 1717, he waxed enthusiastic about the latest French and Italian styles and sought to incorporate them in the construction of the city. Most significantly, in 1714 the construction of wooden building was banned in St Petersburg and, to ensure that there would be a sufficient number of masons free to work on the city, all stone construction outside the new capital was banned.

The irregular, unplanned development of the city until 1716 led Peter to order Trezzini to create a unified city plan designed around Vasilevsky Island. However, this plan was never implemented as Trezzini's star began to wane. Peter recruited Frenchman Jean Baptiste Alexandre LeBlond from Paris and both he and Trezzini focussed their efforts on Vasilevsky Island, despite people far preferring to live across the river on the higher, better connected Admiralty Island. Menshikov's pink palace was at this time the finest in the city, far grander than Peter's Winter Palace as the tsar himself hated living in vast quarters, preferring simple cottages throughout his life.

AFTER PETER

Peter's wife Catherine, an illiterate peasant from Lithuania, had no interest in or talent for city planning. Her two-year reign produced no significant new buildings in the city, with the exception of Trezzini's Third Winter Palace, although it was also too short to have been particularly detrimental either.

Peter's grandson Peter II moved the capital back to Moscow in 1727 and seemed determined to reverse Peter's reforms. Luckily he died young from smallpox and his successor, Empress Anna, moved the capital back to St Petersburg and oversaw the completion of many of Peter's unfinished projects, including the **Kunstkamera** (p109) and the **Twelve Colleges** (p111). Most significantly of all, she hired Italian Bartolomeo Rastrelli as chief architect, a decision of huge importance to the city's look today. His major projects under Anna's reign were the **Manege** (p88) and the Third Summer Palace, which was unfortunately destroyed and replaced by Tsar Paul's eccentric **Mikhailovsky Castle** (p91) in 1797, although his greatest work was yet to come under Elizabeth.

Alexander Nevsky Monastery (p102)

Anna made a great deal of difference to the face of St Petersburg in other ways too. She ordered all nobles in the city responsible for paving the street in front of their properties, thus ensuring the reinforcement of the Neva Embankment and several other major thoroughfares.

A massive fire in 1737 wiped out the unsightly and run-down wooden housing that surrounded the Winter Palace, thus freeing up what is now the historic centre for the centralised city planning that would be implemented under Empress Elizabeth, Peter the Great's granddaughter.

ELIZABETH & THE AGE OF RASTRELLI

Elizabethan St Petersburg was almost entirely the work of Rastrelli, whose Russian baroque style became synonymous with the city and is still in evidence today. Rastrelli's crowning glory, however, was the remodelling of the **Winter Palace** (p88); he had also completed its previous incarnation under Empress Anna. He completed his work in 1762 shortly after Elizabeth's death, but the palace survives largely as he created it (despite a serious fire in 1837). One major difference was the colour – under Rastrelli it was painted yellow and white.

Rastrelli's second major landmark was the **Anichkov Palace** (p90) on the corner of Nevsky pr and the Fontanka, after which he became the city's most fashionable architect and commissions soon followed to build the **Stroganov Palace** (p97), the **Vorontsov Palace** (southeast of Gostiny Dvor on Sadovaya ul; p92), **Kamennoostrovsky Palace** (p115), the magnificent **Smolny Cathedral** (p101), the **Catherine Palace** (p191) at Tsarskoe Selo, and the extension of LeBlond's **Grand Palace** (p188) at Petrodvorets. Rastrelli's interiors in the last of these projects were so over the top that some commentators have suggested that it was an ironic comment on Elizabeth's insatiable thirst for opulence and pointless grandeur, although it would seem unlikely that a man as astute as Rastrelli would have so pointedly bitten the hand that fed him.

Rastrelli's baroque style would go out of fashion quickly following Elizabeth's death in 1761. But he was responsible for some of the most stunning and enduring buildings in the city, and for contributing much to the Italianate appearance of contemporary St Petersburg. Rastrelli cast a long shadow over successive architects for decades after his fall from favour.

CATHERINE THE GREAT

Catherine, despite her fondness for Elizabeth, was no great fan of her increasingly elaborate and sumptuous displays of wealth and power. Catherine's major philosophical interest in the Enlightenment, which in Western Europe had brought the neoclassical style to the fore, meant that she began her long reign by departing with baroque architecture and introducing neoclassicism to Russia.

The first major neoclassical masterpiece in Catherine's St Petersburg was the building housing the Academy of Fine Arts on Vasilevsky Island, designed by Jean-Baptiste-Michel Vallin de la Mothe. Catherine employed a wider group of favoured architects than Elizabeth; as well as foreigners such as Vallin de la Mothe, Scot Charles Cameron and Italians Antonio Rinaldi and Giacomo Quarenghi, she also commissioned many home-grown architects such as Ivan Starov and Vasily Bazhenov, whom Peter the Great's investment in teaching and foreign education had helped to produce.

Catherine's plan included making the Palace Embankment the centrepiece of the city and to this end she had the **Little Hermitage** (p69) built by Vallin de la Mothe, followed by the **Old Hermitage** (p69), the **Hermitage Theatre** (p69) on the other side of the Winter Canal and then Quarenghi's magnificent **Marble Palace** (p88). Catherine also extended the development of the embankment west of the Winter Palace, to what is now the English Embankment (Angliyskaya nab), creating a marvellous imperial vista for those arriving in the city by boat.

The single most striking and famous of Catherine's additions to the city was Etienne-Maurice Falconet's **Bronze Horseman** (p87), an equestrian statue to Peter the Great on Senate Sq (now pl Dekabristov). Falconet worked on the statue for a staggering 22 years and returned to Paris an angry, frustrated man, and never even saw this most enduring of St Petersburg's monuments completed.

Other notable additions to the cityscape during Catherine's reign included the new **Gostiny Dvor** (Merchant Yard; p92) shopping arcade, one of the world's oldest surviving shopping centres. While Elizabeth had commissioned Rastrelli to rebuild the arcade that burned down further up Nevsky pr in 1736, Catherine took him off the project and had it completed by Vallin de la Mothe, who created a subtler and more understated neoclassical façade. Starov's **Tauride Palace** (p101), built for Potemkin, was perhaps the purest classical construction in St Petersburg during Catherine's reign and survives today. Its expansive English gardens, realised by William Gould, are open as an unfortunately rather run-down public park today.

ALEXANDRINE ARCHITECTURE

Alexander I (r 1801–25) ushered in the new century with much hope that he would see through Catherine's reforms and be the most progressive tsar yet. Architecture under his reign divides into two schools; that pioneered before the Napoleonic Wars by Andreyan Zakharov, Thomas de Thomon and Andrei Voronikhin, and the Alexandrian Empire style of post-1812 in which a new generation of architects, most famous of whom was Carlo Rossi, created a Russian counterpart to the style that had become so popular in prewar Napoleonic France.

Before the Napoleonic Wars, the two most significant additions to the cityscape were de Thomon's Strelka (the 'tongue of land' that is the tip of Vasilevsky Island) and Voronikhin's Kazan Cathedral on Nevsky pr. The **Strelka** (p110) had been the subject of countless designs and proposals as a centrepiece to St Petersburg, but despite Catherine's efforts, nothing grand enough had been completed. De Thomon rebuilt Quarenghi's Stock Exchange and added the much-loved Rostral Columns to the tip of the island, creating a stunning sight during summer festivities when the columns lit the sky with fire, a tradition that still continues today.

The **Kazan Cathedral** (p92) is a fascinating anomaly in St Petersburg's architectural history. While completed under Alexander I, it had been commissioned by Paul and reflected his tastes and desire to fuse Catholicism and Orthodoxy. As such it is strikingly un-Russian, and borrows many of its features from contemporaneous Italian architecture from Rome and Florence.

Following the Napoleonic wars, several projects of true genius were initiated. Most obvious of these is the **General Staff Building** (p88) on Palace Sq, realised by Carlo Rossi, the greatest architect of his age working in Russia. The Italian, even more than Rastrelli, has defined the historic heart of St Petersburg with his imperial buildings. He created the sumptuous General Staff Building that managed to complement Rastrelli's Winter Palace without outshining it; its vast length broken up by white columns creates one of the greatest squares in the world. Rossi also designed and built the magnificent triumphal arch that leads from Bolshaya Morskaya ul into the Palace Sq (and makes up part of the General Staff Building itself, connecting the two buildings over the street). The final touch to Palace Sq was added by Auguste Montferrand, who designed the **Alexander Column** (p88), a monument to Russia's 1812 trouncing of Napoleon. Rossi's other great achievement under Alexander I was the Mikhailovsky Palace and Gardens (now the **Russian Museum**; p93) for the tsar's brother and the Mikhailovskaya Sq (now Arts Sq) in front of it.

Kazan Cathedral (p92)

NICHOLAS I

Rossi's genius continued to shine through the reactionary rule of Nicholas I. In fact, Nicholas was the last of the Romanovs to initiate mass municipal architecture and so Rossi remained very much in favour locally, despite Nicholas's personal preference for Slavic-revival style that was very popular in Moscow.

Rossi's largest projects were the redesign of Senate Sq (now pl Dekabristov) and what many consider to be his finest work, Alexandrinskaya Sq (now pl Ostrovskogo), the **Pushkin Theatre** (p93) and Theatre Street (now ul Zodchego Rossi). The latter ensemble on Theatre Street is particularly noteworthy – its width (22m) is the same height as its buildings and the entire street is exactly 220m, or ten times the size of the buildings and the street's width. The view from pl Lomonosova towards the Pushkin Theatre is breathtaking.

However, the building that was to redefine the city's skyline (and remains the highest structure in the historical heart to this day) was Montferrand's **St Isaac's Cathedral** (p89). The cathedral is unique – an Orthodox church built in a classical style, it is the fourth largest cathedral in Europe and took over three decades to construct.

During Nicholas' reign St Petersburg finally gained its first permanent bridge across the Neva. Originally called the Annunciation Bridge and completed in 1850, it's now known as Lieutenant Schmidt Bridge and connects Admiralty Island to Vasilevsky Island. Another step to modernity was taken with the building of Russia's first railroad, linking the capital to Tsarskoe Selo. A more useful line to Moscow began service in 1851, and to accommodate it the Nikolaevsky Station (now known as the **Moscow Station**; p103) was opened on pl Vosstaniya.

Other projects completed during Nicholas' reign had a mainly military theme: Stasov's **Trinity Cathedral** (p102) for the barracks of the Izmailovsky Regiment, which features the city's most pleasing cupola – painted in deep ink blue and hovering mesmerisingly over the Fontanka despite its dire need for restoration; the **Narva Triumphal Gates** (p120), another monument to the 1812 defeat of Napoleon; and the **Moscow Triumphal Arch** (p120) commemorating victory against the Ottoman Empire in 1828. One final masterpiece of the era was Shtakenschneider's mouthful, the **Beloselsky-Belozersky Palace** (p98) on the corner of the Fontanka and Nevsky pr.

IMPERIAL ST PETERSBURG

The reigns of Alexander II and III saw few changes to the overall building style in St Petersburg, although under Alexander II industrialisation led to the filling in of several canals, most significantly the Ligovsky Canal (now one of the city's busiest streets, Ligovsky pr). Fortunately for the appearance of the city, a plan to fill in what is now Griboedova Canal proved too expensive to execute and the canal remains one of the city's most charming.

Alexander III's main contribution to the city was the Church of the Resurrection of Christ, referred to by one and all as the **Church on Spilled Blood** (p91), built as it was on the site of his father's assassination in 1881 by terrorists. Alexander III insisted the church be in the Slavic revival style, which explains its uncanny similarity in silhouette to Red Square's St Basil's Cathedral. Architects Malyshev and Parland erected the pompous church so beloved

Unique St Petersburg Buildings

The city is full of architectural gems, although some are more obvious than others. The following are a few truly quirky buildings that are worth the effort to see.

- **Communications Workers' Palace of Culture** – A fantastic anomaly on the Moyka River, this constructivist edifice is a must see. Nightmare or gem, you decide.
- **Vitebsk Station** (p210) – Russia's first train station is a charming and seductive place built in the mid-19th century. Check out the recently renovated tsar's waiting room for some tsarist grandeur.
- **House of Soviets** (p119) – High Stalinism's best representative in the city, this spooky place on Moskovsky pr is right out of *1984*. The frieze depicting the working people's struggle is fantastic.
- **Chesme Church** (p119) – Many consider this gothic masterpiece to be St Petersburg's single most impressive church. Despite its small size, its magnificent colour scheme and sense of movement (it appears to rise out of the ground perhaps about to take off) are enormously striking.
- **Church of St John of Kronshtadt on ul Nekrasova** (p98) – The façade of this unique church is wonderful – Byzantine meets Muscovite revival – and completely atypical of its time.
- **Tower House, pl Tolstogo** – One of the many *style moderne* masterpieces on the Petrograd Side, Tower House rises majestically over Kamennoostrovsky pr with its balconies and unusual crenellations borrowed from English medieval castles.

by visitors to the city, and in its spectacular multi-coloured tiling work there are the first hints of the Russian *style moderne* that was to take the city by storm by the end of the 19th century.

That the ineffective and deeply conservative Nicholas II was to preside over one of the city's most exciting architectural periods was pure chance. As the city became richer and richer during the 19th century the industrialist and merchant classes began building mansions in the feted Art Nouveau style, known in Russia as *style moderne*.

The Petrograd side, the most fashionable at the time, was where the majority of *style moderne* buildings were constructed, and wandering the back streets here reveals a huge number of late-19th-century and early-20th-century Art Nouveau buildings. Nicholas II's mistress before his marriage, the ballet dancer Mathilda Kshesinskaya, lived in one of the most fabulous *style moderne* buildings, a mansion on Kamennoostrovsky pr that now houses the **Museum of Political History** (p113).

Church on Spilled Blood (p91)

SOVIET ARCHITECTURE

As in all other spheres, the collapse of tsarism and the communist coup in October 1917 changed everything in architecture. The beleaguered city stopped all major building projects and the vast aristocratic palaces and mansions of the nouveaux riches were either turned over to the state or split up into communal apartments for workers.

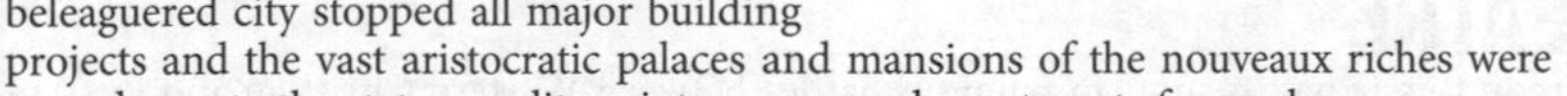

Both Lenin and Stalin detested St Petersburg and the worldly, liberal values it stood for. When the title of capital was returned to Moscow in 1918 as the Germans approached St Petersburg, the city went into a decline that was to last until the 1990s. That's not to say that it was ignored, however: its first Soviet governor, Zinoviev, planned rather unrealistically to construct a vast three-towered skyscraper in the city that would serve as everything from local administration to palace of culture.

Constructivism was the architectural form that found favour under the Bolsheviks in the 1920s. Areas rich with constructivist buildings include around pl Stachek, such as the Kirov Region Administrative Building on Kirovskaya pl; and the incredibly odd Communication Workers' Palace of Culture on the Moyka Canal.

Once Stalin was in total control from 1927 he initiated a policy of relocating the centre of newly renamed Leningrad to the south of the historic heart, considering the opulence of the imperial centre a potentially corrupting influence on the people. His traditional neoclassical tastes prevailed, creating Stalinist architecture, the prime example of which is the vast House of the Soviets, around which the new city centre was to be built. Begun by Noy Trotsky in 1936, although not finished until after the war (by which time Trotsky had himself been purged), this magnificently sinister building is a great example of Stalinist neoclassical design (similar in many ways to the imperial neoclassicism pioneered a century beforehand) with its columns and bas-reliefs. It was never used as the Leningrad government building as the plan was shelved after Stalin's death in 1953. A combination of WWII and Stalin's old age saved many buildings of great importance, including the Church on Spilled Blood, which was slated for destruction before the German invasion of the Soviet Union intervened. Other churches and historical buildings were not so lucky, though.

During the eras of Khrushchev and Brezhnev, St Petersburg's cultural (ie imperial) heritage was cautiously respected as the communist leadership took a step back from Stalin's excesses. However, between the 1950s and 1970s huge swathes of the city outside the historic centre were covered with high-rise Soviet apartment buildings, which for many will be the first and last thing they see in the city. Examples of archetypal post-Stalinist Soviet architecture include the Oktyabrsky Concert Hall next to pl Vosstaniya and the horrifically bland **Finland Station** (p116).

CONTEMPORARY ARCHITECTURE

Contemporary building efforts have been focussed since the end of communism on the reconstruction of imperial-era buildings, many of which were derelict and literally falling down due to 70 years of neglect. Some success stories include the renovation of the **Grand Hotel Europe** (p92), the **Mikhailovsky Castle** (p91), the **Beloselsky-Belozersky Palace** (p98), the **Anichkov most** (p98), the **Grand Choral Synagogue** (p105), the **Smolny** (p101), the **Spaso-preobrazhensky** (p101), **Nikolsky** (p106) and **Vladimirsky** (p99) cathedrals, and the on-going mammoth renovation of **Gostiny Dvor** (p92).

As so much energy has gone into preservation efforts for the historic centre a modern St Petersburg architecture has not emerged, most newly constructed buildings being a bland modern style recognisable throughout Russia in post-1991 buildings.

One building that has certainly created much controversy is the new Mariinsky Theatre building, to be erected behind the present theatre on Teatralnaya pl. This remarkable building will totally break with St Petersburg's architectural tradition (and in doing so inevitably enrage many more traditional residents, who point out that even the Soviets didn't have the nerve to alter the imperial centre beyond the bare minimum). Dominique Perrault's unique design is a black marble theatre wrapped in a vast irregular golden glass dome, the so-called 'golden envelope'. Without doubt the first major architectural addition to the city in the 21st century, Mariinsky II is due to open in 2008.

THEATRE

Theatre in Russia has its roots in religious battles between Western Christian and Russian Orthodox churches, which were vying for members as early as the 16th century. Because Jesuits used dramatic scenes to propagandise and spread their message, the Russian Orthodox Church found it had to do likewise in order to stop an exodus to Catholicism. Over the centuries that followed, drama was almost exclusively used in a similar fashion by schools and the Church, until tsars and nobility began importing tragedy and comedy from the West.

Vaudeville – biting, satirical one-act comedies that had been created on the streets of Paris and poked fun at the rich and powerful – found its way into Russia in the 19th century and the practice of using theatre to put forth the Party or church line on social issues came under attack by playwrights like Pushkin and Mikhail Lermontov. Other writers, such as Gogol, Alexander Griboyedov and Alexander Ostrovsky, wrote plays that attacked not just the aristocracy but the bourgeoisie as well.

Anton Chekhov wrote for St Petersburg newspapers before writing one-act, vaudevillian works. Yet it is his full-length plays, especially *Uncle Vanya* and *The Seagull,* which are his legacy. Towards the end of the 19th century, Maxim Gorky's *The Stormy Petrel,* which raised workers to a level superior to that of the intellectual, earned him reverence by the Soviets as the initiator of socialist realism.

The futurists had their day on the stage, mainly in the productions of the energetic and tirelessly inventive director Vsevolod Meyerhold, who was one of the most influential figures of modern theatre. His productions of Blok's *The Fair Show Booth* (1906) and Mayakovsky's *Mystery-Bouffe* (1918) caused sensations at the time, and his 1935 production of Tchaikovsky's *Queen of Spades* was cited as strongly influential by Akhmatova and Shostakovich.

St Petersburg on the Screen

- *October* (*Oktyabr*; Sergei Eisenstein; 1928) Eisenstein's brilliant Marxist epic depicts a largely fictional version of the Russian Revolution, shot in Leningrad using some 11,000 extras. The lighting needs of the production left the entire city without electricity during the shoot, the most famous scene of which – the magnificent storming of the Winter Palace – remains an almost unmatched piece of cinematography.
- *Errors of Youth* (*Oshibki Yunosti*; Boris Frumin; 1978) A fascinating glimpse at life outside the law in the Soviet Union, Frumin's portrait of the Soviet superfluous man follows Dmitry Gurianov's efforts to find his place in life during the period of the Brezhnev stagnation. After dishonesty in the army, boredom in the countryside and a failed affair, he heads to Leningrad where he ends up as a black marketeer. A brave attempt at realism, the film was of course banned.
- *Brother* (*Brat*; Alexei Balabanov; 1997) A cult movie for the post-perestroika generation, Balabanov's huge hit stars late heart throb Sergei Bodrov Jnr as the young Danila Bogrov, a veteran from the Chechen War who comes to St Petersburg to find his brother (the fabulous Viktor Sukhorukov) and ends up taking on the mafia. A gruesome portrait of mid-1990s St Petersburg and the worst excesses of the new Russia.
- *Of Freaks and Men* (*Pro Urodov i Lyudey*; Alexei Balabanov; 1998) A change of gear for Balabanov just a year after *Brother*, this dark art-house film portrays the lives of pornographers in pre-Revolutionary Petrograd. Shot beautifully in sepia tones and in the style of early Russian cinema, there are some astounding scenes, such as the Mongolian conjoined-twin porn stars floating away on an iceberg and a tram crossing the Lieutenant Schmidt Bridge to the strains of Prokofiev. Magnificent, if highly odd.
- *Russian Ark* (*Russky Kovcheg*; Alexander Sokurov; 2002) Filmed in one single 96-minute tracking shot, Sokurov's masterpiece is a highly eccentric film that muses on the history and destiny of Russia through the metaphor of a stroll through the Hermitage. Using 867 actors and after months of rehearsal, he amazingly got the entire film on the second take. Hard work, but the surreal culmination is incredibly moving.

The Soviet period saw drama used primarily as a propaganda tool and when foreign plays were performed it was usually for a reason – hence the popularity in Russia of *Death of a Salesman*, which showed just what Western (US) greed and decadence would lead to. However, just after the revolution, theatre artists were given great, if short-lived, freedom to experiment – anything to make theatre accessible to the masses. Avant-garde productions flourished for a while, notably under the mastery of poet and director Igor Terentyev. Artists such as Pavel Filonov and Malevich participated in production and stage design.

Even socialist theatre was strikingly experimental: the Theatre of Worker Youth, under the guidance of Mikhail Sokolovsky, used only non-professional actors, encouraged improvisation, sudden plot alterations and interaction with audience members, and strove to redefine the theatre-going experience. Free theatre tickets were given out at factories, and halls which once echoed with the jangle of their upper-class audience's jewellery were now filled with sailors and workers. The tradition of sending army regiments and schoolchildren to the theatre continues to this day.

For information on theatre venues, see p160.

CINEMA

The Lenfilm studios on the Petrograd Side were a big centre of the Soviet film industry, producing many much-loved Russian comedies and dramas, and have continued in the post-communist era to work with some success as a commercial film studio. Most famously scenes from the James Bond film *Golden Eye* (1995), featuring Pierce Brosnan as 007 driving around St Petersburg in a tank, were partly shot at Lenfilm. However, the removal of the lavish Soviet-era state funding for filmmaking has inevitably led to torpor in the local industry. Most major Russian films are made in Moscow and are nearly always made with foreign money.

Being one of the most cinematic of cities, it's sad that St Petersburg has made so relatively few appearances on the big screen. Of course there are famous exceptions, such as Sergei Eisenstein's *October* (1928), but the closed nature of the Soviet Union meant that very few films known internationally were made in Leningrad, and since the end of communism a lack of funding has hindered budding young talents in the city from making films.

Despite this there have been some recent Lenfilm successes including Alexander Sokurov's *Russian Ark* and Alexei Balabanov's *Of Freaks and Men*, both of which enjoyed a great deal of critical acclaim in the West. Indeed, Sokurov is being increasingly recognised as Russia's most talented director currently working. A St Petersburg native, his films have taken on a long range of subjects from the dying days of Hitler *(Molokh)* and Lenin *(Taurus)* to his extraordinarily tender films about family relationships: *Mother and Son* and *Father and Son*.

History

History

21ST-CENTURY ST PETERSBURG

St Petersburg began the 21st century in perhaps the most optimistic way possible: on New Year's Eve 1999, ageing President Boris Yeltsin resigned from his job, leaving the country to be run by his young Prime Minister Vladimir Putin, a native of the northern capital. In many countries the home-town of the head of state might well be dismissed as an irrelevance, but in Russia, where the rivalry between Moscow and St Petersburg is one that cuts to the heart of the nation's destiny and world outlook, the significance of a Petersburger as president was lost on nobody, marking a comeback for the long-sidelined northern capital. The city's second great boost was its tercentennial celebrations in May 2003, not to mention the vast amount of federal money that was poured into local restoration and investment, or the boost to tourism that the anniversary created. The celebrations themselves may have been rather forgettable, but the prestige and self-confidence they brought were essential. After a brutal and miserable 20th century that almost saw the city erased from the face of the earth, its greatest minds shot or exiled and its heritage left to fate, the first years of the new century have been overwhelmingly positive ones that look forward to a great future.

FROM THE BEGINNING

CONTEXT

Context is everything in understanding the history of St Petersburg. The city's creation in Russia's northern wilderness was no isolated event; it was the logical result of the continuing debate between the two opposing schools of thought that have conflicted in Russia since the Dark Ages. Without understanding this, the mere facts of St Petersburg's creation and development are meaningless.

Throughout Russia's turbulent history, two general philosophies have stood out, which historians would later characterise as 'Slavophile' and 'Westernising'. These two schools have fought constantly to control Russia's direction and the battle is very much ongoing today.

Broadly speaking, the Slavophile school sees Russia as a unique country on earth, standing aloof between Europe and Asia without being part of either. Its fundamental belief is in Orthodoxy and that Russia has a unique destiny independent of any other countries, save perhaps the other Slav nations, which it considers its natural allies (and, less explicitly, its satellites). Famous Slavophiles have included Dostoevsky and Nicholas II.

The Westernising school has always sought to benefit from European civilisation and innovations in all forms: political, social and technological. Despite the implications of the term 'Westernising', it would be misleading to assume that it was blindly pro-Western or in any way anti-Russian, believing very strongly that this very same Western influence can be fused with Russian traditions and ideas to create something superior to them both. The most famous Westerniser was of course Peter the Great, but others include Catherine the Great, Leo Trotsky, Boris Yeltsin and (cautiously) Vladimir Putin.

Moscow has historically been the seat of Slavophiles – isolated, inland, inward-looking, devout and traditional. Peter the Great created St Petersburg for Westernisers, realising that

TIMELINE 1703	1712
Peter the Great founds St Petersburg	Government institutions begin to move to St Petersburg from Moscow

the only way for them to gain the ascendancy was to start afresh with a clean slate in a new capital where his ideas could bear fruit. St Petersburg was famously described as Peter's 'window on Europe', and its changing fate over the past 300 years has reflected the balance of power between the Slavophiles and the Westernisers.

Essential Reading

If you want to get into the history of the city from its origins to the present day, there's simply no contest: buy Arthur George's superb *St Petersburg: Russia's Window to the Future - the First Three Centuries* (2003). This fascinating, funny and staggeringly comprehensive political, social and cultural history of the city is unrivalled. Squarely putting St Petersburg's history in the context of Russia's ongoing struggle between Slavophiles and Westernisers, it's hard to read without George's passion for all aspects of the city rubbing off.

GENESIS

It is a romantic yet entirely untrue notion that before Peter the Great nothing existed at the mouth of the Neva River. It was strategically vital and access to the Baltic Sea was guarded with fierce jealousy by the Swedes who correctly estimated that if Russia were able to gain an outlet to trade with Western Europe, its subsequent development would soon be so overwhelming as to threaten the Swedish Kingdom from the east.

To forestall Russian development around the mouth of the Neva River, the Swedes captured the lands from the Teutonic Knights in 1330 and built a fortress where the Okhta River runs into the Neva in the present-day suburb of Okhta. If anything, this was the first formalised fort in this location, despite the fact that the Russians took the fortress back just one year later, renamed it Korabelnitsa and used it as a dock for boats trawling the Neva.

The Swedes and the Russians fought over this sorry foothold and the settlements that gradually grew up around it for three centuries without ever reaching a conclusion. In its last incarnation before Peter the Great's arrival on the scene, Korabelnitsa was destroyed, renamed Nyen and became a very important Swedish port on the Baltic, handling much of Russian trade with Finland and Sweden.

While the Swedes were confident in their stronghold, they were unprepared for the chain of events that would ultimately banish them from the Neva for good and see the inexorable rise of the Russian nation as a great power. First there was the ongoing crisis of Muscovy, then the end of the Russian war with Turkey in 1700 and the emergence of two European allies with whom Russia could unite against Sweden in the early 18th century. Then, most importantly of all, there was Peter the Great.

THE CRISIS OF MUSCOVY

Moscow became the capital of what is now modern Russia by developing into the chief town of Rus under the Mongol Horde in the 14th and 15th centuries. Assisting the Mongols to subdue rival Russian towns, Moscow soon began to administer the entire region, earning trust from the Mongols before turning on them and banishing them from Russia for good.

Yet Moscow was hindered in its development by its remote location. Unnavigable from any other European city of significance, it was largely cut off culturally and technologically from the developments of Western Europe. While the Enlightenment flowered in Europe, Muscovy remained in the dark ages. Its medieval Kremlin, insular tsars and religious fanaticism made Moscow a backwards-looking and repressive place, terrified of innovation, reform and development.

Had Peter the Great not come along, Russia would probably have remained an insignificant and insular state and world history might have been very different.

1714	1725
Generally accepted as the year St Petersburg was fully Russia's new capital	Death of Peter the Great

PETER THE GREAT

Peter the Great was born in the Moscow Kremlin in 1672. The son of Tsar Alexei's second wife, Natalya Naryshkina, he was considered by many to be illegitimate due to his mother being the tsar's second wife.

When Tsar Alexei died in 1676, Peter's eldest half-brother Fyodor assumed the throne for a six-year reign, only to die at the age of 20. The heir to the throne, Peter's other half-brother Ivan, was a mentally subnormal, sickly boy who was clearly unfit to rule and Peter was instead proclaimed tsar in 1682. However, with Ivan the prospects of the Miloslavsky family (that of Tsar Alexei's first wife) died, and a fierce power struggle broke out between them and the Naryshkins (Peter's mother's family). This culminated in the rebellion of the Streltsy, the Kremlin guard, who believed Ivan had been killed by the Naryshkins. This brutal revolt marked Peter for life and was a huge factor in turning him against Moscow, witnessing as he did at the age of 10 the butchering of many of his close relatives.

The revolt led to a bizarre compromise. Ivan and Peter jointly ascended the throne of Russia, but Ivan's older sister Sophia – an ambitious, sly woman – was proclaimed Regent. This was actually hugely beneficial to Peter, who, relieved of ceremonial duties (which Ivan fulfilled) and the burden of running the country (Sophia's job), was able to develop his own interests. When in Moscow he spent as much time as possible in the foreign quarter where he got to know a wide circle of European merchants, many of whom would remain his friends for life. Alongside drinking and carousing, European ideas and advances in technology fascinated the young Peter, who realised how far behind the rest of the civilised world Russia was.

Outside Moscow at the royal residence of Preobrazhenskoe, Peter engaged in military games with some 300 soldiers whom he trained up using modern foreign methods to what would become the Preobrazhensky Guards, Peter himself serving with them (he believed he must earn his rank like anyone else). Here he also discovered sailing, the greatest passion of his life.

Ornate railing, Peter's Cabin (p115)

1728	1732
Peter II moves the Russian capital back to Moscow	Empress Anna returns the capital to St Petersburg

However, Peter the Great's idyllic teenage years were ended by his arranged marriage to Yevdokia Lopukhina in 1689 (he was not to meet his true love, his second wife Catherine, until many years later). The marriage acted as a catalyst for Peter to assume power in Russia, though; Sophia was banished to Moscow's Novodevichy Convent and Peter assumed the running of the country.

The Man Behind the Myth

Peter the Great: A Biography, Lindsey Hughes' succinct, comprehensive and hugely readable account of Peter the Great's life and times in Russia is a superb introduction to the key figure in St Petersburg's history. Never pulling punches in its detailed retelling of Peter's less-than-laudable personal life and his often barbaric childishness, Professor Hughes manages to present both the genius and failings of the man in an even-handed manner few historians have accomplished.

In 1697 Peter began his famous Grand Embassy when he left for Western Europe (the first Russian sovereign ever to do so). Travelling 'incognito' (a ruse that never really worked) with some 250 compatriots, Peter visited Amsterdam, London, Berlin, Dresden and Vienna over the course of two years.

In Holland – the country that inspired Peter more than anywhere else – Peter spent four months learning how to build boats in the Amsterdam suburb of Zaandam, taking a huge amount of new knowledge back with him. By the time of his return to Russia, Peter understood the scale of the challenge ahead of him and had already made the psychological break with Moscow he believed was essential to allow Russia to develop.

Peter was now in a position to force through the reforms he'd been musing upon in Europe. His introduction of 'Western dress' (as opposed to the Asiatic dress still usual in Moscow) was followed by the forced shaving of beards and the reform of the Julian calendar to almost universal horror among the *boyars* (nobles) at court. Despite the surface changes to the court, Peter knew that the political culture in Moscow would always resist change and unless he created a new capital city elsewhere, his far-reaching plans could never be seen through.

The beginning of the 18th century saw Russia at war with Sweden, but even at this time, Peter was planning to create a new city in the very area where Charles XII of Sweden was fighting the Russians for control of access to the Baltic Sea.

A CITY IS BORN

The city of Sankt Pieterburkh was created on 27 May 1703. Named in Dutch, Peter's favourite language, and after St Peter, who guards the gates to paradise, Peter from the start referred to the city as his own 'heaven' in direct opposition to what he considered to be infernal Moscow.

The first settlement was built on Zayachy Island (Hare Island), a defensively brilliant stronghold that became the Peter and Paul Fortress, still standing in the same position today. At war with Sweden, the city's defence was paramount and it wouldn't be until Peter's naval victory at Hangö in 1714 that Russia gained full control of the eastern Baltic and Sweden no longer presented itself as a threat to the city's survival.

The first area of the city was built upon what is now the Petrograd Side; here Peter had his own **cabin** (p115) built as well as the Trinity Cathedral (now destroyed) on what is now Troitsky pl, the original central plaza of the city.

Peter's first challenge was a shortage of stone, not to mention a workforce, with which to realise his vision of a great city. This he overcame with sheer resourcefulness. He sent orders to regional governors throughout the empire to supply him with temporary workers, lured skilled workers (offering them free plots of land in the city as well as food and an allowance)

1762	1773
A coup against her husband Peter III brings Catherine the Great to the Russian throne	The Pugachev Rebellion against Catherine the Great curbs her liberalism

The Other Side of Peter

The legend of Peter the Great's genius in Russia often overshadows the tsar's highly unusual personal life and entourage. Peter was in many ways incredibly childish, a consumer of a vast amount of alcohol and ensconced for much of the time among his own bawdy secret society, the 'drunken assembly'. This sybaritic gathering of drinkers included Peter's own inner circle, his closest friend Prince Menshikov, his wife and a number of 'freaks' including dwarves, giants, hunchbacks and other misfits who Peter found himself enormously fond of. Within the drunken assembly Peter, while of course being the real monarch, created a 'Prince-Caesar' whom he addressed as 'Your Majesty' as well as a mock head of the church named the 'Prince-Pope' and a number of other highly eccentric rituals that continue to fascinate historians today. Practical jokes (naked dwarves jumping out at guests from pies, for example), respectable ladies being force-fed alcohol and the humiliation of anyone who fell out of favour were the order of the day. One of the drunken assembly's most famous gatherings was at Menshikov Palace in 1710 when all the dwarves of the empire were summoned to the capital to attend a dwarf wedding. The drunken assembly looked on in hysterics as dozens of dwarves danced, sang and ate at miniature tables.

There was also a darker side to Peter that his admirers often tend to gloss over. Ruthlessly committed to seeing his reforms through, Peter was determined to leave the Russian throne only to someone who was as committed as he was to modernisation. His only son to make it into adulthood, Tsarevitch Alexei, was the product of his first unhappy marriage and was woefully ill-equipped for his destiny. Peter was always disappointed by Alexei's behaviour and instinctive fondness for the very Russian traditions that Peter had gone to so much effort to eradicate. Their troubled relationship (Alexei grew up largely ignored by his father and it was only his second wife Catherine's influence that encouraged Peter to take notice of him) eventually led to Alexei fleeing the country and asking for asylum from Austria-Hungary. Lured back to Russia by Peter's ministers with the promise of forgiveness if he agreed to give up his claim to the throne, Alexei was nevertheless interrogated by Peter personally and tortured horribly, his father believing he was involved in a plot to place him on the throne and reverse his reforms. This scene is captured chillingly in Ghe's magnificent historical painting *Peter I Interrogates Tsarevitch Alexei at Peterhof* (1872), which hangs in the **Russian Museum** (p93). Alexei died from his torture and for three years Peter regularly attended mass for his soul, ultimately believing that his son's death had been necessary to secure Russia's future.

from all over Russia and abroad, and when still more were needed, he emptied the prisons and put criminals to work on the city and even used Swedish prisoners of war (many of whom earned their freedom and remained in the city after the peace treaty between the two nations was signed). Conditions were bleak and many died from the poor working conditions, and disease frequently spread through the workers who lived in cramped and unsanitary quarters. All those coming to St Petersburg by carriage from elsewhere in Russia famously had to bring with them a required minimum amount of stone that would be deposited at the city gates and used for municipal construction.

The court, diplomats and the majority of Russian business moved to St Petersburg, even though most people far preferred Moscow to the discomforts of the new capital. Moreover, the upper classes were thoroughly taken aback at the scale of Peter's further reform of the nobility. Peter was keen to encourage talented commoners to make careers in the services, to supplement the nobles on whom he still largely relied to fill the top posts in the army, navy and civil service. To this end, he granted noble status to commoners who earned promotion to the higher ranks. Birth for the first time counted for little, as state servants were subject to Peter's new Table of Ranks, a performance-based ladder of promotion with only the upper grades conferring hereditary nobility.

Peter mobilised Russian resources to compete on equal terms with the West, a startling achievement given Russia's backwardness. His territorial gains were small, but the strategic Baltic Sea territories added a new class of German traders and administrators that formed the backbone of Russia's commercial and military expansion.

1796	1799
Death of Catherine the Great	Birth of Alexander Pushkin, Russia's greatest poet

By the time of his death in 1725, Peter's city on the Neva had a population of 40,000 (one-eighth of the country's urban population) and 90% of Russia's foreign trade passed through it. The south bank around the Admiralty had become the centre of the now-bustling town. Peter died without naming a successor. Had it not been for a government structure built on the Table of Ranks as well as a professional bureaucracy with a vested interest in its preservation, Peter's reforms might well have died with him.

AFTER PETER

Despite his successes, Peter's legacy was a half-built and ramshackle city, a court and nobility exhausted by his reforms and general discontent with the new capital. It would take a whole generation's passing before most people would recognise the brilliance and vision of the late tsar; in the meantime people remained deeply suspicious. His wife, an illiterate Lithuanian peasant, became Empress Catherine I, whose short reign (1725–27) was unremarkable.

The decline of Peter the Great's dream quickly followed Catherine's death in 1727, when Peter the Great's 11-year-old nephew Peter became Peter II. The young tsar hated St Petersburg, moved the court back to Moscow and looked set to reverse many of Peter I's monumental changes. The population of St Petersburg halved and all building work stopped until even the young tsar realised that too much effort had gone into its creation for it simply to be abandoned. In 1729 he issued a decree commanding all builders and merchants who had left the city to return.

After Peter II's early death from smallpox, Empress Anna Ivanovna (r 1730–40) returned the court and capital to St Petersburg. Following the brief reign of Ivan VI (1740–41), Anna's great nephew who was dispatched in a coup and imprisoned, there came the reign of Peter the Great's granddaughter, Empress Elizabeth (r 1741–61) who created one of the most glittering courts in Europe and whose taste for the lavish included employing chief architect Bartolomeo Rastrelli to create some of the city's most sumptuous buildings and interiors.

Elizabeth was eccentric and contradictory, living a hedonistic lifestyle that revolved around hunting, drinking and dancing. More than anything she loved hosting transvestite balls, possibly because she looked far better as a man than as a woman, and her 20-year reign left the state coffers empty due to her total failure to live within her means. Despite this she also oversaw a start of real sophistication in the city: the bawdy freak show that was once the imperial court gradually became populated by poets, artists and philosophers. Journalism and theatre both gained popularity during her reign, and Elizabeth personally set up the Academy of Fine Art in 1757, an institution that was to come into its own during the rule of Catherine the Great. As Elizabeth's reign came to an end, it seemed that Peter's dream of a truly European city was finally coming to pass.

CATHERINE THE GREAT

The accession to the throne of Elizabeth's mentally unbalanced nephew as Tsar Peter III boded ill for the city that had thrived so irrepressibly under Anna and Elizabeth. Peter was a militaristic fanatic who spent all his time training his own private guards unit and worshipping Prussia, due to his Germanic upbringing. A Lutheran who continued to prefer Lutheranism over Orthodoxy, despite converting, Peter clearly had his days numbered from the word go.

Peter was married to Sophie of Anhalt-Zerbst, who had come from Germany to Russia to marry Peter, taking the name Catherine when she converted to Orthodoxy to become tsarina of Russia. Her wit and intellect made her far more suitable to rule than her imbecilic

1801	1812
A plot against Tsar Paul places Alexander I on the throne	Napoleon's campaign against Moscow falters as the winter cold sets in

husband and she was soon involved in a plot to overthrow Peter, from whom she had been estranged for some time.

With the aid of Grigory Orlov, Peter III was overthrown quickly (and later murdered, although this was against Catherine's wishes). Catherine's subsequent succession to the Russian throne, despite no legitimate claim to it whatsoever, heralded the beginning of a golden age for St Petersburg.

Catherine saw herself very much as Peter the Great's philosophical heir. Indeed, she was extremely enlightened and open to modern ideas, keeping up a famous correspondence with Voltaire and being personally acquainted with many French thinkers of the Enlightenment, including Diderot. Like Peter, Catherine saw herself as an enlightened autocrat whose mission was to lead her people into the new European age. Her long reign saw Russia become a major European power and sowed the seeds for it becoming a world name in the arts during the 19th century.

While legends persist about Catherine's rapacious sexual appetite (rumours of her fondness for horses have been greatly exaggerated), she had only 12 lovers and even if some of them were engaged concurrently, by modern standards she would have appeared quite conservative, if not extraordinarily generous: many of her favourites were given palaces and large estates.

While she was a great exponent of the Enlightenment and westernised Russia in leaps and bounds, she also ensured that any public spirit of liberalism didn't grow unchecked. She made no headway in the question that was so essential to Russia's development: the emancipation of the serfs, the vast majority of the population who were stuck in feudal times because they were tied to a certain landowner's land, living effectively as slaves.

Catherine's most visible bequest was to bring Russia on to the world stage of arts. She freed regulations and restrictions on publishing. She founded the magnificent collection now known the world over as the Hermitage, named after the building adjacent to her magnificent Winter Palace where Catherine kept her paintings and sculptures. And she went on an architectural commissioning spree, inviting dozens of Western European architects to bring neoclassicism to St Petersburg.

However, near the end of her reign the liberalism of her early years noticeably retreated. At first this was due to the Pugachev Rebellion of 1773, when Emilian Pugachev, a Don Cossack in the Volga region claiming to be the overthrown Peter III, began a peasant uprising. The revolt gained massive support in the south and had to be put down by brute force, giving Catherine her first taste of what might come to be if her enlightened policies continued.

Most importantly, however, the French Revolution of 1789 horrified Catherine with its radicalism. Enlightened she may have been, but Catherine was certainly no republican. In the wake of the storming of the Bastille Catherine turned her back on European reform, fearing that something equivalent could soon happen in Russia if the doors to such ideas remained open. This ideological about-face marked a turn in the fortunes of the Westernising school that effectively continued until Boris Yeltsin became President of Russia some two centuries later.

BACKTRACKING

Catherine's death in 1796 finally gave her mentally unbalanced son Paul the chance to rule, something he'd been waiting for since his teenage years. So bitter and resentful at his mother's long reign was Paul that his first acts were to decree that women could never again become sovereigns of Russia and to give his murdered father a state funeral denied him under Catherine. Given Catherine's popularity and success, so obviously thumbing her in the eye was an inauspicious start.

Very much his father's son, Paul was a Prussia-obsessed militarist who ignored the Russian army (save making them wear Prussian-style uniforms) and instead trained his own regiment

1814	1825
Russian troops occupy Paris and Russia becomes Europe's greatest power	The Decembrist Revolt is crushed on Senate Sq

at his residence at Gatchina. He quickly created a near-police state in the city, and under him the carefree gaiety of the city's balls and entertainments evaporated overnight.

Paul's complete disregard for the people of his city proved his undoing. The court believed that the tsar was answerable only to God exclusively when he was doing a good job, and soon a plot was hatched to put his eldest son Alexander on the throne in his place.

Already convinced he was going to be assassinated, Paul had the **Mikhailovsky Castle** (p91) constructed on the Fontanka, complete with elaborate security and even a moat. He managed to survive only 40 days here before being slain in his bedroom at the hands of a large cabal, however, and his son Alexander became the new tsar to popular delight.

Despite Alexander's misgivings about the plot (he never fully got over the guilt of patricide by association), he ascended the throne amid mass celebrations and merrymaking as the city shed the oppressive rule of his father. The start of a new century began with a dashing young sovereign leading one of Europe's great powers: things were looking rosy for St Petersburg.

ALEXANDER I

Alexander I (1801–25) presided over a period of growing prosperity and social content in the first years of his reign. He implemented a series of educational reforms and seemed to have much of his grandmother's spirit of Enlightenment about him.

However, the rise of Napoleon in France was to change the European balance of powers beyond recognition. Hostilities first broke out between Russia and France when Russia allied itself with Austria and Prussia in an ineffective and ill-fated anti-French alliance, which led to a series of Russian defeats. Fearful of popular reaction to the defeats, Alexander pragmatically signed the Treaty of Tilsit with Napoleon in 1807, the terms of which forbade Russia to trade with the British. Despite this Alexander restarted trade with

Lenin statue outside Finland Station (p116)

1837
Alexander Pushkin dies in a duel in St Petersburg's woodland

1851
The first trains linking Moscow and St Petersburg begin running

Britain to Napoleon's rage shortly afterwards. Never one to take things lying down, Bonaparte led what was at the time the largest army ever assembled (some 600,000 men) against Russia in the summer of 1812.

Russia used its size to its advantage, employing the famous scorched earth tactics (burning all crops, removing all livestock from the advancing army's path), which dramatically slowed down the French advance and depleted their supplies. The campaign culminated with a pitched battle at Borodino outside Moscow, where despite an enormous number of casualties there was no outright winner.

Napoleon advanced on Moscow, which he had decided was more strategically important than the capital, a miscalculation that cost him dearly. The Governor of Moscow burned large sections of the city to give the French little to celebrate taking, while Napoleon famously watched the city burn from the Kremlin. With no spoils to plunder and no government or tsar to arrest, Napoleon's victory was rather a pointless one. Moreover, with Alexander in heavily fortified St Petersburg and with no ready source of supplies to undertake an attack, the French had little choice but to retreat.

The Russian army pursued the Grand Army all the way back to Paris, giving Russia a unique military victory from the ashes of defeat. In just a century Russia had gone from being a backwards medieval country on the fringes of the continent to Europe's most powerful nation. While the country was ecstatic about its new international prestige, the returning Russian army who began to arrive in St Petersburg in 1814 had been made very aware of Russia's backwardness by their time in Western Europe. The officers that chased out Napoleon brought back with them a huge number of reformist ideas and a general yearning for some more genuine modernisation measures. From this kernel grew the reformers that were to overshadow Nicholas I's reign, the Decembrists.

NICHOLAS I & THE DECEMBRISTS

Alexander died suddenly in Southern Russia in 1825 with no heir. The throne would have passed to his reformist brother Constantine but for the fact that he was living in Warsaw, having entered into a morganatic marriage with a Polish commoner, and had no desire to rule. Thus it looked certain that Alexander's youngest brother Nicholas, a known conservative, would become the new tsar.

The reformers, who had been meeting for a decade in St Petersburg and even as far afield as Ukraine, took advantage of the time delay, swearing allegiance to Constantine and determined to prevent Nicholas from becoming tsar. On 14 December the plotters assembled in freezing temperatures on Senate Sq (now pl Dekabristov) where a face-off ensued between them and guards loyal to the tsar.

After a stand-off that lasted much of the day and several strokes of bad luck for the rebels, Nicholas I ordered the square to be cleared by force, killing hundreds of the rebels who became immortalised as the Decembrists in the process.

The remainder of Nicholas I's reign was as inauspicious as the beginning. Though he granted title to peasants on state land (effectively freeing them), his foreign policy accomplished little else than to annoy everyone in the Balkans and most of the rest of Europe; and to start the Crimean War in which Britain and France sided against Russia. Inept command on both sides resulted in a bloody, stalemated war. At home, his obsession with military order stifled the capital from expressing any independent thought.

However, Nicholas I's reign is looked back on as a golden age by many – this was when Russia's greatest writers were at work, most importantly Pushkin (who was censored by the tsar himself), but Lermontov and Gogol also shone through during Nicholas' otherwise rather backward rule.

1861	1881
Emancipation of the serfs frees up labour to feed the Russian industrial revolution	A bomb kills Alexander II as he travels home along the Griboedova Canal

ALEXANDER II: THE TSAR LIBERATOR

When Nicholas I died in 1855, St Petersburg was the fourth largest city in Europe, the status it again holds today. His son, Alexander II (r 1855–81), put an end to the Crimean War, which had revealed the backwardness behind the post-1812 imperial glory. The time for reform had come and he engaged it on all levels of society.

The serfs were freed in 1861. Of the land they had worked, roughly a third was kept by established landholders. The rest went to village communes, which assigned it to individuals in return for 'redemption payments' to compensate former landholders – a system that pleased no-one. While little seemed to have changed at the time, the emancipation of the serfs was the great historical event of Russia's 19th century, finally ending feudalism and allowing Russia to become a major industrial nation. Railroads and factories were built and cities expanded as peasants left the land. Nothing, though, was done to modernise farming methods and the peasants found their lot had not improved in half a century.

Russia expanded enormously, taking in Central Asia and beginning to worry the British by encroaching on India. In the east, Russia acquired a long strip of Pacific coast from China and built the port of Vladivostok, but sold the 'worthless' Alaskan territories to the US in 1867 for just $7.2 million.

The loosening of restrictions and rapid change in the make-up of Russian society took its toll, however. Industrialisation and the emancipation of the serfs brought a flood of poor workers into St Petersburg, leading to overcrowding, poor sanitation, epidemics and festering discontent. Revolutionary sentiment was rife and radicals were plotting the overthrow of the tsarist government as early as the second half of the 19th century. After seven attempts on his life, Alexander II was assassinated in 1881 in St Petersburg by a terrorist bomb. Today on the site you can see the **Church on Spilled Blood** (p91), which was built so that mass could be said for the late tsar's soul.

THE LAST TSARS

The last Alexander (and the penultimate tsar of Russia) was the most conservative and autocratic yet. Seeing what his father's reforms had led to, Alexander III (r 1881–94) quickly vetoed the constitutional reforms that his father had been about to institute at the time of his death and introduced a series of ultra-conservative measures. Despite this hardened autocrat on the throne, St Petersburg's economic development, now more in the hands of the new merchant classes than the authorities, continued to thrive and this was a period of enormous industrialisation for the city.

When Alexander III died unexpectedly in 1894, his son Nicholas became tsar, to Nicholas' horror. Completely unready for the responsibility, he panicked openly to his family and eventually resolved to continue his father's unpopular policies. Of all the ineffective and vacillating tsars of the 19th century, none was less fit to be ruler of Russia than the immature, reactionary Nicholas II. Few people could be said to have only themselves to blame for their fates, but when Nicholas II and his entire family ended up being shot in 1918 by revolutionaries in Siberia, it can pretty squarely be seen as the consequences of his catastrophic decision-making from his first day on the throne.

At Nicholas' coronation in 1896, a huge crush in the vast crowds killed over a thousand people – an unprecedented disaster that many interpreted as a bad omen for the tsar's reign. Worse, Nicholas refused to cancel celebrations that night and so earned himself no popularity by dancing the night away as Moscow mourned its dead.

Nicholas II married one of Queen Victoria's many granddaughters, Princess Alexandra of Hesse, a woman even more conservative and backwards than the tsar himself, whose religious extremism and superstitious nature meant that she frequently relied on quacks

1904	1905
Russo-Japanese War begins and disaster for Russia ensues	Nicholas II orders troops to fire on thousands of protesters on 'Bloody Sunday'

and other phonies. Most famous of these was of course Grigory Rasputin (see the boxed text, p55).

The soaring economic successes of late-19th-century St Petersburg suddenly went into terrible decline at the turn of the century, leaving much of the urban proletariat out of work and angry. Nicholas II looked to a short successful war with Japan as a means of uniting the country behind him and bringing the damaging last few years since his father's murder to a close. Nothing could have been worse: the Russo-Japanese War that followed was quick, humiliating and devastating; nearly the entire Russian navy was obliterated. The butchering of young Russians caused a huge political backlash and the series of defeats took their toll in the form of ever-increasing civil unrest in St Petersburg. Under the terms of the peace treaty signed on 5 September 1905, Russia not only gave up Port Arthur, the larger half of Sakhalin Island and other properties, but also recognised Japanese predominance in Korea.

THE 1905 REVOLUTION & WWI

In the aftermath of the Russo-Japanese War, St Petersburg became a hotbed of strikes and political violence. There soon followed the 1905 revolution, sparked by 'Bloody Sunday' on 9 January 1905, when a strikers' march to petition the tsar in the Winter Palace was fired on by troops. The group, led by Father Georgy Gapon, was made up of about 150,000 workers who were imploring for better living conditions. The protesters were fired upon throughout the

Rasputin & the Royal Family

No name is quite as synonymous with debauchery and mysticism as that of St Petersburg's 'mad monk' Grigory Rasputin (1869–1916), the Siberian peasant who became one of the most powerful men in the Russian Empire due to his enormous influence over Tsar Nicholas II and his wife Alexandra during the last days of the Russian empire.

Rasputin was born into poverty in a small village east of the Urals and after a dissolute boyhood and a marriage that was soon over, he discovered religion and, more importantly, the controlling power it could have over its devotees. Becoming a 'fool in God' and wandering through Russia, Rasputin had a school of Christianity that engaged in a practice euphemistically called *radeniye* (joy), which entailed group sex and general promiscuity for the sake of the guilt and ensuing repentance that would follow.

Coming to St Petersburg, he met with Nicholas and Alexandra in 1905 after becoming fashionable among the ladies at court. He began (apparently successfully) to control Tsarevitch Alexei's haemophilia, quickly becoming a member of the Romanov inner circle, something that scandalised all St Petersburg given his origins and filthy appearance (he never took to wearing fine clothing or washing despite his wealth and power). Attempts to turn the imperial family against him failed and by 1916, with Nicholas overseeing the disastrous war effort and often out of Petrograd, Rasputin assumed day-to-day control of Russia.

Prince Felix Yusupov and the tsar's cousin Grand Duke Dmitry were leaders of a plot to dispatch Rasputin by poisoning him while he was a guest at the Yusupov Palace. The plot, which can be re-enacted in gory detail by taking a Rasputin Tour at the **Yusupov Palace** (p107), misfired somewhat. The first attempt on his life was through poison, which had no visible effect. Next Yusupov shot Rasputin at close range, which seemed to do the job, although shortly afterwards the plotters noticed Rasputin hobbling out of the palace. Next Rasputin was bound and beaten repeatedly before being thrown through a hole in the ice on the Moyka. When police found him two days later, he had broken free of the rope and had drowned in the river, despite the gang's best efforts at killing him themselves.

Rasputin was buried secretly at Pushkin, although apparently not before his penis was removed and preserved in a jar – the highly impressive results of which can be seen at the **Museum of Erotica** (p100). Yusupov was exiled for his crime, although to avoid scandal given the gang's immense popularity and the public loathing for Rasputin, the tsar avoided a big trial. The aura of mysticism remains, however, and there is an enormous number of books about this strangest of players in Russian history.

1914	1916
WWI begins; St Petersburg changes its name to the less Germanic Petrograd	Rasputin is drowned by plotters who invite him round to the Yusupov Palace for tea

city; estimates of the number of dead reach into the thousands. Despite the thorough witch-hunt for revolutionaries that followed, the incident galvanised and united opposition factions against the common enemy: the tsar.

In the months to follow, peasant uprisings, mutinies (most famously that aboard the Battleship *Potemkin*) and other protests across the nation abounded. Social democrat activists in St Petersburg and Moscow formed soviets, or 'workers' councils'. The St Petersburg Soviet, led by the Mensheviks (Minority People, who in fact outnumbered the Bolshevik, or Majority People's, party) under Leo Trotsky, called for a massive general strike in October, which brought the country to a standstill.

Russian Dates

All dates given in this chapter are 'new style', ie correspond to the current Gregorian calendar used worldwide. Other history books will often give different dates for events in Russia's past: until 1700 Russia dated its years from 'creation', meaning that 1700 was known to most as 7208. Peter instituted a reform to date the years from the birth of Christ, but when Europe abandoned the Julian calendar altogether in favour of the Gregorian calendar in the 18th century, Russia did not follow suit, making Russian dates 13 days out of sync from European dates by 1917. Finally, 31 January 1918 was followed by 14 February 1918 and all post-1918 Russian dates have been identical to those in the West.

These protests resulted in Tsar Nicholas II's grudgingly issued 'October Manifesto', which, along with granting hitherto unheard of civil rights, created the (largely powerless) State Duma, Russia's elected legislature. Despite his concession, Nicholas II detested the Duma and stymied its work at all junctures, infuriating its members and much of the population of St Petersburg.

At the start of WWI in 1914, the city's name was changed to the Russian-style Petrograd in a brief wave of patriotism (or at least anti-German sentiment, despite the name St Petersburg being Dutch in origin). The city's population was 2.1 million. A few years later, after countless defeats on the battlefield and literally millions of lives lost in the unpopular war, Petrograd would again be the cradle of revolution.

1917 & ALL THAT

The events in Petrograd in 1917 changed world history forever. The year saw two revolutions – that of February and that of October, and in the space of one year the world's biggest country went from being a tsarist police state to a communist one.

With the deprivations caused by the war, along with a breakdown in the chain of command, morale was very low in early 1917. People were also incensed at the strong influence Rasputin had on the throne, via the Empress Alexandra. Nicholas II was blamed for failures of the Russian armies. Political fragmentation had resulted in a reincarnation of the Petrograd Soviet of Workers & Soldiers Deputies, based on the 1905 model. Workers' protests turned into a general strike and troops mutinied, forcing the end of the monarchy.

On 1 March Nicholas abdicated after he was 'asked to' by the Duma. The Romanov dynasty of over 300 years officially came to an end. A short time later, Nicholas II and his entire family were exiled to Yekaterinburg, east of the Ural Mountains, where they were later murdered and buried in a mass grave. Some of the bodies were exhumed and re-buried at the **Peter and Paul Fortress** (p114) in 1998.

A provisional government announced that general elections would be held in November. The Petrograd Soviet started meeting in the city's Tauride Palace alongside the country's reformist Provisional Government. It was to Petrograd's Finland Station that Vladimir Lenin travelled in April to organise the Bolshevik Party. The Smolny Institute, a former girls' college in the city, became the locus of power as the Bolsheviks took control of the Petrograd Soviet, which had installed itself there.

1917	1918
The February Revolution is followed by the Bolshevik coup in October; Lenin takes power	Lenin moves the capital to Moscow

During the summer, tensions were raised considerably by the co-existence of two power bases: the Provisional Government and the Petrograd Soviet. The Bolsheviks' propaganda campaign was winning over a substantial number of people who, understandably, thought that the slogan 'Peace, Land and Bread' was a good maxim by which to live. Tensions were high; Lenin thought that it was now time for a Soviet coup. But a series of violent mass demonstrations in July, inspired by the Bolsheviks but in the end not fully backed by them, was quelled. Lenin fled to Finland, and Alexander Kerensky, a moderate Social Revolutionary, became prime minister.

In September the Russian military Chief-of-Staff, General Kornilov, sent cavalry to Petrograd to crush the Soviets. Kerensky's government turned to the left for support against this insubordination, even courting the Bolsheviks, and the counter-revolution was defeated. After this, public opinion massively favoured the Bolsheviks, who quickly took control of the Petrograd Soviet (chaired by Trotsky, who had joined them) and, by extension, all the Soviets in the land. Lenin (who had cowered in Finland through all this) again decided it was time to seize power and returned from Finland in October.

The actual 'Great October Soviet etc etc' revolution wasn't nearly as dramatic as all those red-tinted, massive Soviet canvases dedicated to the event would have you believe. Bolsheviks occupied key positions in Petrograd on 24 October. Next day, the All-Russian Congress of Soviets appointed a Bolshevik government. That night, after some exchanges of gunfire and a blank shot fired from the cruiser *Aurora* on the Neva (a symbol of the navy's allegiance to the uprising), the Provisional Government in the Winter Palace surrendered to the Bolsheviks.

Armistice was signed with the approaching Germans in December 1917, followed by the Treaty of Brest-Litovsk in March 1918 that surrendered Poland, the Baltic provinces, Ukraine, Finland and Transcaucasia to the Germans. This negotiation for a separate peace with Germany enraged the Allied forces, who would later back anti-Bolshevik fighters in a nose-thumbing effort to punish the revolutionaries for taking their ball and going home.

CIVIL WAR

There was wide dissent after the revolution and a number of political parties sprang up almost immediately to challenge the Bolsheviks' power. The power struggle began peacefully in the November elections for the Constituent Assembly; the Socialist Revolutionaries won a sweeping victory, only to have the assembly shut down by a very angry Lenin. A multi-sided civil war erupted. Trotsky founded the Red Army in February 1918 and the Cheka, Russia's secret police force designed to fight opposition, was established.

The new government operated from the Smolny until March 1918, when it moved to Moscow, fearing attacks on Petrograd from outside and from within. The loss in status was a crushing blow to the city, already suffocating from food shortages and unrest, and one that still affects it today. By August 1920, the population of the city had fallen to 722,000, only one-third of the pre-revolutionary figure. Civil war ravaged the country until 1921, by which time the Communist Party had firmly established one-party rule thanks to the Red Army and the Cheka, which continued to eliminate opponents. Those who escaped joined an estimated 1.5 million citizens in exile.

The Bolsheviks instituted a number of reforms, including modernising orthography and introducing the use of the Gregorian calendar in 1918. But the 1921 strikes in the city and a (bloodily crushed) revolt by the sailors of nearby Kronshtadt helped bring about Lenin's more liberal New Economic Policy (NEP).

Petrograd was renamed Leningrad after Lenin's death in 1924. After a long struggle for the soul of the party, Stalin defeated Trotsky and his supporters to become the USSR's sole leader by 1927. He initiated one of the most painful periods in Russian history with the

1920	1922
Population of St Petersburg falls to 722,000, one-third of the pre-revolutionary figure	The Union of Soviet Socialist Republics (USSR) is born

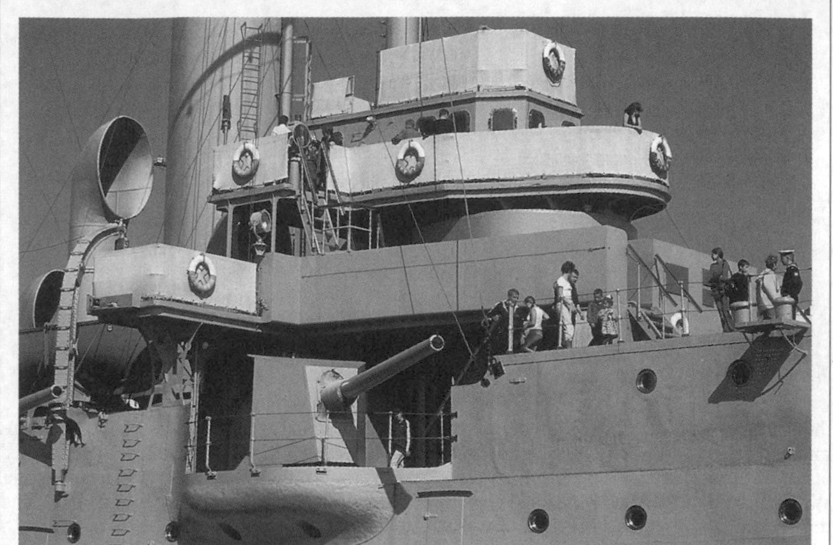

Visitors on Cruiser Aurora (p112)

collectivisation of the land, which led to millions of deaths from starvation. By the end of the 1920s, he had instituted the first five-year plan, which made Leningrad a centre of the Soviet Union's industrialisation programme. By 1939 the city had a population of 3.1 million people and was producing 11% of Soviet industrial output.

THE TERROR

When popular and charismatic local party boss Sergei Kirov was shot by an assailant as he left the Smolny on 1 December 1934, Stalin's 'great terror' began, a movement designed to eliminate his enemies (real and perceived) which culminated in a series of show trials in Moscow that shocked the world.

Stalin showed his true brilliance as a Machiavellian operator by simultaneously ordering the assassination of Kirov and using his 'outrage' to settle political scores in Leningrad, which to Stalin was still a dangerous bastion of cosmopolitanism and Western thinking. In the wake of Kirov's murder alone, some 30,000 citizens were arrested and deported to camps from the former capital. Successive waves engulfed the city: in 1935 it was the turn of anyone from an aristocratic background, for example. People changed, their everyday lives marked by a deep dread that every morning they were saying goodbye to their loved ones forever, or that they'd be woken in the middle of the night by the feared knock at the door – the preferred time of day to arrest people, as fewer people would witness the scene and the victim would be disorientated.

Nikolai Yezhov, the loathsome local NKVD chief who carried out Stalin's orders without so much as a second thought, was the dark force who controlled the fates of thousands during this time. The period became known as the *yezhovshchina,* and alongside the hundreds of

1924	1934
Death of Lenin; Petrograd changes its name to Leningrad in his honour	Leningrad party boss Sergei Kirov is shot on Stalin's orders; the terror begins

Top Soviet History Reads

- *Ten Days That Shook the World* by John Reed – This classic eyewitness account of the Russian revolution by American journalist John Reed makes for a fascinating read.
- *Lenin* by Robert Service – The definitive biography of a man whose ruthlessness was so overshadowed by Stalin, this book reminds us exactly where the dark fervour of communist Russia originated.
- *The Russian Revolution from Lenin to Stalin* by EH Carr – A classic introduction to the Russian revolution, this succinct yet profound analysis of the period 1917–29 is a great starting point for anyone wanting to understand just how the people's revolution resulted in Stalinism.
- *The 900 Days: The Siege of Leningrad* by Harrison Salisbury – *De rigueur* for any city resident during their first year here, this book is not for those with just a passing interest in the blockade, but for those who know their city and want to vicariously suffer its darkest hours in a forensic reconstruction.
- *Stalin: The Court of the Red Tsar* by Simon Sebag Montefiore – This superb new biography illuminates Stalin's fascinating inner circle and describes what really went on day to day in the Kremlin through the reign of communism's Genghis Khan.

thousands of unknowns who were imprisoned or killed, much of the city's once world-famous intelligentsia was similarly liquidated: artist Kazimir Malevich, silenced and depressed, died of natural causes in 1935 and his funeral was seen as that of the entire Petrograd avant-garde. Writer Boris Pilnyak was shot in 1938, writer Osip Mandelshtam died in a camp in 1939, and theatre director Vsevolod Meyerhold was tortured and then shot in 1940.

WWII

While the terror lessened after 1939 as it became abundantly clear that the country's economy was suffering from the sheer numbers of people taken from the workplace to camps, it was Hitler's invasion of the Soviet Union in June 1941 that put an end to it.

Stalin had concluded a non-aggression pact with Nazi Germany in 1939 and was for some inexplicable reason blind to Hitler's potential for treachery. As many an observer has wryly pointed out, Stalin suspected his own officers but blithely had faith in a megalomaniac foreign dictator. Despite a massive amount of intelligence suggesting the Germans were planning an invasion, Stalin never countenanced the possibility and so shocked was he when German divisions numbering over three million men rolled confidently across the Soviet border on the morning of 22 June 1941, he had what has been described as a nervous breakdown on the spot, leaving the USSR without a leader at its most critical moment in history.

Moreover, the purges of the previous seven years had taken such a massive toll on the Red Army that it was no match for Hitler's efficiently organised and motivated troops. By July the Germans were approaching Leningrad – taking the leadership by surprise with the speed of their advance. Shortly afterwards, Leningrad was to be plunged into its darkest hour.

THE BLOCKADE

Preparations for defending the city from the Germans were slow in coming. Indeed, city party boss Andrei Zhdanov remained on holiday in Sochi for a further five days after the German invasion and, in typical Soviet style, little happened without him.

Once Zhdanov was back on the scene though, a huge general mobilisation began and the city's citizens began working to fortify and defend the city. St Isaac's magnificent golden

1941	1942
The Soviet Union is invaded by its 'ally' Adolf Hitler; the siege of Leningrad begins	On 9 August, a starving orchestra performs the Leningrad premiere of Shostakovich's Seventh Symphony

dome was painted grey to avoid being made an obvious target and in a manner as miraculous as the survival of St Paul's in London during the blitz, it too came through the war unscathed. The Hermitage was progressively emptied of its treasures – two trains containing over a million items left the city that summer carrying priceless artwork to refuge in the Urals. Historical sculptures, including the *Bronze Horseman*, were buried or covered with sandbags and defensive lines around the city were created in an attempt to slow the advance, even though the advancing troops outnumbered local militias by more than two to one.

By the end of August, the blockade had begun. Zhdanov had been slow to evacuate Leningrad, preferring instead to utilise the city's residents in the creation of civil defence installations. This meant that by the beginning of the blockade, a mere 600,000 people had been evacuated, leaving some three million people in the city with completely inadequate food supplies and winter looming.

Stalin decided not to abandon Leningrad, mainly because of the propaganda value the capitulation of the city bearing Lenin's name would bring to Hitler (a similar worry made both sides fight so hard for Stalingrad three years later). More importantly Stalin wanted Hitler to concentrate his forces in surrounding Leningrad, rather than turn his attention south to Moscow, which was the centre of Soviet power but still woefully ill-prepared for war.

Food was practically nonexistent in the city and at one point rations were limited to 175g of sawdust-laden bread a day. People ate their dogs and cats; even rats and birds disappeared from the city. A fallen horse would be butchered in minutes and carried home in pieces by starving citizens. The paste behind wallpaper was scraped off and eaten; leather army belts were cooked until chewable. Cannibalism started in the shelters for refugees from the neighbouring towns; without ration cards, they were among the first to die and strange-flavoured meat went on sale at the Haymarket. People exchanged precious jewels and antiques for a loaf of bread. The exhausted and starved literally fell over dead on the streets. There were periods when over 30,000 people died of hunger each day.

More than 150,000 shells and bombs dropped on the city, the effects of which are still visible on some buildings (notably on the west wall of St Isaac's Cathedral and the northwest corner of Anichkov most). Still, life went on. Concerts and plays were performed in candlelit halls, lectures given, poetry written, orphanages opened, brigades formed to clean up the city. Most famous was the 9 August 1942 concert of Shostakovich's Seventh Symphony by the Leningrad Philharmonic, nationally broadcast by radio from the besieged city. According to survivors, random acts of kindness outnumbered incidents of robbery and vandalism, and lessons learned about the human spirit would remain unforgotten for a lifetime.

Hitler's confidence about 'wiping the city of Leningrad from the face of the earth' (he even had invitations to victory celebrations at the Astoria Hotel printed up, planning to have the swastika flying over the city by the summer of 1942) was misplaced. Even starving the population into submission did not work: thanks largely to the freezing of Lake Ladoga, to the northeast of Leningrad, a stream of food and supplies ('The Road of Life') reached the city and the Germans began a retreat after a 29-month siege. On 27 January 1944, Zhdanov announced that the blockade was finally over. Leningrad had survived by the skin of its teeth, over a million civilians had been starved to death and the city lay in virtual ruins.

POST-WAR LENINGRAD

In true St Petersburg style, Leningrad residents immediately began the hard tasks of rebuilding the city, clearing rubble and of course, burying the dead. With over a million dead, mainly buried in mass graves in what is now the **Piskaryovskoe Cemetery** (p117), there was a severe need for the city to be repopulated. By the end of the war, its population stood at just over 600,000, down some three million from 1940, and it wasn't until 1960 that the population

1944	1953
With one million dead from starvation, Leningrad emerges from its darkest hour as the Germans retreat	Death of Stalin

exceeded prewar levels. The centre and most of the inner surrounding areas were slowly repaired, and eventually the outlying areas were lined with concrete apartment blocks.

Despite giving Leningrad the title 'Hero City' (to this day proudly displayed on pl Vosstaniya, making it the first thing people see when arriving from Moscow by train) for its role in the war, the city continued its decline in the post-war period. Stalin, as antipathetic towards the city as ever, saw plans by Zhdanov and other city politicians to rejuvenate Leningrad on a massive scale as a waste of time. While other Soviet cities such as Moscow, Stalingrad and Minsk had enormous amounts of money poured into their reconstruction after the holocaust of war, Leningrad was assigned peanuts. Instead of investment, the unfathomably cruel Stalin launched yet another purge on the city, liquidating the very people who had so heroically saved the city from falling into Hitler's hands.

THE THAW

When Stalin finally died in 1953, an exhausted, terrorised Russia slowly began to return to some semblance of normality. Beria, Stalin's bloodthirsty henchman, was arrested and shot and relative liberal Nikita Khrushchev assumed full power by 1956. Khrushchev immediately began the process known as the thaw, denouncing Stalin's crimes in a secret speech at the Communist Party congress that year.

While the terror stopped and Russia opened up to the outside world to a degree Leningrad remained marginalised, although its poets and artists were as active as ever, with a new post-war generation including Joseph Brodsky coming into their own. Moscow remained deeply suspicious of all non-party artists and clampdowns were heavy. Most famously, Brodsky was tried and convicted of being a 'social parasite' (ie not having a job, illegal in the Soviet Union) in 1964 and was sent into exile in the far north.

STAGNATION

Often referred to as the restalinisation of the Soviet Union, a coup against Khrushchev in 1964 brought Leonid Brezhnev to power. Brezhnev quickly ended the thaw by exiling a number of the USSR's most famous writers including Brodsky and Alexander Solzhenitsyn. Brezhnev also indicted other writers and viciously silenced critics of the Kremlin, including Andrei Sakharov, the nuclear scientist who had become a vocal supporter of the country's nascent human rights movement. Shortly afterwards the Soviet invasion of Czechoslovakia in 1968 brought an end to Dubček's Prague Spring, thus preventing any reform to the communist system coming from any of the Soviet Union's European satellite states.

Economic decline, mass corruption and general malaise set in by the early 1970s. It was clear that the socialist system was not working, communism had not been attained and that people were hungry for change. It was equally clear that this change was not to come for a while, however, as the average Politburo member's age was over 70 (the youngest was a 56-year-old unknown named Mikhail Gorbachev) and reform was not on the agenda.

During this time in Leningrad the city's now legendary underground emerged. While the intelligentsia had always had networks of dissent even under Stalin, by the 1970s a mass movement – rock and roll – had been created. Beginning with the wide private circulation of Beatles tapes in the 1960s, by the early '70s Leningrad had a local rock scene that soon began to worry the Kremlin due to its enormous popularity. Today, many of the groups formed in Leningrad during the 1970s continue to make music and remain popular throughout the country.

Following Brezhnev's death in 1982 (many joked that it wasn't noticed until 1984) there were two General Secretaries in quick succession – Yuri Andropov (1982–84) and Konstantin Chernenko (1984–85). Both were already old by the time they took office and both died

1956	1960
Nikita Khrushchev takes the reigns; the thaw begins	The Piskaryovskoe Cemetery containing the mass graves of blockade victims finally opens

Reburying the Past

On 17 July 1998, in a controversial ceremony partially snubbed by the Church and the State, the remains of Tsar Nicholas II, his wife, three of his five children, their doctor and three servants were buried in the Romanov family crypt at the SS Peter and Paul Cathedral within the fortress of the same name. A 19-gun salute bid them a final farewell. The ceremony was contentious for many reasons – political, religious, scientific and financial.

While President Boris Yeltsin and then-General Alexander Lebed were in attendance, together with many Romanov family members, other politicians downplayed the event; and Patriarch Alexei II held his own, rival service in Sergiev Posad, outside Moscow, with a few renegade Romanov descendants in attendance.

The burial, which Yeltsin called an expiation of Russia's common guilt, set off touchy debates on monarchism (to be or not to be?) as a potential solution to the country's state of turmoil (most say: 'not to be'). It also raised debate about the authenticity of the royal remains, despite tests and DNA analyses done since they were unearthed in 1991 which 'prove' they are the royal family's.

After the execution of the Romanovs in Yekaterinburg in July 1918 by a firing squad estimated at 11 men, the bodies were dumped down a mine shaft 30km away. Grenades were tossed in after them in an unsuccessful attempt to collapse the mine. The bodies were then dragged out, doused unevenly with acid and buried quickly in a swamp – all except for two of the children, Maria and Alexei, whose remains were allegedly burned and disintegrated completely. The Dom Ipateva, in which the Romanovs had been held and killed, was destroyed in 1977 by the then head of the city's Communist Party, one Boris Yeltsin, on, he says, orders from the Politburo.

The burial of the nine bodies provided an at-best partial closure to an 80-year-old tragedy. Plans by the Orthodox Church to canonise the tsar and his family within a few years do little to alleviate dissatisfaction felt on all sides. Yet many see the burial as a proper step towards finally settling Russia's restless soul – the next, last and most important, say the superstitious, is to move that waxy-looking bloke off Red Square and place him by his dear old mum in St Petersburg.

in power, neither making any real stab at change. This led to the appointment of a largely unknown reformer named Mikhail Gorbachev.

PERESTROIKA

Gorbachev's programme of reform that followed the death of Chernenko in 1985 resulted in the dissolution of the USSR within six years. A committed communist, Gorbachev's intentions were never to bring down the Soviet Union, but he believed that democracy and communism could coexist.

Gorbachev sacked most of the Brezhnevite Politburo, appointed a brand-new generation of reformers and made public his policy of *glasnost* (openness) to a delighted Soviet public.

The shock of the Chornobyl nuclear disaster in April 1986 fuelled the drive towards political restructure. It had taken a very un-*glasnost*-like 18 days to admit the (underplayed) extent of the disaster to the West, even longer to the neighbouring Warsaw Pact countries. It is worth noting that a now unclassified KGB document, commissioned and signed by Yuri Andropov on 21 February 1979, predicted the disaster more than seven years before it occurred.

It was becoming clear that no leader who relied on the Party could survive as a reformer. *Perestroika* (restructuring) became the new cry. This meant limited private enterprise and private property, not unlike Lenin's New Economic Policy, and further efforts to push towards decentralisation.

The forces unleashed by Gorbachev's laudable but awkwardly instituted reforms precipitated the fall of the Soviet Union. The reduced threat of repression spurred a growing clamour for independence: first in the Soviet satellite states of Eastern Europe, then followed

1964	1964
Poet and future Nobel laureate Joseph Brodsky is labelled a 'social parasite' and sent into exile	Coup against Khrushchev brings Leonid Brezhnev to power

by the Baltic republics, Moldova and the Caucasian republics. The floodgates, once opened, were impossible to close, despite occasional shows of force.

THE 1991 COUP

On 19 August 1991, a group of hardline communists staged what was perhaps the most inept coup of the 20th century. While Gorbachev was on holiday at his Crimean dacha, it was announced in Moscow that a 'state of emergency' was in effect; a self-appointed Committee of the State Emergency announced that it was in power.

Tanks and armed soldiers appeared on the streets of Moscow and Yeltsin joined a group of protesters at the Russian Parliament's headquarters, the White House. When tanks approached, Yeltsin, in full view of CNN, leapt aboard one and implored its crew to use their heads and hold their fire. As hordes of protesters grew the disorganised plot crumbled.

As hundreds of thousands of St Petersburg protesters filled Dvortsovaya pl, Mayor Anatoly Sobchak, who had earlier talked a group of soldiers out of obeying their Moscow-issued orders to arrest him, appeared on local TV denouncing the coup and asking local residents to do the same. Fearful but determined residents spent a jittery evening awaiting tanks that never appeared.

When Yeltsin proclaimed the Communist Party an illegal organisation, what fragile threads remained of the Soviet Union were ripped apart. On 25 December 1991, Gorbachev resigned and the Soviet Union was officially pronounced dead. Next day, the Russian Federation's flag of red, white and blue flew over the Kremlin.

Vladimir Putin: St Petersburg's Prodigal Son

St Petersburg has few admirers more emphatic about loving the city than the Russian President Vladimir Putin. Speculation was at one point rife that Putin wanted to make the historically monumental decision to move the capital back to St Petersburg from Moscow, reversing Lenin's largely expedient transfer of the honour there in 1918, although this prediction never came to pass.

Putin was born on 7 October 1952 into a poor family in Leningrad. Before the war his parents lived in nearby Peterhof, his mother being evacuated to the city as the Germans approached. After the war, which both his parents survived, the family moved to 12 Baskov per, a side street off ul Mayakovskogo.

He went to school in the neighbourhood, and took a law degree at Leningrad State University before working in Moscow and East Germany for the KGB. He returned to his home town in 1990 as assistant to the rector of Leningrad State University. He then enjoyed a meteoric rise through local politics and by 1994 he was deputy to former St Petersburg mayor Anatoly Sobchak. Here Putin famously replaced the portrait of Lenin in his office with one of Peter the Great.

When Sobchak lost the mayoral election to his one-time deputy Vladimir Yakovlev it came as a huge shock to both Putin and Sobchak. While the latter disappeared abroad due to worries about being made to stand trial for alleged corruption offences, Putin made his way to Moscow where he took on a minor role in Boris Yeltsin's Kremlin. A similarly meteoric rise through the ranks here led to Putin taking over the FSB (the post-communist KGB) in 1999 – a hugely significant role in a country where the secret services continue to exercise enormous power and influence. Finally, after Yeltsin sacked his previous two prime ministers in quick succession, Putin – a complete unknown – was offered the post. When Yeltsin finally resigned as president on New Year's Eve 1999, Putin was appointed acting president and the rest is history. Since then he has won two presidential elections and remains hugely popular among the Russian people, despite being vilified by the intelligentsia for his attitude towards the press.

Putin's fondness for his home town is undiminished, although even someone with as much unchecked power as the president clearly hasn't got the energy to move the capital back to St Petersburg again. Instead, Putin is keen to show off the city – often receiving foreign leaders here. Tony Blair watched the premiere of the Mariinsky's *War and Peace* with Putin here, while EU leaders stayed at the presidential retreat in Strelna during the EU-Russia summit in 2003.

1985	1986
A little-known reformer named Mikhail Gorbachev becomes the country's leader	Chornobyl nuclear disaster

Smolny Institute (p101)

ST PETERSBURG REBORN

After a popular vote in 1991, the citizens of Leningrad overwhelmingly endorsed Mayor Sobchak's plan to change the city's name for the fourth time in the 20th century, this time back to the original St Petersburg.

The 1990s were a hard time for the city, which along with the rest of Russia had to live through the dark days of early 1990s economic reforms, a bitter medicine that finally seems to be paying dividends a decade later. With the communist authorities no longer all-powerful, criminal groups gained a firm grip on various areas of commerce in the city, becoming known to one and all as 'the Mafia'. More than most cities in Russia during the 1990s, St Petersburg was afflicted by high rates of criminality, and excessive gang violence and contract killings.

Mayor Sobchak, who ultimately wasn't cut out for the economic challenges of running an ailing city the size of St Petersburg, was defeated by his former deputy Vladimir Yakovlev in 1996, bringing a new power shift to the city. Yakovlev's time in the Smolny was marked by allegations of corruption and cronyism, not to mention more violence. The assassination of both his deputy Mikhail Manevich and Duma deputy Galina Starovoitova in 1997 and 1998 respectively horrified, yet ultimately didn't surprise, Petersburgers long accustomed to violence.

However, Yakovlev's time in power did see the city finally making progress economically, balancing its budget and attracting investment from overseas in significant amounts. The Russian economic collapse in August 1998 seemed to many to be the last straw as the myth of Russian democratic and market reform came tumbling to the ground. Many predicted a

1991

The entire city mobilises to resist the communist coup in Moscow

1991

Leningrad becomes St Petersburg again by popular referendum

total collapse of the state, which thankfully did not occur, the unpredictable and eccentric Yeltsin finally resigning in 1999 for the young, teetotalling former KGB officer Vladimir Putin. Whatever else can be said about Putin's less than democratic tendencies, there's no doubt that for the first time in living memory Russia has a youthful, popular leader with a mandate for change. With five years of successive economic growth at around 6%, there's little doubt that St Petersburg is finally getting to the place Peter the Great intended for it three centuries ago.

2000	2003
St Petersburg native Vladimir Putin is elected President of Russia	St Petersburg celebrates its 300th birthday with huge celebrations

The Hermitage

The Hermitage

There are art galleries, there are museums, there are the great museums of the world and then there is the Hermitage. An unrivalled collection of art treasures housed in the magnificent palace from which the Romanov tsars ruled the Russian Empire, the **State Hermitage** (☎ 311 3465; www.hermitagemuseum.org; Dvortsovaya nab 34) will inevitably be the focus of any first visit to St Petersburg, and rightly so. Fully living up to its reputation and taking several repeat visits to get any way through its staggeringly varied and fascinating collection, the Hermitage demands a great deal of your time and however much you give you'll inevitably come out wishing for more.

The enormous collection almost amounts to a history of Western European art, from the pottery of Upper Egypt to the jewellery of Bronze Age civilisations and a full range of artists such as Rembrandt, Rubens, Picasso and Matisse, and schools including the Florentine and Venetian Renaissance, impressionism and post-impressionism. There are also prehistoric, ancient Greek and Roman, Russian and Oriental sections, plus excellent temporary exhibitions. The wealth of the collection itself is limitless – as much as you see in the museums, there's about 20 times more in its vaults. Some famed Fabergé jewels, for example, are only on display during certain temporary exhibitions.

The vastness of the place – five main buildings, of which the Winter Palace alone has 1057 rooms and 117 staircases – and its huge number of visitors (more than three million annually) demand a little planning. It may be useful to make a reconnaissance tour first and then return another day to enjoy your favourite parts. You can spend a whole visit just looking at the staterooms where Nicholas II and his family spent their last days before the revolution, never even scraping the surface of the art collection itself.

Winter Palace

The State Hermitage consists of five linked buildings along riverside Dvortsovaya nab – from west to east they are the **Winter Palace**, the **Little Hermitage**, the **Old Hermitage** and **New Hermitage** (sometimes grouped together and called the **Large Hermitage**), and the **Hermitage Theatre**. The art collection is on all three floors of the Winter Palace and the main two floors of the Little and Large Hermitages. The Hermitage Theatre is open for special events, mainly concerts.

Though the rooms listed in our room-by-room guide should, in principle, be open during your visit, occasionally some will be closed without warning for maintenance or other mysterious reasons. If the painting you came to Russia to see is inaccessible, ask one of the guards when it is expected to open again.

HISTORY

THE IMPERIAL ERA

The present baroque/rococo Winter Palace was commissioned from Rastrelli in 1754 by Empress Elizabeth. Yet it had three predecessors, which all stood near the embankment between the Admiralty and the tiny Zimnaya Canal. The first was built in 1711 but was replaced by number two, built between 1716 and 1720. Peter the Great died in that one in 1725 (it was situated at the site of the present-day Hermitage Theatre). Empress Anna decided to have another stab at it in the early 1730s, engaging a young Bartolomeo Rastrelli. It was enthusiastically built upon and redeveloped in the 1740s, but (lucky for us) the whims of Empress Elizabeth were still not satisfied.

Elizabeth ordered Rastrelli to give it a final go in 1754, closely supervising the ensuing building's construction and design. Sadly, she didn't survive to occupy it. She was living in a temporary residence specially built for her by Rastrelli, a so-called Wooden Hermitage (between present-day Bolshaya Morskaya ul and the Moyka near Nevsky pr) and died there in December 1761, only a few months before the Winter Palace was finally completed.

Catherine the Great and her successors didn't much care for Rastrelli's baroque interiors and had most of the rooms completely remodelled in classical style by the 1830s. They didn't touch the exteriors, however, and left the Jordan Staircase and the Cathedral alone.

The classical Little Hermitage was built for Catherine the Great as a retreat that would also house the art collection started by Peter the Great. At the river end of the Large Hermitage is the Old Hermitage, which also dates from her time. At its southern end, facing Millionnaya ul, is the New Hermitage, built by Nicholas I to hold the family's still-growing art collection and the only part of the Hermitage to be occasionally open to the 'decent' public (ie the upper classes and bourgeoisie) until after 1917.

The Hermitage Theatre (where plays would be performed for the imperial family) was built in the 1780s by the classicist Giacomo Quarenghi, who thought it one of his finest works. Rossi later reworked it.

In December 1837 a devastating fire broke out in the heating shaft of the Field Marshals' Hall; it burned for over 30 hours and destroyed a large portion of the interior. Most of the imperial belongings were saved, thrown out of windows or dragged outside to sit in the snow. Nicholas I vowed to restore the palace as quickly as possible, and by using as many as 10,000 exhausted workers at a time had it pretty much looking like it had before in only 15 months. Architects and designers Stasov and Bryullov headed the operation. Huge furnaces burned day and night inside the palace, raising the temperature to nearly 30°C to dry the paint faster. In winter, workers fell seriously ill, some even dying, from the drastic drop in temperature after leaving the building.

From Catherine's time on, the palace was used as the imperial family's residence (her soon-to-be-murdered husband Peter III was its first inhabitant, but for only three months). There were some exceptions: Catherine's son, Paul I, had an entire castle built for himself (the Engineers' Castle) only to be murdered in it after 40 days of occupancy; and Alexander III and Nicholas II both preferred to spend their time at the Anichkov Palace (Nicholas II eventually resided most of the time in the Alexander Palace in Tsarskoe Selo).

AFTER 1917

After the February 1917 Revolution, the seat of the Provisional Government under Karensky was placed here, but only for a few months before they were arrested. During the revolution, the Bolsheviks took the Winter Palace, but the dramatic storming portrayed in all those Soviet paintings or in Eisenstein's film *October* never occurred. Three shells struck the building, bullet holes riddled the square side of the palace and a window was shattered on the 3rd floor before the Provisional Government was arrested in the Small Dining Room behind the Malachite Hall on 26 October 1917.

The Bolsheviks renamed the Winter Palace the Palace of the Arts. In November 1918, on the revolution's first anniversary, several thousand participants arrived in the city for a congress of peasants. Most were housed in the Palace of the Arts. In a vulgar show of contempt for the palace's previous owners and all they had stood for, they filled all the bathtubs and many valuable Oriental and Saxon vases with their own excrement.

In 1922 the Winter Palace was officially transferred to the State Hermitage and before WWII part of it was used to house the Museum of the Revolution. The Soviet period saw the Hermitage transformed into one of the world's greatest museums.

Throughout the 1990s, thanks partly to partnerships with foreign museums and donors, the museum has been able to renovate its heating and temperature control system, install a new fire detection system, fit its windows with a thin sheath of UV-filtering plastic, and to begin the first thorough, digitised inventory of its mammoth collection. There are major plans for further renovation and the museum is now actively promoting itself abroad with branches in London and Amsterdam.

In 2002 the museum itself was used very fittingly as a set for one of 21st-century Russia's first major works of art, Alexander Sokurov's magnificent film *Russian Ark*, the first feature length film in history to be shot using one unbroken tracking shot.

Today the museum receives some three million visitors a year, and now also encompasses the east wing of the General Staff Building, the Menshikov Palace and the Summer Palace.

ADMISSION

The main entrance to the Hermitage for individuals is through the courtyard of the Winter Palace from Palace Sq. Just inside are four ticket counters, flanking a very useful information booth where you can get free colour maps of the entire museum in most major European languages.

That the admission price is R350 (much higher for a foreigner than for a Russian) is just something you'll have to grin and bear. However, ISIC card-holders and visitors under the age of 17 get in for free, whatever their nationality. Also, foreigners working or residing in Russia (and who can show proof of this) get in for the Russian price – R100. You need to pay an extra R100 to take photographs and R350 to use a video camera.

The museum is open from 10.30am to 6pm Tuesday to Saturday and 10.30am to 5pm Sunday. The ticket counter closes one hour before closing time.

The queues can be horrendous in summer – try to get there as early as possible to avoid an unpleasant wait. Sometimes, enterprising Russians will 'sell' you their place at the front of the line – you may get a few nasty looks but it's not illegal. A far better way to queue jump is to reserve your ticket online at www.hermitagemuseum.org. Here you can order tickets and pay for them by credit card, after which you will receive a voucher for entry via email which you can show to the ticket collectors and go straight in.

TOURS & INFORMATION

If the museum's sheer size seems overwhelming you can join a tour, which whizzes round the main parts in about 1½ hours but at least provides an introduction to the place in English. It's easy enough to 'lose' the group and stay until closing time.

The museum's **excursion office** (☎ 311 8446, 213 1112; 🕒 11.30am-1pm & 2-4pm) is down the corridor to the left as you enter, up the stairs and straight to the end of the small corridor (don't turn right towards the cloakroom). People who have booked with the excursions office use the Dvortsovaya nab entrance, although you won't be able to use this without booking first, in which case use the main courtyard entrance to get to the office.

You can either call in advance (suggested) or show up and hope to be able to arrange a guided tour through the museum in English, German or French, a thematic tour, or to book a place in groups to see the Golden Collection.

Immediately after ticket inspection you can rent a Walkman with recorded tours in English, German, French, Italian or Russian, including a general orientation (R250), and tours of the Flemish and Dutch collections, 'Impressionism to Picasso', and 'Unknown Masterpieces Revealed' (prices vary).

You'll trip over all the book stalls and souvenir kiosks set up throughout the museum, but be aware that things are sold at a big mark-up – you can buy most books and postcards at half-price outside or at any bookshop. In the museum's lavish main shop you can stock up on Hermitage T-shirts, mugs, calendars, figurines and *palekh* painted boxes – not to mention fine-looking imitation Fabergé eggs and sumptuous chess sets. Books of all kinds are rife, including a *Hidden Treasures Revealed* and a Hermitage-produced guide to the museum, available in many languages.

There's a small café on the 1st floor, opposite an interactive centre with computer terminals offering a virtual tour of the museum and the opportunity to search for the location of your favourite painting. These are to the right of the Jordan Staircase. Final proof that we've reached the modern age can be found in Café Max, an Internet café.

There are several toilets on the 1st floor only: downstairs by the cloakroom (old and stinky – you'll think you're at a train station), near the café, next to room 99, and by both the State and Council Staircases.

A ticket booth in the basement near the cloakroom sells tickets for events at the Hermitage Theatre.

Much of the Hermitage is now wheelchair-accessible, though that may entail having you and your wheelchair carried upstairs by museum staff. There are wheelchairs available on site. Note that the wheelchair entrance is on the square side of the building; there is a special lift there for that purpose. It's best to call in advance (☎ 110 9079) if you require any assistance, so someone will be there to open the gates. Otherwise, ring the bell and hope for the best.

Note that Russians number their levels in the same way as in the USA. There is no ground floor as such – the ground level is known as the 1st floor. We therefore have followed the Russian/US system.

THE COLLECTION

Many objects in the Hermitage's collection, which tops the three million mark (only 5% to 10% of the entire collection is ever on display at one time), were obtained thanks to

The Jordan Staircase

This magnificent creation of Bartolomeo Rastrelli is the main staircase of the Winter Palace and a great introduction to the opulence typical of the tsars. From the main gallery the staircase of white marble divides into two flights that cling to the walls before meeting again on the 2nd floor. Ten solid granite columns support the marble structure, which is lined with sculptures brought back from Italy by Peter the Great. During the 18th century the staircase was known as the Ambassadorial Staircase, as visiting foreign dignitaries would enter the palace here for audiences with the tsar. However, in the 19th century it became known as the Jordan Staircase as the imperial family would use it to descend to the Neva River for the celebration of Christ's baptism in the River Jordan on 6 January every year. At these ceremonies in a marquee set up on the ice, a hole would be cut through to the water and the emperor would drink a cup of (completely filthy) water, after it had been blessed by the Metropolitan of St Petersburg. Despite the worries of the tsar's doctors, the ceremony continued throughout the imperial era and, miraculously, no tsar is recorded to have ever become ill as a result.

shrewd negotiating and as a result of forced nationalisation (a diplomatic term for state-sponsored looting).

Though Peter the Great had purchased some Rembrandts and other objects of art, the Hermitage's collection really began with Catherine the Great, one of the most voracious art collectors of all time. She managed some amazing deals. In 1779, for example, she bought a series of valuable paintings by Poussin and others from the famous Walpole collection in England (Sir Robert Walpole was Britain's first prime minister). She convinced – somehow – his grandson to give her the paintings of her choice (she chose 15 Van Dycks!) in exchange for a large, framed portrait of herself! At the time this caused a scandal, as the collection had been destined to form the foundation of a national gallery in Britain.

Six years later, she acquired 250 Roman busts, marble sculptures and bas-reliefs from a director of the Bank of England; and immediately purchased 1120 important drawings by architect Charles-Louis Clérisseau when she found out that the Emperor Joseph was interested in buying them. She also had thousands of objects commissioned, including furniture, dinner services, portraits and some 32,000 copies of glass gemstones.

Nicholas I also greatly enriched the Hermitage's collection of treasures, which he opened up to the public for the first time in 1852. But it was the post-revolutionary period that saw a threefold increase in the collection. Many valuable private collections were seized by the state and nationalised, namely those of the Stroganovs, Sheremetyevs, Shuvalovs, Yusupovs and the Baron Stieglitz. These considerably swelled the Hermitage's coffers in a matter of years. Most remarkable was the 1948 incorporation of post-impressionist and impressionist paintings from the renowned collections of Moscow industrialists Sergey Shchukin and Ivan Morozov.

However, a number of major works by Rembrandt (15), Rubens and van Eyck were sold in the 1920s and 1930s to bolster the cash-strapped new government and to purchase machinery for Stalin's drive to industrialisation. Ironically, this was at the height of a world recession, so the paintings fetched laughably small sums for the standards of the time.

In 1995 the Hermitage displayed, for the first time, some of the sweetest war booty seen in the 20th century. 'Hidden Treasures Revealed' was comprised entirely of art captured from German private collections by the Red Army in 1945, including works by Monet, Degas, Renoir, Cézanne, Picasso and Matisse – almost all of which had never been publicly displayed. There was a political debate at the time as to whether the paintings should be returned to Germany, but evidently a resolution has since been found, as most of these paintings are now on permanent display in rooms 143–146 under the coy moniker 'French Paintings from the 19th and 20th centuries'.

Introductory Itinerary

If your time at the Hermitage is limited, the following rooms include the unmissable highlights of the collection:

- **Room 100:** Ancient Egypt
- **The Jordan Staircase:** directly ahead when you enter from the main entrance inside the Winter Palace by the ticket offices.
- **Rooms 178–197:** the staterooms for the apartments of the last imperial family
- **Room 204:** the Pavilion Hall
- **Rooms 207–215:** Florentine art, 13th to 16th centuries
- **Rooms 217–222 & 237:** Venetian art, 16th century
- **Room 229:** Raphael and his disciples
- **Rooms 239–240:** Spanish art, 16th to 18th centuries
- **Rooms 244–247:** Flemish art, 17th century
- **Rooms 249–252 & 254:** Dutch art, 17th century
- **Rooms 228–238:** Italian Art 16th to 18th centuries
- **Room 271:** the imperial family's cathedral

Concentrate the rest of your time on the fabulous 3rd floor, particularly rooms 333–350 for late 19th-century and early 20th-century European art.

WINTER PALACE, 1ST FLOOR

Rooms 1–33: Russian prehistoric artefacts

Room 11: Palaeolithic (500,000 to 12,000 BC) and Mesolithic (12,000 to 3000 BC). **Room 12:** Neolithic (4000 to 2400 BC) and Bronze Age (2000 to 500 BC), including petroglyphs from 2500 to 2000 BC taken from the northeastern shores of Lake Onega after archaeological expeditions in 1935. **Room 13:** Bronze Age, western steppes, 4000 to 2000 BC. **Room 14:** Bronze Age, southern Siberia and Kazakhstan, 2000 to 900 BC; fine bronze animals. **Rooms 15–18:** culture and art of the Scythians, who lived in what is presently the south of Russia from the 7th to 3rd centuries BC. There's the stunning Golden Stag, which once formed part of an iron shield – but the best Scythian material is in the Golden Rooms Special Collection. **Rooms 19 & 20:** forest steppes, 7th to 4th centuries BC. **Rooms 21–23 & 26:** material from Altai Mountains burial mounds, including **26:** human and horse corpses preserved for over 2000 years complete with hair and teeth; and **24:** Iron Age, Eastern Europe, including Finno-Ugrians and Balts, 8th century BC to 12th century AD. **Room 33:** southern steppes tribes 3rd century BC to 10th century AD – some fine Sarmatian gold.

Rooms 34–40 & 46–69: Russian east

Rooms 34–39: Central Asia, 4th century BC to 13th century AD. **Rooms 55–66:** Caucasus and Transcaucasia, 10th century BC to 16th century AD, including Urartu (room 56), 8th to 6th centuries BC, discovered in digs in 1911 and 1916; Dagestan (room 59), 6th to 11th centuries AD; and 14th-century Italian colonies in Crimea (room 66). **Rooms 67–69:** Golden Horde, 13th to 14th centuries.

Room 100: Ancient Egypt

An excellent collection, including clay plates from 5000 BC and wooden figurines from about 2000 BC, much of it uncovered by Russian archaeologists. Of particular interest is a wonderfully disturbing 10th century BC mummy. Sadly there is no labelling in English except the signs saying 'Please Do Not Touch'.

LITTLE HERMITAGE, 1ST FLOOR

The little staircase at the end of room 100 will bring you into the Little (or Small) Hermitage, which on this floor used to house the palace stables and riding school. Most of it is off-limits, but **room 101** has displays of Roman marble and mosaics under restoration.

Pavilion Hall (p78)

LARGE HERMITAGE, 1ST FLOOR

Rooms 106–131: Ancient classical culture

Rooms 106–109 & 127: Roman sculpture, 1st century BC to 4th century AD, including **107:** Jupiter Hall (a statue of the god sits near the middle – look for his pet eagle), a sumptuous space with portraits of sculptors

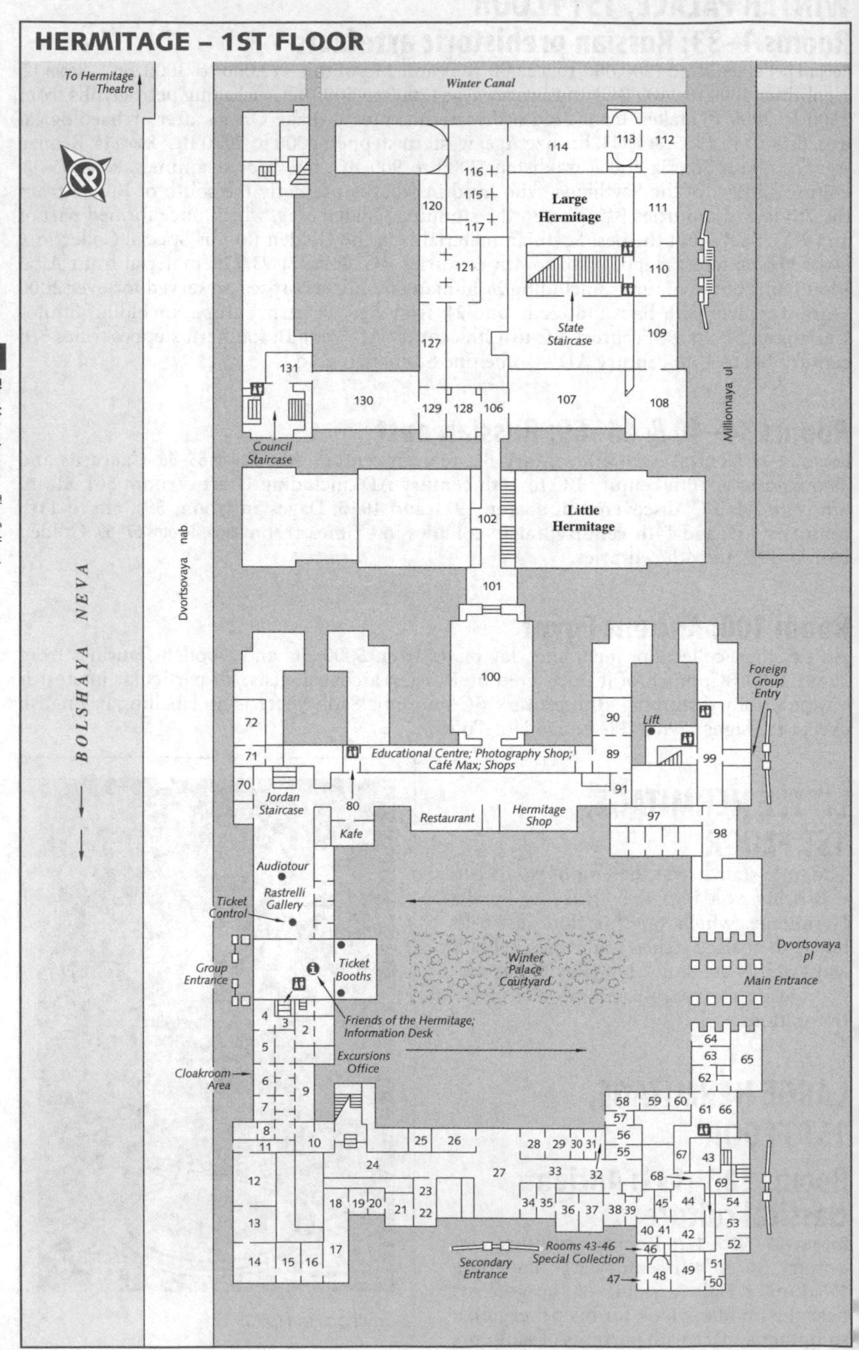
HERMITAGE – 1ST FLOOR
To Hermitage Theatre
Winter Canal
Large Hermitage
State Staircase
Council Staircase
Little Hermitage
Millionnaya ul
Dvortsovaya nab
BOLSHAYA NEVA
Educational Centre; Photography Shop; Café Max; Shops
Jordan Staircase
Restaurant
Hermitage Shop
Kafe
Lift
Foreign Group Entry
Audiotour
Rastrelli Gallery
Ticket Control
Ticket Booths
Group Entrance
Friends of the Hermitage; Information Desk
Excursions Office
Cloakroom Area
Winter Palace Courtyard
Dvortsovaya pl
Main Entrance
Secondary Entrance
Rooms 43-46 Special Collection

on the ceiling (can you spot Michelangelo?) and a near-intact ancient Roman sarcophagus; **108:** architect Leo von Klenze wanted the room to reflect the courtyard of a Hellenistic or Roman house, and so it is filled with Greco-Roman decorative art; **109:** features the *Tauride Venus,* acquired by Peter the Great from Pope Clement XI and which resided in the Tauride Palace until the mid-19th century; **127:** a great statue of Octavian Augustus from the 1st century AD. Though done near the end of his life, it was a stroke of brilliant, eternal PR to portray him as an omnipotent, young, muscular man, sitting half-naked with a sceptre in one hand and a ball in the other. **Rooms 111–114:** Ancient Greece, 8th to 2nd centuries BC, mostly ceramics and sculpture, though beautiful **111**, designed by von Klenze, was initially meant to be used as a library – hence the portraits of famous philosophers high up on the walls. **Rooms 115–117 & 121:** Greek colonies around the northern Black Sea, 7th century BC to 3rd century AD; **Room 128:** the huge 19th-century jasper Kolyvanskaya Vase from Siberia is one of the highlights of the museum. The vase, which weighs 19 tonnes, was designed by Avram Malnikov and made by craftsmen of the Kolyvan Lapidary Works in the Altai Mountains over 14 years. It took nearly 800 men to position it where it sits now, in a luscious yet subdued room with magnificently subtle lighting. **Rooms 130 & 131:** ancient Italy, 7th to 2nd centuries BC, including Etruscan vases and bronze mirrors. Room **130** is known as the Hall of Twenty Columns, for obvious reasons, and was recently beautifully renovated. There's almost no labelling in any language, however.

LARGE HERMITAGE, 2ND FLOOR

Rooms 206–215: Florentine art

From room 131, head up the Council Staircase (Sovietskaya Lestnitsa – its name derives from the members of the State Council who most often used it in the 19th century). At the top is **room 206** where a marble, malachite and glass triumphal arch announces the beginning of the Italian section, 13th to 16th centuries. **Room 207:** Ugolino Di Tedice's *The Crucifixion*, from the first half of the 13th century, is the earliest example in this collection, but Simone Martini's *Virgin of the Annunciation* from either 1339 or 1342 is the room's subtly crafted standout. **Room 209:** 15th-century paintings, including Fra Angelico. **Room 213:** 15th and early 16th centuries, including two small Botticellis (commissioned by Lorenzo Medici), Filippino Lippi, Perugino. **Room 214:** Russia's only two paintings by Leonardo da Vinci – the *Benois Madonna* (1478) and the strikingly different masterpiece *Madonna Litta* (1490), both named after their last owners. Note also the room's beautiful jasper columns and the doors with tortoiseshell and copper inlays. **Room 215:** features art by Leonardo's pupils, including Correggio and Andrea del Sarto.

Room 216: Italian Mannerist art

Works from the 16th century; also a nice view over the little Winter Canal to the Hermitage Theatre.

St Sebastian

One of Titian's last paintings, *St Sebastian* (1575) tells in part the story of the saint who attempted to convert Emperor Diocletian to Christianity and who was tied to a tree, shot with arrows and left for dead. According to the Catholic tradition, Sebastian survived his ordeal and returned to Rome to preach to Diocletian, who had him beaten to death then and there.

However, the painting takes up the popular Renaissance theme of Sebastian's suffering in the wilderness with arrows hanging from his flesh. Alone in an empty, dark place and waiting for death, the religious intensity of the painting overcomes the tragedy with Sebastian's faith shining through as he looks to heaven. The colouring, based on the contrast of dark and purple-yellow tones, supports the tragic atmosphere of the scene. While the topic may be tragic, Titian refuses to flinch from it, hoping instead to demystify the horror of the worst human suffering by showing it to us in full. The painting is to be found in room 221, 2nd floor, Large Hermitage.

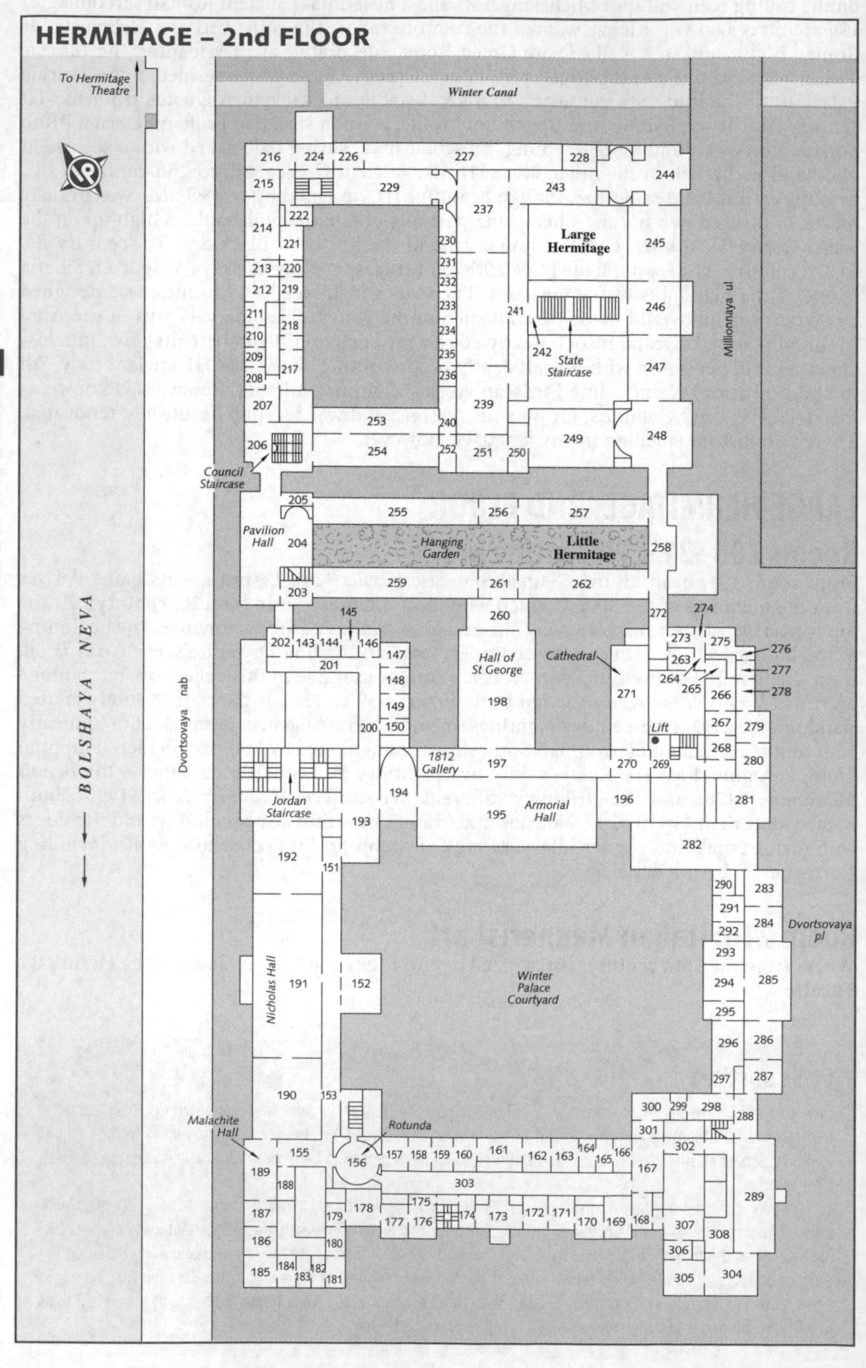
HERMITAGE – 2nd FLOOR
To Hermitage Theatre
Winter Canal
Large Hermitage
State Staircase
Millionnaya ul
Council Staircase
Pavilion Hall
Hanging Garden
Little Hermitage
Hall of St George
Cathedral
Lift
1812 Gallery
Jordan Staircase
Armorial Hall
BOLSHAYA NEVA
Dvortsovaya nab
Nicholas Hall
Winter Palace Courtyard
Dvortsovaya pl
Malachite Hall
Rotunda

Rooms 217–222: Venetian art

Mainly 16th century. **Room 217:** Giorgione's *Judith.* **Room 219:** Titian's *Portrait of a Young Woman* and *Flight into Egypt,* and more by Giorgione. **Room 221:** more Titian, including *Dana* and *St Sebastian.* **Room 222:** Paolo Veronese's *Mourning of Christ.*

Rooms 226 & 227: Loggia of Raphael

Quarenghi's sumptuous 1780s copy of a gallery in the Vatican with murals by Raphael was built at the request of Catherine the Great, who so liked what she saw in the Vatican, she decided to build her own (there weren't many souvenirs to take back home then). These copies were done on canvas – note the royal touch of russification here and there, like the replacing of the Pope's coat-of-arms with the Romanov dynasty's two-headed eagle. The Tyrolese Christopher Unterberger headed a team of artists who drew the murals.

Rooms 228–238: Italian art, 16th to 18th centuries

Room 228: 16th-century ceramics. **Room 229:** Raphael and disciples, including his *Madonna Conestabile* and *Holy Family,* plus wonderful ceramics and decorations, as well as Russia's only Michelangelo, a marble statue of a crouching boy. **Room 237:** 16th-century paintings, including Paolo Veronese and Tintoretto. The high vaults and frieze are decorated with arabesque stucco. **Room 238:** 17th- and 18th-century painters including Canaletto and Tiepolo; also two huge 19th-century Russian malachite vases. Rooms 237 and 238 have lovely ceilings.

Rooms 239–240: Spanish art, 16th to 18th centuries

Room 239: Goya's *Portrait of the Actress Antonia Zarate,* Murillo's *Boy with a Dog,* Diego Velazquez' *Breakfast;* **Room 240:** one of El Greco's last paintings, the marvellous *St Peter and St Paul.*

Rooms 241–243: Marble sculptures & Knights' Hall

Room 241: sculptures by Antonio Canova and Albert Thorwaldsen. **Room 242:** mainly taken up by the State Staircase, surrounded by walls of yellow marble. **Room 243:** the slightly creepy Knights' Hall; Western European armour and weaponry from the 15th to 17th centuries, featuring four 16th-century German suits of armour atop armoured horses.

Rooms 245–247: Flemish art, 17th century

Room 245: savage hunting and market scenes by Snyders. **Room 246:** Van Dyck portraits. **Room 247:** a large room displaying the amazing range of Rubens, including *Descent from the Cross, Bacchus, The Union of Earth and Water, Portrait of a Curly-Haired Old Man* and *Roman Charity.*

The Return of the Prodigal Son

Painted during the last year of Rembrandt's life, *The Return of the Prodigal Son* (c 1669) arguably represents the height of Rembrandt's mastery of psychology in his paintings. Taking the famous story from the Gospel, Rembrandt creates a scene of enormous tragedy as the prodigal son returns home having wasted his inheritance and his youth to find the mercy and forgiveness of his father. This solemn baroque masterpiece is an extremely moving portrait of unquestioning parental love and mercy.

The old man (near death, much like the painter) clearly forgives his son by placing his arms over his shoulders. Likewise, his filthy, poor son is truly repentant; he kneels before his father and his vulnerability and contrition is further suggested by his one bare foot. The assembled men behind the father look disapproving, but they are placed in shadow while father and son enjoy the full glow of Rembrandt's light.

You'll find the painting in room 254 on the 2nd floor of the Large Hermitage building.

Rooms 248–252 & 254: Dutch art, 16th to 18th centuries

Room 249: Tent Hall, designed by Leo von Klenze, including landscapes and portraits by Ruisdael, Hals, Bol, Steen (whose *Idlers* is a memorable highlight) and others. **Room 250:** 18th-century Delft ceramics. **Room 254:** 26 Rembrandts ranging from lighter, more detailed early canvases like *Abraham's Sacrifice of Isaac* and *Dana* to *The Holy Family* of 1645, and darker, penetrating late works like *The Return of the Prodigal Son* and two canvases entitled *Portrait of an Old Man*. There's also work by Rembrandt's pupils, including Bol.

LITTLE HERMITAGE, 2ND FLOOR

Room 204: Pavilion Hall

A sparkling, airy white-and-gold room with 28 chandeliers, tables, galleries and columns. The south windows look on to Catherine the Great's hanging garden, the north onto the Neva; the floor mosaic in front of them is copied from a Roman bath. Roman and Florentine mosaics from the 18th and 19th centuries, and the amazing Peacock Clock (James Fox; 1772) – a revolving dial in one of the toadstools tells the time, and on the hour (when it's working) the peacock spreads its wings and the toadstools, owl and cock come to life. It's demonstrated to the curious every Wednesday at 5pm.

Room 258: Flemish art, 17th century

This long corridor used to be the only entrance to the Little Hermitage from the Winter Palace – it was along here that Catherine the Great would flee the business of the day to have a rest, accompanied or not.

Other rooms

Room 259: Western European applied art, 11th to 15th centuries. **Rooms 261–262:** Dutch art, 15th and 16th centuries.

WINTER PALACE, 2ND FLOOR

Rooms 143–146: French painting, 19th & 20th centuries

This is most of what used to be called the Hidden Treasures Revealed exhibit. It boasts oil paintings captured by the Red Army from private collections in Germany, including works by Monet, Degas, Renoir, Cézanne, Picasso and Matisse, almost all never before publicly displayed.

Rooms 147–189: Russian culture & art

Rooms 147–150: 10th to 15th centuries. **Room 151:** long hallway lined with portraits of the imperial family from Peter the Great onwards. Look out for the very masculine picture of Catherine the Great in her guard's uniform on her horse Brilliant. **Room 152:** closed at the time of writing. When it reopens there are plans to display the art of ancient Rus here. **Room 153:** items relating to Peter the Great. **Rooms 155–166:** late 17th and early 18th century, including **155:** Moorish Dining Room; **156:** rotunda; **157–first half of 161:** Petrovsky Gallery, displaying personal effects and equipment used by Peter the Great as well as some beautiful early 18th-century furniture; **161:** an ivory chandelier that was partly built by the Great Guy himself. It was in this room in 1880 that there was an attempt on the life of Alexander II – a bomb had been set off in the room below, killing 11 soldiers (the tsar had wandered into another room at the time). Khalturin, the young revolutionary who planted the bomb was executed, but got belated tribute for his great deed by the Soviets, who renamed Millionnaya ul after him; **162:** mosaic of Peter by Lomonosov and a globe dating from 1733; and **163–166:** furniture and household goods from the Winter Palace during the 18th century. **Rooms 167–173:** Russian culture 1700–1800 (spot the bizarre 1772 tapestry image of Australia in room 167).

Rooms 175–187 (Start at 187 and work your way back): rooms occupied by the last imperial family, now displaying 19th-century interior design, including **176:** the Children's Room; **177:** the neoclassical Sitting Room; **178:** Winter Palace Library: the wonderful gothic interior was completed in 1894. This was where Nicholas II spent much of his time – check out the sublime walnut ceiling; **179:** Smoking Room with a décor that looks uncannily like that of a student dorm; **180:** sitting room; **181:** Pompeii Dining Room; **182:** Gothic Study; **183:** boudoir featuring some incredibly ugly baroque furnishings; **184:** study, sitting room and boudoir; **185:** Music Room; **186:** sitting room and study; **187:** Palace Drawing Room; the griffin-motif furniture dates from 1805. **Room 188:** Small Dining Room, completed in 1894. Most significantly this is the room where the Provisional Government was arrested by the Bolsheviks in 1917. **Room 189:** Malachite Hall with two tonnes of gorgeous green malachite columns, boxes, bowls and urns. Designed by Bryullov in 1839, this may be the most impressive of all the palace's rooms. The three figurines on the wall represent Day, Night and Poetry. This was where the last meeting of the 1917 Provisional Government occurred, on the fateful nights of 25 and 26 October 1917 (they were arrested soon after in the Small Dining Room next door).

Rooms 190–192: Neva Enfilade

One of two sets of staterooms for ceremonies and balls. **Room 190:** Concert Hall for small balls, with an enormous, very ornate 18th-century silver tomb (constructed 1747–52) for the remains of Alexander Nevsky. It was commissioned by the Empress Elizabeth. **Room 191:** Great or Nicholas Hall, the palace's largest room, scene of imperial winter balls (5000 guests could be squeezed in here). **Room 192:** Fore Hall, the site of pre-ball champagne buffets; all are now used for temporary exhibitions.

Rooms 193–198: Great Enfilade

The second series of staterooms. **Room 193:** Field Marshals' Hall, with its military-themed chandelier and coach – a real crowd-pleaser. This is where the disastrous fire of 1837 broke out. **Room 194:** Peter the Great's Hall, with his none-too-comfy-looking oak and silver throne. Better is Jacopo Amigoni's portrait of *Peter I with Minerva,* in which the Emperor looks more pleased with himself than with his date. This room was severely damaged by a Nazi shell during the blockade. **Room 195:** Armorial Hall, bright and gilt-encrusted with chandeliers engraved with the coat-of-arms of all the Russian provinces. Also displays of 16th- to 19th-century Western European silver. **Room 197:** 1812 Gallery, hung with 332 portraits of Russian and allied Napoleonic war leaders. **Room 198:** St George's Hall or Great Throne Room – once a stateroom where the imperial throne used to sit, its 800 sq metres are now used for temporary exhibitions. The white Carrara marble was imported from Italy and the floors were crafted from the wood of 16 different tree species. Official receptions and ceremonies were held here.

Rooms 272–289: French art, 15th to 18th centuries

Rooms 272–273: tapestries, ceramics, metalwork. **Room 279:** paintings by Poussin. **Room 280:** Lorrain. **Room 281:** French 18th-century painting. **Room 282:** Alexander Hall, a testament to the victory over Napoleon in 1812. **Rooms 283–285:** Vanloo, Boucher, Watteau and other 18th-century French painters. **Room 286:** Jean-Marc Nattier portraits, including a picture of a very vulnerable-looking Catherine I commissioned by Peter the Great in 1717. **Room 287:** Jean-Antoine Houdon's marble statue of Voltaire. **Room 288:** Jean-Baptiste Greuze and Jean-Honoré Fragonard. **Room 289:** White Hall, a pleasant space built for Alexander II's wedding, with 18th-century furniture and vases. Bryullov designed this in 1838 using a Roman bath as a model. There's also a superb moulded ceiling and a display of 18th-century *bureaux.*

Rooms 298–302: British art, 16th to 19th centuries

Room 298: Gainsborough's *Lady in Blue.* **Room 299:** Reynolds. **Rooms 299–300:** British artists including Sir Joshua Reynolds (room 300). **Room 301:** portraits of the Russian aristocracy by Thomas Lawrence and other British artists. **Room 302:** 18th- and 19th-century English silverware.

> ### Lady in Blue
>
> This is one of the highlights of the Hermitage's considerable collection of English painting and the only painting by Gainsborough in the museum's possession. *Lady in Blue* (c 1780) was bequeathed to the Hermitage in 1912 by art collector Alexei Khitrovo. The woman is unknown, although she may have been the Duchess of Beaufort, which if true would have been strange, given that Gainsborough was married to the illegitimate daughter of the Duke of Beaufort. Up close it is possible to observe the feathery brushstrokes employed by the artist to create this whole – stand back again and all the strokes have faded magically. The strange expression on the face of the woman has been interpreted in many different ways including lust, repentance and ennui. The painting is in room 298, on the 2nd floor of the Winter Palace.

Rooms 303–308: 'Dark Corridor' & surrounding rooms

Room 303: 'Dark Corridor', containing tapestry, 16th to 18th centuries. Take a confusing trail through 167 and 308 to get to **Room 304:** Golden Drawing Room. The ceiling is fabulous, although the gilt walls would make even Donatella Versace blush. Temporary exhibits are held here. **Room 305:** Burgundy Hall, containing English and French Porcelain. **Room 306:** Maria Alexandrovna's bedroom, fit for a princess, with lush red brocatelle (made by Cartier in Paris) used in the curtains and on the walls. **Room 307:** the Blue Bedroom. **Room 308:** off the Golden Drawing Room, this small room houses temporary exhibits.

Other rooms

Rooms 200–202: Western European tapestry, 16th to 19th centuries. **Rooms 263–268:** German art, 15th to 18th centuries, including Dürer and Lucas Cranach the Elder. **Room 269:** Western European porcelain, 18th century. **Room 271:** imperial family's cathedral where many royal weddings took place (here Nicholas II married Alexandra in 1894). It now houses temporary exhibits.

WINTER PALACE, 3RD FLOOR

To view the French art collection in (approximate) chronological order, visit the rooms as follows: 314, 332 to 328, 325 to 315 and 343 to 350. The staircase beside room 269 on the 2nd floor brings you out by room 314. **Room 315** is the Hermitage shop.

Room 316–320: Impressionists & Post-Impressionists

Room 316: Gauguin's Tahitian works. **Room 317:** Van Gogh's *The Bush, The Arena at Arles* (1888) and *Memory of the Garden at Etten* (1888), Douanier Rousseau. **Room 318:** works by Cézanne including *The Smoker* (1890–92) and works by Pissarro including his sublime *Boulevard Montmartre in Paris* (1897). **Room 319:** Monet, including *Meadows at Giverny* (1888) and the wonderful *Waterloo Bridge, Effect of Mist* (1903). **320:** Renoir.

Rooms 321–325 & 328–331: Barbizon school & Romanticism

Rooms 321 & 322: Corot, Courbet, Théôdore Rousseau, Millet. **Room 330:** don't miss *Slave Woman Sold* (1884) by Jean Léon Gerome. **Room 331:** Delacroix and Vernet.

> ### Waterloo Bridge, Effect of Mist
>
> One of the most extraordinary paintings in the entire Hermitage collection, Claude Monet's wonderfully melancholic depiction of light diffused in the London fog over the Thames is a stunning example of his subtle mastery of colour. The view is from Monet's room at the Savoy Hotel in 1903, looking towards Waterloo Bridge. The painting is one of a series of Monet views of London during the late impressionist period and, while it is notable for its theme (Monet nearly always preferred rural landscapes over urban ones), its most striking feature is the analysis of complex colour nuances in flickering, changing light. The painting can be viewed in room 319, on the 3rd floor of the Winter Palace.

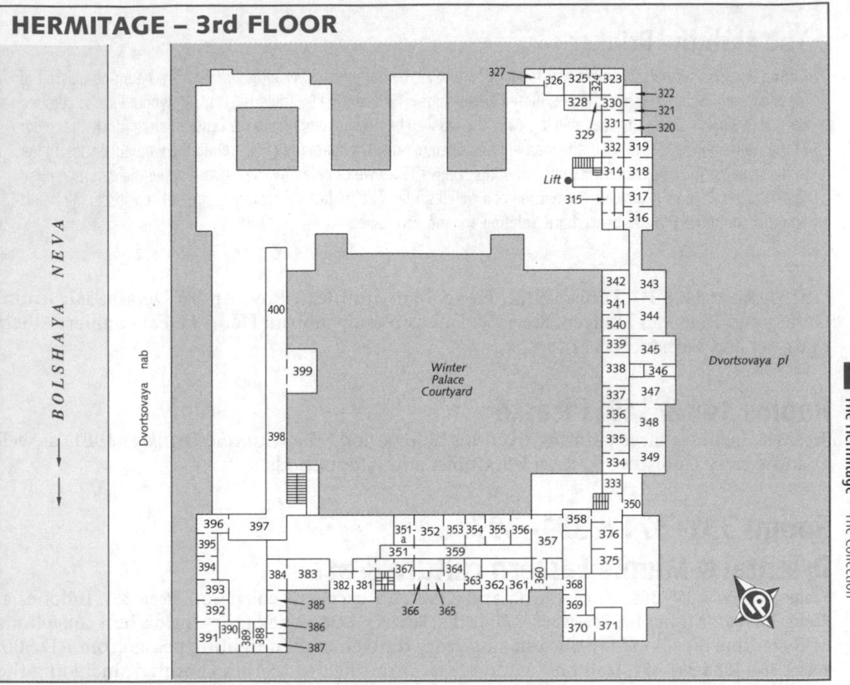

Room 333: Russian art, 20th century

Room 333: Kandinsky's early work including *Winter* (1909) and Malevich's *Black Square*. This is the only room in the entire Hermitage to feature 20th-century Russian art, most of which is housed in the Russian Museum.

Rooms 334–342: European art, 19th century

Includes landscapes by Caspar David Friedrich. **Room 334:** Vincent van Gogh.

Rooms 343–347 & 350: French art, 19th to 20th centuries

Rooms 343–345: 35 canvases of Matisse's work, including **343:** *View of Collioure* (1905); **344:** *The Dance* (1910), *The Red Room* (1908) and *Music* (1910); **345:** *Portrait of the Artist's Wife*

Black Square

This most striking painting of the Petrograd avant-garde was a work of huge significance, marking the beginning of a new art form to be known as suprematism. Kazimir Malevich created several variants of the simple black square against a white background throughout his career, of which this is the fourth and last. *Black Square* (1915) was taken by many as a nihilistic declaration of the 'end of painting'. It caused both outrage and awe when it was displayed, and remains a contentious piece of work today. However, the painting went missing during the Soviet period, mysteriously appearing in Samara, southern Russia, in 1993. Evaluated by experts and confirmed to be one of Malevich's originals, the painting came into the possession of a Russian bank, which went bankrupt in the 1998 financial crisis. Oligarch Vladimir Potanin – in search of some relatively cheap PR – bought the painting for $1 million and donated it to the Hermitage in 2002. It hangs in room 333 on the 3rd floor of the Winter Palace.

The Absinthe Drinker

During Picasso's second trip to Paris in 1901, aged just 22, he painted *The Absinthe Drinker*. This haunting portrait of loneliness and isolation was a theme explored deeply in the 19th century by Toulouse-Lautrec, whom Picasso admired greatly. A lonely woman sits at a table in a café; the red wall behind her reinforcing the sense of discomfort. The colour of the walls and the blue tones of the marble table seem to press the space inwards, around the woman, enclosing her in her hopeless loneliness. In the expression of the subject's face we can identify the outcast, while the deformation of the right hand seems to indicate the tension of a coiled spring. The subject's inert face is similarly enclosed: her hands wrapped around her like serpents, both isolating and protecting her.

(1913). **Rooms 346 & 347:** Louis Valtat, Henri Manguin, Jean Puy, André Derain; **347:** André Derain and Kees van Dongen. **Room 350:** Fauvism and Cubism: Henri Le Fauconnier, Albert Marquet and Fernand Léger.

Rooms 348 & 349: Picasso

Room 348: includes three painting from his blue period, *The Absinthe Drinker* (1901) as well as some early Cubist work. **Room 349:** Cubist and later periods.

Rooms 351–371 & 381–397: Oriental & Middle Eastern culture & art

Rooms 351–357 & 359–364: art of China and Tibet, an excellent collection. **Room 358:** Indonesia. **Rooms 365–367:** Mongolia. **Rooms 368–371:** India. **Rooms 381–382:** one of the world's best collections of Byzantine art – look for the amazing ivory diptych of men fighting beasts from AD 500. **Rooms 383–387 & 391–394:** Iran and Middle East from the 3rd to 18th centuries, including the world's largest collection of Sasanide silver (vases, plates, ornamental wine glasses) from the 3rd to the 7th centuries. These were accidentally uncovered near the Ural Mountains, where ancient merchants had traded furs for them. **Room 388:** Syria and Iraq, 13th to 15th centuries. **Rooms 389–390:** Egypt from 7th to 15th centuries. **Rooms 395–397:** Turkey from the 15th to 18th centuries.

Rooms 398 & 400: Coins

Includes the numismatic collection, boasting over 90,000 coins and medals.

Neighbourhoods

Neighbourhoods

St Petersburg is a tricky city to divide up. While water-loving Peter the Great intended for the Neva River to be the centre of the city with Vasilevsky Island as its glittering centrepiece, the lack of bridges between the islands hindered development, meaning that most people wanted to build on the higher, less flood-prone land around the Admiralty. Even Peter's despotism couldn't change people's preference and the centre of the city is very much now south of the Neva, focused on Nevsky pr between the Hermitage and the Moscow Station.

This book divides the city into nine easily digestible chunks. Begin with St Petersburg's historic heart, an area so dense with museums, palaces and churches that many people can spend days here without leaving. This includes the main part of Nevsky pr, which runs from the Hermitage to pl Vosstaniya (Uprising Sq), as well as including the area stretching from Isaakievskaya pl (St Isaac's Sq) to the Summer Garden. To the east of the historic heart is Smolny, the quiet but historic government district around which the Neva curves on its final approach to sea. Due south of here is Vosstaniya, the area around pl Vosstaniya, where the February Revolution began and containing the second, less dynamic, half of Nevsky pr, the Moscow Station and the wonderful Alexander Nevsky Monastery. To the west of Vosstaniya is Sennaya, which takes its name from the city's Haymarket, or Sennaya pl. This was Dostoevsky's neck of the woods, an industrial area of great poverty and squalor during the 19th century; it remains fascinating and full of characters today. West of both the historic heart and Sennaya is the Mariinsky region, named after the world-famous Mariinsky Theatre and arguably the city's cultural heart. In its quiet historic streets graceful canals wend their way to the sea past some delightful ruins that the city's renovation programme has yet to reach.

On the other side of the Neva River is Vasilevsky Island, the huge triangle of land that Peter the Great eventually decided would be the centre of the city and which now functions as its intellectual heart, housing the university and various other august academic institutions. The Petrograd Side is actually where it all began – Peter's city grew out of the Peter and Paul Fortress and the neighbourhood is a busy residential one today with plenty to keep you interested for a day or two. As well as fashionable, *style moderne*–saturated Petrogradsky Island, this neighbourhood includes the green and pleasant islands to the north: Kamenny, Yelagin and Krestovsky Islands, where Petersburgers relax at the weekend. There's also the Vyborg Side, a huge swathe of land north of the Neva River. Rather industrial and residential, it does however boast a couple of sights well worth visiting, including the charming Sampsonievsky Cathedral and the city's century-old Buddhist temple.

Back over the Neva, to the south of all the districts, the area imaginatively named Southern St Petersburg encompasses the modern communist city, still largely looking like Leningrad rather than St Petersburg. This vast area includes some wonderful historic oddities, Stalinist monoliths and parkland.

Griboedova Canal and Church on Spilled Blood (p91)

Russian Street Names & Addresses

We use the Russian names of streets and squares in this book to help you when deciphering Cyrillic signs and asking locals the way. To save space the following abbreviations are used:

bul – bulvar бульвар – boulevard

nab – naberezhnaya набережная – embankment

per – pereulok переулок – side street

pl – ploshchad площадь – square

pr – prospekt проспект – avenue

ul – ulitsa улица – street

sh – shosse шоссе – road

St Petersburg addresses can be horribly long and have the potential to really confuse first-timers to the city. You'll generally be given a street name and house number, and when visiting friends, a flat number *(kvartira* or *kv)* as well. In some big buildings you'll be given a *podyezd* (entrance) number, and in massive ones, a *korpus* (building within a building) number too. You'll then also have to remember the door code (most houses use the old Soviet manual system where you must push down all numbers simultaneously, which when there's a four-digit code can be quite a challenge after a few vodkas). Further confusion can be added if the house is located on a street corner, in which case the house number of the two intersecting streets will be given. For example, ul Lenina 25/8 is where ul Lenina 25 meets house 8 of whichever street it bisects. Finally, many addresses in St Petersburg will be given with either the suffix PS (ПС) or VO (ВО). These abbreviations stand for Petrograd Side (Петроградская сторона) and Vasilevsky Island (Василевский остров) respectively. This is particularly essential with addresses on Bolshoy pr, which runs on both islands. The ultimate St Petersburg address is therefore: ul Lenina 25/8, korpus 2, podyezd 3, kv 49, code 4950, PS. Fun stuff.

ITINERARIES

One Day

There's only one place to start a tour of St Petersburg and that's by entering **Dvortsovaya pl** (Palace Sq; p88) from Bolshaya Morskaya ul and seeing the incredible **Winter Palace** (p88). Having only one day in the city shouldn't prevent you from making a whistle-stop tour of the **Hermitage** (p67) – don't miss the Jordan Staircase, the State Rooms or the modern European art on the 3rd floor. You should then make for the **Church on Spilled Blood** (p91) and cross the magnificent Neva River via the Troitsky most to see the city at its most Venetian, visiting the **Peter and Paul Fortress** (p114). Heading back, go across Birzhevoy most to Vasilevsky Island's **Strelka** (p110), then continue over the Neva on Dvortsovy most to see the **Admiralty** (p87), the **Bronze Horseman** (p87) and **St Isaac's Cathedral** (p89) before catching some of the city's nightlife at popular bars **Tsynik** (p155) or **Che** (p154).

Three Days

With two more days you'll be far less rushed and be able to take in the city's best sights without too much of a hurry. This way you can do day one over two far more leisurely days, devoting much of at least one day to the Hermitage. On day three try to visit one of the city's palaces – the spectacular interiors at the **Yusupov Palace** (p107) or the fascinating Petrine décor in the **Menshikov Palace** (p109) are obvious favourites. Take a cruise on the canals, stroll in the **Summer Garden** (p90) and make a trip to the far end of Nevsky pr to see the pious **Alexander Nevsky Monastery** (p102).

One Week

This is an ideal amount of time to start getting to know the city – you certainly won't be bored. On day four, prepare to be overwhelmed by the collection at the **Russian Museum** (p93), then stroll north to the Petrograd Side and take in some of the *style moderne* architecture on Kamennoostrovsky pr, checking out one of the interesting museums such as the **Kirov Museum** (p113), **Cruiser Aurora** (p112) or the **Kunstkamera** (p109). The next day, make a trip out of town to see one of the tsarist palaces: **Petrodvorets** (p188) is the most popular and visually most spectacular, while **Tsarskoe Selo** (p191) has more interesting interiors. Day six can be spent exploring other areas of the city – try the **Smolny Cathedral** (p101), the **Chesme Church** (p119) and the gorgeous, yet largely unvisited **Sampsonievsky Cathedral** (p118). Round the week off with some shopping on Nevsky pr, a visit to a *banya* (p163) and an evening of ballet at the **Mariinsky Theatre** (p159).

ORGANISED TOURS

If the size or foreign feel of St Petersburg is intimidating rather than exciting, or if you just prefer to stand back and let someone else do the navigating, consider doing a half- or full-day tour of the city. These tours can give you a great idea of what's your thing and what isn't, they can whiz you past the summer lines at the Hermitage and will often show you things you wouldn't have the time or inclination to see alone.

The best tours we have seen and ones that receive a steady stream of positive feedback from readers, are the excellent **Peter's Walking Tours** (www.peterswalk.com). This innovative company run by Peter Kozyrev and his fantastic team of English-speaking guides offers a huge number of thematic tours of St Petersburg on foot. The tours leave from either the HI St Petersburg Hostel, or Quo Vadis on Nevsky pr. Prices range from R400 to R550 per person for the various tours and best of all, no advance booking is required – just show up at the appointed time and place. Check the website for the latest details, but tours range from a three-hour Peter's Top Five walk to a six-hour tour that uncovers the history of the Leningrad blockade. From late April to early September there is a bicycle tour as well. Eco-friendly and fun, these city tours will shatter your prejudices if you are an inveterate independent traveller.

Other options include **Eclectica** (☎ 279 2410; www.eclectica.ru; Ligovsky pr 1, office 313; metro Pl Vosstaniya), which offers a huge range of literary and architectural tours; and **Monomex Tours** (☎ 445 1690; www.2russia.com) who specialise in truly esoteric sociological tours such as Russian Child Rearing Practices, Care for the Elderly and Police Enforcement Tactics – certainly offering something new to see if you get bored of the Hermitage!

HISTORIC HEART

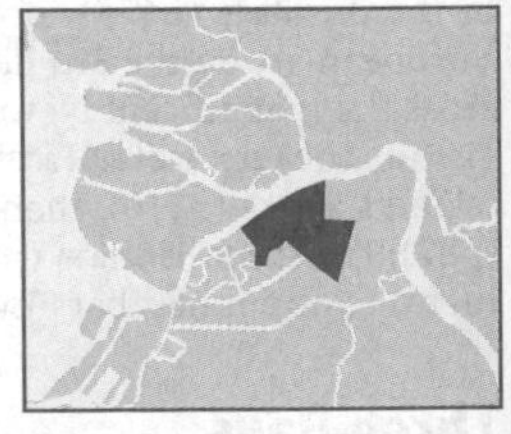

Eating pp139–52; Shopping pp165–72; Sleeping pp173–84

To many, this area is St Petersburg with its fabulous architecture, dazzling museums, graceful canals and the awesome Nevsky pr. Despite its vast cultural wealth, however, and unlike many other cities of similar historic significance, this is still a thriving residential neighbourhood where locals carry on their daily business without so much as a glance at the visitors who flock here. Get off the main streets and squares and you'll see old, crumbling, painfully beautiful St Petersburg as it has been since the early 18th century.

Orientation

The historic heart takes in the left bank of the Neva, from the Fontanka to Isaakievskaya pl (St Isaac's Sq). It is divided neatly in two by Nevsky pr, which runs down the middle to pl Vosstaniya, and is also crisscrossed by the Moyka, Kanal Griboedov and several smaller canals. Due to the density of the area, this section is subdivided into three sections according to the waterways that characterise it. These are: Within the Moyka, Between the Moyka & Fontanka, and Outside the Fontanka.

Transport

The city's most anticipated transport resource is the Admiralteyskaya metro station, which will be a boon for visitors if it ever opens, located as it is just moments from the Winter Palace and St Isaac's Cathedral. However, until then, most people will arrive in the historic heart at Nevsky Pr/Gostiny Dvor metro station (the most convenient for the main sights), or further down Nevsky, Mayakovskaya/Pl Vosstaniya station. Dostoevskaya/Vladimirskaya station also serves the historic heart. Arriving by train from Moscow at the Moscow Station, you'll find yourself on the threshold of the historic heart too.

WITHIN THE MOYKA

The core of the historic heart, this is where the big palaces and some of St Petersburg's most recognisable buildings stand. Of course, most people's first stop here is the **Hermitage**, for which there's a separate chapter (p67) detailing its vast array of treasures. All the sights here are most easily reached from Nevsky Pr metro station.

ADMIRALTY Map pp246-9

Admiralteysky pr 1; closed to the public

The gilded spire of the old Admiralty across the road from Dvortsovaya pl (Palace Sq) is a prime St Petersburg landmark. Gorokhovaya ul, Voznesensky pr and Nevsky pr all radiate outwards from it. This spot was the headquarters of the Russian navy from 1711 to 1917. Now it houses the country's largest military naval college. In late 2000, funeral services were held here for some of the victims of the tragically sunk *Kursk* submarine, past graduates of the college. Despite the spire's solid gold appearance, it's actually made from wood and almost rotted through before restoration efforts began in 1996.

The Admiralty was reconstructed between 1806 and 1823 to the designs of Andreyan Zakharov, and with its rows of white columns and plentiful reliefs and statuary it is a foremost example of the Russian Empire style. One feature you can get a close look at is the nymphs holding giant globes flanking the main gate. Its statue-filled gardens (laid out from 1872 to 1874) and fountain (1877) are particularly lovely in summer, where it's a main centre of general merrymaking. Busts and statues of Glinka, Lermontov, Gogol, other cultural figures – and Hercules – dot the gardens. The building itself is closed to visitors.

BRONZE HORSEMAN & PLOSHCHAD DEKABRISTOV Map pp246-9

The most famous statue of Peter the Great was immortalised as the *Bronze Horseman* in the poem by Pushkin. With his mount rearing above the snake of treason, Peter's enormous statue stands at the river end of pl Dekabristov. The statue was sculpted over 12 years for Catherine the Great by Frenchman Etienne Falconet. Its inscription reads 'To Peter I from Catherine II – 1782'. Many have read significance into Catherine's linking of her own name with that of the city's founder: after all she had no legitimate claim to the throne and this statue is often seen as a method for formalising the philosophical (if not hereditary) link between the two monarchs. The significance of the inscription in both the Latin and Cyrillic alphabets would not be lost on the city's population, still in the process of Westernisation during Catherine's reign. Falconet's original study for the magnificent sculpture can be seen in the **Russian Museum** (p93) and despite completing his lifework here he departed Russia a bitter and angry man – the years of arguing with the head of the Academy of Fine Arts over the finer details of the sculpture had taken its toll and he didn't even bother staying for the unveiling.

The statue has become a much-debated philosophical symbol of the city and Russia itself: is the horse charging forward or rearing back? The snake is trampled on but still alive (some have even rather fancifully suggested that this was an omen predicting the viper of communism). This statue has become the main trademark of the new spirit of St Petersburg.

Most of the west side of the square is occupied by the Central State Historical Archives in the former Senate and Synod buildings, built by Rossi between 1829 and 1834. These institutions were set up by Peter the Great to run the civil administration and the Orthodox Church. Today, the *Bronze Horseman* is a favourite place for wedding parties to be photographed. Hang about long enough and you're bound to see some newlyweds.

The square on which the *Bronze Horseman* stands, pl Dekabristov (Decembrists' Sq), is named after the first attempt at a Russian revolution – the Decembrists' Uprising of 14 December 1825. Inspired by radical ideas from France during the Napoleonic campaigns, young officers who wanted to introduce constitutional monarchy ineptly set up a protest on the very day of the new tsar Nicholas I's swearing-in ceremony. After repeated attempts by Nicholas' ministers to reason with the rebels, they were fired upon. Many officers and bystanders died as a result. Most of the leaders later ended up on the gallows or in Siberia.

DVORTSOVAYA PLOSHCHAD (PALACE SQ) Map pp246-9

There is no contest as to where St Petersburg's heart lies – although no longer really the hub of the city, there can be little doubt that this vast expanse where Nevsky pr meets the Neva River and Palace Embankment is quite simply one of the most beautiful squares in the world, redolent still of the imperial penchant for grandeur almost a century after the end of the Romanov dynasty.

Most impressive of course is the incredible green, white and gold **Winter Palace** (Zimny Dvorets), with its rococo profusion of columns, windows and recesses topped by rows of larger-than-life statues. A residence of tsars from 1762 to 1917, it's now the largest part of the **Hermitage museum** (p67). The best way to approach both the square and palace is to walk up Bolshaya Morskaya ul under the triumphal arch, from where the ensemble is particularly stunning.

On Bloody Sunday (9 January 1905), tsarist troops fired on workers peaceably gathered in the square, thus sparking the 1905 revolution. And it was across Dvortsovaya pl that the much-exaggerated storming of the Winter Palace took place during the October 1917 Revolution.

In the square the 47.5m **Alexander Column**, designed by Montferrand in 1834, commemorates the 1812 victory over Napoleon and is named after Alexander I. On windy days, contemplate that the pillar is held on its pedestal by gravity alone!

The former **General Staff Building** of the Russian army (1819–29) forms an incredible 580m curve around the south of the square in two great blocks joined by arches over Bolshaya Morskaya ul. The arches are topped by a chariot of victory, another monument to the Napoleonic Wars. On New Year's Eve 2000, fireworks set off by revellers on the square landed on the mainly wooden statues and caused severe damage, meaning that the façade was covered in scaffolding for several years. The General Staff Building now houses six **exhibitions** (☎ 314 8260; Dvortsovaya pl 6-8; adult/student R160/free; 🕑 10am-6pm Tue-Sun), of which the former apartments of Count Nesselrode (Nicholas II's prime minister) and French Art of the 20th century: Pierre Bonnard and Maurice Denis are permanent.

MANEGE CENTRAL EXHIBITION HALL

Map pp246-9

☎ 314 8253; Isaakievskaya pl 1; exhibits around R50; 🕑 10am-6pm Fri-Wed

This large white neoclassical building used to be the Horse Guards' Riding School (constructed between 1804 and 1807 from a design by Quarenghi). It now has rotating exhibitions, many of which are worth a look – particularly the annual retrospective of painting, sculpture and installation pieces produced by artists in the city held here in December.

MARBLE PALACE Map pp246-9

☎ 312 9196; Millionnaya ul 5; adult/student R270/135; 🕑 10am-5pm Wed-Mon

Between the Mars Field and the Neva is the Marble Palace, which was built between 1768 and 1785 as Catherine the Great's gift to Grigory Orlov for putting a Moscow rebellion down. It's an architectural gem by Rinaldi, who used 36 kinds of marble and was pained to make them bleed seamlessly into one another. Formerly the Lenin Museum under the Soviets, it is currently a branch of the Russian Museum featuring rotating exhibitions of modern art and a permanent exhibit on foreign artists who were active in Russia in the 18th and 19th centuries.

A monstrous but amusing **equestrian statue** of Alexander III stands plumply in the courtyard outside the main entrance; it became the butt of many jokes after it was erected in 1909 (originally outside the Moscow Station). Even his son Nicholas II thought of shipping it off to Irkutsk, but when rumours started that he wanted to send his dad into Siberian exile, he changed his mind. Sculptor Paolo Trubetskoy said of his work, 'I don't care about politics. I simply depicted one animal on another'.

MARS FIELD Map pp246-9

Marsovo polye

The Mars Field is the open space south of the Troitsky most, about one kilometre north of Nevsky pr along Sadovaya ul. Known as the Tsarina's Meadow (Tsaritsyn Lug) until the 19th century, it became a popular military parade ground under Alexander I, which led to it being renamed.

Don't take a short cut across the grass – you may be walking on graves from the October 1917 Revolution, the civil war, or of later communist luminaries also buried here. An **eternal flame** burns for the victims of the revolution and ensuing civil war. Despite the sad associations, this is a lovely place to stroll and enjoy St Petersburg at its most beautifully open-plan, with the Moyka and Lebyazhya canals meeting at its southeastern corner.

MUSEUM OF POLITICAL HISTORY ANNEXE Map pp246-9

☎ 312 2742; Admiralteysky pr 6/2; adult/student R100/40; 🕑 10am-6pm Mon-Fri

Facing the Admiralty across the street is an annexe of the Museum of Political History (p113) in what was once the grand Fitinhov mansion (1790), later turned into the city administration building, which housed police security service offices. Even poor Lenin spent 10 days in a jail cell in the basement. From 1917 to 1918 Felix Dzerzhinsky, founder of the KGB precursor Cheka, set up his All-Russian Extraordinary Commission here, where many people were interrogated and some shot on the premises. In 2001, a small but interesting exhibit opened on the 2nd floor chronicling the history of police repression in Russia, detailed through documents, photos and short video documentaries. The exhibit will be a bit obscure without a guide. For an English tour, call in advance.

ST ISAAC'S CATHEDRAL Map pp246-9

Isaakievsky Sobor; ☎ 315 9732; www.cathedral.ru; Isaakievskaya pl; admission R250; 🕑 11am-6pm Thu-Tue

The golden dome of St Isaac's Cathedral, looming just south of pl Dekabristov, dominates the St Petersburg skyline. Named after St Isaac of Dalmatia, on whose feast day Peter the Great was born, it is one of the largest domed buildings in the world and over 100kg of gold leaf was used to cover the 21.8m-high dome alone.

French designer Auguste Montferrand began designing the cathedral in 1818, despite the fact that he was no architect. Indeed, it was Montferrand's contacts at court who got the design approved by the tsar and when it was announced to the public, local architects – outraged at the foreign upstart's commission – correctly pointed out a number of technical flaws in the plan. The cathedral took so long to build (until 1858) that Nicholas I was able to insist on a more grandiose structure than Montferrand had planned. The long construction period gave rise to a rumour among locals that the Romanov dynasty would fall were the Cathedral ever completed – something that in the event happened some 60 years later. Special ships and a railway had to be built to carry the granite from Finland for the huge pillars, which each weigh some 120 tonnes. There's a statue of Montferrand holding a model of the cathedral on the west façade, although Nicholas I denied the architect his dying wish, to be buried here, considering it too high an honour for an artisan. Since 1990, after a 62-year gap, services have been held here on major religious holidays and St Isaac's may return

Eternal flame, Mars Field (opposite)

to full Church control before long (like the Church on Spilled Blood, St Isaac's is officially classed as a museum at present).

The church's obscenely lavish interior, covering 4000 sq metres with 600 sq metres of mosaics, 16,000kg of malachite, 14 types of marble and an 816-sq-metre ceiling painting by Karl Bryullov, is definitely an acquired taste and the lack of any religious atmosphere inside makes the entry price enormously inflated. Among the many displays inside there are some interesting photographs of the cathedral throughout its history, including one of the park outside being used to grow cabbages during the Nazi blockade.

Far better value for money is the sublime view of the city from the 43m-high **colonnade** (*kolonnada*; admission R100; 11am-6pm Thu-Tue) around the drum of the dome. You need to purchase separate tickets for this. After you climb the 262 steps, babushki will try to prevent you from photographing the impressive skyline from up there (something about national security), but people sneak shots all the time.

SUMMER GARDEN Map pp246-9

Letny Sad; 314 0374; during summer adult R10, child/student free; 9am-10pm May-Oct, 10am-6pm Oct-mid Apr, closed mid-end Apr

Central St Petersburg's loveliest and oldest park, the Summer Garden is between the Mars Field and the Fontanka. You can enter at the north or south ends. Laid out for Peter the Great with fountains, pavilions and a geometrical plan to resemble the park at Versailles, the garden functioned as Peter's private retreat before becoming a strolling place for St Petersburg's 19th-century leisured classes; commoners were of course not admitted. The fountains were powered by a canal dug from the Ligovsky Canal, which once flowed along present-day Ligovsky pr. The flood of 1777 destroyed them. Though changed since that era, it maintains a formal elegance, with hundreds of lime trees shading its straight paths and lines of statues.

SUMMER PALACE Map pp246-9

Muzey Letny Dvorets Petra I; 314 0456; adult/student R270/70; 10am-5pm Wed-Mon early May-early Nov only

The modest, two-storey Summer Palace in the northeastern corner of the Summer Garden was St Petersburg's first 'palace' (a slight misnomer for a building the size of a fairly large modern home), built for Peter between 1704 and 1714, and still pretty well intact. Little reliefs around the walls depict Russian naval victories. Today it's open as a museum, although rather overpriced. Many rooms are stocked with early-18th-century furnishings. Behind the glass cupboards inside the Green Room, on the 2nd floor, is where Peter used to keep his collections of babies in jars that now draw crowds at the Kunstkamera.

BETWEEN THE MOYKA & FONTANKA

ANICHKOV PALACE Map pp246-9

310 8433; museum admission R60; 10am-5pm Mon-Fri; metro Nevsky Pr

Built between 1741 and 1750, the Anichkov Palace was the city's second-most important, taking up the block between pl Ostrovskogo and the Fontanka (its main façade faces the river and was once joined to it by a canal). It was also twice a generous gift for services rendered – Empress Elizabeth gave it to her favourite Count Razumovsky and later Catherine the Great presented it to Potemkin. A slew of architects, including Rastrelli and Rossi, worked on it. This was Tsar Nicholas II's favourite place to stay in St Petersburg – he far preferred the cosy interiors to the vastness of the Winter Palace. However, it's not nearly as architecturally stunning as many of the city's other palaces and the vast majority of it is closed to visitors.

It became the city's largest Pioneer Club headquarters after 1936 and to this day houses over 100 after-school clubs for over 10,000 children. Today there's a small museum inside, where worthwhile and relaxed tours of the charming palace and grounds can be organised. Otherwise, the palace, as a children's club, is off-limits to casual tourists.

ARMENIAN CHURCH OF ST CATHERINE Map pp246-9

Nevsky pr 42

Continuing with a tradition of non-Orthodox churches being welcome on Nevsky pr, the Armenian merchant Ovanes Lazarian paid for the city's first Armenian church to be erected here in 1771. It was designed and built by German architect Georg Veldten and completed in 1780. The Soviet regime deemed it reasonable to bash the place to bits and install a 2nd floor, which blocked the view of the cupola. The church has been fully restored now, however, and it's open to visitors.

BANKOVSKY MOST Map pp246-9

Named after the Assignment Bank (now a further education institute) on one side of the bridge, the Bankovsky most (1825–26) is one of St Petersburg's loveliest bridges. Suspended by cables emerging from the mouths of golden-winged griffins, the wooden bridge affords a splendid view up the Griboedova Canal past Nevsky pr to the Church on Spilled Blood. Note the 'no smoking' signs on the bridge; many of St Petersburg's historic wooden bridges have been destroyed by fire.

CHURCH ON SPILLED BLOOD

Map pp246-9

☎ 315 1636; Konyushennaya pl; adult/student R250/125; 🕑 11am-6pm Thu-Tue; metro Nevsky Pr

The multi-domed Church on Spilled Blood has become one of the more visible symbols of St Petersburg since it reopened to the public in 1997. Built in memory of the assassination of Tsar Alexander II, who was blown up by the People's Will terrorist group in 1881, the Church of the Resurrection of Christ as it is officially called was intended as a private place of mourning for the life of the tsar.

It was the Bolsheviks who threw the ornate doors of this amazing candy-cake structure open to the people and, not built to withstand thousands of visitors, its interior quickly began to suffer. Following the closure of churches by Stalin in the 1930s, the church was used to store various items from potatoes to theatre sets. Its decades of damage and neglect were finally recognised and a restoration programme began, very progressively given a political climate still very cold to religion, in the early 1980s. It's now most commonly known as the church that took 24 years to build and 27 to restore and it should not be missed for its 7000 sq metres of mosaics by over 30 artists that line the walls inside. On the very spot of the assassination is a marble bust of Alexander (some tourists have mistaken this for a bust of Stalin!). However, if your budget's tight, stick to gawking at the superbly polychromatic Russian Revival style marvel, the only one of its kind in the city.

A few facts: there are 20 granite plaques on the façade which record, in gold letters, the main events of Alexander's reign; the steeple is 81m high; the mosaic panels about half-way up detail scenes from the New Testament; and the 144 mosaic coats of arms each represent the provinces, regions and towns of the Russian Empire of Alexander's time, which all joined in mourning the death of the tsar.

The church's reopening in 1997 was a huge boost for the city's self-confidence and despite the high price of entry it should not be missed.

ENGINEERS' CASTLE Map pp246-9

Inzhenerny Zamok; ☎ 313 4173; www.rusmuseum.ru; Sadovaya ul 2; adult/student R270/135, photos R100; 🕑 10am-6pm Wed-Sun, 10am-5pm Mon; metro Nevsky Pr

A much greater Summer Palace used to stand across the canal from the south end of the Summer Garden. But Rastrelli's almost fairytale, wooden creation for Empress Elizabeth was knocked down in the 1790s to make way for the brick Engineers' Castle of Paul I. The son of Catherine the Great, Tsar Paul was born in the wooden palace and wanted to build his own residence on the same spot, so torched the old one and had the current edifice created, complete with defensive moat as he (quite rightly) feared assassination. But this erratic, cruel tsar only got 40 days in his new abode before being assassinated by plotters in 1801. The style is a somewhat bizarre take on a medieval castle, quite unlike any other building in the city. In 1823 it became a military engineering school (hence the name), whose

Engineers' Castle (above)

most famous pupil was Fyodor Dostoevsky. Now owned by the Russian Museum, who has restored it to its former glory, there's a movement to refer to it again as the Mikhailovsky Castle (Mikhailovsky Zamok), although most people still refer to it as the Engineers' Castle. As a wing of the Russian Museum, the castle is currently being used to display court portraits of the tsars and their families as well as other leading figures in Russian history. This is the first National Portrait Gallery in Russia and is a fascinating collection for anyone interested in the tsarist period.

GOSTINY DVOR Map pp246-9

Nevsky pr 35; metro Gostiny Dvor

The arcades of Gostiny Dvor department store stand facing the clock tower of the **former Town Duma** on Dumskaya ul, which was the seat of the pre-revolutionary city government. One of the world's first indoor shopping malls, the 'Merchant Yard' dates from between 1757 and 1785, stretches 230m along Nevsky (its perimeter is over 1km long) and is another Rastrelli creation, although not as elaborate as many, finished as it was in a more sober neoclassical style by Vallin de la Mothe. Gostiny Dvor began getting a face-lift (which is still ongoing, such is the scale of the task) in the late 1990s and the inside is now quite fashionable. On weekend afternoons, you can watch the traditional spectacle of lunatic-fringe political groups proselytising their messages out front. It's the Hyde Park Corner of St Petersburg; in other words, get your Stalin calendars here. Facing Gostiny Dvor across Sadovaya ul is the **Vorontsov Palace** (1749–57), another noble town house by Rastrelli. From 1810 it was the most elite military school in the empire. It's still a military school for young cadets; on weekends you can watch mothers pass food parcels to their sons through the wrought-iron front gates.

GRAND HOTEL EUROPE Map pp246-9

☎ 329 6000; www.grandhoteleurope.com; Mikhailovskaya ul 1/7; metro Gostiny Dvor

Standing proud as a peacock on the corner of Nevsky and Mikhailovskaya ul, the Grand Hotel Europe is the city's premier hotel and the only one in the city to be a true tourist attraction in itself. Built between 1873 and 1875, it was redone in *style moderne* in the 1910s and completely renovated from 1989 to 1991. It is one of the city's architectural gems, boasting shameless splendour; marble and gilt, sweeping staircases and antique furnishings.

KAZAN CATHEDRAL Map pp246-9

Kazansky Sobor; ☎ 311 4826; www.kazansky.ru in Russian; admission free; 🕒 11am-7pm

This most atypical of St Petersburg's cathedrals was commissioned by Tsar Paul shortly before he was murdered in a coup. It reflects his eccentric desire to unite Catholicism and Orthodoxy in to a kind of 'super-Christianity' as well as his fascination with the Knights of Malta, a group he was a member of. The great, 111m-long colonnaded arms of the neoclassical Kazan Cathedral reach out towards Nevsky pr. Andrey Voronikhin, a former serf, built the cathedral between 1801 and 1811 and his design was influenced by St Peter's in Rome. His original plan was to build a second, mirror version of the cathedral opposite it on the other side of Nevsky, but this never materialised. The square in front has been the site for political demonstrations since before the revolution.

The cathedral is dark and traditionally orthodox inside and is well worth entering. It holds daily services (at 9am and 6pm), and it is free to wander through and gaze up at the daunting 80m-high dome. The two statues out front are of the victorious Napoleonic War field marshall Mikhail Kutuzov (whose remains are buried inside the cathedral), and his friend and aide Mikhail Barclay de Tolly.

LUTHERAN CHURCH Map pp246-9

Nevsky pr 22

Across Nevsky pr, tucked in a recess between Bolshaya and Malaya Konyushennaya uls, is the lovely Lutheran Church built for St Petersburg's thriving German community in the 1830s. Distinguished by a four-column portico and topped with a discreet cupola, this was turned into a swimming pool in the 1950s (the high diving board was placed in the apse) – but is that worse than using it to store vegetables, as it had been since the 1930s? The church is open to visitors, having been restored beautifully. Check out the photos from its chlorine era just inside.

PLOSHCHAD ISKUSSTV (ARTS SQUARE) Map pp246-9

Just a block east of the Griboedova Canal is the quiet pl Iskusstv (Arts Square), named after its cluster of museums and concert halls. A **statue of Pushkin**, erected in 1957, stands in the middle of the tree-lined square. The square and Mikhailovskaya ul, which joins it to Nevsky pr, were designed as a unit by Rossi in the 1820s and 1830s.

The **Brodsky House-Museum** (☎ 314 3658; pl Iskusstv 3; adult/student R200/100; 🕒 11am-5pm Wed-Sun) is a former home of Isaak Brodsky, one of the favoured artists of the revolution. It has some 800 lesser-known works by top 19th-century painters like Repin, Levitan and Kramskoy.

The **Museum of Ethnography** (☎ 313 4420; Inzhenernaya ul 4/1; adult/student R200/100; 🕒 10am-6pm Tue-Sun) displays the traditional crafts, customs and beliefs of the over 150 peoples who make up Russia's fragile ethnic mosaic. There's a bit of left-over Soviet propaganda going on here, but it's a marvellous collection: the sections on Transcaucasia and Central Asia are fascinating, with rugs and two full-size *yurts* (nomads' portable tent-houses). The Special Storeroom has some great weapons and rare devotional objects. A guide makes a lot of difference to how much you understand on your visit.

PUSHKIN FLAT-MUSEUM Map pp246-9

☎ 311 3531; nab reki Moyki 12; adult/student R200/50; 🕒 10.30am-6pm Wed-Sun

Pushkin's last home (he only lived here for four months) is beside one of the prettiest curves of the Moyka River, north of Nevsky pr. This is where the poet died after his duel in 1837. His killer was a French nobleman, Baron d'Antès, who had been publicly courting Pushkin's beautiful wife, Natalya. The affair was widely seen as a put-up job on behalf of Tsar Nicholas I, who found the famed poet's radical politics inconvenient – and who, rumour has it, may himself have been the one really stalking Natalya. The little house is now the Pushkin Flat-Museum and includes a Russian-language tour (English tours can be arranged in advance). The apartment has been reconstructed to look exactly as it did in the poet's last days. For the morbid, on display are his death mask, a lock of his hair and the waistcoat he wore when he died.

PUSHKIN THEATRE & PLOSTROVSKOGO Map pp246-9

Rossi's neoclassical Pushkin Theatre (formerly the Alexandrinsky), at the south end of the square, is one of Russia's most important. In 1896 the opening night of Chekhov's *The Seagull* was so badly received here that the playwright fled to wander anonymously among the crowds on Nevsky pr. The square in front of it is named after early Russian playwright Ostrovsky, whose plays are still performed inside the theatre today.

An enormous **statue of Catherine the Great** (1873) stands amid the chess, backgammon and sometimes even mahjong players that crowd the benches here. At the Empress' heels are renowned statesmen of the 19th century, including her lovers Orlov, Potemkin and Suvorov.

This airy square, commonly referred to as Cathy's Garden (Katkin Sad), was created by Carlo Rossi in the 1820s and 1830s. Its west side is taken up by the lavish **National Library of Russia**, St Petersburg's biggest with some 31 million items, nearly a sixth of which are in foreign languages.

Behind the theatre, on ul Zodchego Rossi, is a continuation of Rossi's ensemble. It is proportion deified: the buildings are 22m wide, 22m apart and 220m long. The **Vaganova School of Choreography** situated here (at No 2) is the Kirov Ballet's training school, where Pavlova, Nijinsky, Nureyev and others learned their art.

RUSSIAN MUSEUM Map pp246-9

Gosudarstvenny Russky Muzey; ☎ 311 1465; www.rusmuseum.ru; Inzhenernaya ul 4; adult/student R270/135, photos R100, audio guide R250; 🕒 10am-6pm Wed-Sun, 10am-5pm Mon, ticket office closes 1hr before closing time

While the Hermitage spreads its net across the cultures of the world, the Russian Museum, as its name suggests, focuses solely on Russian art, from primitive Church icons to contemporary commercial art. The collection is magnificent and although lacking many of the better-known paintings that can be found in its only real rival, the Tretyakov State Gallery in Moscow, the Russian Museum's range is arguably more even.

If your time in the city is limited and you think only the Hermitage is a must-see, try your utmost to accommodate some time for this gem of a museum; your appreciation of Russian culture will be much deepened by it. Moreover, it's easily done in a half-day visit unlike the vast and sometimes overwhelming Hermitage.

The Mikhailovsky Castle was designed by Carlo Rossi and built between 1819 and 1825 for Grand Duke Mikhail (brother of Tsars Alexander I and Nicholas I) as compensation for not being able to have a chance on the throne. It later became Russia's first public gallery, formed from the collection begun by Tsar Alexander III – a bust of whom greets you on the magnificent main staircase – and opened by Nicholas II on 7 March 1898. The Benois building, now connected to the original palace and accessible through an entrance on nab

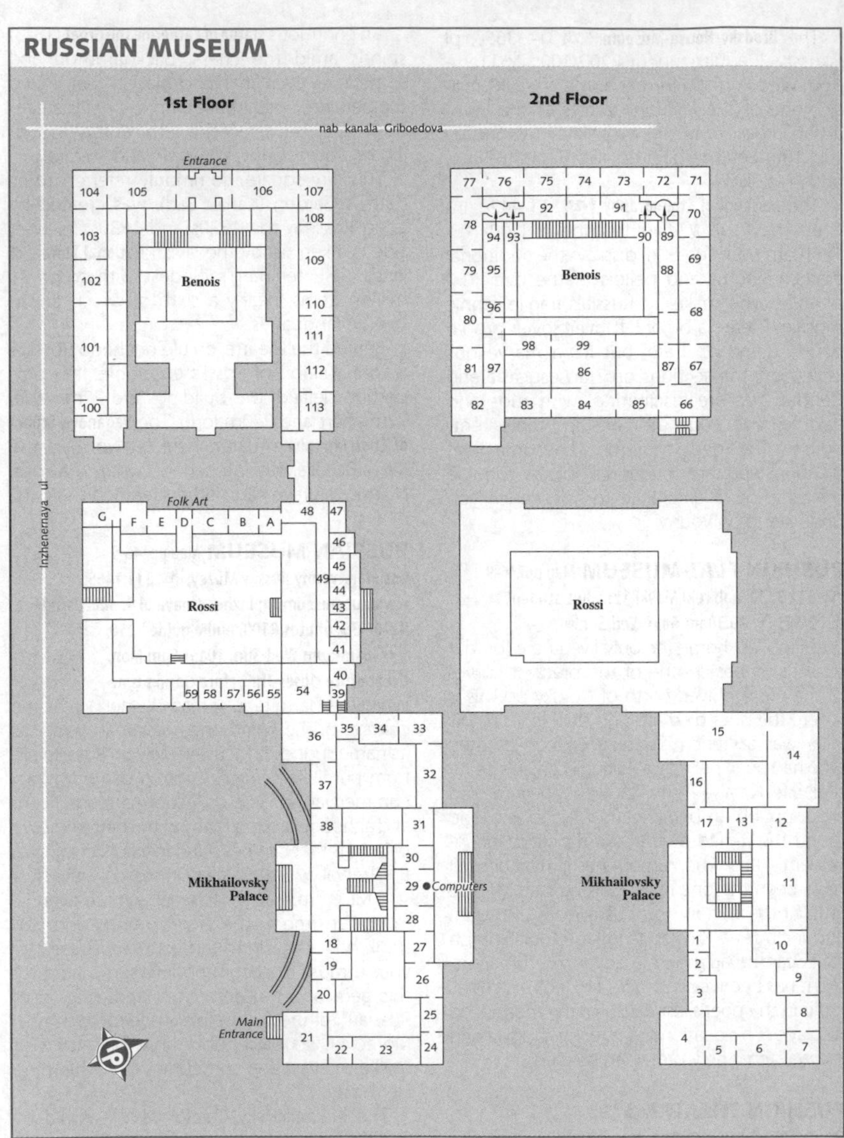

kanala Griboedova, was constructed between 1914 and 1919. The building is most impressively viewed from the back, during a late-night stroll through the pleasant Mikhailovsky Gardens behind it.

The museum currently boasts over 400,000 items in its collection and now owns three other city palaces where (largely) temporary exhibitions are also held: the Marble Palace, the Stroganov Palace and the Engineers' Castle. It has also realised grandiose plans for the various properties: in 2002, all 8.7 hectares of the already lovely Mikhailovsky Gardens were redesigned according to the original 19th-century plans, and the moat that surrounded the Engineers' Castle was redug.

Coming into the museum via the ground floor entrance to the right of the main façade go up the magnificent main staircase to the 1st floor, as this is where the chronological ordering of the exhibits begins. Despite its magnificence, the ceiling above the main staircase must surely win the title of worst trompe l'oeil in St Petersburg hands down.

Rooms 1–4 Church Icons The first four rooms of the museum encapsulate a succinct but brilliant history of Russian icon painting over the past eight centuries, including work from the three major schools of Russian icon painting: Novgorod, Muscovy and Pskov. Room 2 has *St George and Scenes of His Life,* while Room 3 features Russian master Andrei Rublev's massive *Peter and Paul* as well as his *Praise of the Mother of God*. Room 4 is notable in its departure from earlier styles. Compare *Old Testament Trinity with Scenes from Genesis* with the completely atypical *Our Father*.

Room 5 Petrine Art Peter was a great patron of the arts and almost single-handedly brought the Western eye to Russian painting, as witnessed by the massive jump in style from ecclesiastical to secular subjects between Rooms 4 and 5. The room includes three busts of Peter and three portraits, including the moving *Peter I on His Deathbed*.

Rooms 6–10 Post-petrine Art and the Rise of the Academy Room 6 includes some charmingly odd canvases in very strange shapes as well as mosaic portraits of both Peter and Catherine the Great. There's also a wonderful moulded portrait of Elizabeth I, Peter's daughter. The centre of the room is taken up by a huge portrait of the ill-fated Peter III, although look out for the impressive bust of Prince Menshikov here too. Room 7 has a sculpture of *Empress Anna with an Arab Boy* as its most obvious feature, but don't miss the tapestry celebrating Peter the Great's victory at Poltava or the ridiculously stylised tapestry portrayal of Africa. These rooms also display the early works of the St Petersburg Academy of Art, who borrowed the European classical aesthetic for their work.

Room 11 The White Hall This shoebox was Grand Duke Mikhail's drawing room. It's crammed with little art but a wonderfully ornate interior, if gilt is your scene. Even if not, the sheer scale is impressive.

Rooms 12–17 The Academy By the early 19th century the Academy of Art was more and more influenced by Italian themes given the unfashionability of France. In Room 12 look for Vladimir Borovikovsky's magnificent *Catherine II Promenading in Tsarskoye Selo*. Room 14 is truly spectacular, including enormous canvases such as Ivan Ayvanovsky's *The Wave* and Karl Bryullov's incredible *The Last Day of Pompeii* and *The Crucifixion*.

Some modernity then begins to creep in with Ivanov's smaller paintings, all of which are grouped together on one side of Room 15. *Four Nude Boys, Old Man Leaning on a Stick* and *Boy Getting out of a Stream* all mark a notable departure in terms of detail and representation. Another highlight of the room is Ramazanov's 1854 bust of writer Nikolai Gogol. In Room 17, Alexei Venetsianov's *Reapers* would have gone down rather well a century later during the socialist realist period!

Rooms 18–20 Rural Landscapes The 'genre painting' that became fashionable among St Petersburg's upper classes at the turn of the 19th century took (an incredibly idealised) rural Russia as its theme.

Rooms 21–22 Room 21 contains the enormous canvases *Phrina at the Poseidon Celebration in Elesium* by Genrikh Semiradsky and Konstantin Flavitsky's *Christian Martyrs at the Colosseum*. Room 22 contains Alexei Savrasov's rural Russian scenes.

Room 23–25 The Wanderers The Wanderers (Peredvizhniki) were a group of academy artists who saw their future outside the strict confines of that strictest of institutions. They wandered among the people, painting scenes of realism that had never before been seen in Russian art.

Room 26 Nicholas Ghe This room includes the incredibly dark *Peter I Interrogating Tsarevitch Alexei in Peterhof,* one of Russian art's most famous historical paintings. This relates to the tumultuous relationship between the despot and his son; Peter could not understand Alexei's character, so different from his own as it was. However, Alexei foolishly went abroad and sought support from foreign leaders to place him on the throne of Russia. Peter, paranoid by his later years, managed to convince Alexei to return home unpunished if he renounced his right to the succession. While Alexei kept his side of the bargain, Peter had his own son tortured to death as he attempted to extract information about 'plotters' against him.

Rooms 27–32 Contemporaries of the Wanderers, landscape artists such as Ivan Shishkin were still popular. These rooms also document the rise of populist art, which had a strong social conscience and sought to educate the public. The best examples of this are Vladimir Makovsky's *The Condemned* and *The Doss House*.

Rooms 33–35 Repin Considered by most Russians to be the greatest artist the nation has ever produced, Ilya Repin (1844–1930) was a member of the Wanderers, but went on to outgrow the movement and produce key works of Russian realist and populist art. His masterpiece is *Barge Haulers on the Volga,* an unrivalled portrait of human misery and enslavement in rural Russia. Unfortunately it's often on loan abroad, but the Russian Museum is its home. Other Repin highlights here are *A Negro Woman, Sadko* and a marvellous portrait of a barefoot Leo Tolstoy.

Room 36–38 Russian Historical Art These rooms display the late-19th-century vogue for historical painting with mystical overtones. Particularly romantic are Vasily Surikov's huge *Yermak's Conquest of Siberia* and *Suvorov Crossing the Alps.*

Room 39 Vereshchagin and Russian Orientalism The 19th century saw a massive extension of the Russian empire as vast swathes of Central Asia were tamed and brought under the tsar. This created great interest in the east and its then completely mysterious culture and traditions. Vereshchagin's *After the Success* and *After the Defeat* depict different sides of the Russian conquest, with brutality against the enemy being the order of the day on both sides.

Room 40-47 Late-19th-Century Russian Art These rooms display the large number of complementing and contradictory styles fashionable in St Petersburg, before the explosion of the avant-garde changed not only Russian art but art around the world. These include Arkhip Kuindzhi landscapes (40–41), Vladimir Makovsky (42), rural scenes by Sergei Ivanov and Appolinary Vasnetsov (43), Isaak Levitan (44), Andrei Ryabushkin (45) and bright paintings of peasants by Mallianvin.

Room 48 Mark Antokolsky's *Ivan the Terrible* and *Death of Socrates* are on display either side of yet another souvenir stand. From here you enter the Benois Wing to your right or continue straight ahead for the comprehensive account of Russian folk art, featuring everything from kitchen equipment to window frames.

Room 49 This long corridor has displays of various religiously themed tapestries from the 14th to the 17th centuries.

Room 54 Repin's tsarist portraits, featuring the enormous *Ceremonial Sitting of the State Council on 7th May 1901, Marking the Centenary of Its Foundation.* Around the walls are individual portraits of its members.

Rooms 55–59 Sculpture in storage, but behind glass walls, so still visible. Most interesting here is Etienne Falconet's model for his *Bronze Horseman,* which stands overlooking the Neva on pl Dekabristov.

Benois Wing

The Benois Wing marks the beginning of the modern era in painting – the Russian Museum's superb collection of late-19th-century and early-20th-century avant-garde art is here, while downstairs exhibits of contemporary Russian art are held.

Room 66 Vrubel The father of modern Russian art, Mikhail Vrubel (1856–1910) is celebrated in

Russian Museum

this room with such ground-breaking works as *Lady in Lilac, Epic Hero* and *Demon in Flight*.

Room 67 Mikhail Nesterov and the truly unusual work of Nikolai Roerich.

Room 68 Look out for the wonderful *Portrait of Sergei Diaghilev with his Nanny* (1906) painted by Leon Bakst. Konstantin Somov's *Portrait of Rakhmaninov* (1925) is full of dark menace.

Room 69 This room has Roerich and Alexander Golovin.

Rooms 70–71 Valentin Serov works here include a 1909 portrait of Anna Pavlova.

Room 72 This room features two sublime paintings by Konstantin Korovin (1861–1939): *White Night in Northern Norway* and *Portrait of Shaliapin*. There are also pictures of nature by Stanislav Zhukovsky and Mikhail Larionov's wonderful late impressionist *Rose Bush after the Rain* (1904).

Room 73-74 Boris Kustodiev Kustodiev's *Portrait of Alexander I* (1906), painted long after the tsar's death, as well as the infinitely more accessible scenes of provincial Russian life. *Autumn in the Provinces, Little Blue House,* and *Maslenitsa* (Shrove Tuesday) are all deliciously rich and playful pictures.

Room 75 Various painters including Nikolai Milioti and Roerich are featured here.

Room 76 Kuzma Petrov-Vodkin Take a look at Petrov-Vodkin's homoerotic *Boys* (1911) and *Thirsting Warrior* (1915) as well as his wonderful portrait of Anna Akhmatova. Petrov-Vodkin was a unique painter – spanning the two centuries and surviving the Russian revolution.

Room 77 Nathan Altman This room is devoted entirely to Nathan Altman, one of the most brilliant stars of the Russian avant-garde.

Room 78–79 Art Between the Revolutions Here is displayed art from 1905 to 1917. The explosion of styles and creative inspiration is evident. Look out particularly for Mikhail Larionov's *Venus* (1912, Room 79) as well as Natalia Goncharova's paintings *Laundresses* (1911, Room 79), *The Evangelists* (Room 79) and *A Factory* (1912), which clearly exhibits the avant-garde's mythification of the industrial that was later to be hijacked by socialist realism. Georgian primitivist Niko Pirosmani's *Prince With a Horn of Wine* (1909) also hangs here.

Room 80 Cubism and Futurism Alexander Rodchenko's *Black on Black* (1918) as well as paintings by Lev Bruni and Lyubov Popova are here. Do not miss Pavel Mansurov's *American Inhabitant*.

Room 81–82 Late Avant-Garde Painting Here is an unrivalled selection of Russian art of the late 1920s and early 1930s. Kazimir Malevich's works of great simplicity sit uncomfortably opposite Pavel Filonov's disturbed and crowded representations of Russian life. Meditating in the middle is Malevich's famous *Black Square* (1925), the third of a series of four. Room 82 contains the last of the avant-gardistes, including David Shterenberg and Vladimir Lebedev.

Room 83 Early Soviet Art This room gives a tantalising suggestion of the many interesting directions that Soviet art promised to take before socialist realism became the only acceptable style in painting by the late 1930s. Here Petrov-Vodkin and Malevich both attempt suitably Soviet themes; the two highlights of the room are Yury Pimenov's terrifying *Disabled Veterans* (1926) and Malevich's *Portrait of a Shock Worker* (1932).

Room 84–85 Socialist Realism Now that it's all in the past, this is a fascinating look back at the committee-created artistic form demanded by Stalin. While Alexander Samokhvalov's *Militarized Komsomol* (1933) and Arkady Plastov's *Holiday at a Collective Farm* (1937) demonstrate amply just how straitjacketed Soviet art became so quickly, there is nevertheless an impressive amount of individualism in many of the other paintings in the room. Alexander Drevin's *Construction of a Railway Bridge in Yerevan* (1933) is a good example. Room 85 is devoted to Soviet art of the 1940s. Here, as you would expect, themes of war are taken up.

SINGER BUILDING Map pp246-9

Nevsky pr 28

Opposite the Kazan Cathedral stands one of St Petersburg's most marvellous buildings, the headquarters of the Singer sewing machine company which opened a factory in the Russian capital in 1904. The building also housed the American consulate for a few years prior to WWI. Until recently the Singer Building provided a home to St Petersburg's premier bookstore, Dom Knigi, although this has now moved further down Nevsky pr to smarter premises (p167) and the Singer Building is currently a rather uninteresting shopping arcade. The wonderful Singer globe and emblem has now finally been restored after spending all of the 1990s under scaffolding.

STROGANOV PALACE Map pp246-9

☎ 314 6424; Nevsky pr 17; adult/student R270/135; 🕓 10am-6pm Wed-Sun, 10am-5pm Mon

One of the city's loveliest baroque exteriors, the green and white Stroganov Palace was designed by court favourite Rastrelli in 1753 for one of the city's leading aristocratic families. Most famously, the Stroganovs' chef created a beef dish served in a sour cream and mushroom sauce here that became known to the world as beef Stroganov. The building is now owned by the Russian Museum, which is in the process of a full refurbishment and already has temporary exhibitions on display. There's a fairly bad waxwork museum and a novelty restaurant in the courtyard, both of which are mediocre, although the courtyard itself is worth a look.

OUTSIDE THE FONTANKA

Nevsky pr crosses the Fontanka on Anichkov most and heads down to pl Vosstaniya. There are fewer historical buildings here but the commercial bustle is as strong as ever.

ANICHKOV MOST Map pp246-9

With famous 1840s statues of rearing horses at its four corners symbolising man's struggle with and eventual taming of nature, this is one of the city's most striking bridges. To witness pure artistic revenge, take note of the southwestern horse's genitals: unlike his anatomically correct companions, his naughty bits are in the image of the sculptor's unfaithful wife's lover (another version has it that it's Napoleon's profile). The horses were removed and fully restored in 2001, but the anatomical peculiarity thankfully remains.

BELOSELSKY-BELOZERSKY PALACE Map pp246-9

☎ 315 5636; Nevsky pr 41; admission R120; 🕑 11am-6.30pm; metro Gostiny Dvor

A photogenic backdrop to Anichkov most is provided by the newly renovated 1840s Beloselsky-Belozersky Palace. The palace was formerly a home of Communist Party officials and is now the Historical Museum of Wax Figures, which is a hoot; if you ever questioned the legitimacy of the 'body' in Lenin's tomb in Moscow, you'll know for sure after you see this. There are two displays: 'Russia from the 7th to 18th Centuries' and 'From Alexander to Putin'. Unfortunately the rest of this wonderful building remains closed to the public.

CHURCH OF ST JOHN OF KRONSHTADT Map pp246-9

☎ 273 9619; www.leushino.ru in Russian; ul Nekrasova 31; admission free; 🕑 9am-6pm; metro Mayakovskaya

This extraordinary building has one of the most striking exteriors in the city – its Byzantine façade is totally incongruous with the rest of the street, although few people seem to notice it, hemmed in on both sides by other terraced buildings on ul Nekrasova. The church once had the whole building, but currently it shares the premises with a hospital. Go past the waiting patients to the 2nd floor where you can see the small church and chat with the charming nuns who look after it.

MUSEUM OF ANNA AKHMATOVA IN THE FOUNTAIN HOUSE Map pp246-9

☎ 272 2211; Liteyny pr 53; adult/student R120/80, tour in Russian, English or French (call ahead) R350, photos R50; 🕑 10am-5.30pm Tue-Sun; metro Mayakovskaya

Housed in one wing of the delightful Sheremetyev Palace (1750–55) is this touching and fascinating literary museum. St Petersburg's most famous 20th-century poet lived here for some 30 years, as this was the apartment of her common-law husband Nikolai Punin.

The apartment is on the 2nd floor and is filled with mementos of the poet and correspondence with other writers including Boris Pasternak. It's also an interesting chance to see the interior of an (albeit atypical) apartment from the early to mid-20th century, complete with furnishings – the kitchen is particularly interesting.

There's a contemplative and peaceful atmosphere to the apartment. Downstairs there is a bookshop and video room where you can watch Russian (and some English) language documentaries on the lives of Akhmatova and her contemporaries while drinking a cup of tea or coffee. It also sells audiotapes of Akhmatova's works read by famous Russian actors. There's another Akhmatova museum located in Tsarskoe Selo.

MUSEUM OF THEATRICAL & MUSICAL ARTS Map pp246-9

☎ 272 4441; nab reki Fontanki 34; adult/student R150/75; 🕑 noon-6pm Wed-Sun; metro Gostiny Dvor

In the Sheremetyev Palace itself is a branch of the Museum of Theatrical and Musical Arts, which has a collection of musical instruments from the 19th and 20th centuries, some beautifully decorated. The Sheremetyev family was famous for the concerts and theatre performances they hosted at their palace, which was a centre of musical life in the capital in the 18th century.

A Walk Down Nevsky Prospekt

The Soviets bit off more than they could chew when they renamed Leningrad's vast main thoroughfare '25th of October Avenue' in honour of their revolution. Even Stalin couldn't manage to make the name stick and to many people, Nevsky pr is and always will be Russia's most famous street, running 4.7km from the Admiralty all the way to the Alexander Nevsky Monastery, from which it takes its name. The inner 2.5km to Moscow Station is St Petersburg's seething main avenue, the city's shopping centre and focus of much of its entertainment and street life. Pushing your way through the crowds on Nevsky pr is an essential St Petersburg experience, and if you happen to be in the city on a holiday evening (like City Day on 27 May), the sight of thousands of people pouring like a stream down its middle is one you'll not soon forget.

Nevsky pr was laid out in the early years of St Petersburg as the start of the main road to Novgorod and soon became dotted with fine buildings, squares and bridges. The kink in the vast avenue was unintentional – road builders coming from Novgorod hadn't quite got their sums right, thus where the two work teams met (at present-day pl Vosstaniya) there were a few red faces.

At the turn of the 20th century it was one of Europe's grandest boulevards, with sidewalks paved with cobblestones and a track down the middle for horse-drawn trams (Russia was the fourth country in the world to have them), on either side of which were wooden paving blocks installed to muffle the sound of the horse-drawn carriages – an innovation that was apparently the first of its kind in the world and for which Nevsky pr was dubbed the quietest main street in Europe. Today, things here are a bit noisier – traffic roars past in six lanes and many people find their experience of St Petersburg is defined by constantly walking up and down the thoroughfare that – try as you might – you just can't avoid.

You'll see all of human life here – street hawkers, beggars, religious and political activists trying to convert people to their causes, dour-faced shoppers, people selling their pets and shoes, and the new rich gliding from boutique to boutique oblivious to everyone else.

VLADIMIRSKY CATHEDRAL Map pp246-9

☎ 312 1938; Vladimirsky pr 20; 🕑 8am-6pm; metro Vladimirskaya

The communists turned this Russian baroque treat into an underwear factory, but since 1990 it has worked as a church and is one of the busiest in town, having been fully restored. It looks fabulous with its amazing onion domes. If you can get past the hordes of babushki and beggars outside, the interiors are stunning (go upstairs to see the main body of the church).

SMOLNY

Eating p147; Shopping p172; Sleeping pp178–9

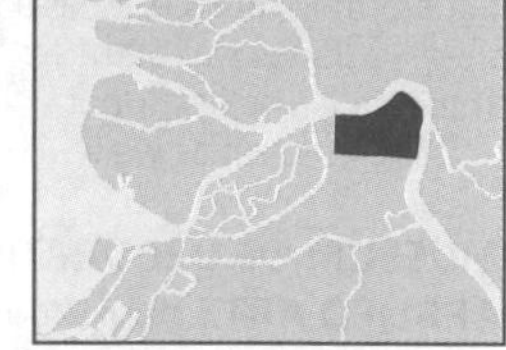

The Smolny district takes its name from the Russian word for tar, *smol,* as this neighbourhood was the site of the city's tar pits, originally producing tar for the Admiralty's ship building in the 18th century.

Peter the Great toyed briefly with making the area centre of his city, before changing his mind two times and finally settling on Vasilevsky Island. Before this, however, wide streets were laid out in the area, many of which were going to be split up with canals, which explains why several streets in the neighbourhood are so wide and still have medians today.

Later it became a fashionable residential area, particularly after Grigory Potemkin moved into the Horse Guards Palace (now the Tauride Palace) completed as a gift for him by Catherine the Great in 1789.

Served rather inconveniently by public transport, Smolny is nevertheless the city's political and diplomatic centre – St Petersburg governor Valentina Matvienko's office is at the Smolny Institute and a large number of foreign consulates are located on or around ul Furshtatskaya. The atmosphere of the neighbourhood remains quiet but smart and residential. The young Vladimir Putin spent his youth playing on these streets; his family lived at Baskov per 12.

Transport

The Smolny neighbourhood suffers from a considerable lack of public transport, aside from the Chernyshevskaya metro station at its heart. To get to the furthest reaches of the area by the Cathedral, you're best taking any *marshrutka* up Suvorovsky pr.

BOLSHOY DOM Map pp246-9

Liteyny pr 4; not open to the public; metro Chernyshevskaya

Noi Trotsky's monolithic design for the local KGB headquarters (and current Interior Ministry headquarters) is referred to by everyone as the 'Bolshoy Dom' or 'the Big House'. It's a fierce-looking block of granite built in 1932 in the late-constructivist style and was once a byword for fear among the people of the city: most people who were taken here during the purges were never heard of again. Employees who have worked here include current president Vladimir Putin during his days as a KGB man.

FLORAL EXHIBITION HALL Map pp246-9

☎ 272 5448; Potymkinskaya ul 2; admission R50; 11am-7pm Tue-Wed & Fri-Sun; metro Chernyshevskaya

One of the finest ways to momentarily escape from a St Petersburg winter is to head for the Floral Exhibition Hall, an indoor tropical paradise just northwest of the **Tauride Gardens** (opposite). Check out the 'monster tree' to the right of the entrance. It has a wishing well and there's a flower stall at the front of the building. There's a florist next door and one diagonally across the street as well.

MUSEUM OF DECORATIVE & APPLIED ARTS Map pp246-9

☎ 273 3258; Solyanoy per 13; adult/student R100/50; 11am-5pm Tue-Sat; metro Chernyshevskaya

This is one of the most impressive museums in the city and is as beautiful as you would expect a decorative arts museum to be. In 1878 the millionaire Baron Stieglitz founded the School of Technical Design and wanted to surround his students with world-class art to inspire them. He began a collection that was continued by his son and was to include a unique array of European and Oriental glassware, porcelains, tapestries, furniture and paintings. It eventually grew into one of Europe's richest private collections. Between 1885 and 1895, a building designed by architect Messmacher was built to house the collection and this building also became a masterpiece. Each hall is decorated in its own, unique style, including Italian, Renaissance, Flemish and baroque. The Terem Room, in the style of the medieval Terem Palace of Moscow's Kremlin, is an opulent knockout.

After the revolution the school was closed, the museum's collection redistributed to the Hermitage and Russian museums, and most of the lavish interiors brutally painted or plastered over, even destroyed (one room was used as a sports hall). The painstaking renovation continues to this day, despite receiving no funding from the Ministry of Education under whose direction it falls, being connected to the Applied Arts School next door.

The objects on display are simply breathtaking, from medieval handcrafted furniture to a rare collection of 18th-century Russian tiled stoves to the contemporary works of the students of the arts school. Their surroundings merely match their magnificence.

MUSEUM OF THE DEFENCE & BLOCKADE OF LENINGRAD Map pp246-9

☎ 275 7208; Solyanoy per 9; admission R70; 10am-5pm Thu-Tue, closed last Thu of month

This museum opened just three months after the blockade was lifted and boasted 37,000 exhibits, including real tanks and aeroplanes. But three years later, during Stalin's repression of the city, the museum was shut, its director shot, and most of the exhibits destroyed or redistributed. Not until 1985's *glasnost* was an attempt made to once again gather documents to reopen the museum; this happened in 1989. The displays contain donations from survivors, propaganda posters from the time and an example of the sawdust-filled tiny piece of bread Leningraders had to survive on. English excursions are available if booked in advance.

MUSEUM OF EROTICA Map pp246-9

☎ 320 7600; Furshtatskaya ul 47; admission free; 8am-10pm; metro Chernyshevskaya

This superbly quirky museum is housed in the clinic of venereal disease doctor and chief of the prostate research centre of the Russian Academy of Natural Sciences Igor Knyazkin, who began assembling a collection of sexually themed trinkets his patients had given him over the years. The exhibit's highlights include what is purported to be Rasputin's preserved penis (which clocks in at an astounding 30cm), the bone of a sea lion's penis and various statuettes of people and animals in a variety of sexual positions.

SMOLNY CATHEDRAL Map pp240-1

☎ 271 9182; pl Rastrelli 3/1; adult/student R200/100; 🕑 11am-5.15pm Fri-Wed; metro Chernyshevskaya

If baroque is your thing, then look no further than the sky-blue Smolny Cathedral, an unrivalled masterpiece of the genre that ranks among Rastrelli's most amazing creations. The cathedral is the centrepiece of a convent mostly built to Rastrelli's designs between 1748 and 1757. His inspiration was to combine baroque details with the forest of towers and onion domes typical of an old Russian monastery. There's special genius in the proportions of the cathedral (it gives the impression of soaring upwards), to which the convent buildings are a perfect foil. In stark contrast, the interior is a disappointingly austere plain white. Inside is a small art gallery and temporary exhibitions are held in the body of what was once a working cathedral. Entry to both is included in the cathedral ticket price. However, the main reason to enter is to climb the 63m belfry (included in the entry price) for stupendous views over the city.

SMOLNY INSTITUTE Map pp240-1

☎ 276 1461; pl Proletarskoy Diktatury 3; 🕑 by appointment only 10am-6pm Mon-Fri; metro Chernyshevskaya

Built by Quarenghi between 1806 and 1808 as a school for aristocratic girls, the Smolny Institute had fame thrust upon it in 1917 when Trotsky and Lenin directed the October Revolution from the headquarters of the Bolshevik Central Committee and the Petrograd Soviet, which had been set up here. In its Hall of Acts (Aktovy zal) on 25 October, the All-Russian Congress of Soviets conferred power on a Bolshevik government led by Lenin, which ran the country from here until March 1918. In 1934, Leningrad Party chief Sergei Kirov was assassinated on Stalin's orders as he left the building, sparking the notorious Leningrad purges. Today the Smolny remains a seat of power and St Petersburg governor Valentina Matvienko runs the city from here. Surprisingly the name 'Dictatorship of the Proletariat Sq' remains despite the rather different political credo associated with local powerbrokers today.

SPASO-PREOBRAZHENSKY CATHEDRAL (CATHEDRAL OF THE TRANSFIGURATION OF OUR SAVIOUR) Map pp246-9

Spaso-preobrazhensky Sobor; Preobrazhenskaya pl; 🕑 services 10am & 6pm; metro Chernyshevskaya

Beautifully restored and repainted both outside and in, the interior of this marvellous yellow church just off Liteyny pr is one of the most overwhelming in the city and certainly St Petersburg's most golden. The grand gates bear the imperial double-headed eagle in vast golden busts – reflecting the fact that Empress Elizabeth ordered its construction in 1743 where the Preobrazhensky Guards (the monarch's personal protection unit) had their headquarters. Architect Vasily Stasov rebuilt the church from 1827 to 1829 in the neoclassical style and it is dedicated to the victory over the Turks in 1828-29. The fence surrounding the church is made from captured Turkish guns!

TAURIDE PALACE & GARDENS

Map pp240-1

The Tauride Gardens, also known as the City Children's Park, is a lovely – if run-down – place for a stroll and there are some rusty rides for the kiddies. The view across the lake at the fine Tauride Palace (Tavrichesky Dvorets), built between 1783 and 1789 for Catherine the Great's lover Potemkin, is a fine sight, although unfortunately the palace itself is off-limits to visitors.

The palace, in the park's northeast corner, takes its name from the Ukrainian region of Crimea (once called Tavria), which Potemkin was responsible for conquering (the palace was a thank-you for that acquisition). Paul I turned the place into a barracks, which ruined most of the lavish interiors. Between 1906 and 1917 the State Duma, the Provisional Government and the Petrograd Soviet all met here; in the 1930s it housed the All-Union Agricultural Communist University, a fate that would have horrified Catherine the Great. Today it is home to the Parliamentary Assembly of the Member States of the CIS (Commonwealth of Independent States). The gardens are located a block and a half east of Chernyshevskaya metro.

Just east of the gardens, on Shpalernaya ul, is one of the last remaining statues of Felix Dzerzhinksy, founder of the infamous Cheka, KGB predecessor.

VOSSTANIYA

Eating p148; Sleeping pp179–80

The mostly residential Vosstaniya region takes its name from pl Vosstaniya (Uprising Sq), where the February Revolution began in 1917. Mainly home to the poor in imperial times, large swathes of the area are taken up by industrial wasteland, home to many large factories and the Moscow Station, St Petersburg's busiest.

The area includes the lesser-known final one kilometre of Nevsky pr, known locally as Staronevsky (Old Nevsky) despite being no older than Nevsky proper. Staronevsky is famous for being the closest St Petersburg has to a red light district and in the evening this far quieter and less commercial stretch of the city's main avenue is busy with prostitutes.

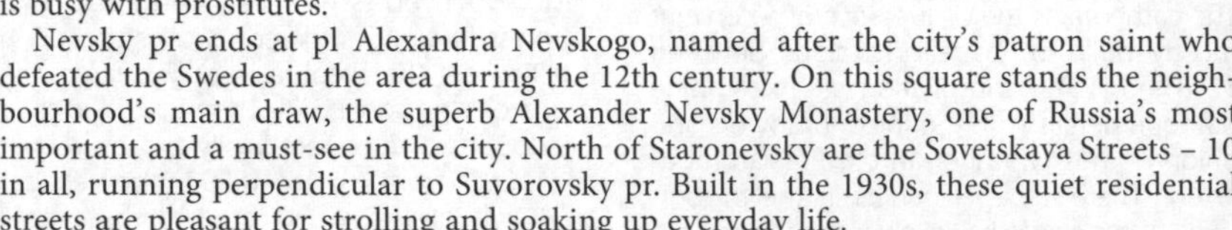

Nevsky pr ends at pl Alexandra Nevskogo, named after the city's patron saint who defeated the Swedes in the area during the 12th century. On this square stands the neighbourhood's main draw, the superb Alexander Nevsky Monastery, one of Russia's most important and a must-see in the city. North of Staronevsky are the Sovetskaya Streets – 10 in all, running perpendicular to Suvorovsky pr. Built in the 1930s, these quiet residential streets are pleasant for strolling and soaking up everyday life.

ALEXANDER NEVSKY MONASTERY

Map pp244-5

Lavra Alexandra Nevskogo; pl Alexandra Nevskogo; ☎ 274 0409; 179/2 Nevsky pr; admission free; metro Pl Alexandra Nevskogo

This fascinating working monastery, in whose grounds the graves of some of Russia's most famous artistic figures can be found, is entered from pl Alexandra Nevskogo opposite the Hotel Moskva. It was founded in 1713 by Peter the Great, who wrongly thought this was where Alexander of Novgorod had beaten the Swedes in 1240. In 1797 it became a *lavra,* the most senior grade of Russian Orthodox monasteries. Today it is open to the public and, sadly, the courtyard is filled with homeless beggars hoping for the charity of visitors.

You can wander freely around most of the grounds, but you must buy tickets from the kiosk on your right after entering the main gates to enter the **graveyards** (☎ 271 2635; admission R40; 🕒 11am-6pm Fri-Wed Mar-Sep, 11am-3.30pm Fri-Wed Oct-Feb).

Transport

The two metro stations in the neighbourhood are both useful: Pl Vosstaniya/Mayakovskaya is on Pl Vosstaniya, while Pl Alexandra Nevskogo is at the far end of Nevsky pr and has its entrance opposite the Alexander Nevsky Monastery. The Moscow Station is also in the neighbourhood and is where most people coming from Moscow will arrive.

The **Tikhvin Cemetery** (Tikhvinskoe kladbishche), on the right as you enter, contains the most famous graves. In the far right-hand corner from its gate, a bust of Tchaikovsky marks his grave. Nearby are Rubenstein, Borodin, Mussorgsky, Rimsky-Korsakov (with by far the most eccentric of all the tombstones) and Glinka. Make a right after entering and you'll reach the tomb of Dostoevsky.

The **Lazarus Cemetery** (Lazarevskoe kladbishche), facing the Tikhvin across the entrance path, contains several late great St Petersburg architects – among them Voronikhin, Quarenghi, Stasov, Zakharov and Rossi. Scholar and polymath Mikhail Lomonosov is also buried here.

Across the canal in the main *lavra* complex, the first main building on the left is the 1717–22 baroque Annunciation Church (Blagoveshchenskaya tserkov), now the **City Sculpture Museum** (☎ 274 2517; admission R30; 🕒 11am-5pm Fri-Wed). It features a large collection of the original models and designs for the city's sculptures and monuments.

About 100m further on is the monastery's 1776–90 classical **Trinity Cathedral** (Troitsky Sobor; ☎ 274 1612; 🕒 open for worship from 6am Sat, Sun & holidays, closed for cleaning 2-5pm; early liturgy from 7am, late liturgy from 10am, all-night vigils from 6pm). Hundreds crowd in here on 12 September to celebrate the feast of St Alexander Nevsky. His remains are in the silver reliquary by the main iconostasis. Behind the cathedral is the **Nicholas Cemetery** (🕒 9am-9pm summer, 9am-6pm winter), a romantically overgrown field where many of the cathedral's priests are buried.

Alexander Nevsky Monastery (opposite)

Opposite the cathedral is the **Metropolitan's House** (1775–78), residence of Metropolitan Vladimir, the spiritual leader of St Petersburg's Russian Orthodox community. In the surrounding grounds is a smaller cemetery where leading Communist (ie atheist) Party officials and luminaries are buried. On the far right of the grounds facing the canal is St Petersburg's **Orthodox Academy**, one of only a handful in Russia (the main one is at Sergiev Posad, near Moscow).

GUVD MUSEUM Map pp246-9

☎ 279 4233; ul Poltavskaya 12; tour for up to 20 people R600; 🕓 10am-5pm Mon-Fri; metro Pl Vosstaniya

For police enthusiasts, the great but little-known GUVD Museum chronicles the history of criminality and law enforcement by the Ministry of Internal Affairs in Leningrad/St Petersburg. This balanced, fascinating exhibit, featuring photos, costumes and weapons in several large halls, will acquaint you with interesting titbits about gang bosses and the Mafia's reign of terror in the 1920s through the fight to control illegal abortions and alcohol production. You'll need to get a guided tour for this, booked in advance by telephone and available in English. If you understand Russian, you can join an already-arranged group; if not, bring along a translator.

MOSCOW STATION Map pp246-9

☎ 168 4905; pl Vosstaniya 2; metro Pl Vosstaniya

This handsome station, originally named the Nikolaevsky Station after Nicholas I, under whose reign the first rail link to Moscow was opened, is St Petersburg's most important. Even if you aren't going to visit Moscow the inside is well worth a look. The vast ceiling frieze in the second of the three halls is an interesting piece of Stalinist art celebrating the Soviet Union's accession to the Olympic movement in 1952.

The main hall contains a bust of Peter the Great welcoming people to his city (the vast majority of Russians arrive here by train). Until 1991 there was a bust of Lenin here, which was replaced far more appropriately by one of the city's founder the same year. The Moscow Station is mirrored at the other end of the line by the Leningradsky Station in Moscow, which can be disorientating when you get off the train at the other end!

SENNAYA

Eating pp148–9; Shopping pp170–1; Sleeping pp180–1

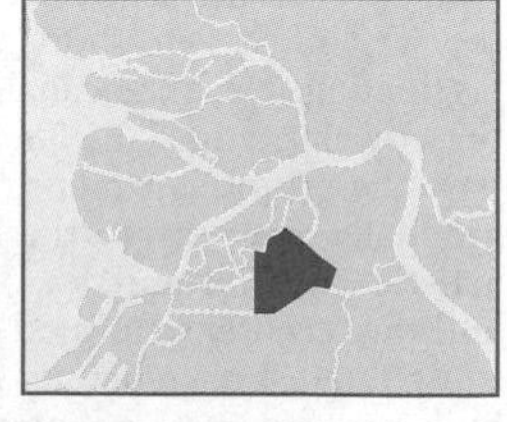

More infamous than famous, this neighbourhood includes the once incredibly run-down Haymarket, which was the centre of Dostoevskian St Petersburg. This area was home to the poor workers and peasants who were new arrivals in the city, living in rat-infested basements and sleeping 10 to a room in shifts. A huge face-lift for the city's tricentennial celebrations in 2003 modernised and cleaned up the area virtually beyond recognition. Today the Sennaya area is a hodge-podge of different environments, from the gorgeous Fontanka River and its stunning façades to the wasteland of the Obvodny Canal, the chaos of Sennaya pl and the commercial bustle around the shopping hub at Five Corners (Pyat Uglov).

Transport

The Sennaya neighbourhood is well served by four busy metro stations. Most convenient is Sennaya Pl/Sadovaya right on Sennaya pl, while Tekhnologichesky Institut, Pushkinskaya and Ligovsky Pr are scattered about elsewhere in the neighbourhood, making it no problem to get about.

RAILWAY MUSEUM Map pp246-9

☎ 315 1466/76; Sadovaya ul 50; admission R50; 11am-5.30pm Sun-Thu; metro Sadovaya

While people loving the real thing will head to the **Museum of Railway Technology** (p120), this well-loved place is for anyone loving model trains. Here you'll find a great collection of Soviet train models (although they'll only be turned on if you order a guided tour in advance, available only in Russian). There's also a luxurious train carriage's interiors on display and a statue of Lenin.

RIMSKY-KORSAKOV FLAT-MUSEUM

Map pp246-9

☎ 113 3208; Zagorodny pr 28; adult/student R50/30; 11am-6pm Wed-Sun

The composer Nikolai Rimsky-Korsakov's apartment has been lovingly re-created to look the same as it did when he spent the last 15 years of life in it (he died in 1908). As well as furniture, the museum contains many of his personal effects and even his batons. The composer's tradition of holding concerts here on Wednesday evenings continues, although you are unlikely to see Stravinksy, Glazunov, Scriabin or Rachmaninoff perform their latest compositions here today.

SENNAYA PLOSHCHAD Map pp246-9

St Petersburg's Haymarket was the city's filthy underbelly immortalised by Dostoevsky, who lived in the neighbourhood and set *Crime and Punishment* here. Until a recent face-lift, the square remained a magnet for the homeless, beggars, pickpockets and drunks, as well as being overloaded with makeshift kiosks and market stalls. Chaotic and dirty, it was the armpit of the city. Despite a big clean-up effort by city authorities in time for the tricentennial in 2003, Sennaya pl retains a fundamental insalubriousness. Be on your guard walking around here at any time, but particularly at night.

The peripatetic Dostoevsky, who occupied around 20 residences in his 28-year stay in the city, once spent a couple of days in debtors' prison in what is now called the Senior Officers' Barracks, just across the square from the Sennaya pl metro station. At the site of the metro station there was once a large cathedral that dominated the square.

YUSUPOV GARDENS Map pp246-9

Due west of the square along Sadovaya ul are the charming Yusupov Gardens, a pleasant park with a big lake in the middle. The building set back behind the gardens is the **Old Yusupov Palace** (not to be confused with the Yusupov Palace on the Moyka where the Yusupov family moved from here in the 18th century). The Old Yusupov Palace is closed to the public and used mainly for official receptions. The park is open daily though and is a very pleasant place to stroll.

MARIINSKY

Eating p149; Shopping p171; Sleeping p181

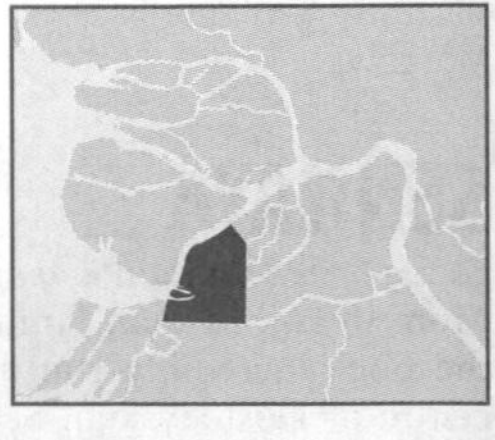

Named after the renowned Mariinsky Theatre, the area to the west of St Petersburg's historic heart is charming and fascinating. Here the canals that run through the centre of the city empty into the Gulf of Finland, quietly meandering past the crumbling mansions and forgotten churches that gradually give way to the city's docklands. St Petersburg's artistic, musical and Jewish communities all gather here, and the recently renovated Grand Choral Synagogue, just off ul Dekabristov, is one of the most interesting religious buildings in the city. With the new Mariinsky Theatre being built and progressive renovation of some of the city's long forgotten palaces and churches here, the Mariinsky neighbourhood of St Petersburg looks set for some big changes in the near future. Unfortunately one of the planned improvements is not the introduction of a metro line – the whole area has a somewhat languorous feel, as there's not a single metro station in it!

Transport

Your feet come in handy here, as the Mariinsky district is terribly served by the metro. In most cases, the nearest station is Sennaya Pl/Sadovaya, but it's hardly convenient for most parts of the area. If you are staying here, get to grips with the *marshrutkas,* trams or city buses that run through the neighbourhood. If you are just visiting, enjoy the walk.

ALEXANDER BLOK HOUSE-MUSEUM

Map pp242-3

☎ 113 8633; ul Dekabristov 57; adult/student R50/25; 🕑 11am-6pm Thu-Mon, 11am-5pm Tue; metro Sadovaya

The flat where Alexander Blok spent the last eight years of his life is now the Alexander Blok House-Museum. After paying in the vestibule downstairs, go to the 1st floor where you'll be given a pair of slippers and go up to the 3rd floor to see Blok's original apartment.

The 3rd floor has been preserved much as it was when Blok lived here with his wife Lyubov (daughter of Mendeleev). Back on the 1st floor, where Blok's mother lived after the original inhabitants fled the Bolsheviks in 1917, there is an art gallery and some original copies of Blok's work. You can also see the room where Blok died (his death mask is on display, as well as a drawing of Blok on his deathbed, drawn on the last page of the poet's pad). There are regular chamber concerts performed here, worthwhile especially for the subdued charm of the flats – and the lovely views out onto the Pryazhka River.

GRAND CHORAL SYNAGOGUE

Map pp246-9

☎ 114 1153, 114 0078; Lermontovsky pr 2; 🕑 services 10am Sat; metro Sadovaya

The Grand Choral Synagogue is one of the most striking of the city's buildings and is located just off ul Dekabristov. From an original design by Stasov, the superb edifice opened in 1893 to provide a central place of worship for St Petersburg's growing Jewish community. Its cupola is 47m high and the cream, chocolate and light blue painted exterior bears more than a passing resemblance to a luxurious cake. It was fully revamped in 2003 with money donated by an American benefactor. Visitors are welcome outside times of prayer, but both men and women should bring something with which to cover their heads, men entering on the ground floor and women on the 1st. The interior is just as spectacular as the exterior and can seat 1300 people. There is an interesting display in the vestibule of photographs and documents detailing the building's history.

MARIINSKY THEATRE Map pp246-9

☎ 326 4141; www.mariinsky.ru; Teatralnaya pl; tours by arrangement; box office 🕑 11am-7pm; metro Sadovaya

Known throughout the world during the Soviet reign as the Kirov, the Mariinsky Theatre resumed its original name in 1992, though the ballet company still uses the name Kirov. Built in 1859, the Mariinsky has played a pivotal role in Russian ballet ever since. Outside performance times you can usually wander into the theatre's foyer and maybe peep into its lovely

Jewish St Petersburg

By the end of the 19th century, Jews had considerable power in the community and widely supported the overthrow of the tsarist autocracy. However, the vast majority also opposed the Bolsheviks and after 1917 a repression began that was to last for the next 70 years. By 1922 all Zionist organisations were made illegal, Jewish schools were nationalised and the teaching of Hebrew banned. The Lensoviet (Leningrad City Council) finally ordered the closure of the synagogue in 1930, but relented after only six months due to an international outcry.

During the Nazi blockade the Jewish community continued to meet for daily prayer and to bury the dead here. While the Nazis never took Leningrad, of course, a chilling foreshadowing of what would have happened took place in Tsarskoe Selo, just outside the city, where following annexation by German troops all 800 Jews in the town were summarily shot in the park of the royal palace. A memorial to the dead has now been set up, although the exact location of the murders remains unknown.

Despite some residual chauvinism and even outright hostility (the synagogue has been routinely graffittied with swastikas by local skinheads) the Jewish community in the city is well integrated and thriving. Many 'refuseniks' who went to Israel in the 1980s and 1990s have in fact returned to the safety and prosperity of the new Russia in the face of the ongoing Middle East conflict.

auditorium. To organise a full tour fax a request to Dr Yuri Schwartzkopf at ☎ 314 1744 and call back for an answer. The Mariinsky has a state-of-the-art website, so there's no problem reserving tickets online well in advance of your trip to ensure you can see a performance. Decent seats start at R800. If you are Russian or can pull off being Russian, you can buy a ticket for a fraction of that price. However, unlike other theatres in town you won't be able to buy tickets at a *teatralnaya kassa* (general theatre box office) – the Mariinsky only sells direct from its own ticket office or via the website.

Construction of a new Mariinsky Theatre (p9) is under way and the incredible and controversial new building is due to open in 2008. Elsewhere around Tealtranaya pl you will find the **Rimsky-Korsakov Conservatory**, which faces the Mariinsky. Surrounding the square is an area of quiet canals and side streets.

Northeast of Teatralnaya pl, before it twists southwest, the Griboedova Canal runs under yet another beautiful beast-supported suspension bridge, the **Lviny most**, with chains emerging from the mouths of lions.

NABOKOV MUSEUM Map pp246-9

☎ 311 4502; www.nabokovmuseum.org; Bolshaya Morskaya ul 47; adult/student R100/20, admission free Thu 11am-3pm; 🕑 11am-6pm Tue-Thu, 11am-5pm Fri, noon-5pm Sat & Sun; metro Sadovaya

This lovely 19th-century town house was the suitably grand childhood home of Vladimir Nabokov, infamous author of *Lolita* and arguably the most versatile and least classifiable of modern Russian writers. Here Nabokov lived with his wealthy family from his birth in 1899 until the revolution in 1917, when they sensibly left the country. The house features heavily in Nabokov's brilliant autobiography *Speak, Memory,* in which he refers to it as a 'paradise lost'. Indeed, he never returned, dying abroad in 1977. There's actually relatively little to see in the museum itself, save for some charming interiors (don't miss the gorgeous carved oak ceiling in the library) and the various displays of Nabokov-related artefacts. The museum is more of a cultural centre hosting festivals and special events, exhibiting art, assisting students and academics and even enjoying a brief spell as a members-only nightclub in 2001.

NIKOLSKY CATHEDRAL Map pp246-9

☎ Nikolskaya pl 1/3; 🕑 9am-7pm; metro Sadovaya

This ice-blue church just south of the Mariinsky Theatre and surrounded on two sides by canals is one of the most picture-perfect in the city. The baroque spires and golden domes make this one of the city's best-loved churches, and one of the few that continued to work during the Soviet era when organised religion was effectively banned.

Nicknamed the Sailor's Church (Nicholas is the patron saint of sailors), it contains many 18th-century icons and a fine carved wooden iconostasis. A graceful bell tower overlooks the canal, which is crossed by the Staro-Nikolsky most (from this bridge, you can see at least seven bridges, more than from any other spot in the city).

PALACE OF GRAND DUKE ALEXEY ALEXANDROVICH Map pp242-3

Dvorets Velikogo Knyazi Alekseya Alexandrovicha; ☎ 114 3330; nab reki Moyki 211; not officially open to the public; metro Sennaya Pl

This fabulous derelict mansion at the very far end of the Moyka River belonged to Alexander II's son and is literally disintegrating while awaiting a saviour. Used as a Pioneers' Palace during the communist era, the building has sat empty ever since and is closed to the public. Built in 1895 by Maximilian Messmacher, the building is fascinatingly odd – asymmetrical and a blend of many different styles, perhaps reflective of the character of Grand Duke Alexey himself.

The resourceful may well be able to pay the security guard to let them in and give them an ad hoc tour of the once lavish staterooms. While all the furniture has now been removed from the palace, many of the once stunning fittings and ceilings remain, and the result is far more reminiscent of daily life for the Romanov dynasty than the crowded museum palaces found elsewhere in St Petersburg. The Chinese Hall and the Grand Duke's office all boast spectacular wooden interiors, while the ceilings of the ballroom and Banqueting Hall are also impressive. Most interesting of all though is Grand Duke Alexey's enormous bath, which is beautifully inlaid with tiling.

RUSSIAN VODKA MUSEUM Map pp246-9

☎ 312 3416; www.vodkamuseum.ru; Konnogvardeysky bul 5; admission R50, English tour R100; 🕑 11am-10pm; metro Sadovaya

This small museum has a definite commercial interest – it's sponsored by local vodka producers Flagman and Russky Standard; and – surprise, surprise – they turn out to be rather key in the entire history of vodka-making, cropping up far too often for comfort in the displays. However, it's still an interesting place to look around, with some fascinating pictures, advertisements and machinery. There's a little café where decent food is served to accompany a huge range of vodkas; and there's a big range of novelty vodka to buy as souvenirs, although at prices higher than you'll find elsewhere in the city in normal *produkty* stores.

STATE MUSEUM OF THE HISTORY OF ST PETERSBURG Map pp246-9

☎ 571 7544; Angliyskaya nab 44; adult/student R60/30; 🕑 11am-5pm Thu-Tue

This superb museum is often overlooked by visitors as it's somewhat off the beaten tourist path, but it's a great place for anyone who is interested in the city's history – particularly that of the 20th century. Inside, as well as temporary exhibitions you'll find a permanent display of artefacts from the city in the early 20th century, particularly detailed when recounting the years immediately following the revolution. There are no labels in English with the exhibits, but you can ask for an explanatory guide that can be lent out from the ticket office downstairs.

TRINITY CATHEDRAL Map pp242-3

Troitsky Sobor; 7A Izmailovsky pr; 🕑 9am-7pm Mon-Sat, 8am-8pm Sun & holidays, daily liturgy at 10am, also service at 5pm Fri-Sun & holidays; metro Tekhnologichesky Institut

The stunning deep-blue cupola of the Trinity Cathedral is visible from all over this area of the city and looks incredible in the evening sun when viewed across the Fontanka River. Up close its poor state of repair is clearly visible, but at 83m high the cupola is still impressive. On the corner of Krasnoarmeyskaya ul and Izmailovsky pr you can see one of the cathedral's pavilions, featuring a restored mini-cupola emblazoned with the golden stars which were once visible on the main cupola of the cathedral.

Construction of the vast cathedral began in 1828, to a design by Stasov. The cathedral was consecrated in 1835 and functioned as the chapel for the Izmailovsky Guards, who were garrisoned next door until Stalin's terror forced it to close in 1938. It reopened in 1990 and a slow but careful restoration effort has been under way ever since. The cathedral's interior is decidedly bare – the white painted walls are unlike most more traditional Orthodox churches. However, it's definitely worth a visit and Dostoevsky buffs will be interested to know that this is the church where the great man married his second wife, Anna Snitkina, in 1867.

YUSUPOV PALACE Map pp246-9

☎ 314 9883; nab reki Moyki 94; adult/student/under 16 yrs R300/250/150, murder of Rasputin tour adult/student extra R130/100; 🕑 11am-5pm; metro Sadovaya

If you have time to visit only one palace in the city, the Yusupov Palace would be a particularly good choice. The palace became the residence of the illustrious Yusupov family after they moved from another fine house on Sadovaya ul, confusingly still sometimes referred to as the Yusupov Palace as well. This spectacular place has some of the most perfectly preserved 19th-century interiors in the city and a fascinating history as well, most notoriously as the place where Rasputin met a gruesome end. Its last Yusupov owner, the eccentric Prince Felix, was a high-society darling enamoured of cross-dressing and often attended the Mariinsky and society balls as a woman.

The palace was built by Vallin de la Mothe in the 1760s and the interiors, which were redecorated later, are sumptuously rich, with many halls painted in different styles and decked out with gilded chandeliers, silks, frescoes, tapestries and some fantastic furniture. The admission price to the palace includes an audio tour in English as well as a number of other languages. The highlight of the tour, which begins on the 1st floor before taking in the ground floor, is visiting the palace's delightful private theatre (where ballet dancers including Anna Pavlova have performed and where tourist-oriented music and dance shows are still regularly held in the evenings). Other stunning interiors can be found in the palace's Turkish Study and the Moorish Room, both of which were created to reflect the Yusupov family's Muslim origins.

In 1916 Rasputin was murdered here in the grizzliest possible way by Felix Yusupov and some fellow plotters, considering the 'mad monk' to have become too powerful (p55). The Murder of Rasputin Tour lasts 30 minutes and is available twice a day in English (1.15pm and 5.15pm). There are only 20 places available on each tour.

VASILEVSKY ISLAND

Eating pp149–50; Shopping p172; Sleeping pp181–2

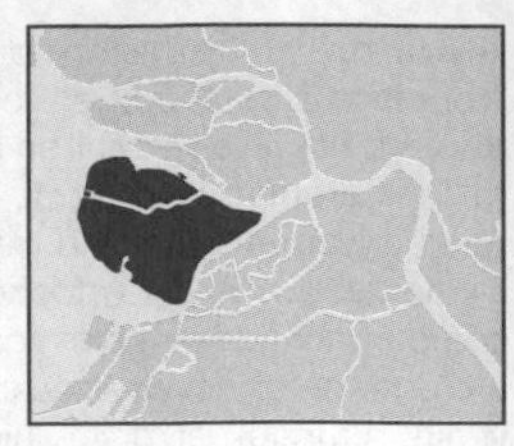

This triangular island, originally gifted to Prince Menshikov by Peter the Great, is a fascinating place. While its sharp nose (the Strelka) feels very much like part of the bustling city centre, go a few blocks back and things calm down noticeably, while even further back it becomes spookily empty before giving way to Soviet-era mass housing. There's a huge amount to see here and everyone should make time to see some of Vasilevsky Island's historic sights.

ACADEMY OF ARTS MUSEUM

Map pp246-9

☎ 213 6496, excursions ☎ 213 3578; Universitetskaya nab 17; adult/student R60/30, excellent Russian-language excursions R100; 🕑 11am-6pm Wed-Sun

The Russian Academy of Arts Research Museum doesn't get many visitors but is well worth exploring. It's easy to spot – look for the two imported Egyptian **sphinx monuments** outside, said to be about 3500 years old. Boys would live in this building from the age of five until they graduated at age 15 – it was an experiment to create a new species of human: the artist. It mostly worked; many great Russian artists were spawned here, including Ilya Repin, Karl Bryullov and Anton Losenko. But the academy's conservatism (it was founded on the idea that art must serve the state) led to the creation of the Peredvizhniki (Wanderers) in 1863 when 14 students left to found the new movement.

Inside are works by academy students and faculty since its founding in 1757, including many studies, plus temporary exhibitions. Make sure to visit the 3rd floor, and the models for the original versions of Smolny, St Isaac's, and the Alexander Nevsky Monastery; and take a peek into the fabulous old library – you'd think you were in Oxford.

CENTRAL NAVAL MUSEUM **Map pp246-9**

☎ 328 2502; www.museum.navy.ru; Birzhevaya pl 4; adult/student R100/15; 🕑 10.30am-5.30pm Wed-Sun

The Old Stock Exchange is now the Central Naval Museum. This is a grand, expansive museum full of maps, excellent model ships, flags and photos of the Russian navy up to the present day – a must for naval enthusiasts. The highlight of the display is *Botik*, Peter's first boat and in his own words the 'grandfather of the Russian Navy' – it's an emotional pilgrimage for many. Other interesting exhibits include a pre-turn-of-the-20th-century submarine (a two-seater!) and some big oars.

Transport

Vasilevsky Island has two metro stations and most sights are walkable from the well-located Vasileostrovskaya. The second station is the far less useful Primorskaya. Sportivnaya metro station, on the Petrograd Side, can also be very useful for reaching some parts of the island.

GEOLOGICAL MUSEUM **Map pp242-3**

☎ 312 5399, excursions ☎ 328 9248; Sredny pr 74; admission free; 🕑 10am-5pm Mon-Fri

With over one million exhibits, prehistoric rock and dinosaur fragments, animal skulls and mammoth tusks, the Geological Museum is more than just a collection of impressive rocks and gems (though it's that too – check out the mesmerising blue charoyite and the 1.5m-long crystal from the Altai mountains). To see all the fantastic pieces here you'd have to walk 3.5km! The real tourist draw is a huge map of the Soviet Union made entirely of precious gems. The winner of the Paris World Exposition Grand Prix in 1937, this 26.6-sq-metre, 3½-ton mosaic took more than 700 people to create, combining amethysts, diamonds, granite, rubies and other gems from 500 different places in the USSR. It later sat in the Hermitage's St George's Hall for 34 years. There's also a precious-gem hammer and sickle nearby, which reflects whatever glory of those days existed much more effectively than those appearing on souvenir pins and rusty metal plaques. It's a great museum.

MENDELEEV MUSEUM **Map pp246-9**

Muzei-Kvaritra I arkhivy D. I. Mendeleeva; ☎ 328 9744; Mendeleevskaya liniya 2; adult/student R60/30; 🕑 11am-4pm Mon-Fri; metro Vasileostrovskaya

This museum is dedicated to the father of the periodic table of elements, chemist and eclectic inventor Dmitri Mendeleev. His cosy study has been lovingly preserved and you can see his desk (where he always stood rather than sat) and even some early drafts of the periodic table.

MENSHIKOV PALACE Map pp246-9

☎ 332 1112; Universitetskaya nab 15; adult/student R200/100, photos R100; 10.30am-5pm Tue-Sun; metro Vasileostrovskaya

The first stone building in the city, the Menshikov Palace was built to the grandiose tastes of Prince Alexander Menshikov, Peter the Great's closest friend throughout his life and the first governor of St Petersburg. Menshikov was of humble origins (he is said to have sold pies on the streets of Moscow as a child), but his talent for both organisation and intrigue made him the second-most important person in the Russian Empire by the time of Peter's death in 1725. His palace, built mainly between 1710 and 1714, was by far the city's smartest residence at the time (compare Peter the Great's tiny Summer Palace!), something which Peter was quite happy with, hating luxury as he did. The palace was used by Peter for official functions and its interiors are some of the oldest and best-preserved in the city.

While the ground floor is a rather uninspiring collection of historical artefacts belonging to Menshikov, the 1st floor is fascinating – superbly preserved with its original fittings and some stunning Dutch tile interiors (to fortify the rooms against humidity due to Menshikov's tuberculosis), original furniture and the personal effects of Menshikov. Each room has a fact sheet in English you can borrow to explain its history. Vavara's Chamber is particularly evocative of how the aristocracy lived during Peter's time: in relative simplicity if you compare it to the excesses of the Yusupov Palace.

The main room in the palace is the magnificent Grand Hall, where balls and great banquets were held, as well as the famous meetings of the 'drunken assembly' and the notorious dwarves' wedding (p50).

MUSEUM OF ANTHROPOLOGY & ETHNOGRAPHY (KUNSTKAMERA) Map pp246-9

☎ 328 1412; www.kunstkamera.ru; Universitetskaya nab 3, entrance on Tamozhenny per; adult R100, student & child R50; 🕑 11am-5pm Fri-Wed, last entry 4.45pm, closed last Tue of month

This fascinating and ghoulish place is an essential St Petersburg sight, although not one for the faint-hearted. The blue-and-white building with the steeple was Russia's first museum, founded in 1714 by Peter himself. In contrast to the Museum of Ethnography, this museum is about peoples outside the former USSR, with

Menshikov Palace (above)

wonderfully kitsch dioramas and displays on the cultures of Asia, Oceania, Africa and the Americas, including rare objects from around the world. However, most people skip these displays and head straight for the old anatomy theatre at the building's centre.

Here in a large room with an attractive green ceiling is Peter's Kunstkamera (from the German for 'art chamber', a misnomer if ever there were one). This collection of preserved 'monsters' began as a private interest when Peter bought the collection of Dutch anatomist Frederik Ruysch during his 'Great Embassy' in Europe, but it soon became a public spectacle. By opening the collection of malformed babies, conjoined twins and various other truly horrendous specimens of nature gone wrong, Peter aimed to educate the notoriously superstitious Russian people. Rather than the result of the evil eye or sorcery, Peter wanted to demonstrate that the malformations were due to 'internal damage as well as fear and the beliefs of the mother during pregnancy' – a slightly more enlightened interpretation. Vodka and wine were given out to encourage the poor to visit, while Peter ordered any peasants giving birth to malformed babies to bring them to him for inclusion in the museum in return for generous compensation.

There's an interesting interactive computer in the corner detailing some truly amazing 'monsters' in drawings from the early pioneer of preservation Ulysses Aldrovandi of Bologna. Think twice about bringing young children here and definitely give the Kunstkamera a wide berth if you are pregnant yourself.

MUSEUM OF ZOOLOGY Map pp246-9

☎ 218 0112; Universitetskaya nab 1/3; adult/student R100/30, Thu free; 🕑 11am-6pm Sat-Thu

To the left (south) of the exchange is the Museum of Zoology, reputed to be one of the biggest and best in the world, with incredibly life-like stuffed animals from around the world. There are some 40,000 animal species on display in realistic dioramas, including wild camel, a gigantic ram, mammoths and an extinct southern elephant. One of the highlights is a complete 44,000-year-old woolly mammoth thawed out of the Siberian ice in 1902.

PEOPLE'S WILL D-2 SUBMARINE MUSEUM Map pp242-3

Narodovolets; ☎ 356 5277; Shkipersky protok 10; admission R150; 🕑 11am-5pm Tue-Sun

Opened as a fun, unique museum, the *People's Will* (Narodovolets) D-2 Submarine was one of the first six (diesel-fuelled) submarines built in the Soviet Union. It was in action between 1931 and 1956, and proudly sank five German ships. The tour you're obliged to take (in Russian) will take you through the charming sub to see how the crew of 53 lived and worked.

PUSHKIN HOUSE Map pp246-9

☎ 328 1901; www.pushkinhouse.spb.ru in Russian; nab Makarova 4; guided tours by arrangement (minimum R300); 🕑 10am-4pm Mon-Fri

The old Customs House, topped with statues and a dome, is now called Pushkin House and is home to the Institute of Russian Literature and a Literary Museum with exhibits on Tolstoy, Gogol, Lermontov, Turgenev, Gorky and others. The archives contain the richest collection of medieval Russian manuscripts in the world. The place is not keen on people off the street; call in advance to book a tour in English or Russian.

STRELKA Map pp246-9

The oldest parts of Vasilevsky Island are its eastern 'nose', the Strelka (tongue of land), where Peter the Great first wanted his new city's administrative and intellectual centre, and the embankment facing the Admiralty. In fact, the Strelka became the focus of St Petersburg's maritime trade, symbolised by the white colonnaded Stock Exchange. The two Rostral Columns, archetypal St Petersburg landmarks, are studded with ships' prows and four seated sculptures supposedly representing four of Russia's great rivers, all reachable from this point: the Neva, the Volga, the Dnieper and the Volkhov. These were oil-fired navigation beacons in the 1800s (on some holidays gas torches are still lit on them). The area remains an intellectual centre, with the St Petersburg State University, the Academy of Arts and a veritable 'museum ghetto'.

The Strelka also has one of the best views in the city: you look left to the Peter and Paul Fortress and right to the Hermitage, the Admiralty and St Isaac's Cathedral.

TEMPLE OF THE ASSUMPTION

Map pp242-3

Uspenskoe Podvore Optina Pustin; ☎ 321 7473; cnr nab Leytenanta Shmidta & 15-ya linii; 🕑 open daily

This is a stunning neo-Byzantine church (1895), built on the site of a previous monastery by architect V Kosyakov. It was closed in 1934 and from 1957 was turned into the city's first – and very popular – year-round skating rink! The 7.7m, 861kg metal cross on the roof was only replaced in 1998.

TWELVE COLLEGES Map pp246-9

West of the Museum of Anthropology and marked by a statue of scientist-poet Mikhail Lomonosov (1711–65) is Mendeleevskaya liniya and the skinny, 400m-long Twelve Colleges building. One of St Petersburg's oldest buildings, it was meant originally for Peter's government ministries and is now part of the university, which stretches out behind it. Within these walls Dmitri Mendeleev created his periodic table, populist philosopher Nikolai Chernyshevsky studied, Alexander Popov created some of the world's first radio waves and a young Vladimir Putin sat a degree in law.

PETROGRAD SIDE

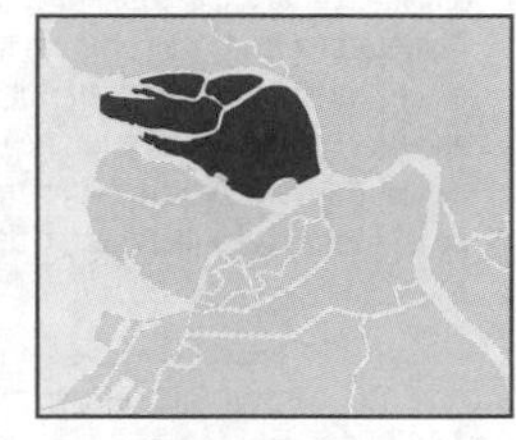

Eating pp151–2; Shopping pp171–2; Sleeping p182

The Petrograd Side (Petrogradskaya Storona) is a cluster of delta islands between the Malaya and Bolshaya Neva channels, of which five are significant: Zayachy (Hare), Petrogradsky, Krestovsky, Kamenny (Stone) and Yelagin Islands. On little Zayachy Island, Peter the Great first broke ground for St Petersburg and built the Peter and Paul Fortress, while Petrogradsky Island is the main commercial hub of the area. Krestovsky, Kamenny and Yelagin Islands (collectively known as the Kirovsky Islands) make up the city's greenest and most pleasant place to stroll.

PETROGRADSKY & ZAYACHY ISLAND

While Zayachy Island is where Europe's fourth-largest city grew from, there's only space today for the fascinating Peter and Paul Fortress. Most of the area's sights are on Petrogradsky Island, the far larger island to the north. This fabulous area has sparkling architecture (just stroll up Kamennoostrovsky pr for a *style moderne* treat), a happening main street (Bolshoy pr) and lots of refreshingly uncrowded, green areas. The name comes from the period of WWI when St Petersburg changed its name to the less Germanic-sounding Petrograd. During this period, the area became the fashionable place to live – something attested to by the large number of mansions built here.

ALEXANDROVSKY PARK Map pp238-9

metro Gorkovskaya

Alexandrovsky Park, a rather sleazy mini Las Vegas on the Neva, is packed with casinos, bars and other entertainments. It can be fun and full of people during the summer though and there's plenty to do here. The **St Petersburg Zoo** (☎ 232 4828; Alexandrovsky park 1; adult/child R80/15; 🕑 summer 10am-7pm, winter Tue-Sun 10am-4pm) is full of miserable animals and happy kids. The lack of funds is pitifully evident, but all things considered it's pretty well kept. It's the world leader in polar bear births (since 1993, over 100 have been born here). Near the zoo is a large **amusement park**, complete with Ferris wheel, bumper cars, petrol-powered go-carts, small roller coasters and the like. The **Planetarium** (☎ 233 5312; Alexandrovsky park 4; shows R50, children under 7yrs free; 🕑 10.30am-6pm Tue-Sun) has cool 50-minute shows throughout the day at 1½-hr intervals.

ARTILLERY MUSEUM Map pp246-9

Voyenno-istorichesky Muzey Artilerii; ☎ 232 0296; Alexandrovsky park 7; adult/student R150/75, photos R50, temporary exhibits extra; 🕑 11am-6pm Wed-Sun; metro Gorkovskaya

Across the moat from the Peter and Paul Fortress, in the fort's original arsenal, is the Artillery Museum, which chronicles Russia's military history. It's a great place if you like weapons: it seems to have one of everything right back to the Stone Age. It also has Lenin's

Transport

The vast area of the Petrograd Side is excellently served by five metro stations: Gorkovskaya, Petrogradskaya, Sportivnaya, Chkalovskaya and Krestovsky Ostrov. Almost nowhere is too far from one of these stations to make it relatively easily walkable.

For Children

If your kids usually nod off at the mention of the word 'museum', that will change in St Petersburg. The Kunstkamera inside the **Museum of Anthropology & Ethnography** (p109) is an all-time favourite for its display of jarred and pickled mutants (although not suitable for kids under six, who could well come away with nightmares). The **Artillery Museum** (p111), with its exciting display of tanks, missiles, cannons and other hardware is another winner, while the **Museum of Zoology** (p110) has some of the best stuffed animal and dinosaur displays anywhere. The **Kirov Museum** (opposite) has an exhibit of how children lived in the Soviet era. Both the **Hermitage** (p67) and **Russian Museum** (p93) can provide tours specially geared to children (even in English!) if contacted in advance.

The **Botanic Gardens** (below) offers year-round, unexpected treats, and the **Floral Exhibition Hall** (p100) near Smolny also has great tropical plants to gawk at. Then, of course, there's the **zoo** (p111), **circus** (p161) and the **Planetarium** (p111), all of which hold special kids' programmes. The **D-2 Submarine** (p110) will wow them too.

The city's parks are first rate; there's a full-scale amusement park in the **Alexandrovsky Park** (p111) behind the Peter and Paul Fortress, and a much more humble one in the **Tauride Gardens** (p101) with a small children's park. There's a great children's playground on the east side of Bolshaya Pushkarskaya ul, Petrograd Side. And there are rowing and pedal-boat rental outlets behind the **Peter and Paul Fortress** (p114) and on **Yelagin Island** (p116).

armoured car, which he rode in triumph from Finland Station.

There's a superb display of military hardware in the courtyard that you can look around for free if you don't fancy committing yourself to a ticket – kids will love it.

BOTANIC GARDENS Map pp240-1

☎ 346 3639; ul Professora Popova 2; grounds free, greenhouse admission R30; 🕓 11am-4pm Sat-Thu; metro Petrogradskaya

This quiet jungle in eastern Aptekarsky (Apothecary) Island, just northeast of the Petrogradskaya metro station and across the Karpovka Canal, was once a garden of medicinal plants that gave the island its name.

The botanic gardens contain 26 greenhouses on a 22-hectare site and is one of St Petersburg's loveliest strolling grounds and most interesting places to visit – and not just for botanists. The gardens, founded by Peter the Great himself in 1714, offer a variety of excursions to their stunning collection, all the more impressive considering that 90% of the plants died during the war (those 'veterans' that survived have a war medal pinned onto them!).

At the turn of the 20th century, these were the second-biggest botanic gardens in the world, behind London's Kew Gardens. A highlight is the *tsaritsa nochi (Selenicereus pteranthus)*, a flowering cactus that blossoms only one night a year, usually in mid-June. On this night, the gardens stay open until morning for visitors to gawk at the marvel and sip champagne.

Ticket Office Times & Sanitary Days

Russian museums usually allow entry only until one hour before closing time. Therefore never turn up after that time as the ticket office will be closed and you'll get a very gruff *'nyet'* from anyone else on site if you ask to have a quick look around.

Also, if you are travelling around the end of the month, bear in mind that many museums take an extra day off called a *sanitarny den* (cleaning day). You won't be able to visit as (theoretically at least) staff are all mucking in to clean the museum from top to bottom.

CRUISER AURORA Map pp240-1

☎ 230 8440; Petrovskaya nab; admission free; 🕓 10.30am-4pm Tue-Thu & Sat & Sun; metro Gorkovskaya

In the Bolshaya Nevka opposite the Hotel St Petersburg is the *Aurora*, a mothballed cruiser from the Russo-Japanese War, built in 1900. From a downstream mooring on the night of 25 October 1917, its crew fired a blank round from the forward gun, demoralising the Winter Palace's defenders and marking the start of the October Revolution. During WWII, the Russians sank it to protect it from German bombs. Now, restored and painted in pretty colours, it's a living museum that swarms with kids on weekends. It's possible to see the crew's quarters as well as endless communist propaganda and a collection of friendship banners from various eclectic organisations around the world.

KIROV MUSEUM Map pp238-9

☎ 346 0289; Kamennoostrovsky pr 26/28; admission R50, excursions in English (unavailable Sundays) R100; 11am-6pm Thu-Tue; metro Petrogradskaya

Sergei Kirov, one of Stalin's leading henchmen after whom countless parks, plazas, squares and a region of the city are named, spent the last days of his life at this decidedly unproletarian apartment before his murder in 1934 sparked a wave of deadly repression in the country. It is now a fascinating museum showing how the Bolshevik elite really lived. The apartment is a quick journey back to the days of Soviet glory, including choice examples of 1920s technology (the first ever Soviet typewriter is here) and books (20,000 of them), while the General Electric fridge and luxurious polar-bear skins would have been incredible luxuries in the early Soviet era. Ordzhonikidze, one of Stalin's most brutal colleagues from Georgia, used to sleep on the sofa when he was in town.

Don't miss the Party leader's death clothes, hung out for reverence: the tiny hole in the back of his cap was where he was shot (blood stains intact!) and the torn seam on his jacket's left breast was where doctors tried to revive his heart. In the exhibition hall downstairs is a brilliant, lively exhibit on childhood during the Soviet era.

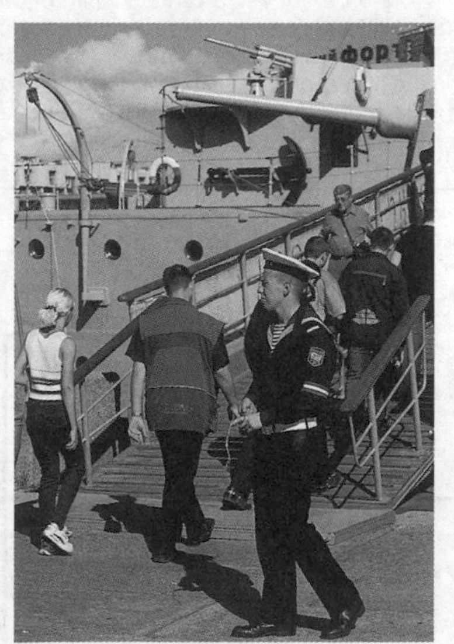

Cruiser Aurora (opposite)

MOSQUE Map pp240-1

☎ 233 9819; Kronverksky pr 7; metro Gorkovskaya

East of the Alexandrovsky Park across Kamennoostrovsky pr is a working mosque (1910–14), modelled on Samarkand's Gur Emir Mausoleum. Its fluted azure dome and minarets have emerged from a painstaking renovation and are stunning. Entering is difficult: *jamat* (congregation) members are highly protective of their mosque, which is a serious place of worship and decidedly not a tourist attraction. Women without a *keemar* (head covering) may not be admitted at all; men need to look neat, dress in long pants and preferably a collared shirt, and politely ask the guard for entry: saying you're a student of religion or architecture is best. If you are asked in, remove your shoes at the stairs (and hope your socks are clean – dirty socks, like dirty feet, may be an insult to the mosque) and do not talk inside. Forget photography. To enter, walk through the gate at the northeast side.

MUSEUM OF POLITICAL HISTORY

Map pp240-1

☎ 233 7052; ul Kuybysheva 4; adult/student R150/50; English guide R240 (minimum 5, maximum 15 people); 11am-5pm Fri-Wed; metro Gorkovskaya

East of Kamennoostrovsky pr is the Kshesinskaya Palace containing the Museum of Political History in Russia. Indeed, the building itself *is* political history – the Bolsheviks made it their headquarters and Lenin often gave speeches from the balcony of this elegant Art Nouveau palace (1904) that once belonged to Mathilda Kshesinskaya, famous ballet dancer and one-time lover of Nicholas II in his pre-tsar days. Go in to see the house itself, the best Soviet kitsch in town (including porcelain with workers' slogans and a watch for astronauts), and some incredibly rare satirical caricatures of Lenin published in magazines between the 1917 revolutions (the same drawings a few months later would have got the artist imprisoned or worse). The main exhibit takes on the subject of Russian politics in the last 40 years – ie from the Brezhnev era to the present day. It's excellently curated, with explanations in English. Elsewhere both the pre- and post-revolutionary period are covered in scrupulous (almost forensic) detail. The Lenin memorial room is highly odd and unchanged since Soviet days, however, with a semi-religious atmosphere. There are also temporary exhibits and you can visit Lenin's one-time office where he worked between the February and October revolutions.

PETER & PAUL FORTRESS Map pp246-9
Petropavlovskaya krepost; ☎ 238 4540; entry to the grounds free, museums adult/student R120/60; 🕙 10am-6pm Thu-Mon, 10am-4pm Tue; metro Gorkovskaya

Founded in 1703, the Peter and Paul Fortress is the oldest major building in St Petersburg. Peter planned it as a defence against the Swedes but defeated them before it was finished (the bottom of the Neva rises in front of it, so banked ships could easily be fired upon). In fact, it has never been utilised in the city's defence – unless you count incarceration of political 'criminals' as national defence (the tsar certainly did, for whatever good it did him).

Its main use up to 1917 was as a prison; one of its first inmates was Peter's own son Alexei, whose torture Peter is said to have personally overseen. Other famous residents were Dostoevsky, Gorky, Trotsky, Bakunin, and Lenin's older brother, Alexander. The entrance to the fortress is on the eastern side of the island, and most worth seeing are the **SS Peter and Paul Cathedral**, with its landmark needle-thin spire, and the **Trubetskoy Bastion**.

The cathedral, though plain on the outside, is radically different from traditional Orthodox churches. Don't miss its magnificent baroque interior. All of Russia's pre-revolutionary rulers from Peter the Great onwards (except Peter II and Ivan VI) are buried here. Nicholas II and his family – minus Alexei and Maria – were the latest, controversial additions (see p63). Peter I's grave is at the front on the right. The 122.5m-high bell tower remains the city's tallest structure.

Between the cathedral and the **Senior Officers' Barracks** is Mikhail Shemyakin's statue of a seated Peter the Great, with somewhat interestingly proportioned head and hands. When the statue was unveiled in 1991 it caused outrage among the citizens of St Petersburg, for whom Peter remains a saintly figure despite his long list of misdeeds, but it's now become something of a local attraction and you'll have to fight your way through family groups to get to him. Local lore has it that rubbing his right forefinger will bring good luck.

In the fort's southwest corner are reconstructions of the grim cells of the Trubetskoy Bastion, where Peter supervised the torture to death of his son. The cells were used by later tsars to keep a lid on original thinking in the empire.

In the south wall is **Nevsky Gate**, a later addition (1787), where prisoners were loaded on boats for execution or exile elsewhere. Notice the plaques showing water levels of famous floods. Outside are fine views of the whole central waterfront. Along the wall to the left, throughout the year on sunny days, you can witness a motley crew of sunbathers (standing's said to give you a *proper* tan); and around the corner, further towards the Troitsky most in winter you can watch people engaging in ice swimming. There are fabulous views of the Winter Palace across the Neva from here.

At noon every day a cannon is fired from **Naryshkin Bastion**, scaring the daylights out of tourists. The **Commandant's House** is an exhibition on the history of the St Petersburg region from medieval times to 1917. The **Engineers' House** has a museum with rotating exhibitions.

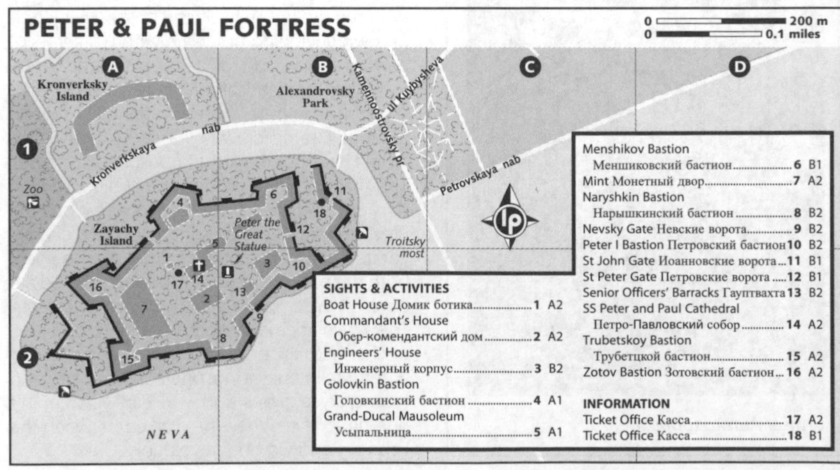

PETER'S CABIN Map pp246-9

Domik Petra Velikogo; ☎ 232 4576; Petrovskaya nab 6; 🕑 10am-5pm Wed-Sun; metro Gorkovskaya

In a patch of trees east of the fortress is a little stone building known as Peter's Cabin. This is St Petersburg's oldest surviving structure, a log cabin built in three days in May 1703 for Peter to supervise the construction of the fortress and city. Peter lived here for several months while the first construction in the city was under way. During Catherine the Great's time, the house was protected by a bricklayer, while during WWII Soviet soldiers would take an oath of allegiance to the city here, vowing to protect it from the Germans, before disappearing to the front. It feels more like a shrine than a museum, but confirms Peter's love for the simple life with its unpretentious, homely feel, visibly influenced by the time he spent in Holland. Its status as the city's oldest sta... building loses something with the vas... monolith behind it, the top of which a... a mobile phone network – it's te... imagine what Peter would have m... Look out for the bronze bust of ... men Zabello in the garden.

SIGMUND FREUD MUS... DREAMS Map pp238-9

☎ 235 2857; www.freud.ru; ... 🕑 noon-5pm Tue & Sun; metro Spo...

One of the most unique exhibits in ... try, itself conceptual and based on abs... tions and ideas, not artefacts, the museum is an outgrowth of the Psychoanalytic Institute that houses it. It aims to stimulate your subconscious via projection as you struggle to read the display symbolising what Freud himself would have dreamt of in a dimly lit, ambient hall. Illustrations to Freud's patients' dreams and other quotations line the small, eccentric, innovative museum.

TELEVISION ANTENNA Map pp240-1

☎ 234 7887; Aptekarsky Island; 🕑 10am-5pm Tue-Sat; metro Petrogradskaya

Leningrad Radio-Tele Broadcasting Centre's antenna, at the northern end of Petrograd Side, is open for excursions to its 50,000-watt transmitter tower. It stands 310m over the city and visitors can access the 200m-high observation deck.

It's a great place to bring kids, and it offers excellent views of the entire city and environs. Individual or group tours can be arranged any time, but there's one fixed every Saturday at 2pm. To reach the TV Antenna from Petrogradskaya metro, take trolleybus No 31 (or bus No 10, 71 or 128) north for two stops. Walk down to the Kantemirovsky most, turn right and walk to the gates facing the river.

TOY MUSEUM Map pp238-9

Muzey Igrushki; ☎ 234 4312; nab Reki Karpovki 32; 🕑 11am-6pm Tue-Sun; metro Petrogradskaya

Since 1997, this privately run museum has been collecting toys from all over Russia and presenting them in three different sections – folk toys, factory toys and those made by skilled artisans. Examples of the latter category include toys made in Sergiev Posad, home of the ubiquitous *matryoshka* (nesting doll), a creation that is often assumed to be far older than it is, being created for the first time only in the 19th century. The Toy Museum is charming and often has very interesting temporary ...xhibits too.

...Y MUSEUM Map pp238-9

...ina 52, flat 24; adult/student ...-6pm, closed Sun & Wed; ...aya

... building (known locally as the ...e' due to its uncanny similarities ... to a large cruise liner) was built in ... height of St Petersburg's lust for *style ...e*. It would otherwise be unremarkable ...t not for the fact that Lenin's wife's family ... here and the great revolutionary himself ... low here before the revolution while organising the workers.

Even if your interest in Lenin is very limited, this is an interesting chance to see inside a bourgeois Petrograd apartment with its delightful turn-of-the-20th-century fittings. The bathroom – where you'll be told with great solemnity that Vladimir Ilyich had a daily splash – is particularly fascinating, as is the original telephone that today still bears Lenin's home phone number on it.

KIROVSKY ISLANDS

This is the collective name for the three outer delta islands of the Petrograd Side – Kamenny, Yelagin and Krestovsky. Once marshy jungles, the islands were granted to 18th- and 19th-century court favourites and developed into elegant playgrounds. Still mostly parkland, they're leafy venues for picnics, river sports and white nights' cavorting; this is the city's oasis.

...ank You For Shopping at W WATERSTONE'S www.waterstones.co.uk

KAMENNY ISLAND Map pp238-9

This island's charm, seclusion and century-old *dachas* (now inhabited by the wealthy, or by the St Petersburg mafiagentsia), combined with winding lanes and a series of canals, lakes and ponds, make a stroll here pleasant at any time of year. At the east end of the island the **Church of St John the Baptist** (1776–81) has been charmingly restored. Behind it the big, classical **Kamennoostrovsky Palace**, built by Catherine the Great for her son, is now a weedy military sanatorium.

KRESTOVSKY ISLAND Map pp238-9

The biggest Kirovsky island, this island consists mostly of the vast **Seaside Park of Victory** (Primorsky Park Pobedy), also pleasant for a walk dotted with sports fields, and the 100,000-seat **Kirov Stadium**. There's not much else to see, although it's useful for transport, having the Krestovsky Ostrov metro station at its centre.

YELAGIN ISLAND Map pp238-9

The whole of Yelagin Island is a park – it's a delightful car-free zone and a fantastic place to wander and relax in summer. Free on weekdays, there's a token fee of R10 at weekends and on public holidays to enter the grounds.

This island's centrepiece is the **Yelagin Palace** (1818–22), built by Rossi for Alexander I's mother, Empress Maria. Rossi also landscaped the entire island for her. The palace is to your right as you cross the footbridge from Kamenny Island.

The very beautiful restored interiors of the **main house** (☎ 430 1131; 1 Yelagin ostrov; adult/student R60/30; 🕒 10am-6pm Wed-Sun) include old furnishings on loan from the Grand Europe and Astoria hotels; don't miss the stupendous 1890s carved-walnut study ensemble from Europe and the incredible inlaid-wood floors. Other nearby estate buildings sometimes have exhibitions, too.

The rest of the island is a lovely network of paths, greenery, lakes and channels – you can rent rowing boats at the northern end of the island – and a plaza at the west end looking out to the Gulf of Finland. Sunsets are resplendent from here. Several small cafés are open in summer.

VYBORG SIDE

Eating p152; Shopping p172; Sleeping pp182–3

Peter the Great had no apparent interest in the far side of the Neva and today, beyond the embankment and Finland Station, among the factories and railway lines, there are few attractions. But there's certainly more than meets the eye, including the mass graves of the blockade victims at the Piskaryovskoe Cemetery, the wonderful Sampsonievsky Cathedral and the world's most northerly Buddhist temple.

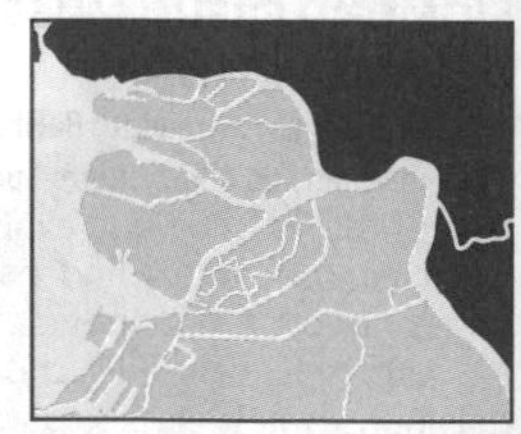

BUDDHIST TEMPLE Map pp238-9

☎ 239 0341, 430 0341; Primorsky pr 91; metro Staraya Derevnya

This beautiful *datsan* (temple) was built between 1909 and 1915 at the instigation of Pyotr Badmaev, a Buddhist physician to Tsar Nicholas II. Money was raised from all over Russia, and as far afield as Thailand and England, by various Buddhist organisations and even gained the support of the Dalai Lama in Lhasa.

The communists shut the temple, arrested many of the monks and used the building as a military radio station until the 1960s when it was taken over by the Zoological Institute and employed as laboratories (the Soviets thrived on using religious buildings for purposes that were particularly humiliating). Thankfully, however, the damage was not particularly profound and the *datsan* was returned to the city's small Buddhist community in 1990, since when it has been renovated. Services are held at 10am daily. Visitors are welcome, although it's best to avoid the services.

FINLAND STATION Map pp240-1

☎ 168 7539; pl Lenina 6; metro Pl Lenina

The Finland Station (Finlyandsky Vokzal) is where Lenin finally arrived in 1917 after 17 years in exile abroad. Here, in the square where his statue now stands, he gave his legendary speech from the top of an armoured car to a crowd who had only heard of but never seen the man. After fleeing a second time he again arrived here from Finland, this time disguised as a railway fireman, and the locomotive he rode in is displayed on the platform. It's not really the same station, as

Transport

Distances are vast on the Vyborg Side, and despite two metro lines and some 14 stations serving it, there can often be big distances to cover on foot. Most useful are the stations Staraya Derevnya and Ploshchad Lenina, both near the Neva and some major sights.

it was in the 1970s in the drabbest possible Soviet style. However, its historic resonance makes it worth a look. Walk out onto the square that still bears Lenin's name and you'll see a marvellous statue of the man himself at the far end.

KRESTY PRISON MUSEUM Map pp246-9

☎ 542 6861, 542 4735; Arsenalnaya nab 7; admission R200 plus passport as security; tours noon, 1.30pm & 3pm Sat & Sun; metro Pl Lenina

Kresty is St Petersburg's main holding prison; if you're busted here, Kresty's where they take you to await whatever it is that awaits you. You wouldn't want to find out: originally opened in 1892 with 1150 individual cells (later reconstructed and designed to hold 2065 inmates), now close to 10,000 poor buggers call it 'home'. Six-bed cells hold 10 to 15 people, sleeping in rotation.

Tours are possible of the prison and small museum. This definitely constitutes a unique day out in the city. You'll be led through the church on the premises, through some of the holding areas, into the inner courtyards where you'll get cat-called by the inmates peeking at you through slats in their cells, and into a great little museum where you'll learn about the past residents (like Trotsky and the entire Provisional Government from 1917). There are also art objects made by prisoners with lots of time on their hands.

Most impressive is a beautiful chess set with a cops and robbers motif made entirely from glazed bits of hardened, chewed bread. Bring your passport and leave your camera at home.

If you opt out of the tour, on any given day you can see inmates' friends and family members lining Arsenalnaya nab and communicating with their incarcerated dear ones. Wives and girlfriends move their arms in what may look like intricate dance moves, but what is in fact a crude code, known to inmates and prison guards alike.

The prisoner makes himself known by holding an article of clothing out the window (only their hands are visible, stuck through the slats or holes in the steel mesh). When the friend down on the street identifies their man, they start waving their arms about, tracing Cyrillic characters in the air. The prisoner waves up and down to signal 'I understand', and side to side to signal 'repeat'.

The inmates have a better way of communicating. Notice those bits of folded newspaper littering the pavement? It's not trash – Russians are neater than that. These have all been flown over from inside the prison with a blowpipe, with a written message folded inside. If you see one of these flying towards you, duck – they fly quick and painfully. Police regularly patrol the embankment and will shoo you away if they think you're lingering.

PISKARYOVSKOE CEMETERY

Map p237

☎ 247 5716; pr Nepokoryonnikh 72; 🕑 10am-5pm; metro Lesnaya/Pl Muzhestva

It's hard work getting to this rather remote cemetery, but as the main place of burial for the victims of the Nazi blockade in WWII, it's an important pilgrimage (it was always one of the first destinations on Intourist bus tours of the city during Soviet times, especially for German tourists).

Originally what is now the cemetery was just an enormous pit where unnamed and unmarked bodies were dumped. Some half a million people were laid to rest here in mass graves between 1941 and 1943. In 1960 the remodelled cemetery was opened and has been an integral part of the city's soul ever since. Every year on Victory Day (9 May) the cemetery is packed out with mourners, many of whom survived the blockade or lost close relatives to starvation.

Entering the main gates, the most striking thing is the music being pumped out of speakers: the ambience is kept solemn yet defiant by, among other symphonic works, Shostakovich's Seventh, which was composed during the blockade and was performed in besieged Leningrad by an emaciated orchestra, several of whom were unable to hold their instruments for the duration of the piece, due to their weakness. As you walk down the main pathway to the statue of an understandably horrified Mother Russia, the scale of the holocaust visited on wartime Leningrad becomes apparent. Very few people make it out here these days and its emptiness, especially on a grey and wet day, is striking. The inscription on the far wall behind Mother Russia is a poem by Olga Bergolts who survived the blockade herself. It reads:

Here lie the people of Leningrad
Here are the citizens – men, women and children –
And besides them the Red Army soldiers
Who gave their lives
Defending you, Leningrad,
Cradle of the Revolution,
Their noble names we cannot number
So many lie beneath the eternal granite
But of those honoured by this stone
Let no one forget
Let nothing be forgotten.

From Lesnaya metro station turn right and walk down the street about 100m and take bus No 123, K-385 or K-33. These go to the Piskaryovka train station, from where it's a further 10 to 15 minutes to walk to the cemetery itself. It may be easier to take a cab from Lesnaya station (reckon on about R150 each way). Getting back to the centre is far easier, *marshrutkas* and buses stop outside the cemetery and will all take you to various metro stations.

SAMPSONIEVSKY CATHEDRAL

Map pp240-1

☎ 315 4361; 41 Bolshaya Sampsonievsky pr; adult/concession R200/100; metro Vyborgskaya

This fascinating pea-green baroque church dates from 1740 and is a beautiful highlight of a remarkably dull industrial area of the Vyborg Side, well worth the trip out here. It's most famous as the place where Catherine the Great is believed to have married her one-eyed lover Grigory Potemkin in 1774 in a secret ceremony attended by just a couple of other people.

Today it's a delightful place, having been repainted and restored to its original glory on the outside. Restoration on the inside is continuing and the job so far has been astonishing. The church's most interesting feature is the calendar of saints, two enormous panels on either side of the nave, each representing six months of the year and every day decorated with a mini-icon of its saint(s). The enormous silver chandelier above the altar is also something to behold, as is the stunning baroque, green and golden iconostasis. Also look out for the handsome frieze of Peter the Great facing the central altar. Move over St Isaac's – this is how to decorate a baroque church with style.

SITE OF PUSHKIN'S DUEL Map p237

Mesto duela AS Pushkina; Kolomyazhsky pr; metro Chyornaya Rechka

This is a point of literary pilgrimage for those who mourn the loss of Russia's poetic genius, Alexander Pushkin, senselessly lost in a duel with the Frenchman Georges d'Antès in 1837. The story has developed a certain mythology around it in the past two centuries: having eaten his final meal at the now *über*–tourist trap Literatornoye Kafe on Nevsky, Pushkin set off by sled on 27 January to this remote piece of woodland to meet d'Antès, a nobleman who has been dismissed as a tsarist stooge, a homosexual and a spy (and possibly all three) by generations of Russian historians. D'Antès had been making public overtures to Natalia Goncharova, Pushkin's wife, and the poet finally decided he had to defend his honour. Pushkin was shot here and after two days of agony, he died at home at his flat on the Moyka. A marble monument now stands on the place where Pushkin was shot and there are always fresh flowers here.

SOUTHERN ST PETERSBURG

Sleeping pp183–4

You have to look relatively hard amid the vast Soviet housing estates, but do so and you'll find plenty of interest to the south of St Petersburg's city centre. This area was picked by Stalin to be the centre of his new Leningrad (he hated the tsarist associations of the historic heart) and from the 1930s building a new city centre began here in earnest. The war and then reconstruction slowed the process down, the plans finally being shelved after Stalin's death in 1953, and his proposed city centre was never completed. However, fascinating testaments to the plan such as the House of Soviets still remain.

Transport

The south of St Petersburg is well served by three metro lines and some 18 stations, making it extremely easy to get to from the centre of the city.

CHESME CHURCH Map p237

☎ 443 6114; ul Lensoveta 12; admission free; 🕑 10am-7pm; metro Moskovskaya

One of the city's most wonderful buildings, this red-and-white Gothic shocker looks not unlike a boiled sweet, with long, vertical white stripes giving the impression that it's rising straight up from the earth like a mirage and shooting upwards. Designed by Yury Felten, it was built between 1777 and 1780 in honour of the Battle of Çesme (1770). The church's remote location is due to the fact that Catherine was on this spot when news arrived of her great victory over the Turks. Ever capricious, Catherine ordered that a shrine be built on the spot to preserve this great moment in Russian history. It now seems particularly incongruous with its surroundings, as Stalin's ill-fated city centre has since grown up around it.

While it's definitely more visually impressive from the outside, do go inside to see some of the icons including a beautiful painting of Christ's arrival in Nazareth.

CHURCH OF THE ASSUMPTION

Map pp242-3

Ul Dvinskaya 7; admission free; 🕑 9am-6pm; metro Narvskaya

This unexpected gem of a church in the city's docklands is a real find. When Tsarevitch Nikolai (later Nicholas II, the last Romanov tsar) was attacked by a Japanese fanatic while on a tour of Asia in 1891, he sustained a serious blow to the head but miraculously survived. The customs officers of St Petersburg's docklands gathered money and constructed a bell tower in thanks for the saving of the heir to the throne.

The church was sanctified in 1899, and the imperial family would annually come here to attend a service of thanksgiving for Nicholas's deliverance. The church was shut from 1935 to 1991. Since its reopening a restoration programme has been under way – the portico and inner cupola have already been fully restored, as have the wonderful golden onion domes that shimmer incongruously in this, one of St Petersburg's most industrial suburbs.

HOUSE OF SOVIETS Map p237

Moskovsky pr 212; not open to the public; metro Moskovskaya

No building in the city can compare in terms of sheer staggering bombast to this Stalinist beauty (or beast, depending on your take). Planned to be the central administrative building of Leningrad when Stalin demanded the city centre be moved south, it was built with the leader's neoclassical tastes in mind. Begun by Noi Trotsky in 1936, although not finished until after the war (by which time Trotsky had been purged), this magnificently sinister building is a great example of Stalinist design with its columns and bas-reliefs. The enormous frieze that runs across the top of the vast building is enormously impressive even now.

The House of Soviets dominates the vast square before it, which features a 1970 bronze statue of Lenin. The House of Soviets was never used as the Leningrad government building as the plan was shelved after Stalin's death in 1953. Today it houses the Moskovsky Region's local administration.

House of Soviets and Lenin statue (above)

KANONERSKY ISLAND Map p237

An original option for a day's walk or picnic is to head to the remote, grassy tip of this island in the city's southwest to watch the big boats head out into the Gulf of Finland. The island once served as part of the city's defence and a shooting training ground, and since 1883 a ship-repairing factory has been located on it. Taking taxibus No 115 outside Sadovaya ul 39 (at Sennaya pl), you get to go under the only tunnel linking two islands in the city. After the last stop, walk for 40 minutes to the very tip of the island. You'll need good shoes, as there's a bit of climbing over rocks involved, but the views are worth it.

MOSCOW TRIUMPHAL ARCH

Map p237

Pl Moskovskiye Vorota; metro Moskovskiye Vorota

The iron Triumphal Arch, 3.5km from the city centre and looking very much like Berlin's Brandenburg Gate but somewhat less than grand in its surroundings, was built by Stasov in 1838 to mark victories over Turks, Persians and Poles. Demolished in 1936, it was rebuilt between 1959 and 1961. Local legend has it that the gate is built on the spot where travellers entering the city in the earliest days had to show that they had brought bricks or stones to be used in the construction of buildings.

MUSEUM OF RAILWAY TECHNOLOGY

Map pp242-3

118 Nab Obvodnogo Kanala; adult/child R150/80; metro Baltiyskaya

A huge treat for trainspotters that lurks in a rather forgotten lot behind the now gutted Warsaw Station, this museum is a wonderful collection of Russian locomotives from the 19th and 20th centuries, including a dining carriage you can go into and some truly ancient steam engines from the late 19th century. Great for kids, too. From Baltiyskaya metro station, walk past the front of the Warsaw Station (with its huge **Lenin statue**) and turn right before the church, making your way through industrial wasteland and you'll eventually find this little gem.

NARVA TRIUMPHAL GATES Map pp242-3

Narvskaya pl; metro Narvskaya

Just outside the Narvskaya metro station you'll see the Narva Triumphal Gates, built between 1827 and 1834 by Stasov as a tribute to Alexander I's defeat of Napoleon in 1812. Standing proudly at one of the city's old gates, this 12-columned monolith is crowned with an angel of victory and decorated with an assembly of valiant warriors.

PLOSHCHAD POBEDY Map p237

Pl Pobedy (Victory Sq), the intended central square of Stalin's Leningrad, is one of the first sights of the city that visitors see on the road from the airport to the city centre, making a deeply Soviet impression for a town as imperial as St Petersburg! The square now houses the vast **Monument to the Heroic Defenders of Leningrad** (☎ 293 6036; Pl Pobedy; admission free; ⏲ 10am-5pm Thu-Tue). This is one of the city's must-see exhibits. Centred around a 48m-high obelisk, the monument (unveiled in 1975) is a sculptural ensemble of bronze statues symbolising the heavy plight of defence and eventual victory. The front line was only 9km from this spot. On a lower level, a bronze ring 40m in diameter symbolises the city's encirclement; a very moving sculpture stands in the centre. Haunting symphonic music creates a sombre atmosphere to guide you downstairs to the underground exhibition in a huge, mausoleum-like interior. Here the glow of 900 bronze lamps creates an eeriness matched by the sound of a metronome (the only sound heard by Leningraders on their radios throughout the war save for emergency announcements), showing that the city's heart was still beating. Large bronze sheets form the Chronicle; changed daily, these are engraved with the events in Leningrad on each day of the blockade. Twelve thematically assembled showcases feature items from the war and siege. An electrified relief map in the centre of the room shows the shifting front lines of the war. Ask to see the two seven-minute documentary films. From metro Moskovskaya, it's a 10-minute walk south.

YEKATERINGOFF PARK Map pp242-3

metro Narvskaya

Just west of metro Narvskaya, along ul Perekopskaya, is the sprawling Yekateringoff Park. Peter the Great had a magnificent wooden palace built here for his wife Catherine in 1711, which was completely destroyed by fire in 1924 after the Soviets had turned it into a party house for young workers. The park, laid out by Montferrand in the 1820s, was later named after the 30th anniversary of the Communist Youth League (a super kitsch statue remains). Today it's a pleasant place for a stroll. There's a children's playground too.

Walking Tours

Walking Tours

St Petersburg is a city that demands to be savoured, and walking here is a delight once you get off the main, traffic-heavy routes. There are over 300 bridges connecting more than 40 islands, a vast river that splits into four, and charming green spaces. The walks outlined in this chapter will drag you away from Nevsky pr to see parts of the city that many casual visitors may miss.

PETER'S CITY

It's hard to imagine this enormous city three centuries ago when the Neva was unbridged and nearly everything else was green, open space. However, many of the buildings Peter built survive today and this walk will help you get to know some of the more interesting ones.

The city known as Sankt Pieterburkh was founded on Zayachy Island, which is where the walk starts, within the walls of the city's first defensive installation, the **Peter and Paul Fortress 1** (p114). Make sure you check out Peter's last resting place in the **SS Peter and Paul Cathedral 2** (p114), and spare a thought for his tragically ill-fated son Alexei, who Peter tortured to death, convinced that he was planning to overthrow him and reverse his programme of Westernisation. He's buried in a crypt below the cathedral that is closed to the public. For a less than flattering look at Peter be sure to look at Mikhail Shemyakin's hyperbolic **statue 3** of a seated, elongated Peter, unveiled in the 1990s in the fortress' courtyard.

Walk Facts

Best time A sunny day to get the best views as you cross the Neva
Start Peter and Paul Fortress
End Menshikov Palace
Food en route Lunch at Restoran (p150) would be suitably imperial
Drink en route Relax with a coffee or cocktail at Russky Kitsch (p150)
Distance About 4km
Time About 2½ hours

Come out of the fortress over the **Lannovsky most 4** and onto **Troitskaya pl 5** (Trinity Sq). This was the intended central square of Peter's city, the centrepiece of which was the enormous Trinity Cathedral, where Peter attended mass when he was in the city but which was later destroyed. The city's most popular pub, the Four Frigates (Peter was a regular!) stood on the square, and this was where the populace would gather to hear edicts, watch executions and enjoy fireworks on feast days.

Bliny kiosk, near Peter and Paul Fortress

Cross the square, on which the most striking building today is the **Mosque 6** (p113) – certainly not there in Peter's day! – and wander down the Petrovskaya embankment to see **Peter's Cabin 7** (p115), generally accepted to have been the first proper structure in the city, and considered by many to be the city's soul. As late as 1941, Soviet soldiers took oaths of loyalty here, swearing to protect the city from the Germans.

Walking back down the embankment, head across the **Troitsky most 8** from where you'll have a magnificent vista of the city

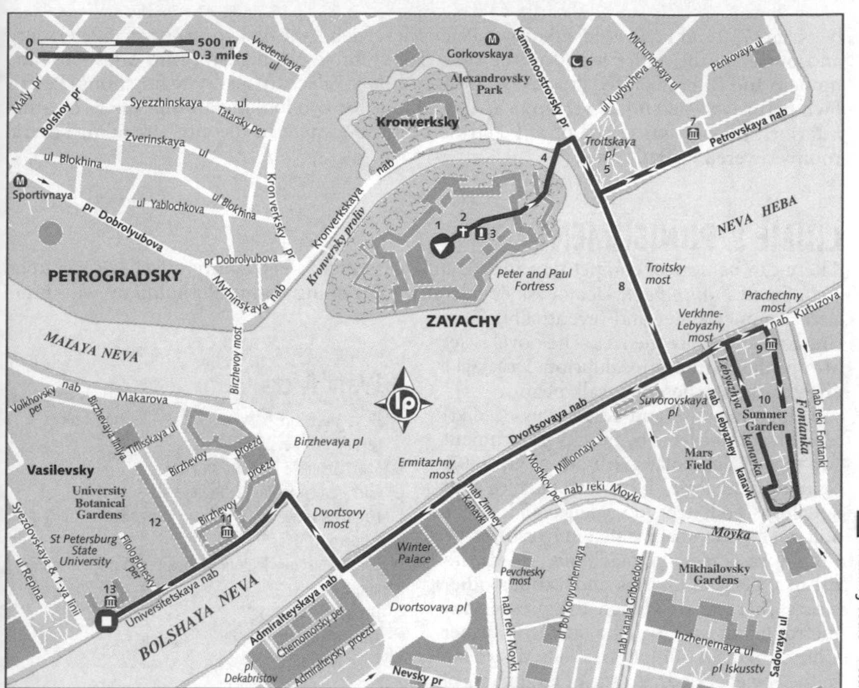

at its most impressively Venetian. This view would please Peter today, as he longed to have the Neva as the centrepiece of the city. However, the bridge itself would not have pleased the tsar – he refused to build bridges across the river, preferring people to use boats instead. Peter passionately believed that his subjects should be familiar with sailing (his greatest passion) and therefore hoped that a lack of bridges would instil an interest among the population. Instead locals congregated on the Admiralty Side, the reason it's the centre of the city today.

On the other side of the river, turn left and follow the embankment until you reach the **Summer Palace 9** (p90), Peter's main residence in the city that stands perfectly preserved in the delightful **Summer Garden 10** (p90); visit the modest Summer Palace before wandering in the garden for a while, imagining the garden parties that Peter and Catherine would have given here for the court, Peter nearly always dressing in his favourite outfit, that of a sailor. Wander out of the garden and walk down the Neva embankment, past the incredible architectural ensemble of the Winter Palace and cross the Dvortsovy most to Vasilevsky Island. Here, take time to visit the **Museum of Anthropology and Ethnography 11** (p109), Russia's first museum, set up by Peter to rid the Russian people of their backwards and superstitious ways by displaying various samples from Peter's extensive collection of preserved, malformed babies. To lure people here, Peter paid for free vodka and wine to be distributed to the visitors, unfortunately something that the modern management have not seen fit to continue.

Continue east to the **Twelve Colleges 12** (p111), a signifcant institution for Peter who had Trezzini begin the magnificent structure in 1722. Peter based his bureaucracy here, and while the separate entrances for each ministry signified their independence, the unified façade highlighted collective responsibility and aims. It is now part of St Petersburg State University.

Continue to the **Menshikov Palace 13** (p109), the last sight on the walk, further down the embankment. Imagine how this vast stone building (St Petersburg's first) must have looked against the open green spaces and ramshackle workers' huts when it was first constructed between 1710 and 1720. Menshikov was Peter's best friend, the first governor of St Petersburg and owner of the entire island at the time. His humble origins gave him a taste for the opulent and Peter tolerated this, using the Menshikov Palace to host state functions (Peter's own palace was functional yet tiny). Spend an hour or two looking around the fascinating interiors, the best preserved of any Petrine décor anywhere in the city, including several rooms covered in Delft tiles.

CRIME & PUNISHMENT

There can be no real competition for the quintessential St Petersburg novel – it has to be *Crime and Punishment*, Dostoevsky's tale of the brooding young Raskolnikov who murders a moneylender and (eventually) faces the dramatic consequences. The novel is set around the gloriously insalubrious **Sennaya pl 1** (Haymarket), where the walk begins.

With a massive (and desperately needed) face-lift administered by the city government for the tricentennial celebrations in 2003, Sennaya's historically notorious filth and squalor is no longer in evidence and yet it's still not hard to imagine that in Dostoevsky's time it was a teeming madhouse, filled with drunks, beggars, thieves and various other sleazy characters. Though the present-day metro station is built on the site of the former Church of the Assumption (1760s; destroyed in the Soviet period), the major landmarks of the day were seedy pubs and inns.

Walk Facts

Best time On busy weekdays the area retains a certain Dostoevskian menace
Start Sennaya Pl metro station
End Srednyaya Podyacheskaya ul
Food en route Have a cheap but delicious lunch at Sumeto (p149)
Drink en route End up at Stolle (p156) for a coffee and cake
Distance 1km
Time About an hour, including stops

The border between reality and fantasy has been smudged irrevocably here: Petersburgers will point out where Dostoevsky lived as quickly as they will the homes of his protagonist Raskolnikov and the old pawnbroker. And snatches of the grim reality of slum life in the mid-19th century can still be gleaned during an hour's walk. The omnipresent stray cats – as permanent a fixture in St Petersburg courtyards as dim light and foul odours – are the gatekeepers to a neighbourhood whose gloominess and squalor have been preserved well enough to make it instantly recognisable, even to Fyodor himself.

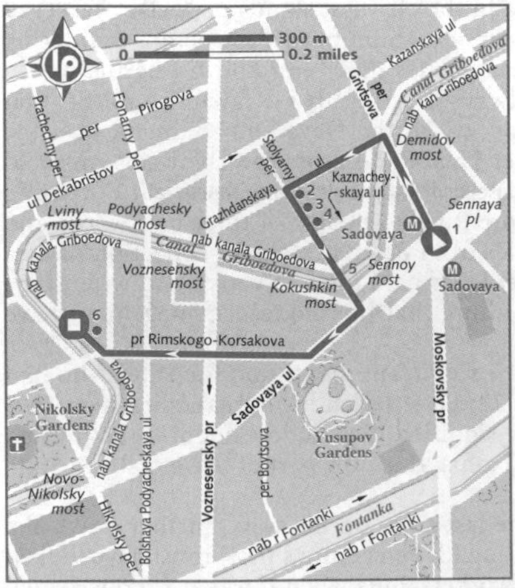

From Sennaya pl, start walking north on per Grivtsova, across the canal, and turn left onto Grazhdanskaya ul and continue to the next corner – **No 5 Stolyarny per 2** is one of the two possible locations of Raskolnikov's attic. The building bears marble plaques in Russian and German marking the waterline reached by the great flood of 7 November 1824, immortalised in Pushkin's poem, *The Bronze Horseman*. There's a plaque that says something to the effect of 'The tragic fate of the people of this area of St Petersburg formed the foundation of Dostoevsky's passionate sermon of goodness for all mankind'. Unfortunately, the door to the stairwell is locked. Those who claim that this is the place go further, saying that Rodya (the diminutive of Raskolnikov's first name, Rodyon) retrieved the murder weapon from a street-sweeper's storage bin inside the tunnel leading to the courtyard.

From that corner, turn south onto Stolyarny per (simply called 'S… lane' in the book) where, at **No 9 3**, you can enter the building of the second possible, and most likely, address. Walk through the tunnel, turn right, use entrance No 2 (up the crumbling stone steps), and walk up four flights until the stairwell ceiling opens upward. Graffiti on the wall (frequently overpainted) often reads, 'Don't Kill, Rodya'. Rodya's flat would have been the padlocked attic on the left-hand side of the 5th floor. In Dostoevsky's time, there were 18 drinking establishments on nearby Stolyarny per alone!

Keep going south along Stolyarny per until you reach ul Kaznacheyskaya. Dostoevsky lived in **three flats 4** on this tiny street alone: from 1861 to 1863 at No 1, and from 1864 to 1867 at No 7. It was from this flat that he wrote *Crime and Punishment*. Dostoevsky spent one month living in the faded red building at No 9, before moving to No 7. It's easy to imagine how he must have been inspired by the human zoo around him to write his dark story.

From whichever flat Raskolnikov lived, he went down Stolyarny per towards the Griboedova Canal. He crossed the **Kokushkin most 5**, where he would stand and gaze into the canal, deep in thought.

Murderer yes, orienteering student no; the route to the pawnbroker's house taken by Rodya is circuitous. After you cross the canal, head straight to Sadovaya ul then turn right. Make your first right turn into pr Rimskogo-Korsakova. Cross Voznesensky pr, and then continue past Bolshaya Podyacheskaya ul and Srednyaya Podyacheskaya; the **pawnbroker's building 6** sits between there and the canal embankment.

The entrance to the building's courtyard is a bit further north on the embankment at nab kanala Griboedova 104. Enter the dank, pot-holed tunnel and head straight for entrance No 5 (flats 22–81).

The building's residents are used to people entering the building to get a look. In fact, brass balls at the corners of the iron banisters are there specifically for visitors, and they end just after the 3rd floor, where her flat (No 74) is on the right-hand side. After the murder, the suspect ran through the tunnel leading to Srednyaya Podyacheskaya.

THE NORTHERN ISLANDS

This is a great way to enjoy the scenery of the Krestovsky Islands and to see some of the quirkier sights of the city as well. Begin the walk at the Chyornaya Rechka metro station, and look out for the **statue of Pushkin 1** that stands on the platform, usually adorned with flowers of some kind. The poet met his end as the result of a duel with the French nobleman d'Antès in woods a short walk away from here.

From the station, turn right down ul Akademika Krylova, walking away from the Chyornaya Rechka (Black Stream). During the late 19th and early 20th centuries there were many factories on the Vyborg Side and the foul industrial by-products pouring into the stream gave the waterway its name.

Walk Facts

Best time Summer
Start Chyornaya Rechka metro station
End Russkaya Rybalka restaurant
Drink en route Beer gardens at Kirov Park
Distance 7km
Time About three hours

Go through the underpass below pr Ushakovskaya and cross the Ushakovsky most over the Bolshaya Nevka, from where there are lovely views of Kamenny (Stone) Island. Look out for the recently restored **Church of St John the Baptist 2** immediately on your left at the end of the bridge and wander through the woods to the **Kamennoostrovsky Palace 3** (p116), which was a gift from Catherine the Great to her son Paul. Obviously lacking somewhat in filial gratitude, Paul was so remarkably bitter about his mother's long reign that he repaid her by decreeing that no woman could ever be Russia's sovereign again.

Make your way down the lovely Malaya Nevka embankment where you'll pass the **Sphinx Monuments 4** on the river bank. Follow the road through the woodland to one of the city's most loved sights, **Peter's Tree 5**, a now-dead oak that stands in the middle of the Krestovka embankment, said to have been planted here by Peter the Great in the city's early years when Kamenny Island was a complete wilderness. It's now unfortunately surrounded by traffic.

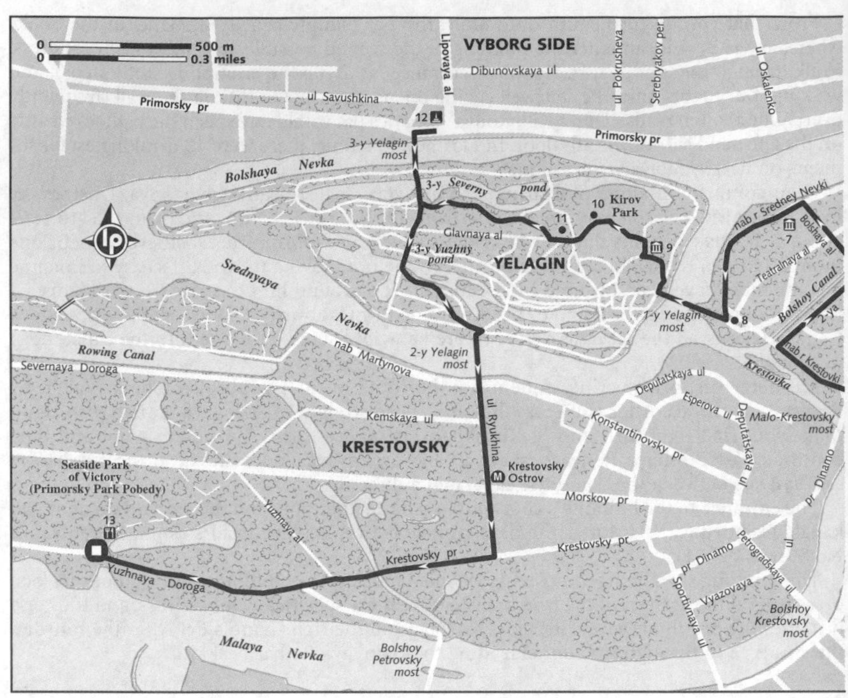

Head along the embankment and down 2-ya Beryozovaya alleya. This lovely street is crammed with 19th-century mansions and villas where the city's rich either lived or had weekend retreats. It's now been taken over by Russia's new aristocrats – yes, the black-windowed BMW classes have co-opted some of these charming houses and either refitted them, or in some scandalous cases, ripped them down and started from scratch. There are several horrific transgressions of good taste here, although some of the new rich have carefully restored these mansions to their former glory. Cross the charming little bridge over the Bolshoy Canal and carry on up Bolshaya al where you'll pass some more charming mansions, including the vast *dacha* (summer house) given over to housing the **Danish Consulate 6** and the fabulous neoclassical **Polovtsev House 7**. Make your way along the embankment to the **Old Theatre Square 8**. The charming building facing to one side of the square would make a superb restoration project for anyone with a few million lying around, and even in its dilapidated state it is quite appealing.

Cross the 1-y Yelagin most (don't be put off by the military-style checkpoint, the barrier is just to ensure that nobody drives onto Yelagin Island which is for pedestrians only). You'll need to pay a token R10 if it's the weekend or a public holiday to gain access. As you cross the bridge you'll see the white neoclassical **Yelagin Palace 9** (p116) designed by Rossi, his first major project for Empress Maria Fyodorovna, mother of Alexander I. Look around inside before continuing the walk around this island, which has something of a holiday-camp feel to it. In classic Russian style, music is pumped out in many of the most isolated, bucolic spots and young couples amble away the afternoon with a couple of bottles of beer and a packet of cigarettes. There are plenty of places to enjoy a beer or to get lost in the woods. Make your way along the pathway behind the back of the **kitchen buildings 10** and **palace stables 11** and wander past the ponds to the 3-y Yelagin most where you can cross back onto the Vyborg Side briefly to visit the fascinating **Buddhist temple 12** (p116) located on Primorsky pr.

Retrace your steps back onto the island, and continue round the ponds, to the southern side of the island. Stop off here for a drink and maybe rent a rowboat to while away some

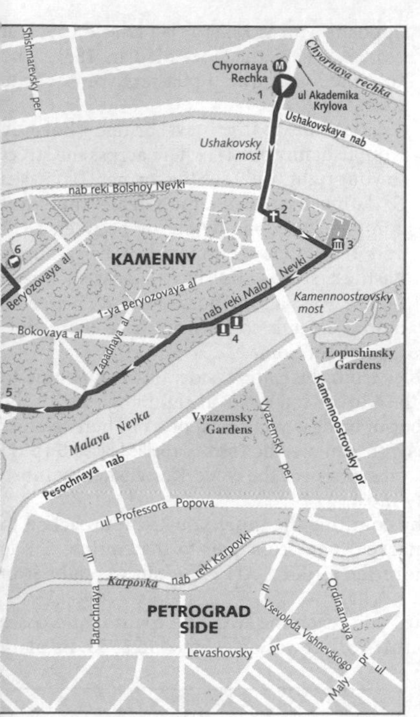

time. Finally, cross onto Krestovsky Island, the last of the three Kirov islands, and carry on straight down to the Krestovsky Ostrov metro station. You can end the walk here or continue for about 1.5km down Krestovsky pr to **Russkaya Rybalka 13** (p152), one of the city's best fish restaurants.

IMPERIAL LUXURY

The most perfect way of seeing Dvortsovaya pl (Palace Sq) and the Hermitage for the first time is to approach them via Bolshaya Morskaya ul. As you turn the corner, behold the **Alexander Column 1**, with the Hermitage complex in the background, perfectly framed under the triumphal double arch. Keep walking towards the square, keeping your eyes fixed on the column and enjoy the visual magic tricks as the perspective changes the closer you get to the arches' opening. Head northeast to the start of Millionnaya ul, and into the **porch 2** covering the southern entrance of the New Hermitage. This was the museum's first public entrance when it opened in 1852. The New Hermitage is one of several buildings in the city with a façade supported by semi-clad musclemen.

Walking northeast again, make the first right turn and walk along the Winter Canal the short block to the Moyka River (glance behind you towards the Neva for another great view). This stretch of the Moyka is lovely. To your right, Nevsky pr is crossed by the Zelyony most, and across Nevsky, catch a glimpse of the **Stroganov Palace 3** (p97). Turn left and walk along the side of the river, past the French Consulate at nab reki Moyki 15. Diagonally

Yelagin Palace (p116)

Walk Facts

Best time Early morning before the crowds arrive
Start Intersection of Bolshaya Morskaya ul and Nevsky pr
End Bankovsky most
Food en route Tinkoff (p145)
Drink en route Kofe Haus (p156)
Distance About 1km
Time About one hour, not counting stops

opposite you is **Pushkin's last home** 4 (p93) at No 12, where the poet died in 1837. The six fluted Corinthian pilasters you see date from the 1770s.

Continue to the next bridge (Bolshoy Konyushenny most), where across the street to your right you'll see the former **Court Stables** 5, dating from Peter the Great's time, but completely redone by Stasov between 1817 and 1823. One of imperial St Petersburg's flashiest streets, Bolshaya Konyushennaya ul (the Russian for horse is 'kon'; hence its name) extends south from here. Turgenev, Rimsky-Korsakov and Chernyshevsky all called this street home.

Continue along the river, looking at the stables from their north side, until you come to a very picturesque ensemble of bridges where the Moyka intersects at right angles with the start of the Griboedova Canal. Count the number of bridges you can spot from here. Across the top of the touristy souvenir kiosk canopies you can see the **Church on Spilled Blood** 6 (p91) looming in the foreground. Head towards this, crossing over the Malo Konyushenny most, which itself is connected to the pretty Teatralny most.

See how much of a foreigner you look like by counting the times you are approached to buy items as you pass through the souvenir market, then cross over to the church. Circle around the church towards your left and admire the striking Art Nouveau wrought-iron fence of the Mikhailovsky Gardens.

Walk south along the Griboedova Canal until you reach the sweet footpath that crosses the canal. Called the **Italyansky most** 7, it dates from 1896, but was redesigned in 1955. Its main purpose seems to be affording photographers a postcard-perfect view of the Church on Spilled Blood. Note the amazing building on the west side of the street at No 13. Originally the **House of the Joint Credit Society** 8 and built in 1890, its richly dressed central cupola was placed to give the appearance of a grand palace.

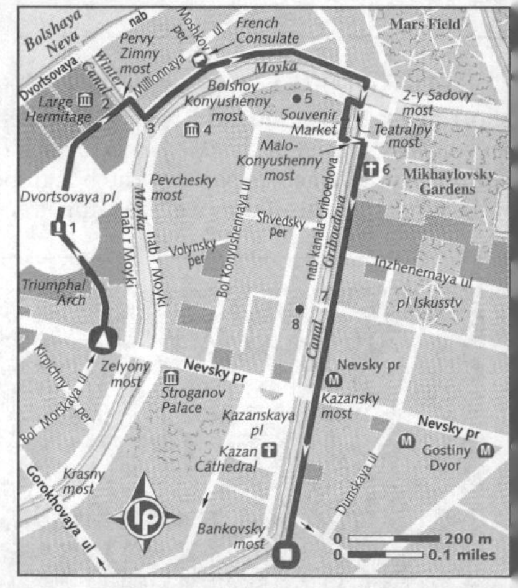

Continue walking down to Nevsky pr, where the old Singer sewing machine company building stands regally on the corner. Cross Nevsky toward the Kazan Cathedral and head to the next bridge, no doubt St Petersburg's most picturesque and most photographed, the Bankovsky most (1826). The cables of this 25.2m-long bridge are supported by four cast-iron gryphons with golden wings. Carry on for a spot of lunch at Tinkoff (p145) on Kazanskaya ul, some way beyond the cathedral.

BEAUTY IN DECAY

Taking in some of the city's most atmospheric ruins, this walk begins on Isaakievskaya pl (St Isaac's Sq). Opposite Hotel Astoria at No 11 is the **former German embassy** 1 (1911), a stunning building done in solid half-columns of granite blocks. There used to be a stone equestrian ensemble on top of the building that was pushed off the roof during anti-German demonstrations at the outbreak of WWI.

Around the corner and a few steps away at 43 Bolshaya Morskaya ul is the **former Italian embassy** 2; Auguste Montferrand built this in 1849 as a mansion for industrialist Demidov. It's now the property of Petrovsky Bank, which hasn't done much to repair the glorious but crumbling Atlantes out the front that are doing their best to keep the whole thing up. Continue down Bolshaya Morskaya ul to the next corner. On the southwest corner you'll find the **Railroad Workers' House of Culture 3**. Built in 1878 as the Reformatskaya Church, it was taken apart and rebuilt to be more in keeping with the railroad spirit. As a result, it has an unusual, piecemeal look (the best views of the building are actually from the other side of the Moyka River).

From the House of Culture, head 200m north to Pochtamtskaya ul where you can see the delightful bridge (added in 1859) that connects two post office buildings. Head for the **Main Post Office 4** and check out the building's lush neoclassical façade (1782–89). The arch across the street was added in 1859. Inside, it's a turn-of-the-20th-century *style moderne* delight.

> ## Walk Facts
> **Best time** Anytime, although the ruins are particularly haunting in the snow
> **Start** Isaakievskaya pl
> **End** ul Dekabristov
> **Food en route** Zolotoy Drakon (p149) for a filling Chinese meal
> **Drink en route** Drop into The Idiot (p149) on the Moyka
> **Distance** About 2km
> **Time** About 1½ hours

Feel free to cruise up and down this ghost town of a street. The scent of faded glory is strong here; the street is full of ruined old buildings, namely No 5 and No 7, which were the post and telegraph building from 1811 to 1917.

Now get back to the Moyka walking along Konnogvardeysky per. Those faded, red Soviet stars you see on rickety metal gates shield your view from several hundred lowly soldiers fulfilling their obligatory military service here. If you loiter long enough, officers will come out to ask what you're up to, so hurry on to the Moyka, turn right and walk along the embankment. Opposite you is the **Yusupov Palace 5** (p107) at No 94 nab reki Moyki, where Rasputin enjoyed his last meal. Let your fantasies roam wild until you get to nab Kryukova kanala. Cross the bridge and keep going along the south bank of the Moyka. Across the river is the island **Novaya Gollandiya 6** (New Holland), one of the city's most mysterious sectors. Except for one day in 2000 when an exhibit of avant-garde art was held there, the island has been closed to the public for the nearly three centuries of its existence.

In Peter's time, it was used for ship-building (its name refers to the place where he learned the trade). It was slowly built up, and in the 1760s to 1780s, the impressive red brick and granite arch was constructed, a prime example of early Russian classicism. In 1893 a large basin was built in the middle of the island. Here, experiments were conducted by scientist Alexei Krylov in an attempt to build a boat that couldn't be capsized. In 1915

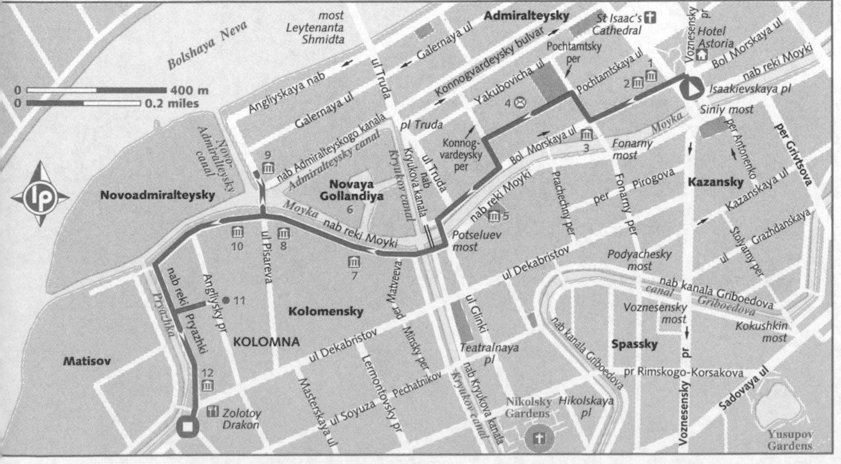

the navy built a radio transmitter here, the most powerful in Russia at the time, and from which the Soviets broadcast their first directives. There are plans to turn the island into a giant art exhibition space.

The surrounding area is home to several old palaces, all in a state of charming decay. Nab reki Moyki 108 (built in 1833) used to be the **Palace of Grand Duchess Kseniya Alexandrova 7**, who was Nicholas II's sister. **Nab reki Moyki 112 8**, a sumptuous building by Victor Shreter from the 1890s, was once considered to be one of St Petersburg's most elite residences. Turn right and over the bridge to the intersection of the Admiralteysky and Novo-Admiralteysky Canals. Here you'll find the **Bobrinsky Palace 9**, built for the son of Catherine the Great and Count Orlov in the 1790s. The building has been left to rot (check out the façade along Galernaya ul); it's now the property of the St Petersburg State University and houses a theatre department.

Best of all, at nab reki Moyki No 122, is the romantic shambles of the **Palace of Grand Duke Alexey Alexandrovich 10** (p106), designed by Messmacher. The son of Alexander II, he was also the Admiral who bore responsibility for the shabby state of the Russian navy before the war with Japan in 1904. The ghosts of the palace's past greatness can best be felt by entering the courtyard around the corner at Angliysky pr 2 and strolling through the palace's former park grounds. If you are keen to see the ruined interior, which is in a shocking state but remains fascinating, then get some cash out and begin making friends with the security guards who'll usually let you have a look around at a price. All of the furniture has been removed, but many of the original fittings and ceilings remain. While here, check out the beautiful **former Dutch consulate 11** at Angliysky pr 8–10.

This district of Kolomna, which stretches south to the Fontanka River, was once full of small wooden houses and was the subject of Pushkin's *Little House in Kolomna* and Gogol's *Portrait*. Continue down to the end of the Moyka River and left along nab reki Pryazhki. Across the tiny river is the rather desolate Matisov Island, named after a miller who lived in a little village located here in Peter the Great's time – he was favoured by the tsar for his reconnaissance efforts, relaying information about approaching Swedish ships. Now the island hosts some factories, a psychiatric hospital and the popular Matisov Domik hotel (p106).

Be sure to check out the Jugendstil gem at nab reki Pryazhki 34. At the corner of ul Dekabristov is the **Alexander Blok House-Museum 12** (p105). Treat yourself to a nice meal at Zolotoy Drakon (p149) across the street and call it a day.

1

1 Singer Building (p97) 2 View from Anichkov most (p98) 3 Late-19th-century architecture, Angliyskaya nab (p40) 4 General Staff Building, Dvortsovaya Ploshchad (p88)

1 *Pavilion Hall (Room 204), Hermitage (p78)* ***2*** *Inside the Hermitage (p67)* ***3*** *Matisse's 'The Dance', Hermitage (p81)* ***4*** *Winter Palace (p69)*

__1__ St Isaac's Cathedral (p89) __2__ Statue at main entrance to Admiralty (p87) __3__ Artillery Museum (p111) __4__ Detail of Mosque (p113)

1 *Trinity Cathedral (p107)* ***2*** *Lenin statue, House of Soviets (p119)* ***3*** *SS Peter and Paul Cathedral (p114) from Troitsky most* ***4*** *Grand Choral Synagogue (p105)*

__1__ Herring dish, Russky Kitsch (p150) __2__ Fasol (p142) __3__ Hermitage Restaurant (p142) __4__ Zov Ilyicha (p145)

1 *Money Honey (p154)* ***2*** *Bar at Hermitage Restaurant (p142)* ***3*** *Griboedov (p156)* ***4*** *Tsynik (p155)*

__1__ Gostiny Dvor (p167) __2__ Folk art shop, Stroganov Palace (p97) __3__ Kuznechny market (p168) __4__ Soviet dolls, souvenir market (p169)

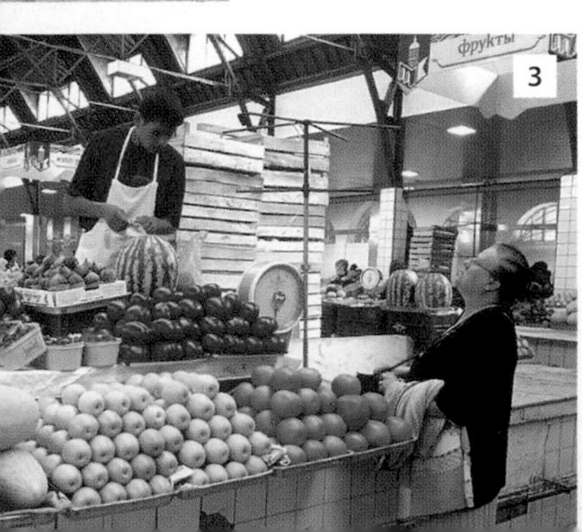

__1__ Transfiguration Cathedral, Kizhi (p200) __2__ Church, Novgorod (p198) __3__ Catherine Palace, Tsarskoe Selo (p191) __4__ SS Peter and Paul Cathedral, Petrodvorets (p190)

Eating

Eating

Yes, yes, one stereotype you'll find hard to avoid before coming to St Petersburg is that of Russian food being terrible. It's certainly no baseless accusation – just a decade ago eating out in town was a fairly joyless experience unless you had unlimited funds and could afford the dining rooms of five-star hotels every night. But how things have changed in just the space of a few years – the new middle class of the city has discovered the joys of eating out, trying authentic foreign cuisine as well as new approaches to traditional Russian dishes, and this has led to a frenzy of openings (not to mention frequent closures) as new trends emerge and others fall from grace. St Petersburg has some truly superb dining today, including an impressively large selection of foreign eateries committed to true authenticity rather than the Russianised cuisine so common until the turn of the century. Whether it's bliny (leavened buckwheat pancakes) on the go, Indonesian with style, takeaway pizza or a five-course *haute cuisine* candlelit dinner you seek, rest assured you'll find it here.

Opening Hours

Going out for breakfast *(zavtrak)* is the kind of bourgeois habit that still raises eyebrows in St Petersburg, where every home seems to have a mother figure providing *kasha* (porridge), and the sheer indulgence of eating croissants and coffee in a café remains extremely foreign. That said there is a small number of cafés and restaurants that open first thing in the morning (see p143).

Most restaurants will open between 11am and noon. Russians tend to have big breakfasts, small, late lunches *(obed)* and large dinners *(uzhin),* so most places that open for lunch have a set menu *(biznes lanch)* that can be served quickly and allows the customer to get back to work within half an hour or so, although you can always eat à la carte and enjoy a longer meal too. It's perfectly normal not to eat lunch until 3 or even 4pm, so restaurants rarely close between the afternoon and the evening.

Given the cheap cost of staff, many restaurants remain open until late at night. Often there are no formal closing times and restaurants and bars stay open *do poslednnogo klienta* (until the last customer). 'Normal' dinnertime is anywhere from 7pm to 11pm. The Russians are relaxed about mealtimes and as many people use restaurants to drink in (Russians always snack while drinking vodka), most places open until at least 11pm. In this chapter opening hours are only listed when an establishment does not operate from noon until 11pm.

How Much?

Cheaper than Moscow, certainly, but beyond that it's impossible to say. Prices have been rising steadily but inexorably in St Petersburg and it's now standard to pay around R500 per main course in a smart restaurant, and around R180 to R250 in mid-range outfits although you can certainly eat well for far less. If you are on a budget, you'll be very well catered for (not to mention in very good company, most locals outside the new middle class find restaurants prohibitively priced and usually only visit them on special occasions, if at all). Comfortably affordable to almost everyone are the *stolovayas* (canteens) that serve up hot meals to workers from all walks of life and are a hangover from Soviet times. Unpretentious and unremarkable, you'll see them on most streets.

Booking Tables

There is rarely a need to book tables in St Petersburg. Provision often outstrips demand and even popular places can be relatively empty on a regular basis. When booking is recommended we note this in reviews. One period when some restaurants may be block-booked for dinner is during the White Nights Festival (p12) in late June, so do call ahead to any smarter or particularly popular restaurants then. An advantage of booking a table is ensuring you have a table as near to (or, let's face it, as far away from) the live music as possible.

Tipping

Anyone unlucky enough to have seen the Soviet concept of 'service with a sneer' (when inscrutable serving staff would bark *'nyet'* at everything you attempted to order until, by a process of elimination, you located the one dish they had available that day) will not recognise the largely very polite and passably efficient staff at most St Petersburg restaurants today.

When and how much you are expected to tip is dictated entirely by the type of establishment. Staff at a *stolovaya* or any basic café will never expect a tip, and may think you highly odd for leaving one. More upmarket places will expect a tip of around 10%, especially from foreigners. However, in practice, waiting staff will be happy with anything, as most Russians do not tip waiters. Increasingly, smarter places are beginning to add a service charge to bills automatically, so check before leaving any extra.

Self-Catering

Cooking for yourself remains hard work in St Petersburg. Finding fresh produce will be the major headache – it's available only at the markets, which usually means a trip out of your way as well as having to visit a supermarket for other goods. Far and away the city's best market is Kuznechny Market (Kuznechny Rynok) next to Vladimirskaya metro station. Luckily, the best supermarket in the city, Lend, is virtually opposite, which makes self-catering a far more attractive prospect if you are staying in the neighbourhood. See Shopping for more information (p165).

HISTORIC HEART

The sheer range of eating options in the heart of St Petersburg is incredible and nothing short of stunning to anyone who knew the city during the 1990s, when its culinary variety was not, let us say, one of the city's salient features. Now you're spoilt for choice – world cuisine, modern and traditional Russian, fast food and even fusion are amply represented. In general, the best places are not on Nevsky pr, which has its fair share of mediocre restaurants, although there are several excellent exceptions. The restaurants listed here are the best in town and deserve to be savoured.

BORSALINO

Map pp246-9 *Russian-European*

☎ 313 5115; Angleterre Hotel, Bolshaya Morskaya ul 39; business lunch R350; 🕑 7am-1am; metro Sadovaya

This excellent bistro inside the ultra-chic Angleterre Hotel has both atmosphere and a regular crowd – rare for hotel restaurants indeed. The menu is extensive including prime rump steak (R800) and an excellent business lunch (R350), all in the lovely setting of the black marble bar overlooking Isaakievskaya pl (St Isaac's Sq).

CAT

Map pp246-9 *Georgian*

☎ 571 3377; Stremyannaya ul 22; mains R200; metro Mayakovskaya

The atmospheric and popular Georgian restaurant Cat (Ket) is very popular both with local Russians and Georgians as well as visitors to the city. The wine list is extensive and food very authentic. Try the *lobio* (bean paste) and *khinkali* (meat dumplings) for a taste of Georgia.

CONGO

Map pp246-9 *African*

☎ 275 9954; ul Zhukovskogo 57; mains R200; metro Pl Vosstaniya

Groovy African-themed Congo features low lighting and predictable leopard-skin décor. The

Top Tables

The hottest places to be seen:

- **Imbir** (p148)
- **Restoran** (p150)
- **Sukawati** (p144)
- **Onegin** (p144)
- **Che** (p148)

food is good, however, and the couscous is particularly excellent. It can get rowdy when there are big parties here, making for great fun.

DA VINCI Map pp246-9 *Russian-European*
☎ **311 0173; www.davinci.spb.ru; Malaya Morskaya ul 15; mains R400; metro Nevsky Pr**
Ostensibly Italian, this is one of those collage restaurants so popular in Russia – there's as much American and Mediterranean food on the menu as Italian, and the entertainment runs the gamut of jazz, Russian folk dancing, female strippers and go-go boys. The eccentrically translated menu is hilarious: try a 'God's Death Omelette' just for the name.

FASOL Map pp246-9 *Russian-European*
☎ **571 0907; www.fasolcafe.ru in Russian; Gorokhovaya ul 17; mains R150; 🕑 noon-midnight; metro Sennaya Pl**
Fasol (Bean) is a chic and upmarket café and dining room on an otherwise rather dull stretch of Gorokhovaya. The minimalist décor and smiling staff are impressive, although weirdly enough beans don't feature on the menu, which sticks to Russian standards with a Euro-twist – the name is a play on the street name, which means 'Pea Street'. Those Russians sure can crack you up.

Fasol (above)

FX Map pp246-9 *Russian*
☎ **571 5956; Gorokhovaya ul 13; mains R150; 🕑 11am-5am; metro Nevsky Pr**
This subterranean naval-themed bar and restaurant is something of an old faithful in town. The full Russian menu is decent and good value, and the beers keep coming late into the night. Live music at weekends can be disturbing, but there's no better place to come for a 1am dinner during the week, as you are nearly always guaranteed a seat.

HARBIN Map pp246-9 *Chinese*
☎ **571 1732; nab reki Moyki 48; mains R400; metro Nevsky Pr**
One of many Harbin restaurants in St Petersburg, named after the northern Chinese city with a large Russian population, this establishment is on the Moyka River and offers decent Chinese food and good service. The real bargain though is the student café run by the same kitchen for a fraction of the price in the next-door Herzen Institute (p146).

HERMITAGE RESTAURANT
Map pp246-9 *Russian*
☎ **314 4772; www.hermitage.restoran.ru; Dvortsovaya pl 8; per dish R550; metro Nevsky Pr**
Superbly located in the Triumphal Arch of the General Staff Building, opposite the Winter Palace, this beautifully laid-out establishment nonetheless may have been conceived on too grand a scale to fill up on a regular basis. Of course it was packed full of dignitaries during the tricentennial celebrations for which it was built, but even its sumptuous menu of Russian and European cooking and wonderful wine list can't sustain such a huge space. Still, there are few places as opulent if you want to dine in style with a big group of friends.

KALINKA MALINKA Map pp246-9 *Russian*
☎ **314 2681; Italiyanskaya ul 5; mains R500; metro Nevsky Pr**
This rather kitsch, folkloric restaurant is in a basement on pl Iskusstv (Arts Sq), and specialises in provincial Russian cooking. Try rabbit à la Russe (R550) or the selection of delicious soups for a great introduction to unembellished Russian cuisine.

KAVKAZ Map pp246-9 *Caucasian*
☎ **312 1665; Karavannaya ul 18; mains R360; metro Gostiny Dvor**
An excellent place, Kavkaz has endured for many years as one of the most consistent and

Top Five Breakfast Joints

- Borsalino (p141)
- The Idiot (p149)
- Marius Pub (p143)
- Mama Roma (p143)
- Bistrot Garçon (p148)

reliable places in town. The food is excellent – Georgian fare with other Caucasian trimmings. Portions are generous and served on large wooden boards. The café is also a pleasant place to stop for coffee and cake.

KHRISTOFOR Map pp246-9 *Russian-Seafood*
☎ 312 9761; Bolshaya Morskaya ul 27; mains R400; metro Nevsky Pr
The enormous ship-shaped bar is the central feature of this excellent, upmarket restaurant – one of the city's best for seafood and fresh fish from the Gulf of Finland. Look out for the parrot, which is likely to be the noisiest creature in this subdued and refined place.

KRISTOFF Map pp246-9 *Russian*
☎ 571 6643; www.kristoff.ru; Kristoff Hotel, Zagorodny pr 9; mains R200; 🕑 24hr; metro Dostoevskaya
This nicely attired, low-lit restaurant has an intimate atmosphere perfect for a date or meal with a few friends. The Russian menu is traditional with some Western imports, and having it open around the clock is a real bonus in this decidedly festive city.

KYOTO Map pp246-9 *Japanese*
☎ 310 2547; www.kyoto.ru; nab reki Fontanki 77; mains R300-800; 🕑 noon until last guest; metro Sennaya Pl
This superb restaurant was serving up sashimi *moriawase* to its appreciative regulars long before the recent vogue for Japanese cuisine hit the city, and will hopefully outlast the places that take their sushi less seriously. It's as authentic as they come, with Japanese staff and a recently refurbished interior. Highly recommended.

LANDSKRONA Map pp246-9 *Russian-European*
☎ 380 2001; Nevsky pr 57; mains R500; metro Mayakovskaya
At the top of the Corinthia Nevskij Palace Hotel, Landskrona is named after a Swedish fort that once existed where St Petersburg now stands. It's a very smart place although it lacks a degree of atmosphere. However, its Mediterranean fare is superb and there's a terrace for outdoor eating.

LA STRADA Map pp246-9 *Italian*
☎ 312 4700; Bolshaya Konyushennaya ul 27; mains R350; metro Nevsky Pr
This bizarrely quiet place has the potential to be very good indeed, and what it lacks in atmosphere it compensates for by serving up some of the best pizza in town. The salad bar is best missed though.

MAMA ROMA Map pp246-9 *Italian*
☎ 314 0347; www.mamaroma.ru; Karavannaya ul 3/35; mains R200; 🕑 8am-11pm; metro Gostiny Dvor
Reliable Italian fare from decent pizza to risotto and pasta is served from this local restaurant. There are also branches at **Moskovsky pr** (192 Moskovsky pr; metro Park Pobedy) and **Petrograd Side** (Bolshoy pr 70/72; metro Petrogradskaya). The lunch buffet is great value and they even do breakfast.

MARIUS PUB Map pp246-9 *Russian-European*
☎ 315 4880; ul Marata 11; mains R300; 🕑 24hr; metro Mayakovskaya
Reliable and rightly popular, Marius Pub is a useful place to know about, as it serves Russian and European pub grub at all hours, and also does a mean breakfast buffet. It functions as the breakfast restaurant to the nearby Helvetica Suites Hotel, and the buffet (R300) is well worth paying for even if you aren't a guest.

MATROSSKAYA TISHINA Map pp246-9 *Russian*
☎ 164 4413; ul Marata 54/34; mains R600; metro Ligovsky Pr
Generally accepted by all to be the city's finest seafood restaurant, it's often completely full. The curious metallic-maritime design complements the excellent menu of grilled, baked and fried fish, and you can even pick which trout or perch you want to end up on your plate.

MILANO Map pp246-9 *Italian*
☎ 314 7348; Karavannaya ul 8; mains R450; metro Gostiny Dvor
Authentic and smart, Milano is one of the city's best Italian restaurants with a large selection of pastas, risottos, fish and meat dishes as

well as a pricey but extensive wine list. The airy, relaxed feel and unhurried service make it more enjoyable than many others in the price range.

NEP Map pp246-9 *Russian*

☎ 571 7591; nab reki Moyki 37; mains R300; metro Nevsky Pr

Unlike most of the other communist-theme restaurants and bars in the city that recall 1970s communism, NEP celebrates the early 1920s, a period of entrepreneurial activity and relative liberalism under Lenin's New Economic Policy, which encourages a kind of Russian vaudevillian decadence. Just next to Dvortsovaya pl (Palace Sq), NEP is decorated in a very cool 1920s style. There's music and cabaret after 8pm from Thursday to Saturday.

ONEGIN Map pp246-9 *Russian*

☎ 571 8384; www.oneginspb.com; Sadovaya ul 11; mains R300-900; 🕑 5pm-2am; metro Gostiny Dvor

The restaurant in town to be seen in at the time of writing, Onegin shamelessly aims itself at the new rich and the superstar classes. Indeed, you really have to be in the know, to know it's there – it's down a small staircase and barely marked at street level. The interior is an incredible feat of staggering nouveau riche hubris, with chandeliers, antique bidets, and the kind of chairs you'd expect Ivana Trump to own. However, the menu really delivers: try crab ravioli (R690), duck filet with glazed forest berries in grape sauce (R480) and marble steak with *foie gras* and fresh asparagus (R870).

ORIENT EXPRESS Map pp246-9 *Russian*

☎ 325 8728; www.orientexpress.ru; ul Marata 21; mains R300; 🕑 noon-midnight; metro Mayakovskaya

You too can take the Orient Express, oh yes. This café (to the left) and restaurant (to the right) is decked out like a luxury train, although anyone who's had the pleasure of the real thing will wonder where the package tourists are. The simple menu is tasty and good value.

PLANETA SUSHI Map pp246-9 *Japanese*

☎ 275 7533; Nevsky pr 94; mains R150-500; 🕑 noon-6am; metro Mayakovskaya

The most centrally located Japanese in town, Planeta Sushi is excellent and remains one of the few popular and relatively non-touristy restaurants on Nevsky. It offers an all-you-can-eat option for just R595 and a discount card for regular customers.

POGREBA MONAKHA

Map pp246-9 *Russian*

☎ 314 1353; Millionnaya ul 22; mains R400; 🕑 11am-until last customer; metro Nevsky Pr

The Monk's Cellar resembles just that – set in a low and dark space below St Petersburg's most glamorous street. The food is rich and traditional – try the excellent smoked salmon and sour cream bliny (R200) and watch out for the monk's skeleton buried under glass at floor level. Bon appetit!

PROPAGANDA

Map pp246-9 *Russian-European*

☎ 275 3558; www.propaganda.spb.ru; nab reki Fontanki 40; mains R300; 🕑 24hr; metro Gostiny Dvor

Constructivism is the theme of this reliable eatery overlooking Anichkov most. Propaganda serves up a mean burger and nice fries as well as a huge array of international dishes. Try salmon *pelmeni* (Russian-style ravioli filled with salmon; R290) and the Kamchatka crab steak (R490) if you fancy something more Russian.

RUSSIAN VODKA MUSEUM TRAKTIR

Map pp246-9 *Russian*

☎ 312 3416; Konnogvardeysky bul 5; mains R180; metro Nevsky Pr

This is an unusual place to dine indeed, the small café inside the Russian Vodka Museum. It's cheap and friendly, however, and you don't have to pay to enter, despite having to walk through the museum to get in. The menu offers standard, tasty Russian home cooking, including a huge range of vodka, naturally.

SHYOLK Map pp246-9 *Asian Fusion*

☎ 571 5078; ul Malaya Konyushennaya 4/2; mains R400; 🕑 1pm until last guest; metro Nevsky Pr

This venue has seen an endless procession of new restaurants, although the latest, Shyolk (Silk) is by far the best looking. Italian dishes complement the mainly Japanese menu and there's a huge, impressive wine list to boot. The whole place is beautifully designed in a comfortably minimalist way.

SUKAWATI Map pp246-9 *Indonesian*

☎ 312 0505; www.sukawati.ru in Russian; Kazanskaya ul 8; mains R160; 🕑 noon-3am; metro Sadovaya

Sleek as you like, the first Indonesian restaurant in Russia has impressed the in-crowd with its beautiful décor and sumptuous, ornately presented dishes. The delicious fare includes

Best Russian Restaurants

- Russkaya Rybalka (p152)
- Staraya Derevnya (p152)
- Staraya Tamozhnya (p150)
- Udachny Vystrel (p145)
- Okhotnichny Klub (p147)

plenty for vegetarians and the wonderful fittings really make this a top restaurant.

TANDOOR Map pp246-9 *Indian*

☎ 312 3886; Voznesensky pr 2; mains R300; metro Nevsky Pr

A pricier and more Russianised Indian menu is offered at Tandoor, just by the Admiralty. The Indian staff speaks English and the décor is charming. The speciality is vindaloo *palek,* a tasty home-made cheese marinated in honey and spices.

TAVERNA OLIVA Map pp246-9 *Greek*

☎ 314 6563; www.tavernaoliva.ru in Russian; Bolshaya Morskaya ul 31; mains R200; metro Nevsky Pr

A superb addition to the St Petersburg dining scene, there is nothing taverna-like about this cavernous place, subtly painted and decorated in an array of Greek styles. The menu is traditional and the food is both excellent value and extremely good, as attested to by the expat Greeks who seem to be regulars.

TINKOFF Map pp246-9 *Russian*

☎ 118 5566; www.tinkoff.ru; Kazanskaya ul 7; mains R400; noon-midnight; metro Sadovaya

Entering huge, factory-like Tinkoff can be like going into a nightclub. Dominated by a microbrewery which makes the eponymous beer – St Petersburg's most fashionable brew – the space is split up into a sushi bar, a large bar area and an open-plan restaurant with German-style beer hall food. The boisterous and sociable dining area has great atmosphere.

UDACHNY VYSTREL Map pp246-9 *Russian*

☎ 311 6949; www.y-v.spb.ru; Gorokhovaya ul 3; mains R450; noon-midnight; metro Nevsky Pr

This is the place to come if you want a hearty hunter's dinner. Definitely not for vegetarians, the beautifully designed wooden interior has bearskins hanging on the wall flanked by other stuffed trophies. One table surrounds a huge grill where diners can watch the various meats being prepared.

VANIL Map pp246-9 *German-French*

☎ 571 9813; ul Rubinshteyna 24; mains R500; metro Dostoevskaya

This exceptionally chic place is wonderful for a relaxed lunch in its beautifully attired dining room. You can watch food being prepared through the glass wall to the kitchen – something that would be disturbing in many places, but is simply reassuring here.

YAKITORIYA Map pp246-9 *Japanese*

☎ 315 8343; www.yakitoriya.spb.ru in Russian; pl Ostrovskogo; mains R300; metro Gostiny Dvor

The Moscow-based Yakitoriya chain now has two branches in St Petersburg; the other is at **Petrovskaya nab 4** (Map pp246–9; ☎ 970 4858; metro Gorkovskaya). With its authentic preparation of a huge range of sushi, and all at great value, it's easy to see why it has been so successful in Moscow, almost colonising the city.

ZOV ILYICHA Map pp246-9 *Russian*

☎ 571 8641; Kazanskaya ul 34; mains R300-400; 1pm-2am; metro Sadovaya

'Lenin's Mating Call' is hands-down the city's most novel novelty restaurant. Worth a visit if you fancy a laugh and decent food too, they show pornography in the toilets and also give you the opportunity to communicate with the person in the next-door cubicle. They even show 'erotic films' in the dining area after 9pm. No under 18s admitted.

Udachny Vystrel (left)

CHEAP EATS

BISTRO OCHAG

Map pp246-9 *Russian-Vegetarian*

☎ 315 8421; Zagorodny pr 2; mains R100; 🕑 10am-10pm; metro Vladimirskaya

Unremarkable but for the fact that it features a vegetarian menu, this airy café is a good place to stop for lunch. Salads and main dishes are available both with and without meat.

BLIN DONALT'S

Map pp246-9 *Russian Fast Food*

ul Zhukovskogo 18; mains R50; 🕑 10am-10pm; metro Pl Vosstaniya

A brilliant attempt to reclaim fast food from the American multi-nationals, Blin Donalt's has somehow avoided legal action from a certain well-known fast-food chain. Here you get fast-food bliny (R12), chicken Kiev (R34) and even borsch (R12) – all as disturbingly unlike the real thing as McDonald's apple pie, but a fascinating comment on post-Soviet Russia.

BLINY DOMIK

Map pp246-9 *Russian Fast Food*

☎ 315 9915; Kolokolnaya ul 8; metro Vladimirskaya

Homely, fun and often very busy, Bliny Domik (Pancake House) has a huge array of calorific savoury and sweet bliny on offer. However, quality has suffered recently and while it's always good to give a long-running favourite the benefit of the doubt, one recent meal was semi-inedible. Also, it's terribly marked on the street, but does definitely exist and remains popular.

CHAYNAYA LOZHKA

Map pp246-9 *Russian Fast Food*

☎ 314 5592; Nevsky pr 44 & 136, ul Vosstaniya 13; mains R100; 🕑 9am-10pm; metro Pl Vosstaniya

Chaynaya Lozhka (the Tea Spoon) is an excellent bliny and salad fast-food joint looking set to become a city-wide phenomenon. It's hugely popular at lunch times, but worth waiting in line for, despite the violent orange of the staff uniform.

GAURANGA

Map pp246-9 *Vegetarian-Indian*

☎ 273 7723; www.gauranga.info in Russian; Ligovsky pr 17; mains R100; noon-9pm; metro Pl Vosstaniya

The decent vegetarian food here is largely inspired by Indian cooking (try the excellent *masala dosa*), although there are several Russian dishes too, and Central Asian favourites such as *plov* (a delicious dish of rice, meat and diced carrots).

Best Cheap Eats in Town

- **Sumeto** (p149)
- **Herzen Institute Canteen** (p146)
- **Chaynaya Lozhka** (p146)
- **Troitsky Most** (p149)
- **Adzhika** (p148)

HERZEN INSTITUTE CANTEEN

Map pp246-9 *Chinese*

Herzen Institute courtyard, nab reki Moyki 48; mains R50-100; 🕑 11am-4pm Mon-Fri; metro Nevsky Pr

Sharing the fruits of the excellent Harbin kitchen next door, this outlet caters to the students of the Herzen Institute who come here in droves at lunch time for ridiculously cheap, but delicious Chinese fare. Things are basic – paper plates and plastic cutlery, but you'll not eat better at these prices.

IL PATIO Map pp246-9 *Italian*

☎ 314 8215; Nevsky pr 32; mains R200; metro Gostiny Dvor

The rebranded Patio pizza chain has a huge presence in the big cities of the former Soviet Union, and Il Patio's St Petersburg outlets keep to the same recipe for success: tasty, filling pizzas, a great salad bar and friendly staff. There's another branch at **Nevsky pr 182** (Map pp244–5; metro Pl Alexandra Nevskogo).

KASHMIR Map pp246-9 *Indian-Vegetarian*

☎ 314 2300; www.kashmir.ru; Bolshaya Moskovskaya ul 8; mains R150; 🕑 11am-11pm; metro Vladimirskaya

A distinctly odd take on Indian food, the chef at Kashmir combines sweet and savoury ingredients with abandon. Kiwi and pineapple with soy-chicken curry, for example, not to mention soy-peacock schnitzel. However, the food's 100% vegetarian, tasty (if unusual) and the incense-infused atmosphere is lovely. Business lunch at R95 is a steal.

NYAM NYAM Map pp246-9 *Fast Food*

☎ 272 7573; Nevsky pr 78; mains R80; 🕑 24hr; metro Mayakovskaya

This is a cheap and cheerful self-service bistro (the name means 'yum yum' in Russian). There's a good range of salads as well as more filling hot dishes.

TEREMOK Map pp246-9 *Russian Fast Food*
Cnr Malaya Sadovaya & Italiyanskaya ul; bliny R40-100; 10am-10pm; metro Gostiny Dvor
Sprinkled all over the city, these bliny kiosks are superb value and serve up great treats to which the crowds of satisfied customers milling about in the immediate vicinity attest. Even though there are set menus for each type of pancake, you can make up your own by just pointing to the fillings you want.

TOLSTIY FRAYER Map pp246-9 *Russian*
314 5921; Kirpichny per 1; mains R150; noon-1am; metro Nevsky Pr
The newer branch of this beer hall on Kirpichny per is the most convenient – providing a fun hideaway for some comfort food and a Baltika beer. The older branch is at **ul Belinskogo 13** (Map pp246–7; metro Gostiny Dvor). The nostalgic communist paraphernalia recalls the days of Brezhnev, but thankfully the staff do not – there are smiles all round and good service.

TRI Map pp246-9 *Fast Food*
595 4153; Italiyanskaya ul 17; mains R150; 24hr; metro Gostiny Dvor
A good place to pick up a sandwich or for a quick lunch, this bizarre enterprise just off pl Iskusstv (Arts Sq) specialises in coffee, tea and wine and there's a hall devoted to each.

U TYOSHI NA BLINAKH
Map pp246-9 *Russian*
311 4947; Zagorodny pr 18; mains R150; metro Vladimirskaya
'Auntie's pancakes' are being served up in so many locations now that it's a wonder she's not dropped dead yet. The cafeteria-style chain is a great place to fill up quickly and cheaply. Although these aren't the best bliny you'll have in St Petersburg, they are tasty and there's a great choice of fillings and sides. Another branch is on **Sytninskaya ul 16** (Map pp238–9; metro Gorkovskaya).

YOLKI PALKI Map pp246-9 *Russian*
273 1594; Nevsky pr 88; mains R150; metro Mayakovskaya
The reliable and affordable Moscow chain finally opened on Nevsky pr at the start of 2004. Kitschly decorated with stuffed animals and fake trees that pour verdure over the tables, it offers affordable Russian standards and a great salad bar (R210). Good for vegetarians.

SMOLNY

There are relatively few restaurants in the Smolny region, but those that are here are of a very high standard and include the ultimate in Russian game restaurants, Okhotnichny Klub (Hunting Club) by the Bolsheokhtinsky most.

CHORNAYA KOSHKA, BELY KOT
Map pp246-9 *Serbian-Russian*
279 7430; ul Pestelya 13/15; mains R500; noon-midnight; metro Chernyshevskaya
Named after the Emir Kusturica film *Black Cat, White Cat,* this ultra-sleek place wins plaudits for contemporary design including exposed brickwork, huge bay windows and chiffon sheets hanging between the tables. Stills from the eponymous film decorate the exposed kitchen. The house speciality is roast suckling pig (R1800), although the rest of the menu is far more reasonably priced. Films are shown daily at 3pm on the giant screen.

GIN NO TAKI Map pp246-9 *Japanese*
272 0958; pr Chernyshevskogo 17; mains R150-500; 11am-6am; metro Chernyshevskaya
Unnervingly enough the entire staff at Gin No Taki greets you in Japanese extremely loudly when you enter the restaurant. That aside, this is one of the city's best and most authentic Japanese restaurants, including an excellent shop next door for all your fresh Japanese food product needs.

OKHOTNICHNY KLUB
Map pp240-1 *Russian*
327 8274; ul Novgorodskaya 27; mains R300-600; metro Chernyshevskaya
Another favourite for hunters – the game menu at the city's Hunting Club is very impressive, and the elegant décor with its red walls, stuffed animals and wooden fittings is exceptionally cosy. A great place to come for a carnivorous Russian meal with all the traditional trimmings.

Best Vegetarian Choices

- **Troitsky Most** (p149)
- **Bistro Ochag** (p146)
- **Kashmir** (p146)
- **The Idiot** (p149)
- Any Georgian restaurant

VOSSTANIYA

Rather dead for restaurants, this largely residential area does, however, have two excellent eateries that happily compensate for the lack of range in the area.

BISTROT GARÇON Map pp246-9 *French*
☎ 277 2467; Nevsky pr 95; mains R500;
🕑 9am-midnight; metro Pl Vosstaniya

While most French restaurants in town are painfully upscale, this gorgeous little bistro is both smart and unpretentious, and prices reasonable given the excellent standard of the cooking. Low lighting, professional staff and a Parisian chef seal the deal.

CHE Map pp246-9 *International*
☎ 277 2467; www.cafeclubche.ru in Russian;
Poltavskaya ul 3; mains R300; metro Pl Vosstaniya

There are few places cooler to hang out at than Che, and while many just come here to drink, the food's very good too. Try the Caesar salad or the pigeon breast cooked in white wine and while the evening away in roomy style.

SENNAYA

Zagorodny pr is swiftly becoming one of the city's best eating streets, now featuring the superb Imbir, delicious and cheap Troitsky Most and the city's best Ukrainian restaurant, the kitsch but delicious Shinok. Two of the best and cheapest Caucasian restaurants can also be found around Sennaya pl.

IMBIR Map pp246-9 *Russian*
☎ 113 3215; Zagorodny pr 15; mains R200;
metro Dostoevskaya

Effortlessly cool, Imbir combines ornate tsarist décor with contemporary design to brilliant effect. Great atmosphere, it's always full of a trendy local crowd, who come here for good coffee and a very reasonably priced menu.

KARAVAN
Map pp242-3 *Caucasian-Central Asian*
☎ 310 5678; Voznesensky pr 46; mains R400;
metro Sadovaya

A superb Central Asian restaurant on the Fontanka, you will see a delicious array of kebabs being prepared on the open barbeques that line the restaurant. Consistently popular, Karavan definitely represents the finer end of kebab dining in town and the menu offers much more besides – try its delicious *golubtsi* (vine leaves stuffed with meat).

KILIKIA Map pp246-9 *Armenian*
☎ 327 2208; Gorokhovaya ul 26/40; mains R350;
🕑 noon-3am; metro Sennaya Pl

This large, cosy Armenian place is excellent value and serves up well-presented, delicious Armenian specialities as well as other Caucasian and Russian dishes. It's especially popular with the large Armenian Diaspora in St Petersburg.

SHINOK Map pp246-9 *Ukrainian*
☎ 571 8262; Zagorodny pr 13; mains R180-350;
🕑 24hr; metro Dostoevskaya

One of the best places to try tasty Ukrainian food in St Petersburg is this friendly, if badly over folksed-up, restaurant. Expect to be transported to the Ukrainian countryside, complete with uniformed Ukrainian peasants.

CHEAP EATS

ADZHIKA Map pp246-9 *Caucasian*
☎ 310 2627; Moskovsky pr 7; mains R100; 🕑 24hr;
metro Sadovaya

Tiny and barely visible from the street, Adzhika serves tasty and cheap Caucasian dishes in a relaxed environment just a few seconds' walk from Sennaya pl. It has a basement entrance – it is there, just look very carefully.

Imbir (left)

SUMETO Map pp246-9 *Caucasian*

☎ **310 2411; ul Yefimova 5; mains R100; metro Sadovaya**

Even if you've never had Dagestani food, you'll see plenty of familiar Caucasian dishes in this quiet but friendly place, from Lula kebab (minced-meat kebab) to fried aubergines with garlic and walnuts in sour cream. Try the pumpkin *chudu* (large pancake) or the selection of Caucasian wines for something new.

TROITSKY MOST

Map pp246-9 *Russian-Vegetarian*

☎ **115 1998; Zagorodny pr 38; mains R120; metro Dostoevskaya**

There are actually five branches of this excellent vegetarian café chain, but the ones listed here are the most centrally located. The Zagorodny pr branch is by far the nicest, with a lovely restaurant as well as a café, while the branch on **Kamennoostrovsky pr** (Map pp240–1; ☎ 232 6693; Kamennoostrovsky pr 9/2; metro Gorkovskaya), facing the bridge after which it is named, is the original (with another branch a couple of blocks away). The mushroom lasagne is legendary among starving local vegetarians.

MARIINSKY

Decidedly quiet, the Mariinsky region does nevertheless have a few excellent restaurants, including expat mainstay The Idiot and the Mariinsky's fashionable restaurant, Za Stsenoy (Backstage).

DVORYANSKOYE GNEZDO

Map pp246-9 *Russian*

☎ **312 0911; ul Dekabristov 21; mains from R1000; metro Sadovaya**

This is the doyenne of the St Petersburg *haute cuisine* world, housed in the Trianon of the Yusupov Palace, a short walk from the Mariinsky Theatre. It's exceptionally stuffy (men shouldn't even think of entering without a tie), but, as previous diners such as Bill Clinton will no doubt tell you, the Russian-French cuisine is exceptional. Reservations recommended.

LE PARIS Map pp246-9 *French*

☎ **571 9545; Bolshaya Morskaya ul 63; mains R600-2400; metro Sadovaya**

Sumptuous and understated, this sleek authentic French restaurant across the Moyka from the Yusupov Palace is a favourite with Mephistophelian city Governor Valentina Matvienko among other local worthies. Expect superb food and soaring prices.

THE IDIOT Map pp246-9 *Vegetarian*

☎ **315 1675; nab reki Moyki 82; mains from R250;** 🕓 **11am-1am; metro Sadovaya**

Most visitors to the city end up at this atmospheric expat institution near the Yusupov Palace at some point during their stay. The food is actually fairly average, and overpriced for what it is (although vegetarians will argue that as one of the very few veggie outlets in the city, it's worth its weight in gold). However, the basement feel, the antiques and the crowd make it an extremely pleasant place to come to eat or drink. Breakfasts are also popular here.

ZA STSENOY Map pp246-9 *Russian*

☎ **327 0684; Teatralnaya pl 18/10; mains R500;** 🕓 **noon-2am; metro Sadovaya**

The Mariinsky's official restaurant is tucked away rather out of sight on one corner of Teatralnaya pl. It's beautifully laid out and the food can be excellent, although the service sometimes comes with a sniff. The major complaint here is that its almost hidden location means it's often empty. You appear to be able to write all over the walls if you are a famous opera singer or ballet dancer. Probably best not to unless you are though.

ZOLOTOY DRAKON

Map pp242-3 *Chinese-Vietnamese*

☎ **114 8441; ul Dekabristov 62; mains R200; metro Sadovaya**

The Vietnamese chefs at Zolotoy Drakon (Golden Dragon) create a potentially enormous range of dishes here at the edge of the city centre, with some 120 dishes on the menu, most of which are very good and reasonably priced.

VASILEVSKY ISLAND

One of the most interesting areas for dining, Vasilevsky Island has it all – boat restaurants, a slew of foreign cuisine from Lebanese to Hungarian and some of the classiest and most innovative Russian restaurants in town (check out Staraya Tamozhnya for a treat or Restoran to increase your cool factor).

BYBLOS Map pp238-9 *Lebanese*

☎ 325 8564; Maly pr 5; business lunch R149; 🕑 11am-11pm; metro Vasileostrovskaya

The only Lebanese place in town, this Vasilevsky Island hideaway is superb and attracts a large crowd for its excellent value lunch, as well as a more relaxed evening clientele. Here you'll find delicious mezze, hummus, *kibbeh*, tabbouleh, *kofta* and of course hookahs and Lebanese wine.

CHARDASH Map pp246-9 *Hungarian*

☎ 323 8588; nab Makarova 22; mains R500; metro Sportivnaya

Named after a Hungarian folk dance, Chardash has a huge menu of Magyar favourites including a good vegetarian selection. The food is great and compensates for the rather crummy décor. There's live music most nights, be warned.

LAIMA Map pp242-3 *German-Russian*

☎ 329 0895; 6-aya liniya 15; mains R250; 🕑 24hr; metro Vasileostrovskaya

Not to be confused with the rather unexciting Laima fast-food restaurant on the Griboedov Canal, this smart and cosy place on Vasilevsky Island's main commercial strip is excellent and combines German *biergarten* fare with Russian cuisine and a great selection of beer.

NEW ISLAND Map pp246-9 *International*

☎ 963 6765; www.concord-catering.ru; moored off Rumantsyevsky spusk, cnr Universitetskaya nab & 1-aya liniya; mains R600; metro Vasileostrovskaya

The list of diners on this smartest of boat restaurants is dizzying – George W Bush, Jacques Chirac and the Queen of Spain have all dined here, while Putin is a regular. With its sumptuous décor and beautifully presented international menu with a strong Italian accent (try the soup of fresh mussels and mushrooms served with champagne sauce to start, for example), you'll cruise the river for two hours while you enjoy your meal. Cruises (R225 per person) depart at 2pm, 6pm, 8pm and 10.30pm from late-April to October.

Best Business Lunches

- **Byblos** (p150)
- **Kashmir** (p146)
- **Borsalino** (p141)
- **FX** (p142)
- **La Strada** (p143)

RESTORAN Map pp246-9 *Russian*

☎ 327 8979; Tamozhenny per 2; mains R400; 🕑 noon-midnight; metro Nevsky Pr

Beautifully designed and lit, Restoran's spelling in Russian with the pre-1917 hard-sign ending suggests it is harking back to the days of Romanov splendour. The Russian cuisine is well realised and beautifully presented, although quality can sometimes be hit and miss. Despite this, Restoran remains one the city's coolest restaurants.

RUSSKY KITSCH Map pp246-9 *Russian*

☎ 325 1122; Universitetskaya nab 25; mains R350; 🕑 noon-midnight; metro Vasileostrovskaya

The wild and often plainly ridiculous design here is purposeful bad taste – Fidel Castro and Brezhnev are kissing in a ceiling painting and the menus are fashioned from butchered copies of Lenin's selected works. Despite this, sitting out on the glass promenade overlooking the river is lovely and the food is good. Bring sunglasses to avoid being dazzled by the design, though.

STARAYA TAMOZHNYA
Map pp246-9 *Russian*

☎ 327 8980; Tamozhny per 1; mains R800; 🕑 1pm-1am; metro Nevsky Pr

The 'Old Customs House' is upscale French dining next to the Museum of Anthropology and Ethnography (Kunstkamera). Famous for its wine list and excellent food, you can see St Petersburg's gold-clad celebrity classes partaking of *filet mignon* and caviar crepes here.

SWAGAT Map pp242-3 *Indian*

☎ 322 2111; Bolshoy pr 91; mains R250; metro Vasileostrovskaya

Northern Indian cuisine in northern Russia – this is the best Indian in town, hands down. Its excellent range of tandoori, tikka, *masala* and curry dishes, superb *kulcha* bread and sour lassi, and an intimate atmosphere with live sitar music after 8pm, makes for a relaxing and delicious night out.

USTRICHNY BAR Map pp246-9 *French*

☎ 323 2279; www.oysters.spb.ru in Russian; Bolshoy pr 8; mains from R500; metro Vasileostrovskaya

This rather unlikely basement bar on Bolshoy pr serves up fresh oysters, champagne and *foie gras*, in case you need to take someone on a date in true eighties style. Six oysters will set you back from R680 and there's also an excellent French wine list to get stuck into.

PETROGRAD SIDE

You won't have any trouble eating well on the Petrograd Side. You'll find the best Chinese and Georgian restaurants in the city here, as well as a few of the more interesting Russian eateries.

AKVARIUM Map pp240-1 *Chinese*

☎ 326 8286; Kamennoostrovsky pr 10; mains R450; ⌚ noon-midnight; metro Gorkovskaya

Located next to Lenfilm, Akvarium is the best Chinese in town, and has prices to match. The décor is exquisite, the staff very professional and the menu far more authentic and innovative than those of other Chinese restaurants around the city.

AQUAREL Map pp246-9 *Fusion*

☎ 320 8600; www.aquarel.net; moored off Birzhevoy most; mains R500; metro Sportivnaya

Housed on a boat moored on the Neva, this is actually one of St Petersburg's finer dining experiences, and the place that pioneered fusion cuisine in the city. The menu encompasses Italian, Russian and Asian ingredients and there are superb views of the Hermitage, Vasilevsky Island and the lights of Birzhevoy most.

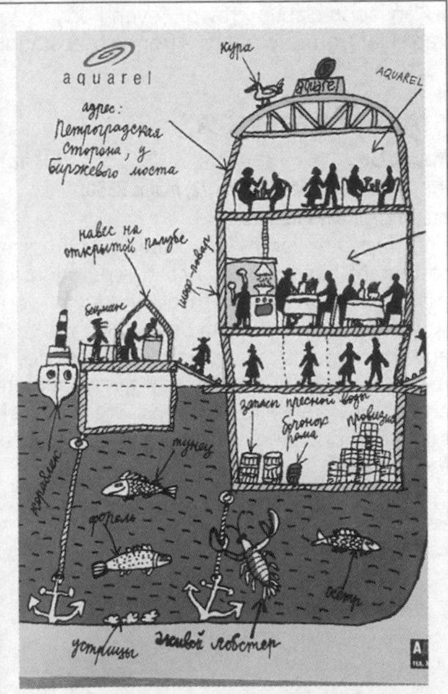

Aquarel advertisement (above)

Best Foreign Eats in Town

- Chinese – **Akvarium** (p151)
- French – **Bistrot Garçon** (p148)
- Georgian – **Salkhino** (p152)
- Indian – **Swagat** (p150)
- Italian – **Milano** (p143)
- Japanese – **Kyoto** (p143)

IVANHOE Map pp238-9 *Russian*

☎ 230 7212; Bolshoy pr 32A; mains R260; ⌚ 24hr; metro Chkalovskaya

Meals are cooked in front of you in a stone oven at this medieval-themed restaurant. A large selection of food and a pleasant, unusual ambience makes this an appealing option. Servings are plentiful, but it's usually so good you'll still want more.

KAFE TBILISI Map pp238-9 *Georgian*

☎ 230 9391; Sytninskaya ul 10; mains R180; metro Gorkovskaya

A Georgian restaurant coming to you charmingly from Soviet central planning, Kafe Tbilisi remains a beloved institution to many residents of the city, its clunky 1970s style and dark décor notwithstanding. Don't miss its *khachapuri* (cheese pie).

NASH PITER Map pp246-9 *Russian*

☎ 233 9771; www.nashpiter.ru in Russian; ul Blokhina 23; mains R250; metro Sportivnaya

Good Russian food with a vegetarian-friendly twist, 'Our Peter' (referring to the local diminutive term for St Petersburg) is a filling and tasty eatery, despite the ubiquitous Fashion TV and painful art on the walls.

NA ZDOROVYE Map pp238-9 *Russian*

☎ 232 4039; Bolshoy pr 13; mains R200; metro Sportivnaya

A bizarre hybrid of tsarist, Soviet and medieval themes coexist at this restaurant brought to you from the relentlessly popular Concord Catering (responsible for Russky Kitsch and New Island, both located on Vasilevsky Island, as well as other venues around the city). Old Russian recipes have been recreated here, including veal stuffed with cherries served over new potatoes in cherry sauce (R200) and Rostov *zrazy* of pike-perch stuffed with crawfish, onions and olives (R180). This is definitely a place to try less standard Russian fare while enjoying a friendly atmosphere.

ODIN Map pp240-1 *Scandinavian*

☎ 974 2220; ul Kuybysheva 28; mains R450; metro Gorkovskaya

A new addition to the dining scene near to the Cruiser *Aurora,* this cosy Scandinavian place's main quirk is that you can catch your own dinner of salmon or sturgeon from the pond that flows under the dining area. If you're lazy, the friendly staff will do it for you. Swedish, Danish and Norwegian standards are all here, and the menu is unsurprisingly fish-heavy.

RUSSKAYA RYBALKA

Map pp238-9 *Russian-Fish*

☎ 323 9813; www.russian-fishing.ru; Yuzhnaya Doroga 11, Krestovsky Island; mains R700; noon-9am; metro Krestovsky Ostrov

This unusual place is set on what was once apparently Prince Menshikov's favourite fishing ground. The idea is simple: you are given a rod and some bait and you catch your dinner from the pond. The chef will bake, smoke or grill your catch and serve it up to you as you like. The interior is cosy and there's an 'anti-fish' menu for those who don't want fish, although that somewhat defeats the point of coming here!

SALKHINO Map pp240-1 *Georgian*

☎ 232 7891; Kronverksky pr 25; mains R300; 11am-11pm; metro Gorkovskaya

This delightful place is for anyone wanting genuine Georgian food on the Petrograd Side. The Adjaran *khachapuri* (cheese pie cooked with runny egg and butter in the middle) is superb, and what the two chefs Ketino and Eka don't know about aubergines ain't worth knowing: try the *baklazhan s orekhami* (aubergine with walnut paste).

VYBORG SIDE

There are few eating options here, but the restaurants listed are all heartily recommended for decent, filling fare and some real atmosphere.

GOSUDAR Map pp240-1 *Russian*

☎ 324 5979; Bolshoy Sampsonievsky pr 32; mains R400; metro Vyborgskaya

This is a traditional-style Russian place with a historic feel. Tasty food is served by attentive staff, although the music can be distractingly loud at times, so book a table on the balcony if possible.

SCHVABSKY DOMIK

Map pp244-5 *German*

☎ 528 2211; Novocherkassky pr 28/19; mains R400; 11am-1am; metro Novocherkasskaya

A combination of three restaurants in one, Schvabsky Domik takes up an entire block. Amid bafflingly awful Bavarian décor you'll be offered standards such as schnitzel, sauerkraut, potatoes galore, sausage and roast pork, as well as more complicated recipes. Visit each of the three dining halls before deciding where to eat as the menus (and the prices) vary quite a bit between them.

SEVEN-FORTY Map p237 *Jewish*

☎ 246 3444; Bolshoy Sampsonievsky pr 108; mains R300; metro Lesnaya/Chyornaya Rechka

Not kosher, but the city's most popular Jewish restaurant, Seven-Forty is a unique place serving traditional, Jewish-Russian home cooking to an appreciative crowd. Seven-Forty is located far from the metro – from either station catch a cab.

STARAYA DEREVNYA

Map pp238-9 *Russian*

☎ 431 0000; ul Savushkina 72; mains R350; metro Chyornaya Rechka

This first-rate family-run traditional Russian restaurant has enjoyed a solid reputation for many years and is worth going out of your way for (from metro Chyornaya Rechka, take any tram three stops or grab a taxi). Service is great, and because it's small, it's very intimate and cosy, so make reservations. The beef with plum and nut sauce, and ham in applesauce, are superb.

Entertainment

Entertainment

Be it highbrow (watching Gergiev conduct *War and Peace* at the Mariinsky), lowbrow (dancing on the tables at Tsynik) or a sweaty in-between (being whipped clean with birch twigs in a *banya*), you certainly won't be short of activities in St Petersburg. The long winters mean that the city's cultural life is particularly lively from October to April, with many big film and theatre festivals, premieres and sporting events. Come summertime, the emphasis noticeably shifts to more hedonistic pastimes when the only thing preventing your bar and club crawl lasting all night is the raising of the bridges over the river. St Petersburg is a great city for entertainment whatever the season and no matter what type you seek.

DRINKING

As with Russian culture in general, drinking is an extremely important part of St Petersburg's social fabric. However, bars have never quite taken off in Russia in the way they have elsewhere in Europe, many Russians preferring to drink with meals or (more commonly) while wandering the streets during the summer months. The bars listed here all have regular crowds and remain consistently popular.

BARS

CHE Map pp246-9

☎ 277 7600; Poltavskaya ul 3; 🕑 24hr; metro Pl Vosstaniya

This is Central Perk meets members-only club – a coffee lounge by day and a packed and popular bar at night featuring live music, DJs and plenty of art 'happenings'. The door policy is erratic – sometimes entry is by club card only, other times it is completely relaxed – although this is just about the only gripe with one of the city's coolest hang-outs.

CITY BAR Map pp246-9

☎ 314 1037; Millionnaya ul 10; 🕑 11am-last client; metro Nevsky Pr

This friendly place is the best and most popular expat place in town – busy every night of the week with foreigners, travellers and Russians who enjoy their company. It's run by the fabulous Elaine, who certainly knows how to throw a good party, and in the quieter moments there's a free book and video lending library.

FISH FABRIQUE Map pp246-9

☎ 164 4857; Ligovsky pr 53; 🕑 3pm-6am, concerts from 8pm; metro Pl Vosstaniya

You don't get any more arty or scruffy than this veritable museum of local boho life in a basement. Here, the young and the not-so-young meet, drink beer and listen to music (playing table football is also something of a rite of passage for anyone wanting to join the local arts scene). DJs or bands play in the evenings and films are shown regularly during the daytime. Enter through the courtyard.

MANHATTAN Map pp246-9

☎ 113 1945; nab reki Fontanki 90; 🕑 2pm-5am; metro Sennaya Pl

In this raucous Fontanka-side basement there's always a sociable, arty/student crowd enjoying the boho atmosphere as well as the (often ear-splitting) live music. There are usually a couple of bands doing sets each evening and DJs keep the crowd happy the rest of the time. The food is surprisingly delicious here too, and there's Internet access.

MOLOKO Map pp244-5

☎ 274 9467; Perekupnoy per 12; 🕑 7pm-midnight; metro Pl Alexandra Nevskogo

An institution in the city – and rightly so – Moloko is the underground club that endured throughout the late 1990s and evolved into the gem it is today. The bar is cheap, the mainly student crowd exceptionally friendly and the better local groups usually play here.

MONEY HONEY Map pp246-9

☎ 310 0549; Apraksin Dvor 14; 🕑 11am-last client; metro Sadovaya

A vital conduit into the teenage rockabilly underbelly of St Petersburg, Money Honey is for kids gone bad as well as those who have invested too much money in Brylcreem and leather jackets. It's a fun and unpredictable place to hang out, famous for brawls and carousing, suitably located in the rather Dostoevskian Apraksin Dvor shopping arcade. Above Money Honey is the far more calm City Club which attracts an older and less ridiculous-looking crowd. To get to either, enter the shopping arcade and head right.

POLITBURO Map pp246-9
☎ 310 9737; ul Yefimova 1; 🕑 10am-last client; metro Sennaya Pl
In case you didn't know, Soviet is hip and nowhere more so than at Politburo, named after the famously grey and faceless communist cabinet. Stalin and Brezhnev stare out at you from old posters, and young students who never had to endure being a pioneer or read the collected works of Lenin enjoy some rose-tinted nostalgia while knocking back bottles of Baltika. There's a discount for anyone who's been awarded the Hero of Labour medal.

PYANY SOLDAT Map pp246-9
☎ 279 1789; ul Nekrasova 44; 🕑 noon-2am; metro Pl Vosstaniya
The name translates as the 'drunken soldier', and while the military-clad staff show no signs of inebriation, the clientele get pretty exuberant by the end of the evening. The well-designed space is industrially themed and features some highly unusual chairs. There's also a decent international menu.

RAYSKY AD Map pp244-5
☎ 164 9333; Ligovsky pr 107; 🕑 24hr; metro Ligovsky Pr
When all other options are exhausted, head to Heavenly Hell – an enduring place whose main selling points are being open 24 hours and cheap as you like. The bar is divided up into Heaven (upstairs) and Hell, down below. As you'd imagine, Hell is a lot more fun.

SHAMROCK Map pp246-9
☎ 318 4625; www.shamrock.spb.ru; ul Dekabristov 27; 🕑 9am-2am; metro Sadovaya
The better of the city's two Irish bars, Shamrock is a nice place with plenty of atmosphere and is not nearly as expat-dominated as some Irish bars abroad can be – it's popular with locals too. Come here for a rowdy night out, live music of varying quality and delicious chips, or just make it here for the great breakfast.

TRIBUNAL Map pp246-9
☎ 314 2423; pl Dekabristov 1; 🕑 4pm-6am; metro Nevsky Pr
This is more your stereotypical Russian bar in the eyes of foreigners – semi-naked women dancing around a mixed Russian and foreign crowd in this popular basement venue next to the *Bronze Horseman*. Women's night on Monday sees male strippers perform too. Turns into a club later on (cover R200 after 10pm Friday and Saturday).

TSYNIK Map pp246-9
☎ 312 9526; per Antonenko 4; 🕑 1pm-3am Sun-Thu, 1pm-7am Fri & Sat; metro Sadovaya
When Tsynik opened at its original venue next to the Moscow Station it was, for a while, the greatest bar in town, swiftly gaining a citywide reputation for drunken mischief and general chaos (dancing on the tables is a tradition long held dear). The second incarnation, just off Isaakievskaya pl (St Isaac's Sq), is less grungy and better run, but lacks some of the anarchy of the past. This is still definitely one of the most fun bars in St Petersburg, with a cool, student-slacker/arty crowd nursing cheap beer and famously delicious *grenki* (black bread fried in garlic).

SPORTS BARS

ALL STAR CAFÉ Map pp246-9
☎ 279 9017; ul Zhukovskogo 33; metro Mayakovskaya
This comfortable, dark sports bar has decent food, including a new sushi bar, and friendly staff; it's a great place to hang out.

PIT STOP Map pp246-9
☎ 314 9334; Sadovaya ul 12; 🕑 24hr; metro Nevsky Pr
Cavernous and slightly sordid, Pit Stop is nonetheless very good fun. You can play pool, watch matches on the big screen and place bets at the in-house *bookmeiker*. Food is unexpectedly excellent, and it's open 24 hours, just off Nevsky.

TIME OUT Map pp246-9
☎ 113 2442; ul Marata 36; 🕑 1pm-5am; metro Vladimirskaya
A small, homely sports pub popular with expats and Russians alike. Come here for a relaxed drink or something to eat while you watch sport on the big screens. Big sporting events can draw huge crowds, so come early.

COFFEE SHOPS & CAFÉS

Over just one decade St Petersburg has evolved from a city where you'd once have been glad to find a café serving Nescafé and condensed milk to one where you can order from a range of coffees that would satisfy the pickiest coffee-lover. While the chains are as strong here as ever, the independent cafés remain the best – we can't recommend fabulous Stolle enough.

CAFÉ RICO Map pp246-9

☎ 164 7214; Nevsky pr 77/1; metro Mayakovskaya

This was one of St Petersburg's first coffee shops and is enduringly popular, serving roasts from across the world and decorated with a funky African–Latin American theme. It can get crowded, but the main location is a great place to stop for coffee at the Vosstaniya end of Nevsky (the entrance is actually on Pushkinskaya ul). Another branch is at **ul Chaykovskogo 47** (Map pp246–9; metro Chernyshevskaya).

IDEALNAYA CHASHKA Map pp246-9

☎ 320 6489; Nevsky pr 15; metro Nevsky Pr

A local legend, the 'perfect cuppa' was one of Russia's first naturally successful chains – ie one that expanded due to demand rather than the fact that the owner was a powerful local fixer. It's no exaggeration to call this chain the Russian Starbucks. Founder Anna Matveyeva discovered the joys of corporate coffee shops while studying in the States and came back determined to bring the concept to her homeland. Of all the branches, the cavernous establishment on the corner of Bolshaya Morskaya ul and Nevsky has the biggest buzz about it, and is packed with students from dawn 'til dusk. Several other locations line Nevsky pr as well as elsewhere in the city centre.

KOFE HAUS Map pp246-9

☎ 312 0510; Bolshaya Konyushennaya ul 13;
24hr; metro Nevsky Pr

This Moscow-based coffee shop chain is taking on Idealnaya Chashka for a battle of supremacy in St Petersburg. Its first premises just off Nevsky are airy and light and the coffee very decent.

STOLLE Map pp246-9

☎ 328 7860; Syezdovskaya & 1-ya linii 50;
metro Vasileostrovskaya

This is hands down the coolest place to come for coffee, although you'd be a fool to come here without sampling one of its magnificent pies too. A huge, open selection greets you – both sweet and savoury. The staff are friendly, the crowd young and attractive, and the coffee superb. There is also an outlet on **ul Dekabristov** (Map pp246–9; ☎ 315 2383; ul Dekabristov 19; metro Sadovaya). The Vasilevsky Island outlet is far more pleasant than the ul Dekabristov one, which at basement level feels slightly cut off from the world.

CLUBBING

All St Petersburg clubs stay open until the very early hours – usually 6am or 7am. Most operate every day of the week. For updates, check the *St Petersburg Times* and look out for posters around town advertising big club events and one-off parties, as these are often some of the best nights out to be had, with famous DJs or good local groups playing. Many of the city's clubs charge an admission fee of R50 to R200. Nearly all clubs serve food, although be aware that a 'crazy menu' is not for ordering food but for choosing women (and sometimes men).

GOLDEN DOLLS Map pp246-9 *Striptease*

☎ 571 3343; Nevsky pr 60; metro Gostiny Dvor

A sleazy institution, Golden Dolls dazzles those passing it at night with neon. There are strip shows, a sauna, bars and a restaurant, all aimed at male pleasure. Most notoriously, for a price you can eat an entire meal off a naked woman's body if you really feel like it.

GRESHNIKI Map pp246-9 *Gay*

☎ 318 4291; nab kanala Griboedova 29;
metro Gostiny Dvor

'Sinners' is St Petersburg's gay mainstay, and is usually very busy at weekends with a friendly crowd who come to watch cabaret and dance to truly awful Russian pop. The three floors are split into dance floor, balcony area and a lounge where there's free Internet access. The club functions on a card system – you pay for everything when you leave.

GRIBOEDOV Map pp244-5 *Alternative*

☎ 164 4355; Voronezhskaya ul 2A; metro Ligovsky Pr

Enduringly cool, the Griboedov club is housed in a bomb shelter and run by local ska group

Dva Samoleta. It functions as a very relaxed and pleasant bar during the early evening, gradually morphing into a raucous and fun club later. Good DJs and live acts cover everything from electronica to trance and reggae.

HALI GALI Map p237 *Cabaret*

☎ 246 9910; Lanskoye shosse 15; metro Chyornaya Rechka

People flock to this very popular cabaret club (or 'erotic theatre' as it styles itself) in the north of the city to see the justly famous show and enjoy a bawdy night out. Unfortunately it's quite pricey and unlikely to appeal to those who don't speak Russian well. The show starts at 9pm nightly.

HAVANA Map pp244-5 *Dance*

☎ 259 1155; Moskovsky pr 21; metro Tekhnologichesky Institut

Consistently popular, Havana is a great place to have a dance and some serious fun while in St Petersburg. There's free popcorn for everyone, and live bands from South America getting the Latin flavour flowing. The only real jeer is the 'no trainers' policy, which, while flouted by half the people inside, always seems to apply to those who *aren't* friends with the doorman.

JAKARTA Map pp244-5 *Dance*

☎ 346 7462; ul Bakunina 5; metro pl Vosstaniya

Greshniki (opposite)

One of the sleekest venues in St Petersburg, Jakarta is a fantastic place where European DJs often spin when they are in town. Unfortunately it takes itself rather seriously – the door policy is one of strict face control, so if you don't look cool, you may not get in.

JET SET Map pp246-9 *Dance*

☎ 275 9288; www.jetset.spb.ru in Russian; Furshtatskaya ul 58B; metro Chernyshevskaya

The club's website is a clue to what makes this place tick: 'Are you a VIP?' it demands, and when you click yes it proclaims 'Thank God!' Jet Set represents the Moscow 'elite' clubbing that many Petersburgers claim to loathe, although quite a few seem to want to be on the guest list. Inside (if you get past the clipboard Nazis) it's sumptuous, with an oriental theme upstairs. You'll see some of the best DJs and musicians here – Portishead and Morcheeba have both performed here.

KABARE Map pp246-9 *Gay*

☎ 114 5056; ul Dekabristov 34; metro Sadovaya

Housed in a Soviet palace of culture behind the Mariinsky Theatre, Kabare has an unpretentious, friendly feel. The music is a blend of Russian and Western pop, there's a karaoke room and plenty of seats in the bar area. The night is focused on the 2am cabaret show, which is among the best in the city if you enjoy seeing men dressed as ageing Soviet pop stars.

LA PLAGE Map p237 *Dance*

☎ 525 6313; pr Kosygina 17; metro Ladozhskaya

A trek from the centre, St Petersburg's beach-themed nightclub is on a big scale, with frequent PAs by Russian pop stars to pull in the wealthy locals. Women have the dubious honour of free entry if they turn up in a bikini.

METRO Map pp244-5 *Dance*

☎ 166 0204; 174 Ligovsky pr; metro Ligovsky Pr

Metro is a St Petersburg legend – it's the city's biggest venue and its innovative management keep it consistently hip for the teenagers who make up its core demographic. The all-female security team is a pleasant change from the usual line-up of meat-heads. The male and female go-go dancers make it gay-friendly, and its student night (Monday) is crammed.

OPIUM Map pp246-9 *Dance*

☎ 312 0148; Sadovaya ul 12; metro Gostiny Dvor

The most talked-about nightspot in town at the time of writing, Opium opened to a big fanfare in 2004 and does not disappoint. It's expensive and extremely elitist, but has excellent music and the in-crowd clawing at the door.

OSTROV Map pp242-3 *Dance*

☎ 328 4857; nab Leytenanta Shmidta 37; metro Vasileostrovskaya

The 'Island' club is on a rather hard-to-reach embankment location on Vasilevsky Island. One of the city's best clubs – professionally run and aimed at a well-off, fashionable crowd without being pointlessly elitist. There are some superb shows on the revolving dance floors. Music is mainly pop and techno, although big-name DJs do occasionally visit.

PLAZA Map pp246-9 *Dance*

☎ 323 9090; nab Makarova 2; metro Sportivnaya

This is the place to come if you really need to show people how shiny your black BMW is. While the clientele have very little to write home about apart from having tonnes of cash, there are often big-name pop stars performing here, and it's frequently the venue for premiere parties and other in-crowd gatherings.

RED CLUB Map pp246-9 *Alternative*

☎ 277 1366; Poltavskaya ul 7; metro Pl Vosstaniya

This relatively recent addition to the local music scene is a welcome one – a great warehouse venue that is a mainstay for local groups and is usually packed out for gigs.

TRI EL Map pp244-5 *Lesbian*

☎ 110 2016; 5-ya Sovetskaya ul; metro Pl Vosstaniya

Russia's only lesbian club has been the subject of much hype (indeed, some taxi drivers seem very keen to discuss little else) and Tri El is a fun, women-only club (although men are allowed on Thursdays and Fridays).

TUNNEL Map pp246-9 *Dance*

☎ 233 4015; cnr Zverinskaya ul & Lybansky per; metro Sportivnaya

A St Petersburg institution, the Tunnel was a hugely influential club in the mid-1990s, when it pioneered techno music in a city where most people's knowledge of Western music stopped with Queen. Closed for several years, it has now reopened in the bomb shelter where it was first born, and plays a mix of electronica and dance.

ART

The centre of the avant-garde movement in Russia at the turn of the last century, to the rest of the world St Petersburg has always been synonymous with art. Ever since the end of communism the city has rediscovered its seething artistic underbelly, and in the mid-1990s musician turned artist Brian Eno even lived here for a year.

St Petersburg's most influential painter (and sometime local Andy Warhol) was Timur Novikov, who died in 2002. Novikov founded the 'Movement for Beauty' in 1990, espousing a neo-academist aesthetic. In 1994 he became the director of the New Academy of Fine Arts, and he continues to cast a long shadow on the city's artistic scene. The following galleries put on regularly changing exhibits of contemporary art and are worth a visit. Other museums that show contemporary art include the Benois Wing of the Russian Museum (p93) and the Manege Central Exhibition Hall (p88), where every December there's a retrospective of the best of the city's art created in the past year.

ART GALLERY BOREY Map pp246-9

☎ 273 3693; Liteyny pr 58; 🕑 10am-6pm; metro Mayakovskaya

There's usually a good show on here, one of the cooler art galleries in town. The bookshop towards the back has very reasonably priced local art and some of the best art books in town.

FREE ARTS FOUNDATION Map pp246-9

☎ 164 5371; Pushkinskaya ul 10; metro Pl Vosstaniya

Galleries have different opening times, but on Saturday afternoons all of them are open. Often referred to simply by its address, this is 'gallery central' as far as modern art is concerned. Occasional performance pieces take place, and this is very much a place to hang out with local artists as well as to actually see art on display and being created.

SOL-ART Map pp246-9

☎ 327 3082; www.solartgallery.com; Solyanoy per 15; 🕑 10am-6pm; metro Chernyshevskaya

In the sumptuous surroundings of the Stieglitz Museum, this is a great place to buy local, contemporary art. There are thousands of paintings to rummage through, and there is a large selection of Russian souvenirs too.

CLASSICAL MUSIC, BALLET & OPERA

Classical music in all its forms is serious business in St Petersburg. Few tourists leave town without seeing a ballet, opera or recital, although a surprisingly small number see something decent – most are likely to see a 'best of' show so often laid on for foreigners. As quality can fluctuate wildly, it's always best to ask locals (*not* local travel agents or hotel staff!) for their recommendations, or to read the reviews in the *St Petersburg Times* whose archive covers most major opera and ballet productions in the city.

Be aware that top ballet and opera shows will cost big bucks. The foreign pricing system is at its most iniquitous here – with vast mark-ups for those without a Russian passport (or officially a 'discount' for Russians). The standard way to buy tickets is from a *teatralnaya kassa* (theatre kiosk), which are scattered about the city. You can also buy tickets at the theatre box offices. The Mariinsky is the exception to this rule – you can *only* buy tickets from the box office (or online via its website).

When choosing what to see, it's usually better to see a Russian opera or ballet rather than a production of a foreign work, as Russian productions of these well-known Western compositions can look very naïve and stylised. A Russian opera such as *Boris Gudonov* or a classic ballet such as *Swan Lake* is likely to be intelligently staged and a fitting experience for a trip to Russia's cultural capital.

HERMITAGE THEATRE Map pp246-9

☎ 110 9030; Dvortsovaya nab 34; metro Nevsky Pr

You are unlikely to see much innovation in the performances produced here, the imperial family's own personal theatre. People come, of course, for the atmosphere and it's safe to say that they don't go away disappointed.

MARIINSKY THEATRE Map pp246-9

☎ 114 4344; www.mariinsky.ru; Teatralnaya pl 1; metro Sennaya Pl

This is easily the most famous and best venue for classical music in St Petersburg and an attraction in its own right whether or not you manage to get tickets to see a performance. Known as the Kirov Ballet during the Soviet era, the Mariinsky troupe confusingly still tours the world under this name as its Soviet-era association with Nureyev, Baryshnikov et al brings more ticket sales! General and artistic director Valery Gergiev has led the venue bravely into the modern world. In 2004 plans were finally signed off to build a new theatre behind the current building, attracting praise and derision from the usual quarters. The new venue is expected to be completed by 2009–10, although the original theatre will continue to function throughout the construction period. Recent successes include the bringing to life of Shostakovich's first opera, *The Nose*.

MUSSORGSKY OPERA & BALLET THEATRE Map pp246-9

☎ 545 4284; pl Iskusstv 1; metro Nevsky Pr

Not on quite as grand a scale as the Mariinsky, the Mussorgsky still delivers the Russian balletic or operatic experience, although most of the time the productions here are no way near as good as those at the Mariinsky.

SHOSTAKOVICH PHILHARMONIA

Map pp246-9

Bolshoy Zal ☎ 110 4257; www.philharmonia.spb.ru; Mikhailovskaya ul 2; metro Nevsky Pr

This is home to world-famous conductor Yury Temirkanov and presents some of the best concerts and festivals in the city in its two halls, the Bolshoy Zal (Great Hall) and the **Maly Zal** (Small

Mussorgsky Opera and Ballet Theatre

Hall; Map pp246–9; ☎ 311 8333; Nevsky pr 30; metro Nevsky Pr). Included in the programme is the superb **Early Music Festival** (p12).

YUSUPOV PALACE THEATRE Map pp246-9
☎ 314 9883; nab reki Moyki 94; metro Sennaya Pl
This delightful place merits a visit no matter what's being shown. Just sitting in this gorgeously attired mini-theatre, which was once a home entertainment centre for one of the city's foremost aristocratic families, is a huge treat.

JAZZ

Jazz has a very large following in the city and there are enough devotees to support some 12 or so clubs around town. The best are listed here, and have traditionally been centred around the Smolny district.

JAZZ PHILHARMONIC Map pp246-9
☎ 164 8565; Zagorodny pr 27; metro Vladimirskaya
This famous venue represents the established, more traditional side of jazz. It has two bands – a straight jazz and a Dixieland – plus foreign guests doing mainstream and modern jazz. There are concerts at 7pm nightly.

JAZZ TIME BAR Map pp246-9
☎ 273 5379; Mokhovaya ul 41; 🕑 noon-2am; metro Mayakovskaya
Charmingly unpretentious, the Jazz Time Bar has small premises on this quiet street set back from the Fontanka. As well as live music every night ranging from jazz-funk, swing and country, there's a good-value business lunch for R99.

JFC JAZZ CLUB Map pp246-9
☎ 272 9850; Shpalernaya ul 33; metro Chernyshevskaya
This excellent club is probably the best of its kind in the city. Small and New York–styled, it could almost be the East Village. It's got a fun crowd, great beer and atmosphere, and really good jazz, blues, improv and folk bands from Russia and around the world.

JFC Jazz Club (below left)

JIMI HENDRIX BLUES CLUB Map pp246-9
☎ 279 8813; Liteyny pr 33; metro Chernyshevskaya
Less of a blues club than a bar-restaurant that has small, intimate concerts, this can be a nice spot when there's a good band playing. The Armenian food is also very good.

NEO JAZZ CLUB Map pp246-9
☎ 273 3830; Solyanoy per 14; 🕑 9am-midnight; metro Chernyshevskaya
A pretty laid-back place with smoother, more mellow live jazz music. Most people come here for supper too (very good Armenian specialities at reasonable prices) and just to chill.

PALITRA ART CLUB Map pp246-9
☎ 312 3435; Malaya Morskaya ul 5; 🕑 11am-last customer; metro Nevsky Pr
This relatively new addition to the jazz scene has a similar line-up to most of the other local bars, although on Sundays there is a special guitar show featuring local experts including flamenco and blues guitarists.

THEATRE

Locals take drama very seriously, and theatre attendance in St Petersburg is far higher than in most cities elsewhere in Europe. Nearly all the drama is of course in Russian, meaning that without knowing the language watching a play may be very hard work. However, the sense of occasion with which the theatre is treated here, the beautiful interiors of the 19th-century buildings and the fascinating cultural experience that seeing a foreign interpretation of a play can be makes it worth a night out, even if you only stay for the first half (and tickets are generally cheap enough to make this perfectly feasible). The best resource for finding out what's on where is the *St Petersburg Times* – the Friday edition (also available online) contains comprehensive listings for every theatre in town. Some of the more interesting and innovative venues are listed here.

BALTIISKY DOM Map pp240-1

☎ 232 6244; www.baltichouse.spb.ru; Alexandrovsky Park 4; metro Gorkovskaya

Known under the Soviets as Lenin Konsomol Theatre, the Baltiisky Dom (Baltic House) was chosen as the new name after communism due to the annual festival of plays from the Baltic countries held here.

BOLSHOY DRAMA THEATRE Map pp246-9

☎ 310 9242; nab reki Fontanki 65; metro Sennaya Pl

Certainly one of the grandest looking of the city's theatres, the BDT was one of the city's first. Its location on the Fontanka is delightful. Here Soviet acting pioneer Georgi Tovstonogov reigned supreme until his death in 1989, and his 1957 staging of Dostoevsky's *The Idiot* is still remembered as one of the peaks of Soviet theatre. During some 40 years of Tovstonogov's direction, the BDT had become the most innovative theatre in town.

KOMMISARZHEVSKAYA Map pp246-9

☎ 311 3102; Italiyanskaya ul 19; metro Nevsky Pr

Named after Vera Kommisarzhevskaya, the great St Petersburg actress who played some of Chekhov's most famous leading ladies, this theatre is another pioneering institution whose recent successes have including putting on the one-man shows of Yevgeny Grishkovets, the current *enfant terrible* of Russian theatre.

MALY DRAMA THEATRE Map pp246-9

☎ 113 2028; ul Rubinshteyna 18; metro Vladimirskaya

The Maly (Little) Drama Theatre, sometimes known as the Theatre of Europe, has perhaps the best international reputation of all the city's theatres. Lev Dodin, probably St Petersburg's most famous director, has put on some of his best productions here including a famously long version of Dostoevsky's *The Devils,* which toured the world to great acclaim, as well as the superb *mise en scène* for Chekhov's *Play Without a Name,* which is sometimes subtitled in English for visitors during summer.

PRIYUT KOMEDIANTA Map pp246-9

☎ 310 3314; Sadovaya ul 27/9; metro Sennaya Pl

This delightful theatre's name means 'the actor's shelter' and it does a pretty good job of fulfilling its role, providing refuge for some of the city's best directors as well as players. It was founded by actor Yury Tomashevsky in the late 1980s; the city gave the theatre the disused cinema on Sadovaya, that it now inhabits. Recent successes have included Peter Shereshevsky's adaptation of Dostoevsky's *The Eternal Husband* and Georgy Vasiliev's ambitious staging of Viktor Yerofeyev's *Moscow Stations,* a sort of Russian *Trainspotting.*

PUSHKIN THEATRE Map pp246-9

☎ 110 4103; pl Ostrovskogo 2; metro Gostiny Dvor

Known to almost everyone as the Alexandrinsky Theatre (after the tsar who had it constructed), this magnificent theatre is just one part of an immaculate architectural ensemble designed by Carlo Rossi, and is well worth seeking out even if you don't see any performances here. This is where Chekhov's *The Seagull* premiered, only to be roundly hated by the public and critics alike. The theatre's interior oozes 19th-century elegance and style, although productions vary enormously in quality these days.

CIRCUS & PUPPET SHOWS

Both the circus and puppetry have a long tradition in St Petersburg and if these are your interests, you'll have no trouble finding a performance.

AVTOVO CIRCUS Map p237

☎ 183 1501; www.circus.com.ru; Avtovskaya ul; metro Avtovo

This rather far-flung enterprise has actually got lots going for it, and the repertoire looks far more contemporary than that of the State Circus in the city centre. Check out the website for the latest programmes.

BOLSHOY PUPPET THEATRE Map pp246-9

☎ 272 8215; ul Nekrasova 10; metro Chernyshevskaya

Founded in 1931, this is the city's main venue for puppets. The theatre has 16 children's shows in its repertoire, and two for adults. It remains very popular, and you'll be offered free tickets if you are staying next door in the **Puppet Hostel** (p179).

PUPPET-MARIONETTE THEATRE

Map pp246-9

☎ 311 1900; Nevsky pr 52; metro Gostiny Dvor

This venue under the arches of central Nevsky has puppet and marionette shows on a varying schedule. Mainly for children, the shows are well produced and professionally performed.

ST PETERSBURG STATE CIRCUS

Map pp246-9

☎ 314 8478; www.ticketsofrussia.ru/theatres/circus; nab reki Fontanki 3; metro Gostiny Dvor

This is the permanent address of the State Circus, whose performers sometimes seem very tired during their rather typical comedy-acrobatic routines. Check the website for the current programme.

THEATRE BOUFFE Map p237

☎ 446 6512; Narodnaya ul 1; metro Lomonosovskaya

This amusing place is located in the middle of nowhere, but is a fantastic place to take younger viewers who will find *Swan Lake* boring. The troupe here specialises in cabaret, farce and skits that are by and large comprehensible even without knowledge of Russian.

CINEMA

Going to the cinema in Russia can be a disheartening experience. Things are gradually improving, but it still seems remarkably acceptable to speak loudly during the film and even to have long and involved conversations on mobile phones. Moreover, there's little on offer for non-Russian speakers, as English-language films are almost universally shown with Russian dubbing rather than the more refined subtitles used in the rest of Europe.

That said, there are sometimes subtitled English-language films being shown – check the *St Petersburg Times* for listings. Also, there are several foreign film festivals run by cultural centres such as the Alliance Française, Goethe Institute and the British Council, with films often shown in the original language. See p10 for information about larger film festivals in St Petersburg.

AVRORA Map pp246-9

☎ 315 5254; Nevsky pr 60; metro Gostiny Dvor

Opening in 1913 as the Piccadilly Picture House, this was the city's most fashionable cinema in the early years of Russian film, and has retained its position pretty consistently ever since. Renamed the more Soviet-sounding Avrora in 1932, it was here that a young Dmitry Shostakovich played piano accompaniment to silent movies. Today it's one of the best in town, and most premieres (to which you can nearly always buy tickets) take place here.

DOM KINO Map pp246-9

☎ 314 0638; Karavannaya ul 12; metro Gostiny Dvor

The House of Cinema shows some of the best films in town – arty Russian and foreign films, as well as some higher brow Hollywood productions. This is also where the British Council holds its British Film Festival. The whole place remains remarkably Soviet in a charming way.

JAM HALL NA PETROGRADSKOY

Map pp238-9

☎ 346 4014; Kamennoostrovsky pr 42; metro Petrogradskaya

Now this is the kind of place that could never have existed in 20th-century Russia. The Jam Hall, inside a less than promising looking palace of culture, has been transformed into a luxury cinema-going experience. With sofa-style seating and tables for your drinks, this is the future and we like it. Pity it mainly shows Hollywood blockbusters dubbed into Russian.

SPORT

Sports fans will have a fairly limited choice when it comes to spectator sports, with soccer and hockey being the only two popularly followed ones.

Other Cinemas

Some other popular cinemas in the city, mainly playing Russian-dubbed blockbusters:

Barrikada (Map pp246-9; ☎ 312 5386; Nevsky pr 15; metro Nevsky Pr)

Crystal Palace (Map pp246-9; ☎ 272 2382; Nevsky pr 72; metro Gostiny Dvor)

Kozilei (Map pp246-9; ☎ 272 8775; Nevsky pr 100; metro Mayakovskaya)

Neo (Map pp242-3; ☎ 103 7525; Bolshoy pr 68B, Vasilevsky Island; metro Vasileostrovskaya)

PETROVSKY STADIUM Map pp246-9

☎ 119 5700; Petrovsky ostrov 2; metro Sportivnaya

Zenith, St Petersburg's main football team, was a sorry lot in the mid-1990s and deserved all those nasty slurs by Spartak (Moscow's team) fans. But under coach Anatoly Davydov's leadership, they won the 1998 Russian Cup, and made it to the nationals again in 2001. After they play at Petrovsky Stadium, you can hear their rowdy legion of loyal fans deafening pedestrians all over town with rally cries, no matter what the outcome of the game. Tickets can often be purchased at any *teatralnaya kassa* or the stadium – posters are usually plastered all over town well beforehand. Ticket prices vary from about R60 to R400.

YUBILEYNY SPORTS PALACE

Map pp246-9

☎ 119 5615; Dobrolyubova pr 18; metro Sportivnaya

The hockey season stretches from September to June, and here's where you can see St Petersburg's top team, SKA. At other times the space hosts expos on tattooing and the like.

HEALTH & FITNESS

Russians tend to split into two definite camps with very few in-betweeners when it comes to health and fitness. Those who do keep fit *really* keep fit (eg teetotalling judo black belt Putin), while those who don't are all-drinking, all-smoking advertisements for a premature death. That said, gyms and pools are increasing in quantity and quality, although by Western standards attendance is still low. Attendance isn't a problem, however, at the traditional *banya* (p164), and nobody should come to Russia without experiencing one – there are plenty of places around town to get whipped naked with birch twigs if that's your thing.

BANYAS

The following *banyas* are all recommended – all are reasonably priced (between R50 and R200 for the communal *banya*, and around R500 for a private one). Most have separate male and female bathing sections, so if you want a go with a mixed group of friends, book a private *banya* or head to places like Kruglye Bani where there are mixed-sex areas. In all places admission includes *tapki* (sandals), *prostinya* (sheet) and *polotentse* (towel).

KAZACHIE BANI Map pp246-9

☎ 112 5079; Bolshoy Kazachy per 11;
🕒 9am-9pm Tue-Sun; metro Pushkinskaya

A very popular and highly recommended *banya* near Vitebsk Station. Although the communal *banya* closes at 9pm, the private one is open through the night.

KRUGLYE BANI Map p237

☎ 550 0958; ul Karbysheva 29A;
🕒 8am-9pm Fri-Tue; metro Pl Muzhestva

There's a fantastic open-air heated pool that is great in the winter evenings. It's popular with expats on Wednesdays.

MITNINSKAYA BANYA Map pp244-5

☎ 271 7119; ul Mitninskaya 17-19;
🕒 8am-10pm Fri-Tue; metro Pl Vosstaniya

This is the last *banya* in the city heated by a wood furnace, just like in the country! Experts swear by it. You'll see lots of tattooed bodies.

NEVSKIE BANI Map pp246-9

☎ 311 1400; ul Marata 5/7; metro Mayakovskaya

A church was torn down to build this. Despite renovations it's not the best, but is conveniently located and cheap.

POSADSKIYE BANI Map pp240-1

☎ 233 5092; Malaya Posadskaya ul 28/2;
🕒 8am-9pm Wed-Sun; metro Gorkovskaya

The most popular *banya* on the Petrograd Side, Posadskiye Bani also includes a Finnish-style dry sauna as well as the traditional Russian *parilka* (steam room).

BEACHES & POOLS

In the stickier months, there's nothing better to do than head for the beach, and there are some perfectly good ones near St Petersburg. If you just want to sunbathe, join the crowds on the southern side of Zayachy Island in front of the wall of the Peter and Paul Fortress, where standing in your swimming costume is the only socially acceptable way to tan for some bizarre reason. You're not advised to swim in the Neva, although many do and don't appear to die.

Purification Through Sweat & Pain

For centuries, travellers to Russia have commented on the particular (in many people's eyes, peculiar) traditions of the *banya*. The closest English equivalents to this word, 'bathhouse' and 'sauna', don't quite sum it up. To this day, Russians (though more men than women) make it an important part of their week. You haven't *really* experienced Russia until you've visited one.

The *banya's* main element is the *parilka* (steam room), which gets so hot it makes the Finnish sauna look like a warm room. Like a sauna, the *parilka* has furnace-heated hot rocks, onto which water is poured using a long-handled ladle-like implement. Often, drops of eucalyptus or pine oil are added to the water. After a burst of scalding steam is released from the burning rocks, everyone stands up, grabs a tied bundle of birch branches *(veniki)* and beats themselves or each other with it. Though it may sound sadomasochistic (and there are theories tying this practice with other elements of masochism in Russian culture) or at the very least painful, the aftereffects are pleasant and cleansing. Apparently, the birch leaves (sometimes oak or, agonisingly, juniper branches are used) and their secretions help rid the skin of toxins.

Banya has a deep tradition in Russian culture ever since it emerged from ancient Novgorod. In folk traditions, it has been customary for bride and groom to take separate *banyas* the night before their wedding with their friends. Midwives used to administer a steam bath to women during delivery, and it was not uncommon to give a hot birch mini-massage to the newborn. There are also many folk proverbs associated with this tradition, including 'the *venik* is everyone's master' and 'the *banya* is a second mother'. The *banya,* in short, is a place for physical and moral purification.

St Petersburg has dozens of public *banyas;* they've existed in the city since Peter the Great himself could be seen running frightfully naked into the snow by the banks of the Neva after a good soaking. The modern tradition is something like this: usually at the same time every week, people go to their favourite *banya* where they meet up with the same people (the Western equivalent would be meeting your work-out buddies at the gym). Many bring a thermos of tea mixed with jams, spices and heaps of sugar (failing this, bottles of beer and some dried fish).

After stripping down in the changing room and wishing *'S lyokogo para'* (something like 'May your steam be easy!') to your mates, you head off into a dry sauna – to get the skin nice and hot – then it's into the *parilka*. After the birch branch bit (best experienced lying down on a bench while someone administers the 'beating'), you run outside and, depending on your nerve, plunge into an ice-cold pool, the *basseyn,* before stammering back into the changing room to hear your mates say *'S lyogkim parom'* ('Hope your steam was easy!'). Then you drape yourself in sheets and discuss world issues before repeating the process (most *banya* experts do this from five to 10 times over a two-hour period).

Otherwise, the lake shore directly west of metro Ozerki is a more pleasant option. Better still, hop on an *elektrichka* from Finland Station to **Sestroretsk** (Map p236) and follow the hordes 10 minutes through the forest to a long and sprawling beach along the Gulf of Finland.

VMF Map pp242-3

☎ 322 4505; Sredny pr 87; 7am-9pm; metro Vasileostrovskaya

This is a huge pool on Vasilevsky Island. As with most pools in St Petersburg you'll have to go to the doctor in residence for a health certificate before you can swim, although this costs peanuts and is usually done in five minutes as long as you don't look ill.

GYMS

MONOLIT Map pp246-9

☎ 273 9882; Mokhovaya ul 47; metro Mayakovskaya

This extremely friendly and professional gym opposite the St Petersburg State Circus aims to get you properly bendy with a huge range of classes from Pilates to belly dancing. A series of 10 classes comes in at R1800, and there are also the basic cardio and weights equipment you'd expect in smart premises such as this.

PLANET FITNESS Map pp246-9

☎ 315 6220; Kazanskaya ul 37; metro Sadovaya

This is St Petersburg's first big gym chain, with six locations so far open throughout the city, graded from three to five stars. Rates and membership details differ from location to location, with the Kazanskaya ul branch, not far from St Isaac's Sq, being the cheapest and most central.

SPORTS COMPLEX Map pp240-1

☎ 238 1632; Kronverksky pr 9A; 90 min for R100; 7am-11pm

The 25m swimming pool, under a glass roof, is heavenly, and you can get in without the usually required medical certificate if you look clean. There's a weights room and aerobics classes, and clubs for every sport imaginable meet here. This place is also a good source of information for spectator sporting events in the city.

Shopping

Shopping

While Moscow has become a shopping destination attracting the cream of world fashion labels, St Petersburg is still rather lagging behind the capital in this sense. Perhaps a fair symbol of the differences between the national and northern capitals, designer stores have not taken off in St Petersburg the way they have in Moscow where Kuznechny most keeps up with Fifth Ave in its sheer variety of flagship designer boutiques. There are some exceptions, however, and an enterprising if unremarkable local fashion scene definitely exists.

There's certainly no shortage of good shops, although there are few that could be called unique. We've included the more original, the most useful and the best bargains. Russian shops are notorious for selling very specific ranges, so if you have lots to buy then a shopping centre may be the answer. Of course, few places can compare to Gostiny Dvor for sheer size, although there are new additions such as the Grand Palace or the Vladimirsky Passazh.

The ubiquitous *produkty* stores throughout the city sell an almost identikit range of both Russian and imported foodstuffs. Trying to self-cater from them can be frustrating, as fresh fruit, vegetables or fresh bread are rarely available. *Supermarkety* (supermarkets) have become increasingly popular and stock a far better range of goods, although they are still less reliable for fresh fruit and vegetables than the city's markets. We've listed some centrally located supermarkets. Far and away the best-stocked and biggest supermarket in town is Lend in Vladimirsky Passazh, while Yeliseyevsky is the closest you can get to Harrod's Food Hall in St Petersburg, with its gorgeous *fin-de-siècle* interiors. You can buy good bread in any *produkty* store or *bulochnaya* (bakery). The standard Russian equivalent of a white loaf is a *gordoskoy baton* or the slightly more expensive *podmoskovny baton*. The city boasts many markets. For fresh fruit and veg, Kuznechny Market really is the best in the city, while for DVDs and anything electrical, head out of the centre to Yunona.

Russia flagrantly ignores international copyright laws much to the delight of Western shoppers who snap up CDs and DVDs at prices unthinkable at home. An average CD will set you back R30 to R60 (€1 to €2), while a DVD is usually around R100 (€3). All labelling is usually in Russian, but DVDs always have the option to switch over to English. Do be aware that bringing pirate DVDs back to your home country could be illegal and you run the theoretical risk of having them confiscated at customs, although you'll have no trouble exporting them from Russia.

For a city of literati there is definitely no shortage of booksellers. If you can read Russian you'll be in for a treat, especially exploring the second-hand shops that can be found in the most unlikely locations. Ask locals for tips – any educated person in St Petersburg is likely to know a whole slew.

The city's more niche-oriented shops offer a huge range of specialist goods, from machine guns to espresso makers.

Opening Hours

Unless stated otherwise, all shops work a roughly 9am to 7pm regime throughout the week, sometimes curtailing hours slightly on Saturday and/or Sunday. Lunch breaks are common, usually 1pm to 2pm, although they vary hugely. Unless otherwise stated, all supermarkets are open 24 hours.

Shopping on Nevsky pr

HISTORIC HEART

The city centre is where the best shopping can be had – just a walk down fabulous Nevsky pr reveals a variety of vast department stores, and some knock-out fashion, music and souvenir boutiques. From DVDs to dapper Russian fashions, you'll find it all here.

505 Map pp246-9 *Music & DVDs*
www.505.ru in Russian; Nevsky pr 72; ⌚ 10am-11pm; metro Mayakovskaya
Excellent range of CDs, DVDs and computer games; and the added novelty of being able to handle the goods yourself, albeit while being watched by about 14 security guards at one time and then having to pass electronic gates to leave which always seem to go off whether or not you've stolen something.

ANGLIA BOOKS Map pp246-9 *Books*
☎ 279 9294; anglia@inbox.ru; nab reki Fontanki 38; metro Gostiny Dvor
The city's only English-language bookshop has a large selection of contemporary literature, history and travel writing. It also hosts small art and photography displays, organises book readings and generally is a cornerstone of expat life here. An excellent shop well worth a visit.

BALTIISKY KHLEB
Map pp246-9 *Bakery*
☎ 331 3220; Vladimirsky pr 19; metro Dostoevskaya
Strangely enough despite the name ('Baltic Bread'), this is a British bakery. The main outlet is in the Vladimirsky Passazh shopping centre, where you can pick up fresh bread, cakes and even ready-made sandwiches on the run. You can take away or eat in the small café area provided.

CANALI Map pp246-9 *Clothing*
☎ 571 5473; Nevsky pr 16; metro Nevsky Pr
Look no further for your super smooth Italian shirts and suits. Canali dresses some of the most dapper men about town and its luxurious Nevsky premises just a short stroll from the Winter Palace is suitably beautiful.

CHAYNY DOM Map pp246-9 *Tea*
☎ 571 2784; ul Rubinshteyna 24; metro Dostoevskaya
This excellent shop sells every possible variety of tea as well as a range of accessories from tea strainers to teapots.

CHOCOLATE MUSEUM
Map pp246-9 *Chocolate*
☎ 327 3693; Nevsky pr 17; ⌚ 11am-9pm
The name is something of a misnomer, as this is a shop and the aim of its displays are to make you salivate and get your cash out (to good effect judging by the crowds). The amazing chocolate designs (including a bust of Lenin in white chocolate for R3000) are worth a look, although only employing black doormen (geddit?!) is a typically Russian idea of humour that will misfire with most Westerners.

DETSKY MIR Map pp246-9 *Children*
☎ 312 7245; Bolshaya Konyushennaya ul 29
Come here for the city's best selection of toys, clothes and games. Now very Westernised and stocking Harry Potter and Lego rather than the arguably more charming Russian toys, although some of these are still available.

DOM KNIGI Map pp246-9 *Books*
☎ 325 6696; Nevsky pr 62; metro Gostiny Dvor
The stalwart of the city's bookshops is Dom Knigi, which for years was one of few places in the country to sell a good range of literature. In the midst of relocating to better but less atmospheric premises on Nevsky pr at the time of writing, its original location in the former Singer building will be missed by the local literati, although its more fearsome shop assistants may well be happily forgotten.

GOSTINY DVOR
Map pp246-9 *Shopping Centre*
☎ 110 5200; www.gostinydvor.ru in Russian; Nevsky pr 35; ⌚ 10am-10pm; metro Gostiny Dvor
One of the oldest shopping arcades in the world, built in the mid-18th century, Gostiny Dvor (the Merchant Yard) has for the past decade been going through a gradual and much-needed restoration and repainting of its exterior, which is finally drawing to completion. Inside, the place retains a largely Soviet feel, although the smarter fashion outlets on the 1st floor are definitely an improvement. Downstairs Gostiny Dvor's endless corridors of counters selling everything from stereos to furnishings remain the order of the day.

GRAND PALACE
Map pp246-9 *Shopping Centre*
☎ 449 9411; Nevsky pr 44; ⌚ 11am-9pm; metro Gostiny Dvor
For once the rather uppity title is deserved – this glittering centre created for St Petersburg's

new rich shopping classes is both grand and palatial. You'll see big names such as Max Mara, Dior and Lacroix here, not to mention the best free toilets available in the city.

HUGO BOSS Map pp246-9 *Clothing*

Boss Man ☎ 315 1237; Nevsky pr 23; Boss Woman ☎ 113 2412; Nevsky pr 47/1

One of the first Western fashion labels to establish itself in St Petersburg, Boss's investment seems to have paid off with both its male and female outlets busy when we visited. Both shops stock the famously classy modern takes on traditional tailoring that the Boss label is so famous for.

INTENDANT Map pp246-9 *Wine*

☎ 571 1510; www.intendant-salon.ru in Russian; Karavannaya ul 18; metro Gostiny Dvor

Intendant is a vintner's with an enormous selection of wines from all over the world. This is a good place to buy some of the better Georgian wines – try a bottle of Saperavi.

ISSKUSTVO Map pp246-9 *Books*

☎ 312 8535; Nevsky pr 16; metro Nevsky Pr

There are several bookshops near the corner of Bolshaya Morskaya ul. In this one is a good selection of maps and art books. There are also posters, calendars, postcards and other good souvenirs on offer.

Caviar – If Buying, Buy Carefully

While nothing is as evocative of Russian imperial luxury as black caviar, be aware that the sturgeon of the Caspian Sea could face extinction due to the unsustainable and illegal plunder of their roe. Official sturgeon catches in the Caspian basin, which account for 60% of the world's caviar supply, fell from 20,000 tonnes in the late 1970s to barely 550 tonnes in 2000. Despite an increase in fishing effort, the declared landings have plummeted by nearly 97% in the last 20 years. While most of the caviar on sale in St Petersburg is legal, if you decide to buy some, buy carefully. Purchase caviar only from shops (not on the street or at markets), only in sealed jars (not loose) and, most importantly of all, make sure the jar or tin is sealed with a CITES (Convention on International Trade in Endangered Species) label, a new international trade-control measure set up to reduce sturgeon poaching. Additionally, under international law, tourists are only permitted to bring home 250g of caviar per person. For more information go to www.cites.org.

KUZNECHNY MARKET

Map pp246-9 *Market*

☎ 312 4161; Kuznechny per 3; 🕑 8am-8pm; metro Vladimirskaya

Visit Kuznechny Market even if you don't want to buy anything – the colours and atmosphere of the city's best and most expensive fruit and veg market are enticing, and the vendors – nearly all from the Caucasus and Central Asia – will charm you into buying by plying you with free samples of fresh fruit as well as *smetana* (sour cream) and delicious honey.

LEND Map pp246-9 *Supermarket*

Vladimirsky pr 19; metro Vladimirskaya

This is the best in the city centre, under the giant Vladimirsky Passazh shopping centre, and you can get everything from fresh pasta and Italian pesto to a reasonably priced bottle of Sancerre. There's also sushi available, not to mention the perch and pike in the aquarium waiting to be someone's supper.

LILIA KISSELENKO

Map pp246-9 *Clothing*

☎ 310 7428; www.kisselenko.ru; Malaya Sadovaya ul 4; metro Gostiny Dvor

Understated chic, Kisselenko uses sublimely simple fabrics to create women's clothing that is at once very linear and quite charming. This is a name to watch out for – she's too sleek and unflashy for the Russian new rich but a magnet for people with good taste.

NAKHODKA

Map pp246-9 *Supermarket*

Nab reki Fontanki 5; metro Gostiny Dvor

A cheap and sprawling supermarket on the Fontanka, Nakhodka (The Find) is an excellent supermarket. What it lacks is a large range of fresh goods, but compensates with a great selection of pre-packed consumables.

OTKRITY MIR Map pp246-9 *Music*

☎ 115 8939; ul Mal Morskaya 16; metro Nevsky Pr

This shop sells a huge range of classical, jazz and world music, all licensed but still very reasonably priced. The staff are delightfully friendly and helpful, and you are free to browse the enormous selection at your leisure.

PARNAS Map pp246-9 *Supermarket*

ul Malaya Sadovaya 3; metro Gostiny Dvor

Parnas is a chain that operates throughout the city. This branch is very conveniently located on

Malaya Sadovaya just off Nevsky, and is usually besieged by teenagers buying beer to drink out on the pedestrianised street. However, there's a good selection of basic foodstuffs here.

PASSAZH

Map pp246-9 *Shopping Centre*

☎ 311 7084; Nevsky pr 48; 🕒 11am-9pm; metro Gostiny Dvor

This charming arcade running between Nevsky and Italiyanskaya ul has little in terms of unique shopping on offer, but it's just a great, characterful place to stroll. Anyone familiar with Moscow's much larger GUM shopping centre will see some similarities in style.

PCHELOVODSTVO

Map pp246-9 *Honey*

☎ 279 7262; Liteyny pr 42; 🕒 10am-6pm Mon-Sat; metro Mayakovskaya

'I came all the way here to buy *honey*?' you ask? But step into this sweet shop and you won't be able to resist. There's many types of fresh honey from Rusisa's Rostov region, products, remedies and creams made from pollen, as well as unique teas, which make nice gifts.

RIVE GAUCHE Map pp246-9 *Cosmetics*

☎ 277 0187; Nevsky pr 81; metro Mayakovskaya

For perfumes, make-up and other luxuries from international names including Chanel, Dior and Givenchy, head to one of Rive Gauche's many outlets around town. With three stores on Nevsky alone, Rive Gauche has cornered this luxury market and its selection is excellent.

SOLDAT UDACHI Map pp246-9 *Military*

☎ 279 1850; www.soldat.spb.ru in Russian; ul Nekrasova 37; metro Pl Vosstaniya

This fascinating shop ('soldier of fortune') sells a huge range of military accoutrement from machine guns (yes, really) to more mundane equipment (binoculars, water bottles) and clothing. There are some great military souvenirs to be had.

SOUVENIR MARKET

Map pp246-9 *Market*

🕒 9am-dusk

This rather uniform set of stalls behind the Church on Spilled Blood is, of course, orientated towards tourists. Here you'll find rows of *matryoshki* (nesting dolls), Soviet flags, military hats, fur caps and T-shirts ('McLenin's' being the current local equivalent of 'I like the Pope, the Pope smokes dope'). Stallholders are multilingual and know how to make a sale. Whatever you do, haggle!

Toy soldiers, Souvenir Market (below left)

SPORTIVNY NA LITEYNOM

Map pp246-9 *Sports Gear*

☎ 272 2170; Liteyny pr 57; metro Mayakovskaya

Another great store with sports clothes, running shoes, camping and hunting supplies, skis and even the occasional mosquito-net hat (which could come in handy in the city, even if it looks a tad odd!).

STOCKMANN

Map pp246-9 *Department Store*

☎ 326 2636; Nevsky pr 25; metro Nevsky Pr

Once a lifeline in the city for foreign residents, this pricey Finnish department store contains both an upmarket food hall and sells men's, women's and children's clothing. There's also a pleasant coffee shop.

TATYANA PARFIONOVA

Map pp246-9 *Clothing*

☎ 113 1415; Nevsky pr 51; metro Mayakovskaya

Parfionova was the first St Petersburg couturier to have her own fashion house back in the 1990s when the Russian new rich turned their nose up at anything not minted in Paris or Milan. She's become a huge local star and at her boutique on Nevsky you'll find her striking monochromatic *prêt-a-porter* designs as well as her famous crimson scarves.

TITANIK Map pp246-9 *Music & DVDs*

☎ 310 4929; Nevsky pr 52/54; ⏲ 24 hr; metro Gostiny Dvor

The chain store Titanik has a great selection of CDs and DVDs, the one drawback being that they are all behind glass and thus, if your Russian isn't good, it's very hard to tell what things are just by reading the spines.

VERSACE Map pp246-9 *Clothing*

☎ 113 4933; Nevsky pr 39; metro Gostiny Dvor

Versace have definitely bagged one of the best retail premises in town: the sumptuous Rossi pavilion of the Anichkov Palace, looking out onto Nevsky. Inside you can expect to see the trademark Versace threads being jealously sought after by the local fashion set.

VLADIMIRSKY PASSAZH

Map pp246-9 *Shopping Centre*

☎ 331 3232; www.vladimirskiy.ru in Russian; Vladimirsky pr; metro Vladimirskaya

Walking into this centre from the chaotic street outside you'll be forgiven for thinking you've passed through a *Buffy*-style portal to another world. This is not Russia as most people know it – sushi bars jostle with cafés and the city's best supermarket, Lend. Rows of empty shops selling identical furs to nonexistent customers remind you that you are in St Petersburg.

VOYENTORG Map pp246-9 *Military Wear*

☎ 314 6254; Nevsky pr 67; metro Mayakovskaya

If army's your thing, you'll do no better than here. It sells original (as well as synthetic) articles of military clothing of all types and varieties (from soldiers' underwear – unused – to officers' caps and parade uniforms). Prices are very reasonable.

YAKHONT Map pp246-9 *Clothing*

☎ 314 6415; Bolshaya Morskaya ul 24; metro Nevsky Pr

Housed in the Fabergé building from where Carl Fabergé dazzled the imperial family and the rest of the world with his extraordinary bespoke designs, Yakhont is carrying on the tradition despite having no link to the Fabergé family. This long, dark salon provides an impressive showcase of their work.

YELISEYEVSKY Map pp246-9 *Supermarket*

Nevsky pr 56; ⏲ 10am-9pm; metro Gostiny Dvor

How many supermarkets can boast being mentioned in *Anna Karenina*? This remarkable shop is a stunner – its *fin-de-siècle* fittings are absolutely gorgeous and it retains a certain snob value in the city, despite its rather inconvenient Soviet shopping style (you have to ask shop assistants to show you goods from behind the glass counters).

Clothing Sizes

Measurements approximate only, try before you buy

Women's Clothing						
Aus/UK	8	10	12	14	16	18
Europe	36	38	40	42	44	46
Japan	5	7	9	11	13	15
USA	6	8	10	12	14	16
Women's Shoes						
Aus/USA	5	6	7	8	9	10
Europe	35	36	37	38	39	40
France only	35	36	38	39	40	42
Japan	22	23	24	25	26	27
UK	3½	4½	5½	6½	7½	8½
Men's Clothing						
Aus	92	96	100	104	108	112
Europe	46	48	50	52	54	56
Japan	S		M	M		L
UK/USA	35	36	37	38	39	40
Men's Shirts (Collar Sizes)						
Aus/Japan	38	39	40	41	42	43
Europe	38	39	40	41	42	43
UK/USA	15	15½	16	16½	17	17½
Men's Shoes						
Aus/UK	7	8	9	10	11	12
Europe	41	42	43	44½	46	47
Japan	26	27	27½	28	29	30
USA	7½	8½	9½	10½	11½	12½

SENNAYA

It's said that you can buy almost anything on Sennaya pl and its seedy side streets, although in the 1990s the suggestion was more about the availability of drugs more than any particularly amazing consumer opportunities. Since the tercentennial clean-up though, lots of smart shops have opened up, particularly in and around the spanking-new Sennaya shopping centre.

BUSHE Map pp246-9 *Bakery*

☎ 312 3578; Razyezhaya ul 13; metro Vladimirskaya/Ligovsky Pr

Despite being an Austrian bakery, Bushe is exceptionally Soviet in style, although it has developed a huge number of local devotees. The cakes are delicious and you should give some of the many varieties of bread a try.

> ### Top Five Speciality Shops
> - Soldat Udachi (p169)
> - Pchelovodstvo (p169)
> - Chocolate Museum (p167)
> - Model Shop (p171)
> - Mir Espresso (p171)

SENNAYA Map pp246-9 *Shopping Centre*
☎ 140 4640; www.sennaya.ru in Russian; ul Yefimova 3; metro Sennaya Pl
An unnervingly American-style mall a short walk from Sennaya pl, this huge place is mainly for fashion, but includes a food hall (and a branch of the ubiquitous McDonald's), a bowling alley and the Patterson department store.

SENNOY MARKET Map pp246-9 *Market*
☎ 310 1209; Moskovsky pr 4; 8am-7pm; metro Sennaya Pl
Cheaper and less atmospheric than Kuznechny, Sennoy Market is centrally located and sells fruit and veg from just south of Sennaya pl.

SNARK Map pp246-9 *Books*
☎ 327 6260; Zagorodny pr 21; metro Dostoevskaya
The friendly Snark chain, which bills itself as a 'book club' and has a less Soviet approach to bookselling, is a great place to browse and has regularly changing themes for kids. Some of its branches sell CDs and DVDs too.

MARIINSKY

Reflecting the unique, arty and cosmopolitan nature of the Mariinsky neighbourhood, you'll find a particularly diverse bunch of shops in this neck of the woods. No ballet or opera fan should miss the unique Mariinsky Art Shop and expat coffee aficionados still thank their lucky stars for life-saving Mir Espresso.

FRANCE BAGUETTE Map pp246-9 *Bakery*
Konnogvardeysky bul 21; metro Sadovaya
This outlet is just one part of a bread factory that makes French-style pastries, such as croissants, *pain au chocolat* and baguettes. Don't go expecting Parisian standards, however, although it's cheap and reliably decent.

KOSHER SHOP Map pp246-9 *Kosher*
☎ 114 1153; Lermontovsky pr 1; metro Sennaya Pl
Serving St Petersburg's Jewish community, the Kosher Shop is conveniently located next to the Grand Choral Synagogue. Although its emphasis is on selling kosher food, the shop also sells books about Judaism in many languages, Jewish music and art.

MARIINSKY ART SHOP
Map pp246-9 *Souvenirs*
☎ 326 4197; inside the Mariinsky Theatre; 11am-6pm on performance days, also open during interval
This small but excellent shop is squarely aimed at tourists and so while it's not exactly cheap, there's a comprehensive range of opera and ballet-related souvenirs including CDs and DVDs, books and posters you won't find elsewhere. Turn right from the main entrance and the shop is at the end on the right.

MIR ESPRESSO Map pp246-9 *Coffee*
☎ 315 1370; ul Dekabristov 12/10; metro Sadovaya
Good quality coffee can be very hard to come by in St Petersburg (although increasingly less so), but come here for the smell alone and stay for the amazing range of coffee from all over the world. As well as espresso machines, there's every conceivable type of coffee maker and caffeine-related accessory.

PETROGRAD SIDE

Full of bustle and energy, the Petrograd Side remains something of a consumer desert, although there are a couple of places that we strongly recommend visiting. The Model Shop will of course be first stop for anyone wanting Russian models of Soviet planes, trains and automobiles.

MODEL SHOP Map pp246-9 *Models*
☎ 116 9077; Artillery Museum, Kronverkskaya nab; metro Gorkovskaya
Inside the Artillery Museum (you don't need to pay for entry to get access to the shop), this is a must for model plane, train and automobile fans. There's a huge range of mainly Russian models in stock and the staff are extremely helpful.

STARAYA KNIGA Map pp238-9 *Books*
☎ 232 1765; Bolshoy pr 19, Petrograd Side; metro Chkalovskaya
Any lover of books will find this superb shop a joy. It's a tiny, musty outfit selling out-of-print and other old books, mainly from the Soviet and pre-Soviet era. Lots of fascinating browsing even if you can't read a word of Russian.

Other Neighbourhoods

Smolny

Comme des Garçons (Map pp244-5; ☎ 275 5832; Suvorovsky pr 47; metro Pl Vosstaniya) Opening a store in St Petersburg was a smart move for Japanese hyper-hipsters Comme, who through a series of high-profile fashion shows in the city have established themselves as the darlings of the local fashion world.

Vasilevsky Island

Techno Sport Centre (Map pp242-3; ☎ 322 6060; pl Morskoy Slavy 1; metro Primorskaya) Way out on Vasilevsky Island, inside the Hotel Morskaya complex is one of the city's best sports supply stores, mainly but not exclusively focusing on seafaring gear. It sells water jets, boats, rubber rafts, motors, water scooters, as well as telescopes, binoculars (Russian and foreign), fishing gear and Nordic Line warm gloves.

Vyborg Side

Polyustrovsky Market (Map pp240-1; ☎ 540 3039; Polyustrovsky pr 45; metro Pl Lenina) Animal lovers will be appalled by this place where animals are bought and sold. Many fluffy young things are caged in horribly small boxes and few are treated with much care. That said, this is the best pet market in the city if you'd like to rescue something cute.

SYTNY MARKET Map pp238-9 *Market*

☎ 233 2293; Sytninskaya pl 3/5; ⌚ 8am-6pm; metro Gorkovskaya

This colourful market on the Petrograd Side sells almost everything from fruit, vegetables, meat and fish inside to electronics, clothing and knick-knacks outside. Its name means 'sated' market, quite understandably.

OUT OF TOWN

Some of the best shopping to be had isn't even in the city itself. IKEA continues to revolutionise the domestic set-up of Russians and expats alike, although the majority of visitors to St Petersburg will be far more interested in bargain hunting (and DVD mass-purchasing) at Yunona, and picking up some bargain porcelain at the Lomonosova China Factory.

IKEA *Furniture*

☎ 332 0055; Murmanskoye Shosse, 12km; metro Ul Dybenko

The Ikeaisation of Russia looks set to carry on exponentially, with a branch of the Swedish behemoth opening in Tatarstan in 2004. Let's face it, though, there's certainly no shortage of houses to redecorate. This gigantic store in the Leningradsky Oblast is like any other, with a vast array of very good value and stylish home furnishings on offer. There's a free shuttle bus from metro Ul Dybenko across the road.

LOMONOSOVA CHINA FACTORY Map p237 *China*

☎ 560 8544; www.lomonosovporcelain.com; pr Obukhovskoy oborony 151; metro Lomonosovskaya

There are great deals on fine china at this factory outlet shop, where you can get anything from the company catalogue at prices lower than in the department stores. There are over 500 items on sale, including lovely teapots (€6) and serving dishes (€20). From Metro Lomonosovskaya, turn left, walk under the bridge to the embankment then left – the factory's ahead. The shop is inside the main door and to the right.

It's easier (though pricier) to shop at the branches in the city centre. Try **Nevsky pr** (Map pp244–5; ☎ 277 4838; Nevsky pr 160; metro Pl Alexandra Nevskogo) or **Vladimirsky pr** (Map pp246–7; ☎ 113 1513; Vladimirsky pr 7; metro Vladimirskaya), but avoid the vast mark-ups made at the Grand Hotel Europe outlet.

YUNONA FAIR Map p237 *Market*

☎ 184 3441; www.spb-unona.ru in Russian; ul Marshala Kazakova 40; ⌚ 10am-8pm Tue-Sun; metro Avtovo, then marshrutka 60 or 80 or Tram 60

It's worth trekking out to Yunona for some of the best bargains you'll ever see. Of course, none of the DVDs or CDs are legal copies (what do you expect for about €2?), and the open sale of weapons may raise a few eyebrows, but this is a fascinating place. It's best to go on Saturdays when there's a vast flea market outside where people sell incredible knick-knacks, antiques and Soviet medals, as well as lots of complete junk, of course.

Sleeping

Sleeping

The 300th anniversary of St Petersburg's founding saw a huge expansion in the city's sleeping options, with a much-needed middle-range gradually developing where before the choice was locked between prohibitive five-star hotels and Soviet fleapits. Top-end accommodation has also been expanded hugely with St Petersburg becoming more and more of a business centre, as well as a destination for more affluent travellers. Flamboyant Anglo-Italian hotelier Rocco Forte's acquisition and revamping of two historic St Petersburg hotels has been spectacular and has raised the bar for other international groups operating in the city.

Accommodation Styles

There are five main types of accommodation in St Petersburg. Most visible are the huge, palace-like four- and five-star hotels that have proliferated in the past few years. These are priced for the business market and may be prohibitive for some travellers (although many offer far better deals through travel agents and hotel websites).

Second is the largely depressing collection of post-Intourist Soviet hotels all slowly adapting to the needs of the modern traveller. Some have done very well (the Sovetskaya, for example) and some are still pretty terrible (the Kievskaya among others). Despite this, there can be some bargains for those who don't mind antediluvian plumbing and resolutely brown furnishing.

Third are the hostels. These began to spring up as St Petersburg started to be a popular backpacker destination in the 1990s and while this may not be Prague, there's now a good choice of centrally located, clean and well-run hostels.

Most uniquely, there are the mini-hotels – a concept that gained currency in the run-up to the tricentennial celebrations in 2003 when it became abundantly clear that there were insufficient beds in the city for the influx of revellers. The ever-resourceful Russian

Renaissance St Petersburg Baltic Hotel (p181)

entrepreneurial sector took over, opening up small, often family-run hotels, many of which are in renovated apartments in very unlikely looking buildings. Today, these make for some of the best-value and most characterful accommodation in the city.

And finally, anyone spending more than a few days in St Petersburg should consider renting a short-term apartment for the duration of their stay. As well as being financially beneficial (especially if there are a few of you), this is a great chance to live life more like the locals, rather than cloistered away in a hotel. As with most things in Russia, it's best to ask around.

Seasonal Pricing & Taxes

Be aware that St Petersburg operates on a roundly enforced system of seasonal pricing. Come early May, nearly all establishments put up their prices by around 20% to 30%, not an insignificant amount. This is of course a good reason to come in the low season (October to April), although some hotels charge on a sliding scale between low and high season – it always pays to ask before you arrive. In this book we have given you the summer prices for each hotel. There's also 18% VAT chargeable on hotel rooms in Russia. Some establishments craftily leave this out when quoting prices – often a good indicator of how (un)professional the establishment is. All prices we quote include VAT, but again, always check with the management when booking. Accommodation prices in St Petersburg are often given in euros (as in this chapter) or US dollars, but payment is usually in roubles.

Reservations

It's always wise to reserve a bed in advance of arrival, and essential during the summer months when St Petersburg is awash with travellers. Indeed, turning up during the White Nights Festival in late June without a reservation is asking for trouble. It usually suffices to call ahead or send an email, but increasingly hotels will ask for a credit card to guarantee a room, and they will charge you for a night's accommodation if you don't show.

However, reservations will often be tied up with visa support, in which case you may already be charged for one night's accommodation in advance.

Visa Support & Registration

Nearly all hotels and hostels in St Petersburg are able to issue an invitation *(priglasheniye)* to potential guests. This is needed to obtain a tourist visa from a Russian embassy abroad (see p217). The same hotel will register your visa for you (something that needs to be done within three days of arrival in Russia), although some cheaper hotels cannot always register visas that were not issued with their invitation. In this case, you need to contact a local travel agency and pay them the approximately €30 fee to register your visa for you.

HISTORIC HEART

In short, this is where you want to be. Many first-time visitors to the city can spend days without leaving this area, with its remarkable museums, churches and canals. There's a huge range of accommodation here, including most of the city's very best hotels. However, there are also a large number of budget places and idiosyncratic mini-hotels that have opened to cater for the huge demand to stay in the neighbourhood.

ANGLETERRE HOTEL Map pp246-9 *Hotel*
☎ 313 5112; www.angleterrehotel.com; Bolshaya Morskaya ul 39; s/d €340/375, ste €435-700; metro Nevsky Pr; Ⓟ
The four-star sister hotel to the five-star Astoria next door, the Angleterre enjoyed a superb renovation by Rocco Forte. Although rooms are sometimes a little small for this price range, the chic cream and red décor, the services and the facilities are all faultless. Rooms overlooking St Isaac's Cathedral are particularly lovely. Romantics will love to know that poet Sergei Yesenin hanged himself in Room 25 after writing a suicide note in blood.

Top Five Sleeps

- **Best Hostel** Nord Hostel (p178)
- **Cheapest Bed in Town** Petrovsky College Student Hostel (p184)
- **Most Romantic Retreat** Grand Hotel Europe (p176)
- **Coolest Hideaway** Kazanskaya 5 (p177)
- **Funkiest Mini-Hotel** Five Corners Hotel (p180)

B&B NEVSKY PROSPEKT

Map pp246-9 *Mini-Hotel*

☎ 325 9398; www.bnbrussia.com; Nevsky pr 11, apt 8; s/d €80/100; metro Nevsky Pr

Superbly located and delightfully furnished with, among other things, what must be the oldest functioning TV and radio in Russia, this B&B is decidedly upmarket, as its prices amply reflect. For this price you get English-speaking staff, use of a shared kitchen and laundry facilities, and free airport transfers.

BED & BREAKFAST *Mini-Hotel*

☎ 315 5635; www.bednbreakfast.sp.ru; prices vary depending on location

Bed & Breakfast run a range of small hotels, apartments for short-term lets and even a hostel throughout the historic heart of St Petersburg. Contact its office for information – its hostels on Kazanskaya ul and Bolshaya Konyushennaya ul are excellent, as are its two mini-hotels on Nevsky pr. Even better value are its flats – a three-bedroom apartment costs from €90 per day.

COMFORT HOTEL Map pp246-9 *Mini-Hotel*

☎ 318 6700; www.comfort-hotel.spb.ru; Bolshaya Morskaya ul 25; s/d €115/135; metro Nevsky Pr

Superbly located, this mini-hotel on one of St Petersburg's most chic streets is welcoming and comfortable, although slightly pricey given its fairly standard facilities. It's excellently located to see nearby St Isaac's Cathedral and the Hermitage, however.

CORINTHIA NEVSKIJ PALACE HOTEL

Map pp246-9 *Hotel*

☎ 380 2001; www.corinthiahotels.com; Nevsky pr 57; s/d €315/355, ste €580-1600; metro Mayakovskaya

Popular with business people and very much a business hotel, the Nevskij Palace is extremely well run and comfortable. On the minus side it lacks the atmosphere of the other 'palace' hotels in town and is set back from Nevsky pr in a characterless glass atrium, although this makes it very quiet.

GRAND HOTEL EUROPE

Map pp246-9 *Hotel*

☎ 329 6000; www.grandhoteleurope.com; Mikhailovskaya ul 1/7; s & d €355, ste €500-3200; metro Gostiny Dvor; (P)

Pricey but spectacular, the Grand Hotel Europe endures as the best hotel in the city. In 1830 Carlo Rossi united the three adjacent buildings with the beautiful façade you see today. History seeps from its marble walls: Tchaikovsky spent his honeymoon here, George Bernard Shaw dined with Gorky in the restaurant and Isadora Duncan lived here during the early 1920s. Today, faultless location, gorgeous rooms and superb service mean that the executive suites with views over pl Iskusstv (Arts Sq) may actually be worth their staggering price tag.

HELVETIA HOTEL SUITES

Map pp246-9 *Hotel*

☎ 571 9597; www.helvetia-suites.ru; ul Marata 11; s/d €210/225; metro Mayakovskaya

A wonderful oasis next door to the Swiss consulate, the Helvetia is located in a secure courtyard just off charming ul Marata, and a stone's throw from Nevsky. What the rooms lack in atmosphere, they make up for in comfort. However, the price still seems high.

HOTEL ASTORIA Map pp246-9 *Hotel*

☎ 313 5757; www.roccofortehotels.com; Bolshaya Morskaya ul 39; s/d €415/430, ste €745-2300; metro Nevsky Pr; (P)

Given a new lease of life by Rocco Forte, who purchased this classic St Petersburg hotel in 1997, the Astoria is the only real rival to the Grand Hotel Europe as the best in town and many argue that it has now surpassed it.

Best Addresses in St Petersburg

- **Hotel Astoria** (p176)
- **Grand Hotel Europe** (p176)
- **Baltic Star Hotel** (p184)
- **Grand Hotel Emerald** (p179)
- **Renaissance St Petersburg Baltic Hotel** (p181)

Guests have spanned the political spectrum from Lenin to George W Bush, and while rates are very steep, there's no doubting that this is a gorgeously designed five-star establishment.

HOTEL DOSTOEVSKY Map pp246-9 *Hotel*
☎ 331 3200; www.dostoevsky-hotel.ru; Vladimirsky pr 19; s/d €155/210; metro Vladimirskaya
Located above the Vladimirsky Passazh, one of the city's most American-style malls, the Dostoevsky is a deceptively enormous place, with some 214 rooms, many of which have gorgeous views of Vladimirsky Cathedral across the road. The panorama from the 7th-floor lounge is breathtaking. Rooms are modern and well designed.

HOTEL SONATA Map pp246-9 *Mini-Hotel*
☎ 380 4090; ul Mayakovskogo 50; s/d €90/100; metro Chernyshevskaya
With two locations in the centre of the city, Sonata is one of the better mini-hotels. Its rooms are large and well designed in a contemporary style. The branch at **Gorokhovaya ul 3** (Map pp246–9; metro Nevsky Pr) is the best for sightseeing and the hotel has particularly spacious rooms.

HOTELS ON NEVSKY ASSOCIATION
Map pp246-9 *Mini-Hotel*
☎ 103 3860; www.hon.ru; s/d from €70/90; metro Nevsky Pr
This excellent group of small hotels provides affordable mid-range accommodation spread over three locations on Nevsky: **Nevsky pr 22** (☎ 312 1206); **Nevsky pr 90** (☎ 273 7314) and **Nevsky pr 91** (☎ 277 1888). Check out the website for more detailed information on each of the hotels, but all can be highly recommended – rooms are en suite and kitchens are available for guests' use.

KAZANSKAYA 5 Map pp246-9 *Mini-Hotel*
☎ 327 7466; www.kazanskaya5.com; Kazanskaya ul 5, 3rd fl; s/d €110/125; metro Nevsky Pr
Perfectly located and beautifully designed, Kazanskaya 5 attracts an in-the-know crowd of artists and musicians staying in the city. Stuffed full of antiques, the understated rooms nonetheless enjoy a thoroughly modern feel with the wooden floorboards and otherwise minimalist décor. There are photography and painting displays throughout the premises and often gatherings of local boho types.

KRISTOFF HOTEL Map pp246-9 *Mini-Hotel*
☎ 571 6643; www.kristoff.ru; Zagorodny pr 9; s/d €120/140; metro Dostoevskaya
Another very good mini-hotel aiming for the higher end of the mid-range bracket, the Kristoff has a very popular Russian-European restaurant downstairs which is worth a visit in its own right (p143). The 15 rooms here are smart and modern with perks including Wi-Fi in the rooms.

NEVSKY INN Map pp246-9 *Mini-Hotel*
☎ 924 9805; www.nevskyinn.ru; Kirpichny per 2, flat 19; s/d €60/75; metro Nevsky Pr
Run by joint British-Russian management, the Nevsky Inn is one of the best mini-hotels in the city. Rooms are clean and comfortable and there's a large modern kitchen that guests can use.

PETRA APARTMENTS
Map pp246-9 *Mini-Hotel*
☎ 312 4379; Gorokhovaya ul 3, apt 18; s & d €100-135, buffet breakfast €7; metro Nevsky Pr
With just five rooms, all of which are embellished with zebra- and leopard-skin print duvets, the Petra apartments are actually typical hotel accommodation, despite the name. The location is brilliant, as is the huge kitchen that guests are free to use.

POLIKOFF HOTEL Map pp246-9 *Mini-Hotel*
☎ 314 7925; www.polikoff.ru; Nevsky pr 64/11; s & d €90-125; metro Gostiny Dvor
With modern, smart design and excellent location, the Polikoff is nonetheless hard to find. Management promises to put a sign up at some point (details, details) but until then, take the brown door from Karavannaya ul and dial 26 for reception. Rooms are quiet and the place is brimming with contemporary cool.

PUSHKA INN Map pp246-9 *Hotel*
☎ 312 0913; www.pushkainn.ru; nab reki Moyki 14; s/d €100/180, apt €180-270; metro Nevsky Pr
Next door to the Pushkin-Flat Museum on the charming Moyka River, the Pushka Inn offers a whole range of accommodation from rooms to apartments. It's a very decent set-up with helpful staff and a great location.

RADISSON SAS ROYAL HOTEL
Map pp246-9 *Hotel*
☎ 322 5000; www.radissonsas.com; Nevsky pr 49/2; s & d €285; metro Mayakovskaya

Opened in 2001, the Radisson now gives the Nevskij Palace a run for its money, offering similarly smart rooms in a more glamorous and atmospheric location. Its position on the corner of Nevsky and Vladimirsky pr means that you feel very much in the thick of things, although the rooms are virtually soundproof.

CHEAP SLEEPS

HERZEN INSTITUTE STUDENT DORMITORY Map pp246-9 *Hostel*

☎ 314 7472; fax 314 7659; Kazanskaya ul 6; s/d €16/40; metro Nevsky Pr

This is the dorm of one of the city's most famous educational establishments and it enjoys a brilliant location behind Kazan Cathedral. Don't expect posters of female tennis stars scratching their bums though – this is a well-run hostel used to foreigners. However, they do not register visas, so you'll need to have had your visa registered elsewhere.

HOTEL NAUK Map pp246-9 *Hotel*

☎ 315 3368; Millionnaya ul 27; s €20-30, d €25-40, tr/q €20/26; metro Nevsky Pr

Just a minute's walk from the Winter Palace, this hotel is Soviet but superb value. Rooms are basic with clean, shared facilities. Despite a R20 charge for a shower, its quads must be one of the city's best deals. Enter via the courtyard and take the terrifyingly old lift to the 3rd floor. Bookings recommended. No English spoken.

NORD HOSTEL Map pp246-9 *Hostel*

☎ 571 0342; www.nordhostel.com; Bolshaya Morskaya ul 10 ; dm/d €24/48; metro Nevsky Pr

The Nord is a winner. Located just seconds from Dvortsovaya pl (Palace Sq), it's a perfect base for exploring the historic centre and a great place for students to take advantage of the free entry to the next-door Hermitage. The dorms are new and comfortable, and expansion is planned. The friendly staff speaks English and there's a shared kitchen and bathing facilities. The double room is excellent value.

ZIMMER FREI Map pp246-9 *Mini-Hotel*

☎ 973 3757, 273 0867; www.zimmer.ru; Liteyny pr 46, apt 23; s & d €18; metro Mayakovskaya

Enter this curious apartment hotel from the unmarked black door on Liteyny pr, not from the elegant courtyard. Very good value, the seven rooms sleep two to four people and share toilet and kitchen facilities. It's rather basic, and still feels more like an apartment than a hotel, but it's excellently located and the charming concierge speaks perfect English.

SMOLNY

The Smolny area is noticeably quieter than the other central districts of St Petersburg. Its charming, historic backstreets make for some pleasant walking, and the Tauride Gardens and Smolny Cathedral are both very attractive features. Stay in Smolny for comfortable, mid-range accommodation. However, it would be a lie to say that this was the most exciting area of the city. Avoid staying out towards the Smolny Cathedral itself if you just want to be near to the museums and main sights, as the area's a bit awkward for transport.

ARBAT NORD HOTEL Map pp246-9 *Hotel*

☎ 103 1899; www.arbat-nord.ru; Artilleriyskaya ul 4; s/d €155/160; metro Chernyshevskaya

Facing the unsightly Hotel Rus, this new, sleek place seems to be showing its neighbour how to run a good establishment. There are comfortable rooms, friendly English-speaking staff and a restaurant downstairs. Set in a residential area, it's a 10-minute walk to Nevsky pr.

AUSTRIAN YARD HOTEL Map pp246-9 *Mini-Hotel*

☎ 279 8235; www.austrianyard.com; Furshtatskaya ul 45; s & d €90-115; metro Chernyshevskaya

You must book ahead to stay in this very private place located next to the Austrian consulate. There are only four rooms, all well equipped with kitchens and bathrooms. It's safe, comfortable and quiet and the local neighbourhood is full of restaurants and cafés.

HOTEL MERCURY Map pp240-1 *Hotel*

☎ 325 6444; Tavricheskaya ul 39; s/d €60/75; metro Chernyshevskaya

This place was once home away from home for out-of-town Party bosses, and its rooms have a certain grandness to them, not to mention a swish location to one side of the Tauride Palace. Staff are friendly enough, although clinging desperately to the hope that the USSR still exists alas it doesn't and the Mercury was empty when we visited. Breakfast not included.

HOTEL NEVA Map pp246-9 *Hotel*

☎ 278 5000; fax 273 2593; ul Chaykovskogo 17; s/d unmodernised €50/65, modernised €70/100; metro Chernyshevskaya

One of the city's oldest functioning hotels, the Neva opened its doors in 1913 and has a spectacular staircase to show for it. Unfortunately the rooms are not quite as grand – but are still comfortable and clean. The location is good, a short walk from the Fontanka and Neva.

HOTEL RUS Map pp246-9 *Hotel*

☎ 273 4683; www.hotelruss.spb.ru; Artilleriyskaya ul 1; s/d €50/62; metro Chernyshevskaya

Something of a hangover from the past, for those who never experienced the joy of Intourist it's almost like a history lesson to visit the Hotel Rus with its brown-carpeted walls, endless corridors and Orwellian scent of cabbage. The rooms are fine, however, having been renovated during the 1990s, while the exterior is a Brezhnevian classic.

CHEAP SLEEPS

PUPPET HOSTEL Map pp246-9 *Hostel*

☎ 272 5401; www.hostel-puppet.ru; ul Nekrasova 12; dm/d €16/40; metro Mayakovskaya

This reliable place is handily located and is affiliated with the long-established HI St Petersburg Hostel. The rooms are basic but clean, with shared facilities including a good kitchen and bathrooms. Free tickets to the puppet theatre (the building once housed a hostel for itinerant puppeteers) are a fringe benefit.

SLEEP CHEAP Map pp246-9 *Hostel*

☎ 115 1304; www.sleepcheap.spb.ru; Mokhovaya ul 18/32; dm €19; metro Chernyshevskaya

This mini-hostel is in the courtyard of a quiet residential street between Liteyny and the Fontanka. The eight-bed rooms are spotlessly clean and all facilities are very good. Airport pick-up is just €10 per person – a great deal if there's one of you, but less so if there's more.

VOSSTANIYA

This is another excellent area to stay in. Taking in the busy hub of pl Vosstaniya (Uprising Sq) and the quieter end of Nevsky pr, this is still very much the city centre and just a walk away from the historic heart. Again, accommodation stretches from five-star to no star – although this is an especially good area for hostels and budget mid-range accommodation.

GRAND HOTEL EMERALD

Map pp246-9 *Hotel*

☎ 140 5000; www.grand-hotel-emerald.com; Suvorovsky pr 18; s/d €295/315, ste €600-1500; metro Pl Vosstaniya; (P)

Less conveniently located than the other five-star hotels in the city, the newly opened Emerald still has considerable charm. Its rooms are lovely, and its décor unashamedly embraces traditional Russian taste for the grand and lavish. Employees are extremely attentive and helpful and the whole place is less full than the other hotels in this price bracket.

HOTEL MOSKVA Map pp244-5 *Hotel*

☎ 274 0020; www.hotel-moscow.ru; pl Alexandra Nevskogo 2; s/d €110/150; metro Pl Alexandra Nevskogo

This enormous 1970s hotel faces off the rather more historic Alexander Nevsky Monastery across the square. A favourite with large tour groups who get big discounts, there's little to attract the independent traveller. Rooms are comfortable, but atmosphere is nonexistent and the location is hardly convenient.

NOVOTEL ST PETERSBURG CENTRE

Map pp246-9 *Hotel*

☎ 335 1188; www.novotel.spb.ru; Nevsky pr 102; s/d €260/275, ste €320-750; metro Mayakovskaya; (P)

The latest big venture in the city centre, this nine-floor hotel brings a further 233 rooms to Nevsky pr, opening in mid-2005. The rooms are superb and the hotel offers all the facilities you'd expect from a high-end venture including a fitness centre and sauna. Breakfast is not included.

OKTYABRSKAYA HOTEL

Map pp246-9 *Hotel*

☎ 277 6330; www.oktober-hotel.spb.ru; Ligovsky pr 10; s/d/ste €75/110/205; metro Pl Vosstaniya

This vast hotel claims to be the oldest in the city, although in its modern incarnation it dates squarely from the October Revolution from which it takes its name. The hotel is divided into two parts – the vast main building facing you as you exit the Moscow Station, and the Oktyabrsky Filial (or annexe), the rather insalubrious building located to your left as you come out of the station. Both locations are fully renovated and now offer a very comfortable standard of accommodation. Rooms at the *filial* are cheaper than those at the main Oktyabrskaya Hotel.

CHEAP SLEEPS

GUESTHOUSE Map pp246-9 *Mini-Hotel*

☎ 271 3089; www.ghspb.ru; Grechesky pr 13; s/d €42/60; metro Pl Vosstaniya

On a quiet street and behind the enormous Oktyabrsky Concert Hall, the Guesthouse is a welcoming and safe private venture with English-speaking staff and pleasant rooms. It will allow anyone who's staying for a few days or more to use the kitchen.

HI ST PETERSBURG HOSTEL

Map pp246-9 *Hostel*

☎ 329 8018; www.ryh.ru; 3-ya Sovetskaya ul 28; dm/d €18/40; metro Pl Vosstaniya

The first hostel of its kind in Russia, the conveniently located and very friendly HI St Petersburg Hostel continues to attract scores of young backpackers. Its dorms are large and clean and the reception includes the travel agency **Sindbad Travel International** (p217). From Moscow Station, it's just a 10-minute walk to the hostel.

SENNAYA

Directly south of the historic heart is the Sennaya region, focused on Sennaya pl (the Haymarket of Dostoevsky's times). Historically the poorer side of town, this area has few accommodation possibilities, although staying here gives you good access to the whole of the city centre, as well as beyond, being well linked by metro to everywhere else.

BEST WESTERN NEPTUN HOTEL

Map pp244-5 *Hotel*

☎ 324 4611; www.neptun.spb.ru; 93 nab Obvodnogo kanala; s €95, d €110-150; metro Ligovsky Pr

This address, on the fourth of the major canals dividing the historic centre, isn't sought-after. Where the others are charming and beautiful, Obvodny Canal is industrial and bleak. The hotel is pretty good value, however, as facilities are excellent and rooms very decent.

FIVE CORNERS HOTEL

Map pp246-9 *Mini-Hotel*

☎ 380 8181; www.5ugol.ru; Zagorodny pr 13; s/d €130/150, ste €150-180; metro Dostoevskaya

Very stylish indeed. The suites at Five Corners are some of the coolest in the city and overlook a trendy hub of streets a short walk from Nevsky pr. Staff are polite and efficient, and expansion is on the cards. The name reflects its location near the 'Five Corners' intersection.

Five Corners Hotel (above)

CHEAP SLEEPS

HOTEL NA SADOVOY

Map pp246-9 *Hostel*

☎ 314 4510; fax 310 6537; Sadovaya ul 53; s/d/tr €30/38/42; metro Sadovaya

Not a hostel in attitude, but with hostel-style accommodation, this central, cheap place has friendly staff who are competent in mime, although alas not English. All rooms have TV, sink and fridge, but there are no other self-catering facilities. Bathrooms are shared but clean.

MARIINSKY

Directly west of the historic heart of St Petersburg, the neighbourhood around the Mariinsky Theatre is characterised by canals as the city tails off into the docklands. There are some charming accommodation options here, but be prepared to cab it, learn the *marshrutka* (minibus) routes, or walk long distances, as there's no metro station in the entire area!

ANNUSHKA HOTEL Map pp242-3 *Hotel*

☎ 103 3092; fax 251 8530; Gapsalskaya ul 2; s/d €70/100; marshrutka K-22 from metro Nevsky Pr or 19 & 115 from metro Sennaya Pl

Having very sensibly ditched its previous name (the Hotel Seamen), the Annushka would be great if it weren't so oddly located. Frankly only seamen and their devotees would want to stay so far out and so near to the port. Despite this, the place is very pleasant, modern and clean. In summer there is a 10-seat speedboat taxi to take guests into the city centre, although it hardly compensates for the poor location.

HOTEL SOVETSKAYA Map pp242-3 *Hotel*

☎ 140 2640; www.sovetskaya.com; Lermontovsky pr 43/1; s/d unrefurbished €50/85, refurbished €85/115

Saddled with an unfortunate name, the Sovetskaya is ironically one of the least Soviet of the former Intourist-run hotels. It has been modernised very well and is aimed largely at tour groups indifferent to its hideous exterior, which frankly, given its position on the otherwise lovely Fontanka River, is a crime.

MATISOV DOMIK Map pp242-3 *Hotel*

☎ 318 5464; www.matisov.spb.ru; nab reki Pryazhki 3/1; s/d €67/110

Unusually located on Matisov Island, 20 minutes on foot from Isaakievskaya pl (St Isaac's Sq), this smart venture is well run, clean and modern. Good English is spoken, and quirks include an onsite museum of 'Olden Days Russia'. A big plus for security, a big minus for location.

RENAISSANCE ST PETERSBURG BALTIC HOTEL Map pp246-9 *Hotel*

☎ 380 4000; www.renaissancehotels.com; Pochtamtskaya ul 4; s & d €215, ste from €300

This is the latest five-star offering for a city that seems to have an insatiable appetite for luxury in all its forms. The Renaissance St Petersburg Baltic may have a stupidly long name, but its sweeping interior and rooms are excellent. It's located just off Isaakievskaya pl (St Isaac's Sq) and some rooms have superb views of the cupola.

CHEAP SLEEPS

DOMIK V KOLOMNE

Map pp242-3 *Mini-Hotel*

☎ 110 8351; www.colomna.nm.ru; nab kanala Griboedova 174a; s/d €50/60

Pushkin's family once rented rooms in this house, and the atmosphere of a large flat remains. Rooms have a homely Russian feel, although facilities are private and guests will be well looked after. Some rooms have lovely views over the canal.

VASILEVSKY ISLAND

Once planned to be the centre of Peter's city, Vasilevsky Island is a large and disparate place. Staying at the tip of the island around the Strelka (tongue of land) and university gives you a great base for exploring St Petersburg, but staying further out is pretty inconvenient. Mini-hotels have flourished here in the charming 'lines' that make up the grid of streets on the east of the island, though, and there's no shortage of space.

PRESTIGE HOTEL Map pp238-9 *Mini-Hotel*

☎ 328 5338; www.prestige-hotels.com; 3-aya Liniya 52; s/d €90/125; metro Vasileostrovskaya

Down-to-earth, simple and smart, the Prestige has well-equipped and large rooms, including one with full disabled access. The staff speak

English and there is none of the pretension of the nearby Shelfort.

PRIBALTIYSKAYA HOTEL

Map pp242-3 *Hotel*

☎ 356 3001; www.pribaltiyskaya.ru; ul Korablestroiteley 14; s & d €100-150; metro Primorskaya

This enormous Soviet creation stands alone on the Gulf of Finland like a hideous mirage at the sparsely inhabited end of Vasilevsky Island. Its location makes it good only for those with their own transport (although most guests are part of tour groups for whom this is no issue). It's a good hotel, however, with comfortable rooms and some lovely views.

SHELFORT HOTEL

Map pp246-9 *Mini-Hotel*

☎ 328 0555; www.shelfort.e-spb.ru; 3-aya Liniya; s/d €60/100; metro Vasileostrovskaya

The Shelfort claims to be a hideaway of the rich and famous on Vasilevsky Island and its staff are very discreet and polite. Despite the rather odd sense of exclusivity, some rooms have great antique fittings, and it is easy to see the appeal.

SPB VERGAZ Map pp238-9 *Mini-Hotel*

☎ 327 8883; www.vergaz.spb.ru; 7-aya Liniya; s/d/apt €90/140/160, breakfast €6; metro Vasileostrovskaya

Staff here are great and the rooms decent and smart. The apartment is a good deal, and includes an office and kitchen, as well as a bedroom and sitting room. All rooms have cable TV and a minibar.

PETROGRAD SIDE

A busy and interesting place to stay to be sure, the Petrograd Side unfortunately has a real lack of decent hotels. Indeed, there's no reason to choose to stay here really, although it's perfectly pleasant with good shops and restaurants to be had if you do.

HOTEL EURASIA Map pp238-9 *Mini-Hotel*

☎ 230 4432; www.eurasia.allcafe.info; ul Gatchinskaya 5; s/d €70/80; metro Chkalovskaya

The Eurasia is one of the better mini-hotels on the Petrograd Side, and is well located for local restaurants and other amenities. Its 18 rooms are comfortable and modern (if perhaps unremarkable) and the staff are very obliging.

LENINGRAD PALACE OF YOUTH

Map pp238-9 *Hotel*

☎ 234 5341; ul Professora Popova 47; s & d €74; metro Petrogradskaya/Chkalovskaya

This vast place provides the quintessential communist holiday experience, although it's up to you whether that's one you really want or not. The perfectly OK, simple and rather sparse rooms are in direct contrast to the extraordinarily silly foyer featuring an indoor jungle, loud dance music, a go-cart track and a bowling alley. It's definitely overpriced for its rooms and location though, as it's a fair schlep to the metro.

CHEAP SLEEPS

PRESTIGE SPORT HOSTEL

Map pp246-9 *Hostel*

☎ 324 7077; www.prestige-hotels.com; pr Dobrolyubova 14; s & d €50-90; metro Sportivnaya

This very well run place is far nicer inside than its exterior might lead you to believe. Its small and simple yet clean rooms are decent value. Not far from Sportivnaya metro, and just a short walk across the river to the Hermitage.

VYBORG SIDE

The Vyborg Side is rather unexciting, and particularly so in the Bolshaya and Malaya Okhta neighbourhoods which make up the right bank of the Neva River before it curves majestically around the Smolny for its final approach to the Gulf of Finland. There's little to be gained from staying out here, although at least metro access to the city centre is perfectly adequate.

DESON LADOGA HOTEL

Map pp244-5 ***Hotel***

☎ 528 5393; www.deson-ladoga.ru; pr Shaumyana 26; s/d €115/135; metro Novocherkasskaya

Rather steeply priced given its location on the wrong side of the Neva in this completely missable residential district, the Deson Ladoga is a five-minute stroll to the metro, however, so getting about is easy. Rooms are pleasant, roomy and still feel new despite being updated in 1996. It's a pleasant enough place if you can negotiate a good deal (unlikely for independent travellers). As it is, the prices are too high to merit staying this inconveniently far from the city centre.

HOTEL ST PETERSBURG

Map pp240-1 *Hotel*

☎ 380 1919; www.hotel-spb.ru; Pirogovskaya nab 5/2; s/d €65/70; metro Pl Lenina

Brought to you from the Soviet central planners' particularly ugly collection, the hotel ironically has some wonderful views of the Neva and historic heart despite itself detracting enormously from the St Petersburg skyline. The place is in the process of modernising itself and rooms are comfortable enough.

NAUTILUS INN Map pp244-5 *Hotel*

☎ 449 9000; www.nautilus-inn.ru; ul Rizhskaya 3; s/d €75/80; metro Novocherkasskaya

Awkward location aside, the Nautilus Inn is a smart and well-run 35-room place. Staff members speak English and the rooms are well equipped and comfortable. The Novocherkasskaya metro station is about 10 minutes away and takes you straight into the city centre.

CHEAP SLEEPS

HOTEL VYBORGSKAYA

Map p237 *Hotel*

☎ 246 9141; fax 246 8187; ul Torzhkovskaya 3; s/d €50/60; metro Chyornaya Rechka

Not in the city centre, but very convenient for the nearby Chyornaya Rechka metro that takes you straight in to the centre, the Vyborgskaya is worth considering if you don't mind old Soviet-style institutions. Dating from 1962, its rooms have been refurbished adequately and it's a short walk to some of the city's nicest green spaces on Kamenny and Yelagin Islands.

SOUTHERN ST PETERSBURG

A good choice for the budget traveller, southern St Petersburg is overflowing with decent, cheap accommodation, including the city's cheapest hotel bed – €9 per night at the Petrovsky College Student Hostel. Well connected to the centre by metro, it's no problem getting about either, and there are a few interesting things to see in the area itself.

HOTEL MIR Map p237 *Hotel*

☎ 108 4910; fax 108 5165; ul Gastello 17; s/d €68/95; metro Moskovskaya

Receiving a full renovation in 2004, the Mir is a short walk from the metro. Unfortunately rooms overlooking the wonderful Chesme Church next door don't have private bathrooms. Prices here are for rooms with bathrooms.

HOTEL PULKOVSKAYA

Map p237 *Hotel*

☎ 140 3900; www.pulkovskaya.ru; pl Pobedy 1; s/d/ste €125/150/210; metro Moskovskaya

Rather poorly located, this nevertheless very smart complex looks out onto the rather uncheery Monument to the Heroic Defenders of Leningrad. There's the making of an excellent hotel here though, were it not for the location nearer to the airport than the historic centre.

HOTEL ROSSIYA Map p237 *Hotel*

☎ 329 3909/00; www.rossiya-hotel.ru; pl Chernyshevskogo 11; s/d €80/90; metro Park Pobedy

Set back from Moskovsky pr, the Rossiya is another Soviet behemoth that has made a fair effort in appealing to market forces. This huge place is next to Park Pobedy metro station, but otherwise rather badly located. It's fine for groups though, and has decent and clean rooms.

CHEAP SLEEPS

ALL SEASONS HOSTEL

Map p237 *Hostel*

☎ 327 1070; www.hostel.ru; Yakovlevsky per 11, 4th fl, door code 369; dm/s/d/tr €11/13/26/39; metro Park Pobedy

The staff of the sadly closed Holiday Hostel near the Finland Station have now moved way south to new premises near Park Pobedy. While not too far from the metro, it's still a way out of the historic centre and thus not particularly convenient. Plans to expand are afoot – at the moment it's hard to even find the entrance. Coming from Park Pobedy it's the second door in the building.

Out of Town

There is no reason to stay outside of the city, save to experience a glimpse of the tsarist lifestyle – something that is on offer at the magnificent **Baltic Star Hotel** (☎ 438 5700; www.balticstar-hotel.ru; Beriozovaya alleya 3, Strelna; s & d €180-390, ste €375-1000, cottage €4200), housed in the grounds of Peter the Great's (and now Putin's) residence at Strelna, 25km to the south of the centre. Suitably for such a grand place, its first guests were the leaders of the EU during the Russia-EU summit in 2003. The main hotel houses 106 beautifully attired rooms, but the VIP cottages on the shore of the Gulf of Finland are really the way to go, each featuring sauna, swimming pool and, of course, staff quarters for your entourage.

HOTEL KIEVSKAYA Map pp244-5 *Hotel*

☎ 166 0456; ul Dnepropetrovskaya 49; s/d without bathroom €20/25, with bathroom €40/50; metro Ligovsky Pr

This rather poorly located place, with a nearby annexe, the **Kievsky Filial** (☎ 166 5811; 40 Kurskaya ul), has made minimal efforts to part with its firmly communist past, although rooms are fair enough and divided into the refurbished and the pre-*glasnost* classic. The two buildings are next to the main bus station.

HOTEL ZARAYA Map p237 *Hostel*

☎ /fax 387 6724; zaraya2003@mail.ru; Yakovlevsky per 11, 5th fl, door code 369; dm €11, s & d €30; metro Park Pobedy

Located above the All Seasons Hostel, the Zaraya essentially offers hostel-standard accommodation, and is overpriced for its location and its facilities, which while very clean, are all shared.

PETROVSKY COLLEGE STUDENT HOSTEL Map pp242-3 *Hostel*

☎ 252 7563; www.teen-tour@petrocollege.ru; Baltiyskaya ul 26; s/d/tr €9/18/26; metro Narvskaya

Not in the centre, but just 10 minutes from Narvskaya metro station, this well-run student hostel is one of the best deals in town for those on a budget. Toilets and showers are shared between four bedrooms, and rooms are clean and simple with access to one of several large kitchens. English is barely spoken, and as reservations are a must, try emailing if you don't speak any Russian. The hostel will register any guest's visa for R220 and can also issue visa invitations.

YUZHNAYA HOTEL Map pp244-5 *Hotel*

☎ 166 1088; fax 166 1087; Rasstannaya ul 26; s/d without bathroom €17/30, with bathroom €27/45; metro Ligovsky Pr

Despite its down-at-heel appearance, the Yuzhnaya Hotel has pleasant staff and prices are cheap enough to make its bare rooms perfectly acceptable. The location is not great, but a tram ride from nearby Ligovsky pr will take you to the metro station in a couple of minutes.

Excursions

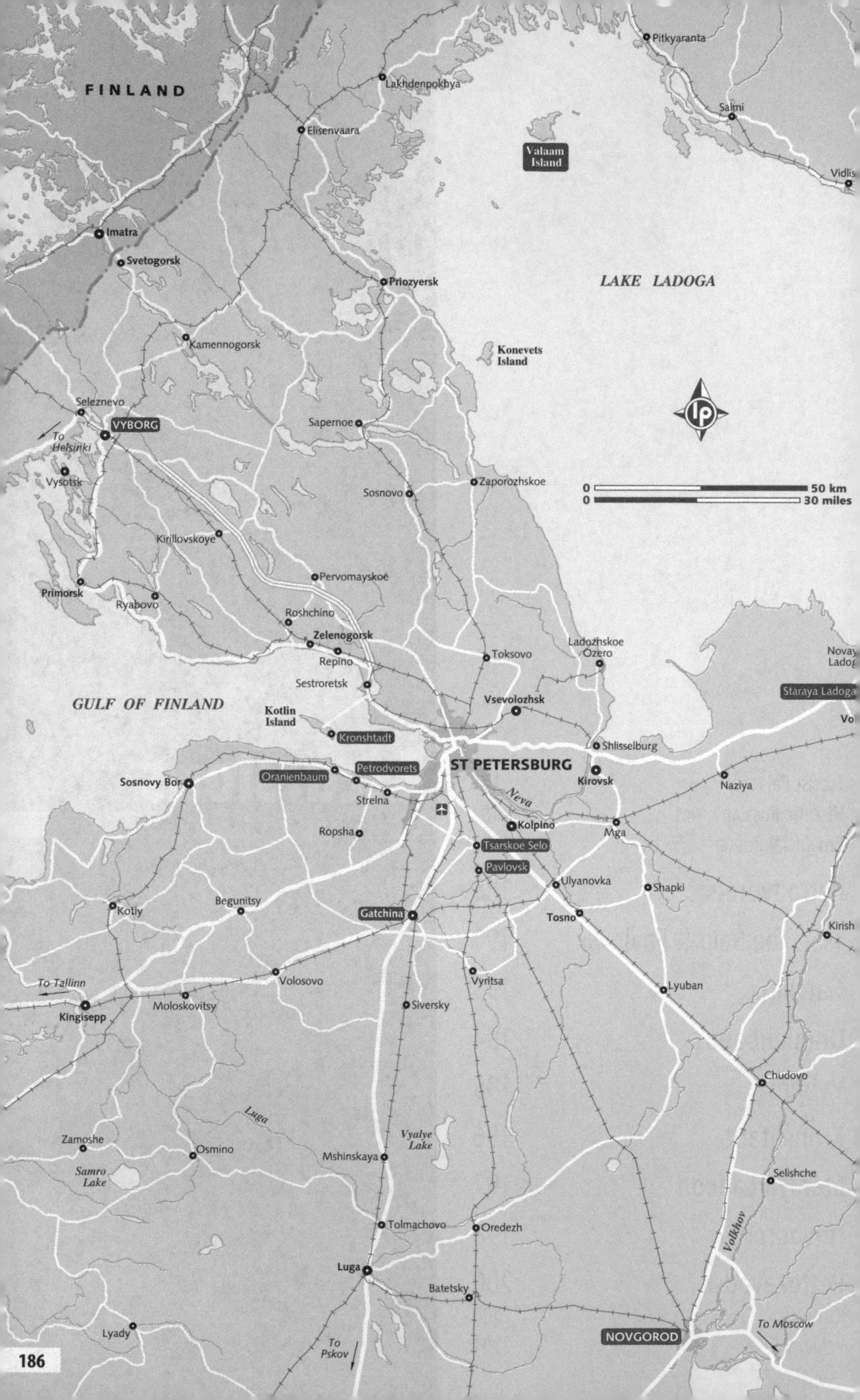

FINLAND
Pitkyaranta
Lakhdenpokhya
Elisenvaara
Salmi
Valaam Island
Vidlis
Imatra
Svetogorsk
Priozyersk
LAKE LADOGA
Kamennogorsk
Konevets Island
Seleznevo
VYBORG
To Helsinki
Sapernoe
Vysotsk
Zaporozhskoe
Sosnovo
0 50 km
0 30 miles
Kirillovskoye
Pervomayskoe
Primorsk
Ryabovo
Roshchino
Zelenogorsk
Repino
Toksovo
Ladozhskoe Ozero
Novay Ladog
Sestroretsk
Staraya Ladoga
GULF OF FINLAND
Vsevolozhsk
Kotlin Island
Kronshtadt
Shlisselburg
ST PETERSBURG
Petrodvorets
Oranienbaum
Kirovsk
Sosnovy Bor
Naziya
Strelna
Neva
Ropsha
Kolpino
Mga
Tsarskoe Selo
Pavlovsk
Ulyanovka
Shapki
Begunitsy
Kotly
Gatchina
Tosno
Kirish
Vyritsa
To Tallinn
Volosovo
Lyuban
Kingisepp
Moloskovitsy
Siversky
Chudovo
Luga
Vyalye Lake
Zamoshe
Osmino
Mshinskaya
Samro Lake
Selishche
Tolmachovo
Oredezh
Volkhov
Luga
Batetsky
Lyady
To Pskov
To Moscow
NOVGOROD

Excursions

Leaving St Petersburg is essential to gain any perspective on Russia: the city has the affectations of a national capital, even though it has not been one for the best part of a century, and is starkly removed from the provincial reality of the rest of the country. Anyone enamoured of the fast pace of progress in the city need only leave for one of the surrounding towns to discover that the rest of Russia is still lagging some way behind. Of course, a far more positive and equally valid reason to leave is that there are plenty of enjoyable day trips to luxurious palaces, fascinating towns and other interesting areas that will enormously enhance your overall experience of St Petersburg. Trains and buses serve all destinations, while in some cases, if there are a few of you, it makes affordable sense to hire a taxi for the journey.

TSARIST PALACES

In the wilderness of the sparsely inhabited Baltic Coast far from Russia's historic centre, Russia's aristocracy, and particularly the imperial family, outdid each other throughout the 18th and 19th centuries trying to create the ultimate summer palace. You are truly spoilt for choice if you enjoy unbelievably opulent interiors, vast, splendid vistas and gorgeously laid-out parklands, woods and temples. While **Petrodvorets** (p188) is the most impressive with its world-famous cascades, the newly recreated amber room at **Tsarskoe Selo** (p191) is also a huge draw, while lesser-known estates such as **Pavlovsk** (p193), **Oranienbaum** (p194) and **Gatchina** (p193) are far less crowded and still enormously impressive.

HISTORIC RUSSIAN CITIES

Further away from St Petersburg are some fascinating cities, most obviously Russia's historic and religious centre at **Novgorod** (p198), one of the most charming cities in the country with its wealth of churches, kremlin and beautiful setting on the Volkhov River, not far from gorgeous Lake Ilmen. For a taste of ancient Rus, a trip to **Staraya Ladoga** (p197), generally thought of as Russia's oldest town, is extremely rewarding. In the town's quaint streets you can find a fascinating fortress, ruined churches and precious architectural relics from Russia's birth as a nation. Far nearer to St Petersburg is **Kronshtadt** (p196), the defensively brilliant outpost of St Petersburg originally called Schlüsselburg by Peter the Great. Here you'll find the neo-Byzantine Naval Cathedral and a pleasant town full of day-trippers from St Petersburg, crowding the relaxed historic streets in the summer and enjoying a change of scene.

PROVINCIAL RUSSIA

For the real Russia, look no further than the country's pleasant provincial towns. Yes, life here is decidedly languorous, but you'll see how the vast majority of the Russian population live, a far cry from their cosmopolitan St Petersburg cousins.

The Finnish-Russian border town of **Vyborg** (p195) has an interesting mixed heritage, having been passed between Russia and Finland constantly throughout its history. It's a run-down but charming town with cobbled streets, a rich architectural heritage and a fascinating 13th-century Swedish fortress. While it's not typically Russian due to its strong Scandinavian influence, it has plenty to offer for an enjoyable day trip.

If you want to travel for a few days within northern Russia, perhaps the most obvious destination is **Petrozavodsk** (p200), the pleasant capital of Russia's Karelia region. From here you can explore the fantastic complex of wooden churches at **Kizhi** (p200) and visit the fascinating **Valaam Transfiguration Monastery** (p201). It's a two- to three-day round trip but well worth the effort.

PETRODVORETS ПЕТРОДВОРЕЦ

This most visually stunning of the tsarist palaces around St Petersburg was first built by Peter the Great, although it was constantly improved upon over the years by his successors to create the astounding ensemble seen today. Comparisons to Versailles abound and it's easy to see why – the sheer scale of the main palace and its incredible garden were heavily influenced by Louis XIV's own summer residence, although the centrepiece, the Grand Cascade, is all Peter's own work. While Petrodvorets is the most popular day trip from St Petersburg for visitors, it's still one undiminished by mass tourism and the fact that it's accessible by hydrofoil from St Petersburg makes it a hugely enjoyable day trip.

The vast palace and grounds you see today are a far cry from the original cabin Peter the Great had built here to oversee construction of his Kronshtadt naval base. He liked the place so much that he built a villa, Monplaisir, and then a whole series of palaces across an estate originally called Peterhof, which has been called Petrodvorets (pet-ra-dvar-*yets*; Peter's Palace) since 1944. All are set within a spectacular ensemble of gravity-powered fountains that are now the site's main attraction.

While Petrodvorets was sadly left in ruins by the Germans in WWII (what you see is largely a reconstruction, the main palace being completely gutted with only some of its walls left standing), it suffered heaviest damage under Soviet bombing raids in December 1941 and January 1942 (according to more recent historians). Hitler, abandoning his hopes for a New Year's victory celebration inside St Petersburg's Astoria Hotel, planned to throw a party here and, as with the Astoria, he drew up pompous invitations. Stalin ordered the place be heavily attacked to thwart this.

Inexplicably, each museum within the estate has different closing days, and some are closed or open only on weekends from October to May. All the museums are open Friday to Sunday, so if at all possible come on a Friday as the place is swarming with visitors at weekends. All the attractions charge separate admissions. Admission to the grounds is payable at the cash booths on the jetty (for those arriving by boat) and outside the gates leading to the Grand Cascade if you come by land.

The uncontested centrepiece is the **Grand Cascade** and **Water Avenue**, a symphony of over 140 fountains and canals partly engineered by Peter himself. The central statue of Samson tearing open a lion's jaws celebrates – as so many things in St Petersburg also do – Peter's victory over the Swedes at Poltava. It was unveiled for the 25th anniversary of the battle in 1735 by Rastrelli. There are trick fountains – each triggered by hidden switches (hidden, that is, by hordes of kids jumping on them) – designed to squirt unsuspecting passers-by.

Between the Grand Cascade and the formal Upper Garden is the **Grand Palace**. Peter's modest project, finished just before his death, was grossly enlarged by Rastrelli for Empress Elizabeth. Many people suggested that Rastrelli's interiors were so obscenely lavish that they were mocking Elizabeth's shameless love of opulence. Later Catherine the Great toned things down a little with a redecoration, although not much: it's now a vast museum of lavish rooms and galleries – a monument above all to the craft of reconstruction (which is still going on). Anything not nailed down was removed before the Germans arrived, so the paintings, furniture and chandeliers are original.

Highlights include the **Chesma Hall**, full of huge paintings of Russia's destruction of the Turkish fleet at Çesme in 1770. Of some

Transport

Distance from St Petersburg 29km

Direction West

Travel Time About 45 minutes

Boat From May to September, a fine alternative is the *Meteor* hydrofoil (R300 one-way, 30 minutes) from the jetty in front of St Petersburg's Hermitage, which goes every 20 to 30 minutes from 9.30am to at least 7pm. Be aware that queues for people taking the boat back to St Petersburg can get very long later on in the day, so don't leave it too late to return.

Bus From Avtovo metro station you can take bus No 424, or bus No 103 from Leninsky Pr metro station. The trip takes about half an hour.

Train *Elektrichki* (suburban trains) leave St Petersburg's Baltiisky Station every 15 to 30 minutes throughout the day. You need to get off at the Novy Petrodvorets Station (not Stary Petrodvorets). From here you can either walk to the palace grounds (about 20 minutes) or take marshrutkas 350, 351, 351A, 352, 353, 354 or 356, getting off at the fifth stop.

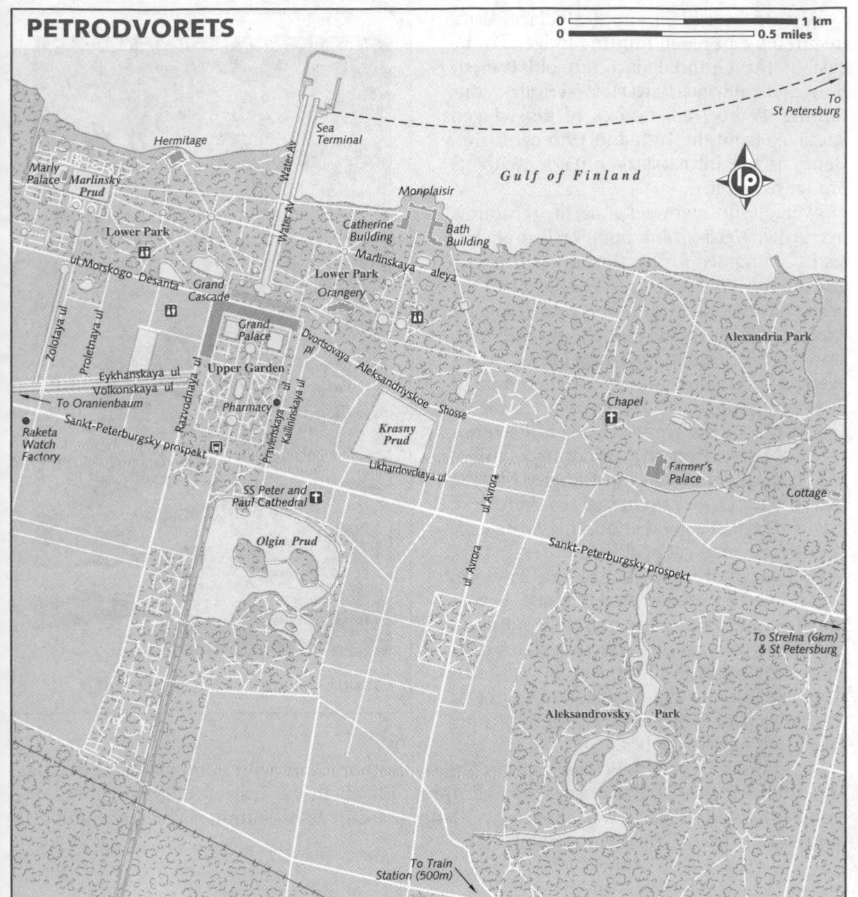

20 rooms, the last, without a trace of Catherine, is the finest – Peter's simple, beautiful study, the only room to be untouched by the Germans. It has 14 fantastic wood-carved panels, of which six reconstructions (in lighter wood) are no less impressive; Peter the Great still looks like the tsar with the best taste.

Tickets are sold inside, near the lobby where you pick up your *tapochki* (slippers to wear over your shoes to avoid damaging the wooden floors).

Peter's outwardly more humble, sea-facing villa **Monplaisir** remained his favourite retreat. It's not hard to see why: it's wood-panelled, snug and elegant, peaceful even when there's a crowd – which there used to be all the time, what with Peter's mandatory partying ('misbehaving' guests were required to gulp down huge quantities of wine as penalties and practical jokes were the order of the day).

To the west of Monplaisir is an annexe called the **Catherine Building**, built by Rastrelli between 1747 and 1755, because Catherine the Great was living here (conveniently) when her husband Peter III was overthrown. On the right side is Quarenghi's 1800 **Bath Building**. The imperial family and their guests once purified body and mind here.

Near the shore, the **Hermitage** is a two-storey pink-and-white box featuring the ultimate in private dining: special elevators hoist a fully-laid table into the imperial presence on the 2nd floor, thereby eliminating any hindrance by servants. The elevators are circular and directly in front of each diner, whose plate would be lowered, replenished and replaced.

Further west is yet another palace, **Marly**, inspired by a French hunting lodge. To the east of the Grand Palace, an old **Orangery** houses the **Historical Museum of Wax Figures**, containing 49 ho-hum figures of big-wigged Russians from the 18th and 19th centuries. Better is the **Triton fountain** outside, with its 8m jet of water.

Even on summer weekends, the rambling, overgrown **Alexandria Park**, built for Tsar Nicholas I (and named for his tsarina), is peaceful and empty. Besides a mock-Gothic **chapel**, the park's diversions include the ruined **Farmer's Palace** (1831), which vaguely resembles a stone farmstead, and the **Cottage** (1829), modelled on an English country cottage, which is now a museum.

Just east of the Upper Garden, the renovated old-style **Pharmacy**, with drawers full of medicinal plants, looks (and smells) like the real thing. You can sip herbal teas here and, if your Russian's good enough, ask the staff about your medical problem.

In Petrodvorets town, the eye-catching five-domed **SS Peter and Paul Cathedral**, across the road and east of the palace grounds, is built in neo-Byzantine style but dates only from the turn of the 20th century. One bus stop west of the main palace entrance is the **Raketa watch factory** with a little boutique selling *very* cool watches.

Grand Cascade, Petrodvorets (p188)

Six kilometres east of Petrodvorets is **Strelna**, another estate with parklands and two palaces built for Peter (later enlarged for Empress Elizabeth by Rastrelli). One of these, the Konstantinovsky Palace, was chosen by Vladimir Putin as his summer residence and also houses an extremely luxurious hotel.

Sights & Information

Alexandria Park (admission free)

Alexandria Park Cottage (admission R150; 🕒 10.30am-5pm Tue-Sun May-Sep, 10.30am-4pm Sat & Sun Oct-Apr)

Bath Building (☎ 427 9129; admission R60; 🕒 10.30am-4pm Wed-Mon May-Sep, 10.30am-4pm Sat & Sun Oct-Apr)

Catherine Building (☎ 427 9129; admission R100; 🕒 10.30am-5pm Fri-Wed May-Sep, 10.30am-5pm Sat & Sun Oct-Apr, closed last Fri of month)

Grand Cascade (🕒 fountains play 11am-7pm from last weekend in May-Sep)

Grand Palace (Bolshoy Dvorets; ☎ 427 9527; adult/student R240/120; 🕒 11am-6pm Tue-Sun, closed last Tue of month)

Hermitage (☎ 427 5325; admission R100; 🕒 10.30am-6pm Wed-Mon)

Marly (☎ 427 7729; admission R75; 🕒 11am-4pm Wed-Mon)

Monplaisir (☎ 427 9129; admission R100; 🕒 10.30am-4pm Thu-Tue May-Sep, closed last Thu of the month)

Pharmacy (☎ 427 9578; 🕒 8am-8pm Mon-Fri, 11am-6pm Sat, 9am-8pm Sun)

Raketa watch factory (☎ 420 5041; Sankt-Peterburgsky pr 60; 🕒 boutique 10am-6pm Mon-Fri, 10am-5pm Sat)

Eating

There are a few cafés scattered around the Lower Park, but none of the venues is particularly outstanding and all are overpriced. You might want to try **Kafe Galereya** (☎ 427 7068; 🕒 10am-8pm), on the west side of Grand Palace, which has caviar-stuffed eggs and strawberries on its menu.

TSARSKOE SELO & PAVLOVSK
ЦАРСКОЕ СЕЛО И ПАВЛОВСК

Few places in Russia are more strongly associated with the country's history and culture than the palaces at Tsarskoe Selo and Pavlovsk. The sumptuous palaces and sprawling parks at these neighbouring complexes, can be combined in a day's visit – but since they're both good places to relax, you might want to take them more slowly.

The first settlement here was prepared as a surprise for Peter the Great by his wife Catherine who took him here to show him the area and then, much to Peter's delight, revealed that she'd already had a house built and furnished for him. While Peter was touched, his passionate love of sailing meant that he was only really happy when he was close to the sea, so it was Catherine who spent time here when Peter was out of the capital.

It was under Empresses Elizabeth and Catherine the Great between 1744 and 1796 that both the palace at Tsarskoe Selo and the estate of Pavlovsk were built and extended. The centrepiece is the vast 1752 to 1756 baroque Catherine Palace (Yekaterininsky Dvorets), designed by Rastrelli. It gradually became the favourite country estate of the royal family and indeed when Russia's first railway line opened in 1837, it was used to shuttle the imperial family between here and St Petersburg. The town changed its name from Tsarskoe Selo (Tsar's Village) to Pushkin in 1937 after Russia's favourite poet, who studied here in the Lycée set up by Alexander I. In the 1990s, the name of the town and the palace changed back to Tsarskoe Selo.

Of the two estates, many find Pavlovsk's park of woodland, rivers, lakes, statues and temples one of the most exquisite in Russia, while its Great Palace is a classical contrast to the florid baroque Catherine Palace.

Transport

Distance from St Petersburg 25km (Tsarskoe Selo) and 29km (Pavlovsk)
Direction South
Travel Time 45 minutes to one hour
Bus A large number of marshrutkas (R17, 30 minutes) leave from outside Moskovskaya metro station in St Petersburg to the town of Tsarskoe Selo's central square all day long. There are also services from Pl Pobedy (bus No 287 or marshrutka No 20). The lines of people returning at the weekend after about 3pm can be horrendous though. From here it's a 20 to 30 minute walk to either palace. Marshrutkas K299 and K545 connect Tsarskoe Selo town and Pavlovsk (a 5- to 10-minute trip).
Train Suburban trains run from Vitebsk Station in St Petersburg, but they're infrequent except for weekends. For Tsarskoe Selo get off at Detskoye Selo Station (R9, zone 3 ticket) and for Pavlovsk (R12, zone 4) at Pavlovsk Station. It's about half an hour to either place.

Catherine Palace

As at the Winter Palace, Catherine the Great had many of Rastrelli's interiors remodelled in classical style. Most of the exterior and 20-odd rooms of the palace have been beautifully restored – compare them to the photographs showing the devastation by the Germans.

Visits normally start with the **State Staircase**, an 1860 addition. South of here, only two rooms (both by Rastrelli) have been restored: the **Gentlemen-in-Waiting's Dining Room** and, beyond, the **Great Hall**, all light and glitter from its mirrors and gilded woodcarvings.

The rooms north of the State Staircase on the courtyard side are the **State Dining Room**, **Crimson** and **Green Pilaster Rooms**, **Portrait Room** and the **Amber Room**. The latter was decorated by Rastrelli with gilded woodcarvings, mirrors, agate and jasper mosaics, and exquisitely engraved amber panels given to Peter the Great by the King of Prussia in 1716. But its treasures were plundered by the Nazis and went missing in Kaliningrad in 1945, becoming one of the art world's great mysteries. In 2004 the strange hoax was revealed – the Amber Room was destroyed in a fire in Kaliningrad while under Red Army occupation. Those responsible for the loss were so terrified of Stalin's reaction that an elaborate myth was created of its disappearance – one that Soviet art historians wasted years trying to solve. In 2004 Putin and German Chancellor Gerhardt Schröder presided over the opening of the new Amber Room, restored largely with German funds, and visitors can again see this spectacular room.

Most of the north end is Charles Cameron's early classical work. The proportions of the **Green Dining Room** on the courtyard side are typically elegant. There are also three rooms

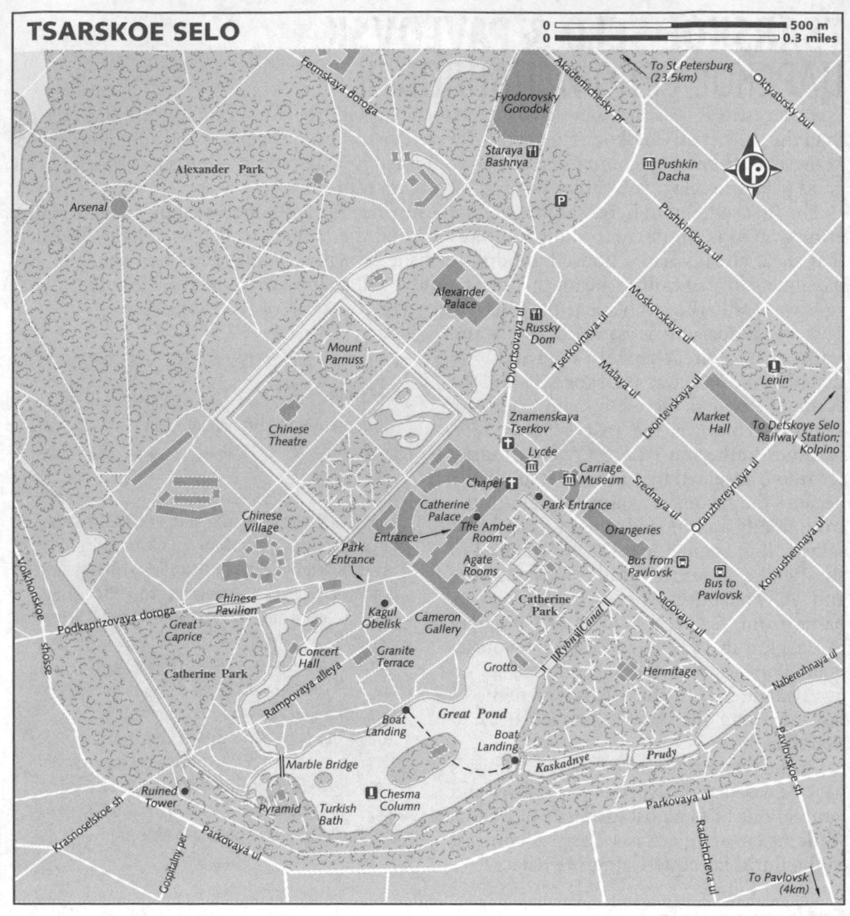

here with fabulous, patterned silk wall-coverings: the **Blue Drawing Room**, **Chinese Blue Drawing Room** and **Choir Anteroom**, whose gold silk, woven with swans and pheasants, is the original from the 18th century.

Tsarskoe Selo Parks

Around the Catherine Palace extends the lovely **Catherine Park.** The main entrance is on Sadovaya ul, next to the palace chapel. The **Cameron Gallery** has changing exhibitions. Between the gallery and the palace, notice the south-pointing ramp that Cameron added for the ageing empress to walk down into the park.

The park's outer section focuses on the **Great Pond**, where you can rent boats in summer. An intriguing array of structures here includes the **Pyramid**, where Catherine the Great buried her favourite dogs, the **Chinese Pavilion** (or Creaking Summerhouse), the **Marble Bridge** (copied from one in Wilton, England) and the **Ruined Tower**, which was built 'ready-ruined' in keeping with a 1770s romantic fashion – an 18th-century empress's equivalent of prefaded denim.

A short distance north of the Catherine Palace, the classical **Alexander Palace** was built by Quarenghi between 1792 and 1796 for the future Alexander I, but Nicholas II was its main tenant. It's the least touristy palace, so in some ways the most pleasant. The overgrown and empty **Alexander Park** surrounds the palace.

Pavlovsk Great Palace & Park

Although designed by Charles Cameron between 1781 and 1786, on Catherine the Great's orders for her son, the future Paul I, the interiors of Pavlovsk's **Great Palace** were largely orchestrated by Paul's second wife Maria Fyodorovna. A royal residence until 1917, the original palace was burnt down two weeks after liberation in WWII by a careless Soviet soldier's cigarette which set off German mines (the Soviets blamed the Germans). As at Tsarskoe Selo its restoration is remarkable.

The finest rooms are on the middle floor of the central block. Cameron designed the round Italian Hall beneath the dome and the Grecian Hall to its west, though the lovely green fluted columns were added by his assistant Vincenzo Brenna. Flanking these are two private suites designed mainly by Brenna – Paul's along the north side of the block and Maria Fyodorovna's on the south. The Hall of War of the insane, military-obsessed Paul contrasts with Maria's Hall of Peace, decorated with musical instruments and flowers.

On the middle floor of the south block are Paul's Throne Room and the Hall of the Maltese Knights of St John, of whom he was the Grand Master.

If you skip the palace, it's a delight simply to wander around the serene park grounds – much less crowded than those at Tsarskoe Selo – and see what you come across.

Sights & Information

Alexander Palace (☎ 466 6071; Dvortsovaya ul 2; adult/student R160/80; 🕑 10am-5pm Wed-Mon, closed last Wed of the month)

Alexander Park (admission free)

Cameron Gallery (adult/student R160/80; 🕑 10am-5pm Wed-Mon)

Catherine Palace (☎ 466 6699; Sadovaya ul 7, Tsarskoe Selo; adult/student R300/150; 🕑 10am-4.30pm Wed-Mon, closed last Mon of the month)

Catherine Park (Yekaterininsky Park; adult/student R60/30; 🕑 9am-6pm)

Great Palace (☎ 470 2155; www.pavlovskart.spb.ru; ul Revolutsii, Pavlovsk; adult/student R240/120; 🕑 10am-5pm Sat-Thu, closed first Fri of the month)

Eating

Avoid the highly mediocre self-service cafeterias at both palaces. There are other options in Tsarskoe Selo and while as expensive as the aforementioned establishments, you are paying for good quality food rather than just because you are caught in tourist traps.

Russky Dom (Russian House; ☎ 466 8838; 3 Malaya ul, Tsarskoe Selo; mains R500; 🕑 noon-midnight) This newcomer's interior is smartly decorated in a contemporary country Russian style. It serves lots of standard dishes including shashlyk, cooked on wood-fired braziers outside.

Staraya Bashnya (☎ 466 6698; 14 Akademichesky pr 14, Tsarskoe Selo; mains R600; 🕑 noon-10pm) The Old Tower consists of just four tables shoehorned into an old watchtower just five minutes' walk north of the Alexander Palace, so you must book.

GATCHINA ГАТЧИНА

The **palace estate** at Gatchina, 45km southwest of St Petersburg, was originally home to Peter the Great's sister Natalya. It changed hands several times after her death until Catherine bought it and gave it to her lover Grigory Orlov for helping her get rid of her husband Peter III. It was later passed on to Catherine's son Paul I, the mentally unstable militarist, who spent most of his time drilling his troops on the parade ground here.

Still impressive, today Gatchina is but a shadow of its former self. The palace, shaped in a graceful curve around a central turret, looks fine from the front, but is falling to pieces around the back. Inside, few of the rooms have been restored (work only began in 1985); the most interesting feature is a tunnel running from the palace to the ornamental lake.

Really, the best reason for coming here is to wander around the leafy park, with its many winding paths through birch groves and across bridges to islands in the lake. Look out for the **Birch House** (Beriozoy Dom), with a façade made of birch logs, and the ruined **Eagle Pavilion** (Pavilion Orla).

In the nearby town there are a couple of interesting churches. The baroque **Pavlovsky Sobor** (ul Gobornaya), at the end of the main pedestrianised shopping street, has a grandly restored interior with a soaring central dome. A short walk west is the **Pokrovsky Sobor**, a red-brick building with bright blue domes.

Transport

Distance from St Petersburg 45km
Direction Southwest
Travel Time One hour
Bus From Moskovskaya metro station bus No 431 (R25, one hour) runs often. In Gatchina it stops on pr 25 Oktyabrya: the park is immediately west.
Train Any suburban train bound for Kalishe or Oranienbaum from Baltiisky Station stops at Gatchina. The palace is a minute's walk from the station.

Sights & Information

Palace estate (☎ 271 13492; admission R270; 10am-6pm Tue-Sun)

Eating

Dom Khleba (ul Gobornaya 2) This excellent bakery and café is one place where you could grab a snack.

Shankhai Kafe (ul Gobornaya 15) This Chinese restaurant closer to the church serves up typically russified Chinese cooking.

ORANIENBAUM ОРАНИЕНБАУМ

Anyone interested in Peter the Great's best friend and oft-rumoured lover, Prince Menshikov, will be fascinated by this testament to Menshikov's growing vanity and general hubris. While Peter was building Monplaisir at Peterhof, Menshikov began his own palace at **Oranienbaum** (Orange Tree), 12km further down the coast, a grand enterprise that eventually bankrupted him. Peter was unfazed by the fact that his subordinate's palace in St Petersburg (the Menshikov Palace) was grander than his own, and likewise Menshikov outdid his master in creating this fabulous place. While not particularly opulent compared to the palaces that Elizabeth and Catherine the Great favoured, by Petrine standards Oranienbaum was off the scale.

Following Peter's death and Menshikov's exile, the estate served briefly as a hospital and then passed to Tsar Peter III, who didn't much like ruling Russia and spent a lot of time there before he was dispatched in a coup led by his wife, Catherine the Great.

Spared Nazi occupation, after WWII Oranienbaum was renamed for the scientist-poet Mikhail Lomonosov. Now known as Oranienbaum again, it doubles as a museum and **public park**, with boat rentals and carnival rides alongside the remaining buildings.

Menshikov's **Grand Palace** impresses the most with its size, though many of its decrepit rooms are still under renovation. Beyond the pond is **Peterstadt**, Peter III's boxy toy palace, with rich, uncomfortable-looking interiors. It is approached through the **Gate of Honour**, all that remains of a toy fortress where he amused himself drilling his soldiers.

Worth a peek also is Catherine's over-the-top **Chinese Palace**. It's baroque outside and extravagantly rococo inside, with a private retreat designed by Antonio Rinaldi including painted ceilings and fine inlaid-wood floors and walls. Check out the blindingly sumptuous **Large Chinese Room**, done up in the 'Oriental' style of the day.

Perhaps Oranienbaum's best feature is the several kilometres of quiet paths through pine woods and sombre gardens, with relatively small crowds; again it's a lovely place for a picnic.

Sights & Information

Chinese Palace (admission R50; 10am-5pm Wed-Mon May-Oct)

Grand Palace (☎ 423 1627; adult/student R50/15; 10am-5pm Wed-Mon May-Oct)

Peterstadt (admission R50; 10am-5pm Wed-Mon May-Oct)

Public park (admission free; 9am-10pm)

Eating

Don't count on being able to get anything beyond snacks or chocolate bars at Oranienbaum. The best option is to pack a picnic and enjoy it in the park.

Transport

Distance from St Petersburg 41km
Direction West
Travel Time 45 minutes to one hour
Bus There are marshrutkas to Oranienbaum from outside metro Avtovo.
Train The suburban train from St Petersburg's Baltic Station to Petrodvorets continues to Oranienbaum. Get off at Oranienbaum-I (not II) Station, an hour from St Petersburg. From the station it's a short walk south, then west at the Archangel Michael Cathedral (Sobor Arkhangela Mikhaila) along Dvortsovy pr until you reach the palace entrance.

VYBORG ВЫБОРГ

One completely refreshing day trip from St Petersburg takes you to Russia's most Scandinavian town, little Vyborg (population 81,000) on the Finnish border. This ancient place has a melancholic, rather forgotten feel to it (the atmosphere of most Russian provincial towns in fact), but is still charming with its quietly crumbling old town, winding cobblestone streets and magnificent fortress. Movie buffs may be interested to know that the critically acclaimed film *The Return (Vozvrashcheniye)* was filmed partly on location here in 2003, with the opening scene taking in the fortress as the young protagonists run through the town.

Before you go, learn to pronounce the town in Russian – *vi*-berk – you must stress the first syllable and try to sound like an aggressive frog. Only by pronouncing it this way will *anyone* be able to understand where you want to go.

Vyborg is built around the romantic, moated Vyborg Castle, built by the Swedes in 1293 when they first captured Karelia from Novgorod. Since then borders have jumped back and forth around Vyborg, giving the town its curiously mixed heritage and explaining the Finnish influence visible in everything from architecture to attitude.

Peter the Great took Vyborg back for Russia in 1710, shortly after establishing St Petersburg as his capital and wanting to secure the region around it. A century later it fell within autonomous Finland and after the revolution it remained part of independent Finland (the Finns call it Viipuri). Stalin took it in 1939, lost it to the Finns and Germans during WWII and on getting it back deported all the Finns. Today it's a laid-back, Finnish-looking city full of Russian fishers, timber-haulers, military men and the usual border-town shady types. Coachloads of Finns arrive for the cheap alcohol every weekend and drunken tourists are something of an inevitability here.

Vyborg Fortress, built on a rock in Vyborg Bay, is the city's oldest building, though most of it now is 16th-century alterations. Inside is a small museum of local studies. Across the bridge is the **Anna Fortress** (Anninskaya Krepost), built in the 18th century as protection against the Swedes and named after Empress Anna Ivanovna. Behind this is the **Park Monrepo Reserve**, a massive expanse of wooded and lake-dotted parkland one could spend a whole day in. Laid out in a classical style, it also has a forest feel to it – as pretty as Pavlovsk's park only wilder. Curved bridges, arbours and sculptures complete the picture.

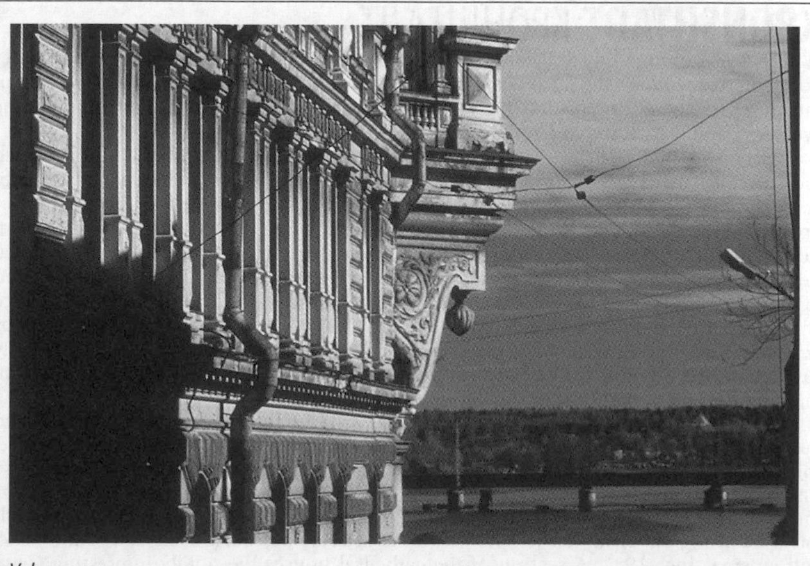

Vyborg

There are lovely streets with centuries-old churches, bell towers and cathedrals, especially along and off ul Krepostnaya, as well as a wealth of *style moderne* buildings that are in a similar state of disrepair. A short walk from the 16th-century castle takes you to the **Kruglaya bashnya** (Round Tower) and the **Spaso-Preobrazhensky Sobor** (Cathedral of the Transfiguration, 1787), all of which are worth visiting.

Sights & Information

Park Monrepo Reserve (☎ 81378-20539)

Vyborg Fortress (☎ 81378-21515; museum R20, tower R20; 🕑 10am-7pm Tue-Sun)

Eating

Bar-Restaurant Nordwest (☎ 81378-25893; mains R120; 🕑 10am-midnight) Slick and just a bit tacky but with a great menu (try its salmon cream soup for R55), this is a good option.

Round Tower Restaurant (☎ 81378-27838; mains R100; 🕑 noon-11pm) Gives you a chance to eat inside one of the town's most interesting buildings. Smartly laid out on the top floor of the tower itself, this is the nicest place in town, with excellent food. The bar stays open 24 hours and can be rowdy.

Sleeping

Bat Hotel (☎ 81378-34537; Nikolaeva 3, Vyborg; s/d €40/50) A very cosy new option is the oddly named Bat, or 'Letuchaya Mysh' as it's known in Russian. The 10 rooms are new and spotless with en suite bathrooms.

Hotel Druzhba (☎ 81378-25744; ul Zheleznodorozhnaya 5; s/d €55/60) This is the old Soviet hotel and is perfectly fine despite its rather forgotten feel.

Transport

Distance from St Petersburg 174km

Direction Northwest

Travel Time Around two to three hours

Bus Hourly buses (2½ hours, R70) run between St Petersburg and Vyborg from the bus stop to one side of Finland Station.

Train Suburban trains (three hours) run roughly every hour from Finland Station to Vyborg's train station, but they are slow and stop frequently. It's best to take one of the rarer express services between the two towns (two hours, three times a day) from here or a Helsinki-bound express from Ladozhsky Station, all of which stop in Vyborg.

KRONSHTADT КРОНШТАДТ

Within a year of founding St Petersburg, Peter – desirous of protecting his new Baltic toehold – started work on the fortress of Kronshtadt on Kotlin Island, 29km out in the Gulf of Finland. Kronshtadt (population 45,100) has been a pivotal Soviet and Russian naval base ever since and was closed to foreigners until 1996.

Soviet history buffs will be interested to visit due to the famous Kronshtadt Mutiny which took place here in 1921 – one of the last overt signs of opposition to the revolution until *perestroika*. The Red Army sailors stationed there, ironically, were the most revolutionary, pro-Bolshevik element in 1917; Trotsky called them 'the pride and glory of the Russian Revolution'. Four years later, though, hungry and poor, the sailors set up a Provisional Revolutionary Committee and drafted a resolution demanding, among other things, an end to Lenin's harsh policy of War Communism. Red Army attempts to stifle the mutiny were at first repulsed, but on 16 March 1921 the mutineers were defeated when 50,000 troops crossed the ice from Petrograd and massacred nearly the entire naval force. Though bloodily suppressed, the event did cause Lenin to relax state pressure and scrap War Communism, marking the end of the Russian revolutionary movement.

The main reason to visit here today is to view up close the exterior of the unusual and beautiful **Naval Cathedral** (Morskoy Sobor; 1903–13). Built to honour Russian naval muscle, this neo-Byzantine styled wonder stands on Anchor Sq (Yakornaya pl), where you'll also find an eternal flame for all of Kronshtadt's sailors and the florid Art Nouveau monument of Admiral Makarov. The cathedral's intricately detailed façade (anchors and all) has a haunting air of mystery – the off-limits interior has been used as a sailors' club and cinema since 1932. A section of the cathedral houses the mildly interesting **Central Naval Museum**.

Otherwise, Kronshtadt is a pleasant place to stroll around. In the harbourside **Petrovsky Park**, 700m southwest of the Naval Cathedral, there's a statue of Peter the Great and you can glimpse Russian warships and even some submarines: be careful about taking any photographs here though. In recent summers Kronshtadt and some of the surrounding sea forts have been the scene of big dance parties, something St Petersburg aims to promote in the future – keep an eye out for posters in the city advertising events out here.

Transport

Distance from St Petersburg 29km
Direction West
Travel Time 20 to 30 minutes
Bus The only proper bus to serve Kronshtadt is No 510 (R20, 30 minutes), leaving regularly throughout the day from outside the Staraya Derevnya metro station on the Vyborg Side. Marshrutkas leave St Petersburg from outside the nearby Chyornaya Rechka: exit the station to your left, cross the street and veer right towards the bus stop where marshrutkas (R30, 20 minutes) or private cars will be waiting. You will arrive in Kronshtadt at the bus stop on the corner of Grazhdanskaya and pr Lenina. From there it's about a 1km walk southeast to the Naval Cathedral.

Sights & Information

Central Naval Museum (☎ 236 4713; admission R100; 🕑 11am-5.15pm Wed-Sun)

Eating

Skazka (pr Lenina 31) Decorated with Disney characters, this is a good choice from the cafés on the town's main drag.

STARAYA LADOGA СТАРАЯ ЛАДОГА

It may look like a sleepy village (population 3000) but once Staraya (Old) Ladoga, located 125km east of St Petersburg on the winding banks of the Volkhov River, was an active participant in the very birth of the Russian nation. Just as the origins of ancient Rus are continually debated, so will Staraya Ladoga's status as 'Russia's first capital'. Nevertheless, its age (historians have given 753 as the village's birth date) and significance remain uncontested.

According to some ancient texts, when the Scandinavian Viking Rurik, along with his relatives Truvor and Sineus, swept into ancient Russia in 862, he built a wooden fortress at present-day Staraya Ladoga and made this his base. Locals even claim the tumulus on the banks of the Volkhov River at the northern end of the village is the grave of Oleg, Rurik's successor.

Archaeological expeditions continue to uncover a wealth of information about the town's past. In 1997 a second 9th-century fortress was discovered 2km outside the village, and it's known that at one time six monasteries worked in this small region. Evidence of Byzantine cultural influences in the frescoes of the village's 12th-century churches point to the town as a cultural as well as historical and commercial crossroads.

The town was known only as Ladoga until 1704, when Peter the Great founded Novaya (New) Ladoga to the north as a transfer point for the materials arriving to build St Petersburg. Protected as a national reserve, the town's basic structure and street patterns have remained virtually unchanged since the 12th century, give or take a few ugly Soviet blocks. The area boasts over a hundred items of archaeological and historical interest, including an ancient fortress and churches. It's a pleasant place to wander for a few hours, particularly in summer when a swim in the river adds to the charm.

Within the **fortress**, at the southern end of the village, you'll find the stone **St George's Church** (Tserkov Georgiya), open only during dry weather to protect the delicate 12th-century frescoes still visible on its walls, and the wooden **Church of Dimitri Solun**. The main tower of the fortress is the **Historical-Architectural & Archaeological Museum** housing a retrospective of the area's history.

John the Baptist Church (Ioanna-Predtechi Tserkov; 1694), located atop the highest hill in the area at the north end of the village, is the only church with a regular weekend service. On this site was a 13th-century monastery. Nearby, beside the riverbanks, is an ancient burial mound and, beneath the church, caves where glass was once made.

Sights & Information

Fortress (Staroladozhskaya Krepost; 9am-6pm Tue-Sun Jun-Aug, 9am-4pm Tue-Sun Sep-May)

Historical-Architectural & Archaeological Museum (☎ 81263-49331; admission R15)

St George's Church (Tserkov Georgiya; admission R30)

Eating

Ladya, a decent restaurant above the general store on the main road through the village, does traditional Russian fare for very reasonable prices.

Transport

Distance from St Petersburg 125km
Direction East
Travel Time Around three hours
Train Unless you hire a taxi to take you there and back (about R1000), you'll need to go by train. Take an *elektrichka* to Volkhov (Volkhovstroy I station) from Moscow Station in St Petersburg (R30, two hours). From Volkhov, take bus /minibus No 23 (R10, 20 minutes) headed towards Novaya Ladoga from the main bus stop outside the station, across the square. The second of three town bus stops lets you off just past the fortress.

NOVGOROD НОВГОРОД

The name means 'new town', but Novgorod was here by the 9th century and for 600 years was Russia's most pioneering artistic and political centre. Today Novgorod (population 240,000) is known mostly for its history, and for some of the most diverse and beautiful architecture in the country. Methodically trashed by the Nazis, it's a sign of the city's historical importance that its old kremlin was one of the Soviet government's first reconstruction projects.

In a sense, Russian history began here. This was the first permanent settlement of the Varangian Norsemen who established the embryonic Russian state. By the 12th century the city, called 'Lord Novgorod the Great', was Russia's biggest: an independent quasi-democracy whose princes were hired and fired by a citizens' assembly, and whose strong, spare style of church architecture, icon painting and down-to-earth *byliny* (epic songs) were to become distinct idioms.

Spared from the Mongol Tatars, who got bogged down in the surrounding swamps, Novgorod suffered most at the hands of other Russians. Ivan III of Moscow attacked and annexed it in 1477 and Ivan the Terrible, whose storm-troopers razed the city and slaughtered 60,000 people in a savage pogrom, broke its back. The founding of St Petersburg finished it off as a trading centre.

Today, Novgorod is an easy and rewarding overnight stop popular with foreign and Russian tourists.

Part park, part museum, part archive, the **kremlin** is worth seeing with a guide. Russian-language guides sometimes hang out at the Millennium monument. The fortress gates are open from 6am to midnight daily; hours for specific sights within the kremlin vary.

Finished in 1052, the handsome, Byzantine **Cathedral of St Sophia** (Sofiysky Sobor) is the town's centrepiece and one of the oldest buildings in Russia. The simple, fortress-like exterior was designed to withstand attack or fire (flames had taken out an earlier wooden church on the site); ornamentation was reserved for the interior. The onion domes were probably added during the 14th century – even so, they are perhaps the first example of this most Russian architectural detail. The west doors, dating from the 12th century, have tiny cast-bronze biblical scenes and even portraits of the artists. The icons inside date from the 14th century and older ones are in the

Transport

Distance from St Petersburg 186km
Direction Southeast
Travel Time Three to four hours
Bus From St Petersburg's Avtovokzal No 2 you can take buses to Novgorod (R145, 3½ hours, 14 daily), arriving at Novgorod's bus station (next to the train station), 1.5km from the centre of town.
Train There is currently one evening train daily from St Petersburg's Moscow Station to Novgorod (R255, 3¼ hours, 5.15pm), which means staying the night. There are also slower trains to/from Vitebsk Station, although timetables vary – check directly with the station (p210).

museum. In comparison the interior frescoes are barely dry, being less than a century old. Services usually take place between 6pm and 8pm daily. Nearby are the 15th-century belfry and a leaning 17th-century clock tower.

Watch the crowds go round and round the **Millennium of Russia Monument**, unveiled in 1862 on the 1000th anniversary of the Varangian Prince Rurik's arrival. The Nazis cut it up, intending to ship it to Germany, but the Red Army saved the day. The women at the top are Mother Russia and the Orthodox Church. Around the middle, clockwise from the south, are Rurik, Prince Vladimir of Kyiv (who introduced Christianity), tsars Mikhail Romanov, Peter the Great and Ivan III, and Dmitry Donskoy trampling a Mongol Tatar. In the bottom band on the east side are nobles and rulers, including Catherine the Great with an armload of laurels for all her lovers. Alexander Nevsky and other military heroes are on the north side, and literary and artistic figures are on the west.

Across a footbridge from the kremlin is old Novgorod's market, with the remnants of a 17th-century arcade facing the river. Beyond that is the market gatehouse, an array of churches sponsored by 13th- to 16th-century merchant guilds and a 'road palace', built in the 18th century as a rest stop for Catherine the Great.

Restored between 1995 and 1999, the Kyiv-style **Court Cathedral of St Nicholas** (Nikolo-Dvorishchensky Sobor; 1136) is all that remains of the early palace complex of the Novgorod princes, from which the area gets its name of Yaroslav's Court (Yaroslavovo dvorishche). The cathedral itself is closed, but an **exhibition hall** in the former trading court gate, across from the cathedral entrance, holds church artefacts and temporary exhibitions of local interest.

On the outside, the 14th-century **Church of Our Saviour-at-Ilino** (Tserkov Spasa-na-Iline) has graffiti-like ornaments and lopsided gables, which are almost playful. Inside are the only surviving frescoes by legendary Byzantine painter Theophanes the Greek (and they came close to extinction when the church served as a Nazi machine-gun nest). Recent restoration has exposed as much of the frescoes as possible, though they are still faint. A small exhibit upstairs includes reproductions with explanations in Russian. Note Theophanes' signature use of white war paint–like markings around the eyes and noses of his figures, and his soul-penetrating expressions. The church itself, east of Yaroslav's Court, is pure Novgorod style (in contrast to the more complex 17th-century Moscow-style Cathedral of Our Lady of the Sign across the street).

Millennium of Russia Monument (above)

Sights & Information

Cathedral of St Sophia (Sofiysky Sobor; 🕒 8am-8pm)

Church of Our Saviour-at-Ilino (Tserkov Spasa-na-Iline; ul Ilina; adult/student R60/30; 🕒 10am-5pm Tue-Sun)

Court Cathedral of St Nicholas exhibition hall (☎ 81622-33465; adult/student R50/25; 🕒 10am-4.30pm Wed-Sun)

Kremlin (☎ 81622-73608, 81622-77187 for information)

Eating

You'll eat decently in Novgorod, where a large number of traditional restaurants cater to both foreign and Russian tourists.

Kafe Charodeyka (ul Volosova-Meretskova 1/1; mains R100-250) A favourite with homesick foreigners, has Tuborg on tap, Irish coffee and pizza, served up in a pleasant atmosphere.

Pri Dvore (ul Lyudogoshchaya 3; mains R50) Cheery little cafeteria with good prepared salads and hot dishes by the kilogram.

Restoran Detinets (☎ 81622-74624; dishes R35-200) Partly in the kremlin wall, this is the place to try for good Russian dishes. Entering the kremlin from the west bank, turn right and follow the wall beyond the WWII memorial and the first few buildings to the restaurant entrance.

Restoran Pri Dvore (☎ 81622-74343; mains R100-200) In the same building as the Pri Dvore around the corner, this smarter restaurant is rather formal, with standard Russian dishes, an English-language menu and weekly lunch specials.

Sleeping

While there aren't many particularly superb deals to be had in Novgorod, you'll have no trouble finding somewhere to stay. A day trip is very rushed, so we recommend that you stay overnight at one of the following hotels.

Beresta Palace Hotel (☎ 8162-158010; beresta@novtour.ru; ul Studencheskaya 2; s/d R2500/3000) Definitely the town's best hotel, the Beresta Palace is run by Best Western and is on the east bank of the Volkhov, a little out of the centre.

Hotel Akron (☎ 8162-136918; fax 816-213 6934; ul Predtechenskaya 24; s/d from R500/750) The rooms here are clean and the modern bathrooms are about the best you'll see for the price.

Hotel Volkhov (☎ 8162-115505; ul Predtechenskaya 24; s/d from R800/1000) Next door to the Akron, the Volkhov targets business travellers and charges a bit more. Rates include breakfast.

Rosa Vetrov (☎ 81622-72033; ul Nonoluchanskaya 27; dm/s/d R150/230/290) Though space is very limited here, this is the town's best and cleanest budget option. Book ahead.

PETROZAVODSK ПЕТРОЗАВОДСК

Nestled on the coast of vast Lake Onega, Petrozavodsk ('Peter's Factory') has a history directly linked to that of St Petersburg, being founded in 1703 – the same year as the northern capital – as an iron foundry and armaments plant. The capital of the autonomous republic of Karelia (the Russian region which borders neighbouring Finland), this is an exceptionally relaxed and pleasant Russian town (population 280,000). Most people come here to visit the magnificent collection of old wooden buildings and churches on Kizhi, an island 66km northeast of the city in Lake Onega.

KIZHI КИЖИ

One of the most stunning sights in European Russia, this island on Lake Onega was a centre of local paganism that was invaded by Christianity in the 12th century. Over the centuries churches have come and gone, but the collection of churches you can visit today date from the 14th to 18th centuries and are fascinating to visit in a half-day trip from Petrozavodsk.

The entire island of Kizhi serves as a museum, the centrepiece of which is the 1714 fairy-tale **Transfiguration Cathedral** (Preobrazhensky Sobor). With its chorus of 22 domes, gables and ingenious decorations to

Transport

Distance from St Petersburg 420km
Direction Northeast
Travel Time Eight hours
Bus It's possible to take one of the daily buses (R200, nine hours) from St Petersburg's Avtovokzal No 2 but it's a hell of a journey.
Train The only enjoyable way to travel to Petrozavodsk is to take the overnight train (R450, eight hours, daily) from Ladozhsky Station, which gets you into Petrozavodsk in the early morning. Trains running between St Petersburg and Murmansk also stop in Petrozavodsk.

keep water off the walls, it is the gem of Russian wooden architecture and amazingly not a single nail is employed in holding it together. Next door is the nine-domed **Church of the Intercession** (Pokrovskaya Tserkov) built in 1764.

The other buildings in the collection were brought from the region around Lake Onega. The 19th-century peasant houses, some more ornate than others, are nicely restored inside. The little **Church of the Resurrection of Lazarus**, from the 14th century, may be the oldest wooden building in Russia. The **Chapel of the Archangel Michael**, with an interesting tent-roofed belfry, has an exhibit on Christianity in Karelia and music students from Petrozavodsk play its bells in summer. There are numerous other houses, barns, windmills and buildings open to exploration.

Kizhi can only be visited easily from early June to late August, when navigation on the lake is open. Hydrofoils (return R260, 45 minutes) make the trip a few times a day from the Petrozavodsk ferry terminal, and as everyone is going to visit the museum the boats are timed to allow plenty of time to see the sights before returning.

Summertime trips can also be booked through St Petersburg agencies, although similar trips at substantially cheaper rates can be booked through the river terminal in St Petersburg (p205).

VALAAM ВАЛААМ

The delightful Valaam Archipelago, which consists of Valaam Island and some 50 smaller ones, sits in northwestern Lake Ladoga. The main attractions here are the 14th-century **Valaam Transfiguration Monastery** (Spaso-Preobrazhensky Valaamsky Monastyr), its cathedral and buildings, and the pleasant town that surrounds it.

There is some dispute about the identity of the first settlers – some sources say that they were 10th-century monks – but most agree that the monastery was first settled in the late 14th century as a fortress against Swedish invaders, who managed to destroy it completely in 1611. Rebuilt with money from Peter the Great, the monastery doubled as a prison.

Many of the monks and much of the monastery's treasure were moved to Finland, which controlled the territory from 1918 to 1940. After 1940, when the territory fell back into Soviet hands again, the Soviet authorities decided they would close the monastery, taking whatever was left and then constructing what they referred to as an 'urban-type settlement' there.

Today the buildings are protected architectural landmarks, but neglect has taken its toll. Many of the buildings are decrepit and in need of repair. There are about 500 residents on the main island, including army service personnel, restoration workers, guides and clergy, most of whom get around in horse-drawn carriages or motorboats.

You can arrange a visit to Valaam via Petrozavodsk through any local travel agency. However, if you want to see both Valaam and Kizhi, you are better off booking a boat trip direct from St Petersburg. Contact any travel agency, book direct at the River Passenger Terminal (p205) or call specialist agency **Solnechny Parus**. Alternatively you can deal with the **monastery's centre in St Petersburg**. It organises a full range of year-round excursions (by boat or helicopter) and can set you up with a place to sleep inside the monastery. It also has combined Valaam/Kizhi tours.

Sights & Information

Kizhi (in Petrozavodsk ☎ 8142-767091; http://kizhi.karelia.ru; admission R350)

Solnechny Parus (☎/fax 812-327 3525; www.solpar.ru; ul Vosstaniya 55)

Valaam Transfiguration Monastery's St Petersburg centre (☎ 812-271 2264; www.valaam.karelia.ru; nab Sinopskaya 34/36)

Eating

Kavkaz (ul Andropova 13; mains R50-250) The city's popular Georgian restaurant. Try the Lula kebab (it looks unappetising but is delicious) and the *khachapuri* (cheese pie).

Petrovsky Restoran (ul Andropova 1; mains R70-200; 11am-2am) This is one of the town's most authentic and cosy places. Try local speciality *myaso po medvednoye* (a meat casserole with potatoes, cheese and mayo; R114).

Saloon Sanches (☎ 8142-763977; pr Lenina 26; mains R120-400; ⏲ 9am-1am) This place serves up a good selection of breakfast omelettes, so it's ideal for early-morning arrivals just off the train.

Sleeping

Unless you are on a cruise you will probably need to spend at least one night in Petrozavodsk, and there are three affordable and decent options.

Hotel Fregat (☎ 8142-764162, 8142-764163; s/d R1500/1650) Located on the lake side of the ferry-terminal building. If you're going to Kizhi, you couldn't be more conveniently located, but its renovated rooms are on the rip-off end of the scale.

Hotel Severnaya (☎ 8142-762080, 8142-780703; http://severnaja.onego.ru/new/eng; pr Lenina 21; s/d/ste R200/720/3000) This is without question your best bet: it's clean, smack in the centre and has very affordable rooms as well as far pricier suites.

Karelia Hotel (☎ /fax 8142-552306; nab Gyullinga 2; s/d/ste R700/1300/1700) A five-minute walk from the ferry terminal, this is a depressing monstrosity but the rooms are clean. Try for a view of the lake.

Directory

Directory

TRANSPORT

AIR

St Petersburg is Russia's second largest air hub, although it lags far behind Moscow in terms of the number of long-haul connections. It's well-connected throughout Europe and the former Soviet Union, but from Asia, Australasia and the Americas you'll usually have to change planes in either Moscow or another European hub to fly into St Petersburg.

Airlines

Any airlines flying to and from St Petersburg not listed below will have an office at **Pulkovo Airport** (☎ 104 3444).

Aeroflot (SU; Map pp246-9; ☎ 327 3872; www.aeroflot.ru; Kazanskaya ul 5)

Air France (AF; Map pp246-9; ☎ 325 8252; www.airfrance.com; Bolshaya Morskaya ul 35)

Austrian Airlines (OS; Map pp246-9; ☎ 331 2005; www.aua.com; Nevsky pr 32)

British Airways (BA; Map pp246-9; ☎ 380 0626; www.britishairways.com; Malaya Konyushennaya ul 1/3-A, office 23-B)

CSA Czech Airlines (OK; Map pp246-9; ☎ 315 5264/59; www.czechairlines.com; Bolshaya Morskaya ul 34)

Delta Airlines (DL; Map pp246-9; ☎ 571 5820; www.delta.com; Bolshaya Morskaya ul 36)

Finnair (AY; Map pp246-9; ☎ 303 9898; www.finnair.com; Malaya Konyushennaya ul 1/3, office B33)

KLM Royal Dutch Airlines (KL; Map pp246-9; ☎ 346 6868; www.klm.com; White Nights Business Centre, Malaya Morskaya 23)

LOT Polish Airlines (LO; Map pp246-9; ☎ 273 5721; www.lot.com; Karavannaya ul 1)

Lufthansa (LH; Map pp246-9; ☎ 320 1000; www.lufthansa.com; Nevsky pr 32)

Pulkovo Express (FV; Map pp244-5; ☎ 303 9268; www.pulkovo-express.ru; 1-aya Krasnoarmeyskaya ul 6)

SAS Scandinavian Airlines (SK; Map pp246-9; ☎ 326 2600; www.scandinavian.net; Nevsky pr 25)

Transaero (Map pp246-9; ☎ 279 6463; www.transaero.ru; Liteyny pr 48)

Airport

St Petersburg has two terminals at its Pulkovo Airport, 17km to the city's south. Pulkovo-1 handles domestic flights and those to some non-Russian cities within the former Soviet Union. Pulkovo-2 is the international terminal; a small, well-run airport which was given a decent face-lift for the tricentennial in 2003. There are plans to build a third terminal here due to increased demand.

There are ATMs in both terminal buildings, although make sure you have euros or US dollars to change just in case they are not working.

To get to the city centre you can take one of two city buses (R7) into the city centre: the K-3 (running every 15 to 20 minutes from 7am to 11pm) that connects Pulkovo-2 to Moskovskaya metro station and terminates in the city centre at Sennaya Pl metro station, or the 13 (6am to 12.45am, every 20 to 30 minutes) that runs to Moskovskaya metro station, from where you can catch a car (see the boxed text on p209) or take the metro to the city centre.

Alternatively, there are several *marshrutkas* (see p208) from both airport terminals to the city centre, or at least the nearest metro station at Moskovskaya. The 3 (to Pushkinskaya metro station), K13 and T11 (both to Moskovskaya metro station) and the K213 (to Sennaya Pl metro station) leave from outside Pulkovo-2, while the K39A (Moskovskaya) and K39 (Pl Alexandra Nevskogo metro station) leave from outside Pulkovo-1.

A taxi here will cost you way over the odds if you haven't reserved ahead. Some of the sharks ask for as much as €50, when a reasonable price would be R600 (€20). Haggling will often do no good, so ask your hotel to book you a taxi or call a local taxi company before you arrive (see p209).

Travel Agents

The following agencies are highly recommended for booking trips to Russia. Even if you only get your visa through them, they can often make things a lot easier for newcomers to Russian bureaucracy.

AUSTRALIA & NEW ZEALAND

Innovative Travel (☎ 03-365 3910; innovative.travel@clear.net.nz; PO Box 21–247, Christchurch) Offers a huge range of tours and good deals on flights to Europe.

Passport Travel (☎ 03-9867 3888; www.travelcentre.com.au; Suite 11A, 401 St Kilda Rd, Melbourne 3004) Australia's recognised Russia specialists organise homestays in St Petersburg as well as dealing with all aspects of the visa process.

Russian Travel Centre (☎ 02-9262 1144; www.eetbtravel.com; 5th fl, 75 King St, Sydney 2000) Also known as Eastern Europe Travel, the Russian Travel Centre offers packages to Russia and can sort out visas and invites.

UK

IMS Travel (☎ 020-7224 4678; www.imstravel.co.uk; 9 Mandeville Pl, London, W1U 3AU) The Russian Travel Centre at IMS Travel has a team of Russian-speaking specialists who can handle almost any travel requirements, including visa invitations, internal flights and transfers on the ground. The centre also has a handy courier service, so you can avoid waiting in line at the Russian embassy in London.

Russia House (☎ 020-7403 9922; www.therussiahouse.co.uk; Chapel Court, Borough High St, London SE1 1HH) Comprehensive services, mainly oriented to business travellers. It can get you a visa in a few hours if you have several hundred pounds to burn. All travel arrangements and visa support can be done here and via its Moscow office.

USA

IntelService Center USA (☎ 1800 339 2118; www.intelservice.ru; 1227 Monterey St, Pittsburgh, PA 15212) With offices in both the USA and Moscow, the IntelService Center has plenty of experience in organising travel in Russia. As well as visa invitations, it can arrange discounted hotel rates and tours.

Travel Document Systems (☎ 1800 874 5100; www.traveldocs.com; 925 Fifteenth St NW, Suite 300, Washington DC 20005) The Washington-based TDS deals exclusively in visa documentation and can fax visa invitations anywhere in the world.

BICYCLE

St Petersburg is a bad place to ride a bike – bumpy, pothole-riddled roads and lunatic drivers not accustomed to seeing cyclists make it a dangerous proposition. It's a very nice pastime outside the centre or through the parks, though, particularly throughout the Kirovsky Islands.

One wonderful bicycle ride – wonderful, that is, once you are south of the airport – is to head due south on Moskovsky pr. Once you pass the airport, you're suddenly in lovely countryside. At the turn-off (there's a statue of Pushkin and the sign points south to Kyiv and east to the town of Tsarskoe Selo), turn left and you'll get to Tsarskoe Selo Palace. It's a long (about 25km) ride, but you can take the *elektrichka* train back to St Petersburg.

Lock your bike before you leave it, preferably with a Kryptonite or other 'U'-type lock and not just a chain and padlock.

If you think biking to Tsarskoe Selo is a heroic feat, check out Dan Buettner's excellent book *Sovietrek: A Journey by Bicycle Across Russia* (1994). His trek across Russia was completed in 124 days in 1990.

BOAT

Ferries

Passenger ferries leave from the **Morskoy Vokzal** (Map pp242–3; ☎ 322 6052; pl Morskoy Slavy 1; metro Primorskaya). To get here more easily, as it's a long way from the metro, take either bus No 7 or trolley bus No 10 from outside the Hermitage.

From here St Petersburg is regularly connected with Helsinki in Finland and Tallinn in Estonia. Less frequent are connections to the Russian Baltic enclave of Kaliningrad and Rostok in Germany. You can buy tickets direct from the ferry companies at the sea port or, a far easier choice, at the central **Paromny Tsentr** (Map pp246–9; ☎ 279 6670; www.paromy.ru in Russian; ul Vosstaniya 19; metro Pl Vosstaniya).

Since 2004, **Tallink** (in Helsinki ☎ 09-228 311; www.tallink.fi) has begun a Helsinki–St Petersburg route (€55, 17 hours). The drag is that it sails via Tallinn on the outbound route, although from St Petersburg, the journey is direct. Boats leave Helsinki every other day at 4pm, arriving later that night in Tallinn and docking in St Petersburg at 9am the next day.

Silja Line (www.silja.fi) operates the Finnjet, which every three to four days connects Rostok, Germany with Tallinn (€96, 25 hours), going on to St Petersburg (€117, a further 11 hours from Tallinn).

Regular ferry services go along the Neva to inland Russia, including cruises to Valaam, Kizhi and Moscow. Prices and schedules vary, so book through a travel agency or the **River Passenger Terminal** (Map p237; ☎ 262 0239, 262 6321; pr Obukhovskoy Oborony 195; metro Proletarskaya).

Bridge Timetable

From May until November all major bridges rise at the following times nightly to allow ships to pass through, meaning you cannot cross the river during these times. Call ☎ 326 9696 for more information. All times are am.

Bridge	Up	Down	Up	Down
Alexandra Nevskogo	2.20	5.05		
Birzhevoy	2.10	4.50		
Bolsheokhtinsky	2.00	5.00		
Dvortsovy (Palace)	1.35	2.55	3.15	4.50
Finlyandsky	2.30	5.10		
Grenadersky	2.45	3.45	4.20	4.50
Kantemirovsky	2.45	3.45	4.20	4.50
Leytenanta Shmidta	1.40	4.55		
Liteyny	1.50	4.40		
Sampsonievsky	2.10	2.45	3.20	4.25
Troitsky	1.50	4.50		
Tuchkov	2.10	3.05	3.35	4.45
Volodarsky	2.00	3.45	4.15	5.45

Water Buses

Surprisingly for a city built on water, there was not until recently any regular form of city water transport in St Petersburg and certainly nothing like Venice's network of *vaporetti*. In summer 2004 four waterbus routes began operation, although with only one per hour and the prices astronomical compared to the metro or even *marshrutkas*, the service is squarely aimed at the tourist market.

Route A Peter and Paul Fortress, the Museum of Anthropology and Ethnography (Kunstkamera), the Admiralty, the Cruiser *Aurora*, the Summer Garden, the Russian Museum's Mikhailovsky Castle, Mars Field (Marsovo Polye), the Alexander Pushkin-Flat Museum and Dvortsovaya pl (Palace Sq).

Route B Kazan Cathedral, the Church on Spilled Blood, the Russian Museum, the Summer Garden, Mars Field, Nevsky pr (Anichkov Palace), the Alexandrinsky Theatre, Nikolsky Cathedral, the Mariinsky Theatre and Sennaya pl.

Route C Stroganov Palace on Nevsky pr, Dvortsovaya pl (Palace Sq), Konyushennaya pl, the Russian Museum (and Mars Field), the Alexandrinsky Theatre, Nikolsky Cathedral, the Mariinsky Theatre and St Isaac's Cathedral.

Route D Admiralty, the Hermitage, Smolny Cathedral, the Okhtinskaya Hotel, the Cruiser *Aurora*, the Peter and Paul Fortress and St Isaac's Cathedral.

Each route takes from one to 1½ hours to complete. At time of writing, a fifth route was soon to be introduced to operate on weekends between the Admiralty and Yelagin Island.

BUS

The city's main bus station is **Avtovokzal No 2** (Map pp244–5; ☎ 166 5777; nab Obvodnogo Kanala 36; metro Ligovsky Pr), a recently remodelled building a little out of the city centre. From here there are buses to towns throughout European Russia and to the Baltic capitals. There are buses from here to Moscow, but all are en route elsewhere. You'll be dropped off in the north Moscow suburb of Khimki. It's far nicer (and the same price) to take the train.

Destination	Duration	Price	Frequency
Helsinki	8hr	R1140	2 daily
Moscow	12hr	R480	1 daily
Novgorod	3½hr	R145	14 daily
Petrozavodsk	9hr	R200	1 daily
Pskov	5½hr	R270	2 daily
Pushkinskie Gory	8 ½hr	R310	1 daily
Rīga	11hr	R500	2 daily
Staraya Russa	5½hr	R220	3 daily
Tallinn	7½hr	R390	7 daily
Tampere	9hr	R1200	1 daily
Velikiye Luki	5hr	R240	3 daily

The other main international bus stop is outside the Baltic Station. From here **Eurolines** (Map pp242–3; ☎ 168 2740; ul Shkapina 10; metro Baltiyskaya) runs buses to Tallinn (R390, five daily), Rīga (R500, daily) and Tartu in Estonia (R360, daily).

Other companies running international bus routes to Helsinki and the Baltics:

Ardis Finnord (Map pp246-9; ☎ 314 8951; Italiyanskaya ul 37; metro Gostiny Dvor) Two daily buses leave from outside its office in the town centre. Departures are at 2.40pm and 10.15pm to Helsinki, and buses to St Petersburg leave at 9am and 11pm.

Ecolines (Map pp244-5; ☎ 315 2550; www.ecolines.ru; Podyezdny per 3; metro Pushkinskaya) Daily overnight bus from the Vitebsk Station to Rīga.

Neofahrt Tour (Map pp246-9; ☎ 118 2189; Oktyabrskaya Hotel, Ligovsky pr 43/45; metro Pl Vosstaniya) Overnight bus leaves from outside the main building of the Oktyabrskaya Hotel at 9.45pm. The bus from Helsinki leaves at 12.45pm, arriving in St Petersburg at 9.30pm.

Saimaan Liikenne (Map pp240-1; ☎ 332 0833; www.savonlinja.spb.ru; ul Chapayeva 5; metro Gorkovskaya) Daily buses to Helsinki.

Bus & Trolleybus

Supporting the metro system is the network of state-run buses and trolleybuses. Both are slow and crowded, but dirt cheap at R7 per trip. You buy tickets on board from a conductor who wears a red armband. These people know the route backwards, so they're nearly always able to help you by telling you when to get off. Trolleybuses No 1, 7 and 10 are useful – they all crawl the length of Nevsky from pl Vosstaniya to the Hermitage. Otherwise, your knowledge of buses will be on a need-to-know basis: if you are staying in a far-flung or badly connected area of town your host will tell you which bus to take to connect you to the city centre or the nearest metro station. If you want to use the buses and trolleybuses you can get a full list of routes from any city transport map – just ask for *karta marshrutov gorodskovo transporta* at any bookshop.

CAR & MOTORCYCLE

St Petersburg's roads are gnarled, its laws are strange and the *semper vigilans* eyes of the DPS goons (traffic cops, seen, seemingly, on every city corner), who are empowered to stop you and fine you on the spot, are always on you. Oh, yeah, they can also *shoot* at your vehicle if you don't heed their command to pull over (a wave of their striped stick towards your car).

Driving Tips

Left turns are illegal except where posted; you'll have to make three rights or a short U-turn (this is safer?). Street signs, except in the centre, are woefully inadequate and Russian drivers make Italian drivers seem downright courteous! Watch out for drivers overtaking on the inside; this seems to be the national sport. Potholes and jagged crevices are everywhere – straddle them.

Emergencies

The law says that when you have an accident you're supposed to remain at the scene until the DPS arrive; in practice, if the damage isn't major, most people would rather leave than add insult (a fine) to injury. **Lenavtotekhnika** (☎ 001) is a towing company that will come and get you 24 hours a day. **Spas** (☎ 327 7001) will do the same.

Fuel

By Western standards, fuel prices are quite low, although they have risen considerably by local standards in the past few years. In addition to state-run filling stations, Neste currently operates over 15 full-service filling stations in and around St Petersburg that charge more for petrol but offer faster service and accept major credit cards. You can get leaded and unleaded fuel at the following places in St Petersburg, although check the website of the main fuel supplier Neste for a full city-wide list (www.neste.ru).

Teatralnaya Pl

Alexandrovsky Park

Maly pr (Vasilevsky Island) 68A

Pulkovskoe sh 38

Moskovsky pr 102A & 156A

Savushkina ul 87

Avantgardnaya ul 86

Parking

In the town's centre, uniformed parking attendants charge about €1 to watch your car for you. There are guarded parking lots outside many hotels now – use them when you can. Never leave anything of value, including sunglasses, cassette tapes and cigarettes, in a car. Street parking is pretty much legal wherever it seems to be; it's illegal anywhere on Nevsky pr. Use common sense – avoid parking in dark side streets and isolated areas.

Rental

Renting a car here is now a pretty simple thing, though it's fairly expensive; the following are some agencies offering self-drive and chauffeured vehicles:

Astoria Service (Map pp246-9; ☎ 112 1583, 164 9622; www.astoriaservice.ru; ul Borovaya 11/13, office 65)

Europcar (Map pp246-9; ☎ 380 1662; www.europcar.ru; nab reki Fontanki 38)

Hertz (☎ 326 4505, 324 3242; www.hertz.spb.ru; Pulkovo Airport Terminal 2)

Pulkovo Rent-a-Car (☎ 332 0101; Pulkovo Airport Terminal 2)

MARSHRUTKAS

The *marshrutka* (a Russian diminutive form of *marshrutnoye taxi*) is king in St Petersburg. These minibuses function like buses, only passengers are free to request a stop anywhere along the route and because of their size they zip through the traffic far faster than normal city buses.

The sheer number of routes is staggering – they connect the city to the suburbs, and far-flung residential neighbourhoods to metro stations, and are often the only public transport serving some parts of the centre (particularly the Mariinsky and Smolny neighbourhoods, where metro stations are almost nonexistent). A *marshrutka* can be a lifesaver if you want to get from one end of Nevsky to the other for next to nothing.

Using a *marshrutka* can be intimidating at first: watch and observe the locals before trying it yourself. Hold out your arm to flag down the *marshrutka* you want. If in doubt state your destination to the driver before getting in: he'll either shake his head and drive off or nod you in. Taking a seat, pass the fare to the driver (if you aren't nearby, pass it to other passengers who will pass it to him). The fare is displayed inside the bus and varies depending on the route, although the average is around R14 – significantly more expensive than a city bus.

When you reach the place you want to be (again, if you don't know the city this makes using *marshrutkas* tricky, but other passengers will always help if you ask), you need to call out to the driver to stop. The standard phrase is '*ostanavityes pozhalsta!*' ('stop please!'). Although if you don't dare shout this out, 'stop please' in English is likely to suffice, as long as it's loud enough.

With over 200 routes in the city centre alone, you'll need to invest in a transport map for a full list in Russian (ask for *karta marshrutov gorodskovo transporta* at any bookshop), or simply learn the routes that take you from where you are staying to where you want to go. Nearly all *marshrutkas* running up and down Nevsky pr go all the way from pl Vosstaniya to the Hermitage, although ask the driver '*Vyess Nevsky?*' ('All of Nevsky?') before getting in.

METRO

The St Petersburg metro is a very efficient four-lined system that is also one of the world's deepest. The network of some 58 stations is most usefully employed for travelling long distances, especially connecting the suburbs to the city centre. Indeed, the historic heart of St Petersburg has only three stations in it.

The flat fare for a trip is R8, but if you're staying for more than a day or two, it's worth buying in bulk. A seven-day pass allowing you to use the metro 10 times is R66, while a month's pass for unlimited travel is R330. If you buy single journeys (ask for '*odin proyezd*'), you will be given a *zheton* (token) that you put into the machine and do not get back – just pass straight through.

If you buy multiple journeys, you will be given a *karta* (card), which will be eaten up by the ticket machine when you use up your last journey.

For those buying season tickets, you can get a *smart karta* (smartcard) that you touch in and out to gain access to the metro.

To anyone for whom Cyrillic is nothing more than pretty little symbols mixed in with the occasional 'English' letter, getting around on the metro can be a bit of an adventure. Some station platforms (10) have outer safety doors, so you can't see the station from an arriving train; also, you can't rely on spotting the signs on the platforms as you pull in, as they are both very infrequent and in Cyrillic.

Listen out for the announcements: just before a departing train's doors close, a recorded voice announces '*Ostorozhno! Dveri zakryvayutsya. Sleduyushchaya stantsia* (name of next station)'. This means 'Caution! The doors are closing. The next station is (name of next station)'. Just before the train stops at the next station, its name is announced. In case you don't catch these, the surest way of getting off at the right station is simply to count the stops.

A confusing aspect of the St Petersburg metro is that where two lines cross and there is a transfer *(perekhod)*, the two stations will have different names. For example, to travel from Gorkovskaya to Mayakovskaya station, you take the blue line south to Nevsky Pr station. Here, you change for the green line and in doing so change from Nevsky Pr station to Gostiny Dvor, where it's one stop to Mayakovskaya. To all intents and purposes it's the same station (you don't need to go outside to change), but has a different name because it's on a different line.

TAXI

One of Russia's most enduring post-soviet traditions is that of 'catching a car'. The shadow economy is thriving and numerous people drive the city streets specifically looking to give people paid lifts in their 1970s Zhigulis and Ladas. See the boxed text (below) for more information about the cultural norms associated with this form of transport.

Nearly all official taxis are unmetered, so if you do flag one you'll have to go through a similar process of negotiation to that involved in catching a car, only the driver will want more money for being 'official'.

If you know in advance that you'll need a taxi, it's easiest to order one direct to your hotel. The operator will tell you the price, which will usually be considerably lower than what a driver will quote you on the street. Some recommended private taxi companies are listed below (all of these work 24 hours). Beware, however, that few controllers are likely to speak English, so it's easiest to ask a Russian friend or hotel employee to place the call.

Neva Taxi (☎ 053)

Nevskaya Zvezda (☎ 970 0202)

Peterburgskoye Taxi (☎ 068)

Taxi Blues (☎ 105 5115; www.taxiblues.ru in Russian)

Taxi Million (☎ 100 0000)

TRAIN

St Petersburg is very well connected to cities throughout Russia, eastern Europe, the Baltics and Finland. The main stations are the Moscow Station (Moskovsky Vokzal), Vitebsk Station (Vitebsky Vokzal), Ladozhsky Station (Ladozhsky Vokzal), Baltic Station (Baltiysky Vokzal) and the Finland Station (Finlyandsky Vokzal). All prices in

A Taxi by any Other Name...

Stand on practically any footpath in town and sticking your arm out, palm facing down, and you can be assured that within less than a minute, a car will stop for you. Usually it's a well-worn little Lada or Zhiguli, but it can be anything – a snazzier car, an off-duty city bus, an army Jeep with driver in camouflage. The driver is most likely someone who drives around a few hours each day trying to supplement their income and bring something extra home to their family. For some, it is the main or only source of income. These are a better (and cheaper) way to cover distances in the city centre than an official taxi.

So, you've stuck your arm out and a car has stopped. This is where the fun starts. You open the door and shout out your destination, say, *'ulitsa Marata!'* The driver looks away for a second and shouts back *'skolko?'* (how much?). You bark back a price and if he's happy with that amount, he'll say, *'sadites!'* (sit down!) at which point you get in and drive off.

It could get more complicated, though. In response to your suggested price, he could answer back a fare 10 or 20 roubles higher, at which point you look away for a second and either say *'davai'* (OK) or else a gruff *'nyet!'*, slam the door shut and wave another car down.

If you feel that the driver is trying to rip you off because of your accent, shut the door. If there's more than one person in the car, don't get in. And if the driver seems creepy, let him drive on. There'll be another car coming in a flash.

Alternatively, the driver might not ask you for a price and just tell you to get in or not depending on whether he wants to go your way. If that's the case, at the end of the ride, you pay him what you think the fare was worth. If your ride is under five minutes long, R50 is acceptable. For a greater distance reckon on paying R100 for anywhere in and around the historic heart. The airport from the city centre should be between R400 and R500.

As a bonus, very often these drivers are very interesting characters you wouldn't ordinarily meet on your trip, and chatting with them about the potholes, how much better things were under the Soviets, their days in the army, how much you earn, Putin, Bush and Blair can be great fun.

the following list are one way, travelling in a *kupe* (2nd class, four people to a cabin with four fold-down beds). However, on trains to Berlin, Warsaw, Prague and Budapest only 1st class is available (two people to a cabin) and thus this is the price we quote. Seating on local trains *(elektrichka)* is just on wooden benches.

Baltiysky Station (☎ 168 2859; Obvodny Kanal 120; metro Baltiyskaya) For local trains including *elektrichkas* to Gatchina (R24), Oranienbaum (R20) and Novy Peterhof (R16; any train going to Oranienbaum or Kalishe stops here).

Finland Station (☎ 168 7687; pl Lenina 6; metro Pl Lenina) For suburban trains to Vyborg (*elektrichka* trains run every hour or two, while the far quicker express trains are a couple of times a day) and other towns in the north of the Leningradsky Oblast. Note: all trains to Finland confusingly now go from the Ladozhsky Station.

Ladozhsky Station (☎ 168 5304; Zanevsky pr 73; metro Ladozhskaya) For trains to Helsinki and northern Russia. There are two daily trains between Helsinki and St Petersburg – the Finnish *Sibelius* and the Russian *Repin* (R1835, 5¾ hours). The *Sibelius* leaves St Petersburg at 7.42am and returns from Helsinki at 4.31pm, while the *Repin* leaves Helsinki at 7.31am, returning from St Petersburg at 3.42pm. Other trains from the Ladozhsky Station go to Karelia and Arctic Russia, including the overnight train to Petrozavodsk (R450, eight hours, daily) and the express services to Murmansk (R1299, 28 hours, daily) and Arkhangelsk (R862, 26 hours, departures Monday, Tuesday, Thursday and Friday).

Moscow Station (☎ 168 4597; Nevsky pr 85; metro Pl Vosstaniya) For trains to Moscow (R600 to R1300 depending on the train, 4½ hours to 10 hours depending on the train, 13 trains daily), most of which leave between 10pm and midnight and arrive in Moscow early the next morning between 6am and 8am. The quickest is the 6.30pm departure that arrives in Moscow at 11pm. There is also a daily train to Novgorod (R255, 3¼ hours, 5.15pm).

Vitebsk Station (☎ 168 5807; Zagorodny pr 52; metro Pushkinskaya) For trains to Rīga (R1100, 12¾ hours, daily at 9.49pm), Vilnius (R1296, 15¼ hours, odd dates of the month at 7.44pm), Kaliningrad (R1047, 27 hours, on even dates of month at 6.13pm), Kyiv (R1054, 24 hours, daily at 8.03pm), Minsk (R915, 15¼ hours, daily at 7pm), Berlin (R4650, 37 hours, departures Tuesday, Friday, Sunday), Warsaw (R2200, 30 hours, departures Tuesday, Friday, Sunday), Prague (R3758, 41 hours, departures Monday, Wednesday, Thursday, Saturday) and Budapest (R5352, 45 hours, once a week on Tuesday). Local trains also leave here throughout the day to Detskoye Selo, the station for Tsarskoe Selo. At the time of writing trains to Tallinn had been withdrawn from service, although if they return they are likely to go from here.

TRAM

The tram network in the city is comprehensive, although you'll notice how empty most trams are – this reflects their relative slowness and propensity to break down or derail. Despite a perfunctory attempt to modernise the fleet of trams for the tricentennial celebrations, the majority are decades old and there's no real reason to use them.

PRACTICALITIES

ACCOMMODATION

Accommodation listings in the Sleeping chapter are ordered by neighbourhood, then alphabetically, with mid-range and top-end places to stay, and 'cheap sleeps' (under €40 for a single or under €60 for a double) listed last. An average double room with an en-suite bathroom during the high season (June to September) will cost €100. Generally we've quoted hotel rack rates, which are nearly always higher than those offered through travel agencies or airlines. Always ask if there are any special offers, and consider booking through a travel agent if you're interested in top-end hotels, as you can save a huge amount in room costs.

BUSINESS HOURS

Government offices are open 9am or 10am to 5pm or 6pm Monday to Friday. Most shops are open Monday to Saturday, often until 7pm or 8pm. Food shops tend to open 8am to 8pm except for an hour break *(pereryv)* sometime in the afternoon; many are open Sunday until 5pm. Food and alcohol shops open 24 hours abound throughout the city.

Most museums shut the ticket office an hour before closing and may shorten hours on the day before their day off. Beware the *sanitarny den* (sanitary day). Once a month, usually near the end (the last Tuesday, for example), nearly all establishments – shops, museums, restaurants, hotel dining rooms – shut down for cleaning, each on its own day and not always with much publicity.

Also, while many businesses claim to open 24 hours *(kruglosutochno)*, beware the highly contradictory technical break *(tekhnichesky pereryf)* – eg a '24-hour' exchange office might shut for a technical break between 2am and 6am!

CHILDREN

Russians love love love children – even the grumpiest babushka will melt and give you preferential treatment when presented with a wide-eyed baby, and you'll have your hands full trying to stop Russian friends spoiling your kids with sweets and chocolate. There's plenty to see and do with kids in town – don't let the stereotypical idea of Russia put you off. Few children are ambivalent about tramping across the frozen Neva, sledging in the Mikhailovsky Gardens or taking a boat trip on the canals. The Railway Museum is another favourite and older kids (not inclined to have nightmares) are likely to love the ghoulish Kunstkamera, although you should definitely avoid it with younger ones.

CLIMATE

St Petersburg's climate is maritime and much milder than its northern latitude would suggest. January temperatures average –8°C; a really cold day will get down to –15°C. It's a windy city though and in some areas exposed to the Gulf of Finland the wind chill is quite fierce, so bring a good warm hat and scarf.

Summer is cool and takes a while to get going: snow in late April is not uncommon as temperatures suddenly drop when the melting ice blocks from Lake Ladoga come floating through the city's main waterways. Warm weather doesn't really start until June to August, when temperatures usually surpass 20°C. On the rare hot days of highs up to 30°C, the city is unbearable and residents flee to the beaches on the north bank of the Gulf of Finland or to their *dachas* in cool but mosquito-infested forests.

The city's northern latitude means long summer days and long winter nights. During White Nights, around the time of the summer solstice, night is reduced to a brief dimming of the lights about 1am, only to

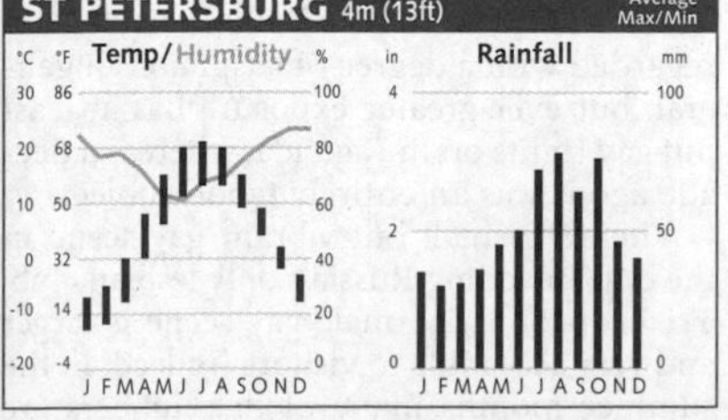

turn to dawn a couple of hours later. In winter the city seems to be in constant dusk.

CONSULATES

Many countries have no diplomatic presence in St Petersburg, instead having their representatives in the capital. If your country is not listed below, contact your embassy in Moscow in an emergency.

Australia (Map pp246-9; ☎ /fax 325 7333; Italiyanskaya ul 1)

Austria (Map pp246-9; ☎ 275 0502; fax 275 1170; Furshtatskaya ul 43)

Belarus (Map pp246-9; ☎ 273 0078; fax 273 4164; nab Robespiera 8/64, office 66)

Canada (Map pp244-5; ☎ 325 8448; fax 325 8393; Malodetskoselsky pr 32B)

China (Map pp246-9; ☎ 114 7670; fax 114 7958; nab kanala Griboedova 134)

Estonia (Map pp240-1; ☎ 102 0924; fax 102 0927; Bolshaya Monetnaya ul 14)

Finland (Map pp246-9; ☎ 273 7321; fax 272 1421; ul Chaykovskogo 71)

France (Map pp246-9; ☎ 312 1130; fax 311 7283; nab reki Moyki 15)

Germany (Map pp246-9; ☎ 327 2400; fax 327 3117; Urshtatskaya ul 39)

Latvia (Map pp242-3; ☎ 327 6054; fax 327 6052; 10-aya liniya)

Lithuania (Map pp246-9; ☎ 327 3167; fax 327 2615; ul Ryleeva 37)

Netherlands (Map pp246-9; ☎ 312 0338; nab reki Moyki 11)

UK (Map pp240-1; ☎ 320 3200; fax 325 3111; pl Proletarskoy Diktatury 5)

USA (Map pp246-9; ☎ 275 1701; fax 110 7022; Furshtatskaya ul 15)

COURSES

St Petersburg is a very popular destination for foreigners wanting to learn Russian. There are a huge number of courses available, from private lessons advertised in the *St Petersburg Times* to full immersion programmes that will billet you with a Russian family and provide a fully structured course at one of the city's universities. Some organisations that organise the latter option are listed here. A bonus of joining one of these courses is that the college hosting you will be able to issue you an invitation for a student visa, and greatly reduce the bureaucratic wrangling you'll otherwise have to deal with yourself.

Herzen State Pedagogical University (Map pp246-9; ☎ 311 6088; www.herzen.spb.ru; Kazanskaya ul 6)

Liden & Denz (Map pp244-5; ☎ 325 2241; www.lidenz.ru; Transportny per 11)

Lingua Service Worldwide (☎ 800 394 5327; www.linguaserviceworldwide.com/russia.htm; 75 Prospect St, Suite 4, Huntingdon, NY 11743, USA)

Russian Language Undergraduate Studies (☎ 01206-524399; www.rlus.co.uk; 2 Mercury Close, Colchester, CO2 9RJ, UK)

CUSTOMS

Customs controls in Russia are relatively relaxed these days. Searches beyond the perfunctory are quite rare. Apart from the usual restrictions, bringing in and out large amounts of cash is limited, although the amount at which you have to go through the red channel changes frequently. At the time of writing it was US$3000.

On entering Russia you will be given a customs declaration *(deklaratsiya),* where you should list any currency you are carrying and any items of worth. List mobile phones, cameras and laptops to avoid any potential problems on leaving Russia.

It's best if you can get your declaration stamped on entry and then simply show the same declaration on exiting Russia. However, sometimes customs points are totally unmanned, so it's not always possible. The system seems to be in total flux, with officials usually very happy for you to fill out declarations on leaving the country if necessary.

DISABLED TRAVELLERS

Disabled travellers are not well catered for in Russia. There's a lack of access ramps and lifts for wheelchairs. However, attitudes are enlightened and things are slowly changing. Major museums such as the Hermitage offer good disabled access.

DISCOUNTS

There are no discount cards currently operating on a citywide basis. Many places dress up the dual-pricing system for foreigners as one price for all, but a 90% 'discount' for being Russian. Therefore, if you have Russian citizenship (or if your Russian is good enough to fool the staff), you'll find museums, theatres and other tourist attractions vastly better value for money.

Student cards have a high rate of hit and miss. Many kindly old ladies at museums will give you the benefit of the doubt if you claim to be a student and look relatively young, others will look at your ISIC card as if it were a document from Mars and throw it back at you with a demand for the full price. The Hermitage is the blissful exception where anyone with a student card from any country gets in for free.

Senior citizens (usually anyone over the age of 60) are also eligible for discounts.

ELECTRICITY

St Petersburg, like the whole of Russia and most of Europe, uses the Continental plug with two round pins. Electricity is 220 volts, 50Hz AC and supply is very reliable. American and Japanese appliances need a 220V to 110V/100V converter.

EMERGENCY

Unless you speak Russian, calling the emergency services in Russia could lead to a rather one-sided conversation. In the first instance always call the following numbers. For serious matters, always contact your embassy as soon as possible if you require assistance or advice.

Ambulance ☎ 03

Fire ☎ 01

Gas Leak ☎ 04

Police ☎ 02

GAY & LESBIAN TRAVELLERS

St Petersburg is Western-looking and relatively liberal, and there's now a general level of recognition towards gay men and, to a lesser extent, lesbians. Both lifestyles are regarded with a degree of suspicion in general, but ever-greater exposure has at least put gay rights on the agenda, whereas a decade ago it was an entirely taboo subject.

There's a small but vibrant gay scene in the city, including Russia's only lesbian club, Tri El (p158). The male gay scene is larger and very accessible to visitors (indeed, in the summer months many of the clubbers are foreigners passing through the city). Look out for regular Chocolate Gay parties held by the Olovo Project (they advertise on billboards around town and on www.xs.gay.ru).

Gay men and women should generally have no problems reserving double rooms, although some older, Soviet-era institutions may automatically change your reservation to a twin when seeing two travellers of the same sex arrive together. Being polite but firm will usually suffice.

HOLIDAYS

Russians love holidays and often organise big dinners or parties to mark events. Those taken particularly seriously are Women's Day, Victory Day and New Year. As a hangover from Soviet times, much of Russia shuts down during the first half of May as the coming of spring is celebrated alongside the official Labour Days and Victory Day.

For a list of festivals and special events in St Petersburg, see p10.

Public Holidays

New Year's Day 1 January

Russian Orthodox Christmas Day 7 January

Defenders of the Motherland Day 23 February

International Women's Day 8 March

Easter Monday Varies

International Labour Day/Spring Festival 1 & 2 May

Victory Day 9 May

Russian Independence Day 12 June

Day of Reconciliation and Accord (the re-branded Revolution Day) 7 November

Constitution Day 12 December

INSURANCE

You'll be asked on your visa application form for details of your insurance policy. Although the Russian Embassy never checks this (or even seems to worry whether or not you attach the policy 'for inspection' as it requests), do be sure that you have comprehensive medical insurance when visiting St Petersburg. If you buy a European policy, check that it covers Russia, or at least European Russia, as some policies have been known not to. While EU citizens are entitled to free medical care in Russia under a reciprocal agreement, for anything other than a minor injury you will want to go to a private doctor and costs soon add up.

INTERNET ACCESS

Russia has a surprisingly high level of Internet access – the majority of people in St Petersburg have access to the Internet somehow and the level of penetration is increasing all the time.

Any computer shop, large supermarket or mobile phone dealership will sell Internet cards, giving you a certain number of hours' access via a phone line. Sometimes this will involve registering your details online, although this is becoming less and less common. Some of the best Internet Service Providers (ISPs) in the city include Cityline and Rossiya Online, although connections can be temperamental due to the city's ancient telephone system.

If you are bringing your own computer, then you'll usually need a US-style telephone connector. However, some older houses will have only a Russian telephone connector – a truly bizarre-looking, five-slot implement. If you find that this is the only way to connect to a Russian phone line, go to a hardware store *(khozyaystevennaya)* and ask for a *russko-amerikansky telefonny perekhodnik*.

For those who just need to check their email a few times while in St Petersburg, there's no shortage of Internet cafés. The larger, best-run ones are in the city centre, although computer centres (mainly filled with bored teenage boys playing war games in the dark) exist everywhere. Some of the best and most centrally located Internet cafés:

Café Max (Map pp246-9; ☎ 273 6655; Nevsky pr 90/92; per hr R60; metro Mayakovskaya)

FM Club (Map pp246-9; ☎ 277 1872; ul Dostoevskogo 6A; per hr R50; 🕑 8am-10pm; metro Vladimirskaya)

Quo Vadis (Map pp246-9; ☎ 311 8011; Nevsky pr 24; per hr R60; metro Gostiny Dvor)

Red Cloud (Map pp246-9; ☎ 595 4138; Kazanskaya ul 30-32; 5 mins for R1; 🕑 11am-8am; metro Sennaya Pl)

LEGAL MATTERS

You are likely to have a brush with Russia's notorious officialdom at some time during your stay. Whether it be a curious policeman who asks to see your papers or an overly officious security guard, men in uniform are, unfortunately, too common a sight in St Petersburg. Most of them are genuinely trying to do their job, although you should always bear in mind that many so-called officers of the law are on the make and will sometimes go to cruel and unusual lengths to extort money from you.

Usually, being polite yet firm will suffice. Follow some simple rules and you'll be fine. Never go anywhere with a policeman unless you are being explicitly arrested. Never let a policeman go through your wallet or insert his hands into your pockets without seeing them first (planting drugs is a well-known ruse). If uncomfortable about the way with which you are being dealt, make it clear that you are about to call your embassy *('ya pozvonyu svoyu konsolstvu')*. Keep a note of your consular details on you in case there is a problem you need help with.

You're not obliged to carry your passport on you at all times (although 99% of Russians will tell you otherwise), but such is the bureaucratic state of Russia, you'll find that nearly everyone does (including foreign residents), creating a climate of suspicion of anyone who does not. The smartest thing is to carry a photocopy of your passport and your Russian visa, and tell any officer stopping you that your documents are being registered *('pasport na registratsii')*.

These small altercations with the bureaucratic state are likely to be the only contact most visitors have with the law. Be aware that drugs-related offences are punished very severely and so you should avoid drugs while in St Petersburg. Russian prisons are extremely unpleasant places. The age of consent in Russia is 16 for both heterosexual and homosexual sex.

MAPS

Lonely Planet publishes a comprehensive St Petersburg City Map that covers the centre of the city in great detail. There's a large number of maps covering the city, all available both abroad at any good travel bookshop and in the city itself. **Dom Knigi** (p167) has the best selection, including maps of transport routes (including *marshrutkas*), and the excellent *Atlas Sankt Peterburg s kazhdym domom* – an invaluable A4 booklet covering the whole city and marking the location of every street number in the city.

MEDICAL SERVICES

Medical care in Russia is basic but comprehensive and, despite the lack of funding for state hospitals, you'll not have trouble getting most drugs or treatments here. Pharmacies are well stocked and even if they don't sell the brand name you are familiar with, they'll often have a chemically identical Russian-produced alternative.

Your number one health priority will be not drinking from the city's water supply (see below). Your second will be to arm yourself with sufficient anti-mosquito spray and other weapons of mass insect destruction to ward off St Petersburg's virulent mozzie population from late April until September.

There are plenty of health resources in the city and you need not worry if you get ill. Medical care is good, although if insured (or just wealthy) you can use the expat health services, which are in a league of their own.

Whatever You Do, Don't Drink the Tap Water

The biggest danger to the average visitor to the city is drinking untreated tap water. In addition to heavy metal pollutants and harmful bacteria, it contains *Giardia lamblia*, a nasty parasite that causes unpleasant stomach cramps, nausea, bloated stomach, diarrhoea and frequent gas. There is no preventative drug. Metronidazole (brand name Flagyl) or Tinidazole (known as Fasigyn) are the recommended treatments. Antibiotics are of no use. Symptoms may not appear for up to several weeks after infection and may recur for years.

To be absolutely safe, only drink water that has been boiled for 10 minutes or filtered through an antimicrobial water filter (PUR brand makes a good portable one). Treat ice with suspicion and avoid fruits and vegetables that may have been washed in the water – those that peel are safest. While accepting tea or coffee at someone's house should be safe, it's best to always stick to bottled water, even for brushing your teeth. Bathing, showering and shaving, though, should cause no problems at all.

If you develop diarrhoea, be sure to drink plenty of fluids, preferably an oral rehydration solution. Imodium is to be taken only in an emergency; otherwise it's best to let the diarrhoea run its course and eliminate the parasite from the body.

Clinics

All the clinics listed below are open 24 hours, unless otherwise stated.

American Medical Clinic (Map pp246-9; ☎ 140 2090; www.amclinic.ru; nab reki Moyki 78; metro Sadovaya)

British-American Family Practice (Map pp246-9; ☎ 327 6030, 999 0949; Grafsky per 7; metro Dostoevskaya)

Euromed (Map pp240-1; ☎ 327 0301; www.euromed.ru; Suvorovsky pr 60; metro Chernyshevskaya)

International Clinic (Map pp246-9; ☎ 320 3870; www.icspb.com; ul Dostoevskogo 19/21; metro Ligovsky Pr)

Medpalace (Map pp246-9; ☎ 272 5291; ul Chaykovskogo 6; 9am-9pm; metro Chernyshevskaya)

Pharmacies

Look for the sign *apteka*, or the usual green cross to find a pharmacy. The following are two central pharmacies open 24 hours.

Apteka (Map pp246-9; ☎ 277 5962; Nevsky pr 83; metro Pl Vosstaniya)

Apteka Petrofarm (Map pp246-9; ☎ 314 5401; Nevsky pr 22; metro Nevsky Pr)

MONEY

The currency in Russia is the rouble (R), made up of 100 kopeks. Notes come in denominations of 1000, 500, 100, 50 and 10R, coins come in 5, 2 and 1R denominations and 50 and 10 kopeks. You can use all major credit and debit cards (including Cirrus and Maestro) in ATMs and in good restaurants and hotels. It's possible to exchange travellers cheques, but for a fee. Euro or US$ cash is the best to bring. Crumpled or old notes may be refused. Most major currencies can be exchanged at change booths across Russia. You may be asked for your passport.

For exchange rates, see the inside front cover.

Banks

Some of the biggest and most reliable banks in St Petersburg are listed here with their head or most central city office. They can all change money, and most change travellers cheques and organise cash advances on credit cards too.

Alfabank (Map pp246-9; ☎ 329 8050; www.alfabank.ru; nab kanala Griboedova 6/2; metro Gostiny Dvor)

Baltiysky Bank (Map pp246-9; ☎ 325 8585; www.baltbank.ru; Sadovaya ul 34; metro Gostiny Dvor)

Bank Moskvy (Map pp244-5; ☎ 112 1033; www.mmbank.ru; Ligovsky pr 108; metro Ligovsky Pr)

Impex Bank (Map pp246-9; ☎ 324 1700; www.impexbank.ru; Nevsky pr 58; metro Gostiny Dvor)

Promstroy Bank (Map pp246-9; ☎ 329 8329; www.icbank.ru in Russian; Nevsky pr 38; metro Gostiny Dvor)

NEWSPAPERS & MAGAZINES

The twice-weekly *St Petersburg Times* is the long-running sister paper to the daily *Moscow Times*, and is a great resource for visitors. While the Tuesday edition can be dry and business-heavy, the Friday edition has theatre, club, cinema and concert listings, worth reading for local gigging stalwart Sergei Chernov's column, 'Chernov's Choice', which sets the weekend agenda.

The rest of the English-language press is barely worth its cover price (free) – the *Neva News* stands out as perhaps the lowest form of journalism, with its clubbing guide shamelessly reprinted from the *St Petersburg Times* and its articles hilariously vacant, including a monthly beauty contest where the prize is always a trip to New Zealand. Another contender is *Pulse*, a glossy magazine published in a Russian and English edition.

In Russian, the pickings are better: glossy bi-weeklies *Afisha* and *Time Out*-affiliate

Dual-Pricing System

The dual-pricing system in Russia still exists, but it's not what it used to be. There is no longer a two-tiered set of prices at hotels, or for train and aeroplane travel within Russia. At museums and large concert halls, however, you'll still be expected to pay many times more than Russians. At some smaller museums, where the need for money is so painfully evident, the price difference may only be R40. However, at the Hermitage (R350 versus R100) or the Mariinsky Theatre, where performances cost about 10 times more for foreigners (and where they'll run after you and holler until you pay the difference if you manage to sneak in with a Russian ticket), the dual-pricing system is very much in evidence. If you have a student or senior citizen discount card you may be able to use it to get the local rate (although some places will honour ISIC and not ITSC cards). Showing your student or business visa can also work. Otherwise you can rest assured that your cash is going to a good cause!

Kalendar, and weekly *Vash Dosug*, sold at newsstands. All have exhaustive listings, and features on local events and personalities.

PHOTOGRAPHY

An enormously photogenic city, St Petersburg usually has people snapping away uncontrollably. All photo stock can be purchased with ease throughout the city. Some good places to stock up on photographic equipment and film:

Komplekt (Map pp246-9; ☎ 110 5313; Gostiny Dvor, Nevsky pr 35; metro Gostiny Dvor)

Patriot (Map pp246-9; ☎ 310 7420; Sadovaya ul 45; metro Sadovaya)

Yarky Mir (Map pp246-9; ☎ 277 3132; Nevsky pr 128; metro Gostiny Dvor)

POST

There are post offices throughout the city where you can buy stamps for letters and postcards, as well as send telegrams should you fancy impersonating your great grandparents. The elegant **Main Post Office** (Map pp246–9; ☎ 312 7460; Pochtamtskaya ul 9; metro Sadovaya) has a beautiful interior and is where to go to send parcels back home. Smaller post offices may refuse to send parcels internationally and, more importantly, parcels have better odds of reaching home from the Main Post Office. Bring whatever you want to send here unwrapped (it will be wrapped and sealed with wax for you). You'll be asked to supply the address you are staying at in St Petersburg, so either put your hotel name and address down or make one up if you are not staying in one.

It costs 10R (€0.30) to send a postcard anywhere in the world and 14R (€0.40) to send a letter anywhere in the world. While the system is slow, it's usually reliable, so don't believe all the horror stories you hear about the Russian postal system.

RADIO

Most of St Petersburg's popular stations play a mix of trashy Euro pop and its even more over-the-top Russian variant. Still, their play-lists can be unexpectedly eclectic. Some of the more popular FM stations include Eldoradio (101.4 MHz), Radio Modern (104 MHz), the grating Europa Plus (100.5 MHz) and the more diversified Radio Nostalgie (105.3 MHz). More Russian content can be heard on Kanal Melodia (91.1 MHz), Russky Shanson (100.9 MHz) and Russkoe Radio (104.4 MHz). Two stations focus on St Petersburg–related news, music and features: Eko Peterburga (91.5 MHz) and Severnaya Stolitsa (105.9 MHz).

SAFETY

Do in general disregard many horror stories you hear about the New Russia and gangsters shooting each other up on the streets. While there has been a problem since the early 1990s with internecine mob warfare and contract killings, the criminal elements responsible have no interest in tourists.

A far bigger threat is petty theft, especially the notorious pick-pocketing in the city centre. Take care among the crowds on Nevsky, around big tourist draws and in the metro, where packed carriages make for rich pickings for the criminally inclined.

One far darker problem is the growth throughout Russia of the skinhead and neo-Nazi movement. You are very unlikely to encounter these thugs, who have committed some disgusting acts of violence against Caucasian (ie dark-skinned people from the Caucasus, not Western Europeans or North American Caucasians) and Central Asian residents of the city. Violence tends to be focused on Hitler's birthday on 20 April – this is a good day for non-white visitors to the city to be very careful, avoid more obscure areas of the city and stick together with friends.

TELEPHONE

Russia's international code is ☎ 7. The international access code from normal phones in Russia is ☎ 8 followed by 10 after the second tone, then the country code. From mobile phones, however, just dial +[country code] to place an international call.

Mobile Phones

The mobile phone revolution in St Petersburg that has taken place in the past few years means that nearly everyone in the city has a phone. There are several large networks, most of which operate on the pay-as-you-go system.

To call a mobile phone from a landline, the line must be enabled to make paid calls (all local numbers are free from a landline anywhere in Russia). To find out if this is the case, dial ☎ 8, and then if you hear a second tone you can dial the mobile number in full. If you hear nothing, hang up – you can't call anywhere but local landlines from here.

Main mobile providers include Beeline GSM, Megafon, MTS-GSM and Skylink. You can buy a local SIM card at any mobile phone shop, which you can slot into your home handset during your stay. SIM cards cost as little as €15, after which you only pay to make (and to a lesser extent, to receive) calls, although prices are very low.

Phonecards & Call Centres

Local phonecards *(taksfon karta)* are available from kiosks and metro stations, and can be used to make local, national and international calls from phone booths around the city. Cards are sold in units of 25, 50 or 100.

Better value for international calls is using a call centre, where you give the clerk the number you want to call, pay a deposit and then go to the booth you are assigned to make the call. Afterwards you either pay the difference or collect your change. There are large numbers of call centres around the city – look for the sign Mezhdunarodny Telefon. The most central is the state-run **Telephone Centre** (Map pp246–9; Nevsky pr 88).

TELEVISION

St Petersburg residents have the choice of several large national channels and the local channel Kultura. The main national channels are ORT (Russian State TV), RTR and NTV. Other channels, such as MTV Russia, broadcast from Moscow are also available to most viewers.

Despite the range, most Russian TV is an appalling mix of South American soap operas dubbed into Russian, Soviet films, straight-to-video Hollywood pap and endless musical concerts. The few highlights have been controversial and satirical programming such as *Kukly* ('Puppets', a carbon copy of Britain's *Spitting Image*) and *Namedni* ('Lately') – all of which have been taken off air due to (explicit or implicit) pressure from the Kremlin (see p19 for more about the relationship between the media and the government).

TIME

St Petersburg is GMT +3 hours, the same as Moscow time. Therefore, when it is midday in St Petersburg, it is 10am in Berlin, 9am in London and 4am in New York. Russia employs daylight savings along with much of the rest of the world.

TIPPING

Tipping remains a fluid concept in St Petersburg. While you should definitely leave a small gratuity for staff at mid-range and smart restaurants (10%), less swanky places and those unused to foreigners will not expect any such tip.

There's no need to tip taxi drivers, with whom you should always agree a price before getting in to their cab. Five-star hotel staff such as doormen and room service staff usually expect a few dollars.

TOILETS

Around nearly all metro stations and tourist attractions there's at least one disgusting blue Portakabin-type toilet manned by an attendant who will charge around 10R for the honour. There are also pay toilets in all main-line train stations and free ones in museums. As a general rule, the more you pay, the worse the smell. It's far better to stop for a drink in a café and use their cleaner facilities.

TOURIST INFORMATION

To this day Russia's only tourist office operates its rather half-hearted attempt at an information booth on Dvortsovaya pl (Palace Sq; Map pp246–9). The staff speak English and there is a variety of leaflets. There is also a range of tourist literature about the city for sale, including in-depth guides to the Hermitage and Russian Museum. Buy them here, as they're half the price of those you'll find on sale inside both museums.

VISAS

Everyone needs a visa to visit Russia and it's likely to be your biggest single headache, so allow yourself at least a month before you travel to secure one. There are several types of visa, but most travellers will apply for a tourist visa, valid for 30 days from the date of entry. Your visa process has three stages – invitation, application and registration.

First of all, to obtain a visa, you need an invitation. For a small fee (usually about €30) most hotels and hostels will issue an invitation (or 'visa support') to anyone staying with them. The invitation then allows you to apply for a visa at any Russian embassy. Costs vary, from €20 for a week's processing to €200 for same day service, so plan as far ahead as possible. If you are not staying in a hotel or hostel, you will need to buy an invitation. This can be done through most travel agents. Some hotels and hostels issue invites for the equivalent cost of one night's accommodation with them.

On arrival in Russia, you will need to fill out an immigration card – a long white form issued at passport control throughout the country. You surrender one half of the form immediately to the passport control, while the other you keep for the duration of your stay and give up only on exiting Russia.

Finally, you are obliged to register your visa within three working days of arrival in Russia. This can nearly always be done by your hotel or hostel, but if staying elsewhere, you'll need to pay a travel agency (about €25) to register it for you. Not registering is a gamble – some travellers report leaving Russia without registration unhindered, but officially you are liable for big fines. It's best not to take chances, especially with the prevailing national security paranoia.

Since 2002, Russia has been running a trial scheme whereby tourists from Schengen countries, Britain, Switzerland or Japan who wish to visit St Petersburg and Moscow for less than 72 hours can get visas on arrival. You must apply at an authorised tour operator in your home country 48 hours before departure. Check with your local Russian consulate for details. As this visa allows such little time in Russia and is only through certain accredited agencies, it's hard to get too enthusiastic about the scheme.

For visas and other travel services, the following St Petersburg travel agencies are recommended:

Infinity (Map pp246-9; ☎ 313 5085; www.infinity.ru; Angleterre Hotel, Bolshaya Morskaya ul 39; metro Nevsky Pr) The St Petersburg branch of this efficient travel agency can help with visas, invites and registration. Staff speak English and can also book you train and air tickets (and deliver them to your door if you are in a rush).

Ost-West Kontaktservice (Map pp246-9; ☎ 327 3416; www.ostwest.com; 105 Nevsky pr; metro Pl Vosstaniya) A reliable outfit, charging €30 to register visas for those not staying in hotels.

Palladium (Map pp246-9; ☎ 279 6584, 279 6644; www.palladium.spb.ru; Hotel Rus, office 160; 1 Artilleriyskaya ul; metro Chernyshevskaya) This small agency deep in the belly of the Hotel Rus can register both tourist visas (€30) and business visas (€50). It also offers short-term apartment rentals around the city as well as all the other normal services. English spoken.

Sindbad Travel International (Map pp246-9; ☎ 327 8384; www.sindbad.ru; 3-ya Sovetskaya ul 28; metro Pl Vosstaniya) The STA agent in St Petersburg is the efficient Sindbad Travel, which can be found inside the HI St Petersburg Hostel. Here you can book air and train tickets, register visas and acquire invitations to help you get a visa issued. English spoken.

WOMEN TRAVELLERS

The most frequent problem faced by foreign women in Russia is sexual harassment. It can be fairly common to be propositioned in public, especially if walking alone at night. This is rarely dangerous and a simple *kak vam ne stydno* ('you should be ashamed of yourself') in a suitably stern manner should send anyone on their way.

That said, Russian men are generally extremely polite, and will open doors, give up their seats and wherever possible help any female out to a far greater degree than their Western counterparts. Women are also very independent and in general you won't attract attention by travelling alone as a female.

WORK

There's a large expat community here and most foreign companies are members of **SPIBA** (Map pp246–9; ☎ 325 9091; www.spiba.spb.ru; Shpalernaya ul 36; metro Chernyshevskaya), the St Petersburg International Business Association. SPIBA seeks to promote the climate of investment and the lot of foreign companies in St Petersburg, and serves as a good first point of contact if you are interested in learning about companies active in the city.

Lots of foreigners and students work part- or full-time as teachers. Look for schools seeking teachers in the *St Petersburg Times'* classifieds section, or contact language schools using the St Petersburg Yellow Pages, on sale at bookshops.

Language

Language

It's true – anyone can speak another language. Don't worry if you haven't studied languages before or that you studied a language at school for years and can't remember any of it. It doesn't even matter if you failed English grammar. After all, that's never affected your ability to speak English! And this is the key to picking up a language in another country. You just need to start speaking.

Learn a few key phrases before you go. Write them on pieces of paper and stick them on the fridge, by the bed or even on the computer – anywhere that you'll see them often.

You'll find that locals appreciate travellers trying their language, no matter how muddled you may think you sound. So don't just stand there, say something! If you want to learn more Russian than we've included here, pick up a copy of Lonely Planet's comprehensive but user-friendly *Russian Phrasebook.*

It's relatively easy to find English speakers in St Petersburg, but your travels will be far more interesting if you at least take the time to learn a few basic words and phrases, and the Cyrillic alphabet – so that you can at least read maps and street signs.

THE CYRILLIC ALPHABET

Russian uses the Cyrillic alphabet, which is not as tricky as it looks. It's well worth the effort to familiarise yourself with it.

The list below shows the letters used in the Russian Cyrillic alphabet with their closest Roman-letter equivalents. If you follow the pronunciation guides included with the words and phrases below, you should have no trouble making yourself understood.

Cyrillic	Roman	Pronunciation
А а	a	as in 'father' when stressed; as in 'ago' when unstressed
Б б	b	as in 'but'
В в	v	as in 'van'
Г г	g	as in 'go'
Д д	d	as in 'dog'
Е е	ye	as in 'yet' when stressed; as in 'yeast' when unstressed
Ё ё	yo	as in 'yore'
Ж ж	zh	as the 's' in 'measure'
З з	z	as in 'zoo'
И и	i	as in 'police'
Й й	y	as in 'boy'
К к	k	as in 'kind'
Л л	l	as in 'lamp'
М м	m	as in 'mad'
Н н	n	as in 'net'
О о	o	as in 'more' when stressed; as the 'a' in 'ago' when unstressed
П п	p	as in 'pig'
Р р	r	as in 'rub', but rolled
С с	s	as in 'sing'
Т т	t	as in 'ten'
У у	u	as in 'rule'
Ф ф	f	as in 'fan'
Х х	kh	as the 'ch' in 'Bach'
Ц ц	ts	as in 'bits'
Ч ч	ch	as in 'chin'
Ш ш	sh	as in 'shop'
Щ щ	shch	as 'fresh chips'
ъ		'hard' sign
Ы ы	y	as the 'i' in 'ill'
ь	-'	'soft' sign
Э э	e	as in 'end'
Ю ю	yu	as in 'Yukon'
Я я	ya	as in 'yard'

PRONUNCIATION

The sounds of а, о, е and я are 'weaker' when the stress in the word doesn't fall on them, eg in вода (*voda*, water) the stress falls on the second syllable, so it's pronounced 'va-*da*', with the unstressed pronunciation for о and the stressed pronunciation for а. Russians usually print ё without the dots, a source of confusion in pronunciation.

The 'voiced' consonants б, в, г, д, ж and з are not voiced at the end of words or before voiceless consonants. For example, хлеб (bread) is not pronounced 'khlyeb', as written, but 'khlyep'. The г in the common adjective endings -его and -ого is pronounced 'v'.

SOCIAL

Meeting People

Hello.
  Здравствуйте.
  zdrastvuitye
Hi.
  Привет.
  privyet
Goodbye.
  До свидания.
  da svidaniya
Please.
  Пожалуйста.
  pazhalsta
Thank you (very much).
  (Большое) спасибо.
  (bal'shoye) spasiba
You're welcome. (ie don't mention it)
  Не за что.
  nye za shta
Yes/No.
  Да/Нет.
  da/nyet
Do you speak English?
  Вы говорите по-английски?
  vy gavarite pa angliyski?
Does anyone here speak English?
  Кто-нибут говорит по-английски?
  kto-nibud' gavarit pa-angliyski?
Do you understand?
  Вы понимаете?
  vy panimayete?
I (don't) understand.
  Я (не) понимаю.
  ya (nye) panimayu
Please repeat that.
  Повторите, пожалуйста.
  paftarite pazhalsta
Please speak more slowly.
  Говорите помедленнее, пожалуйста.
  gavarite pa-medleneye pazhalsta
Please write it down.
  Запишите, пожалуйста.
  zapishyte pazhalsta

Going Out

What's on ...?
Что происходит интересного ...?
Shto praiskhodit interyesnava ...?
  locally
  поблизости
  pablizasti
  this weekend
  на этих выходных
  na etikh vykhadnykh
  today
  сегодня
  syevodnya
  tonight
  вечером
  vyecheram

Where are the ...?
Где находятся ...?
gdye nakhodyatsa ...?
  clubs
  клубы, дискотеки
  kluby, diskoteki
  gay venues
  гей клубы
  gey kluby
  places to eat
  кафе или рестораны
  kafe ili restarany
  pubs
  бары
  bary (or irlandskii bary for 'Irish pubs')

Is there a local entertainment guide?
  Есть обзор мест куда пойти в газете?
  yest' abzor myest kuda paiti v gazete?

PRACTICAL

Question Words

Who?	Кто?	kto?
What?	Что?	shto?
When?	Когда?	kagda?
Where?	Где?	gdye?
How?	Как?	kak?

Numbers & Amounts

0	ноль	nol'
1	один	adin
2	два	dva
3	три	tri
4	четыре	chityri
5	пять	pyat'
6	шесть	shest'
7	семь	sem'
8	восемь	vosem'
9	девять	devyat'
10	десять	desyat'
11	одиннадцать	adinatsat'

12	двенадцать	dvenatsat'
13	тринадцать	trinatsat'
14	четырнадцать	chetirnatsat'
15	пятнадцать	petnatsat'
16	шестнадцать	shesnatsat'
17	семнадцать	semnatsat'
18	восемнадцать	vosemnatsat'
19	девятнадцать	devitnatsat'
20	двадцать	dvatsat'
21	двадцать один	dvatsat' adin
22	двадцать два	dvatsat' dva
30	тридцать	tritsat'
40	сорок	sorak
50	пятьдесят	pedesyat
60	шестьдесят	shesdesyat
70	семьдесят	semdesyat
80	восемьдесят	vosemdesyat
90	девяносто	devenosta
100	сто	sto
1000	тысяча	tysyacha
2000	две тысячи	dvye tysachi

Days

Monday
  понедельник
  panidel'nik
Tuesday
  вторник
  ftornik
Wednesday
  среда
  srida
Thursday
  четверг
  chetverk
Friday
  пятница
  pyatnitsa
Saturday
  суббота
  subota
Sunday
  воскресенье
  vaskrisen'e

Banking

I'd like to ...
Мне нужно ...
mne nuzhna ...
  cash a cheque
  обналичить чек
  abnalichit' chek
  change money
  обменять деньги
  abmenyat' den'gi
  change some travellers cheques
  обменять дорожные чеки
  abmenyat' darozhniye cheki

Where's the nearest ...?
Где ближайший ...?
gdye blizhayshiy ...?
  automatic teller machine (ATM)
  банкомат
  bankamat
  foreign exchange office
  обменный пункт
  abmenniy punkt

Post

Where is the post office?
  Где почта?
  gdye pochta?

I want to send a ...
Хочу послать ...
khachu paslat'
  fax
  факс
  faks
  parcel
  посылку
  pasilku
  small parcel
  бандероль
  banderol'
  postcard
  открытку
  atkrytku

I want to buy ...
Хочу купить ...
khachu kupit' ...
  an envelope
  конверт
  kanvert
  a stamp
  марку
  marku

Phones & Mobiles

I want to buy a phone card.
  Я хочу купить телефонную карточку.
  ya khachu kupit' telefonnuyu kartachku

I want to make a call (to ...)
Я хочу позвонить (в ...)
ya khachu pazvanit' (v ...)
  Europe/America/Australia
  европу/америку/австралию
  yevropu/ameriku/avstraliyu

Where can I find a/an ...?
Где я могу найти ...?
gdye ya mogu naiti ...?
I'd like a/an ...
Мне нужен ...
mnye nuzhen ...
adaptor plug
переходник для розетки
peryehadnik dlya razetki
charger for my phone
зарядное устройство для телефона
zaryadnaye ustroistva dlya telefona
mobile/cell phone for hire
мобильный телефон напрокат
mabil'niy telefon
SIM card for your network
сим-карта для местной сети
sim-karta dlya mestnoi seti

Internet

Where's the local Internet café?
Где здесь интернет кафе?
Gde zdyes' internet kafe?

I want to ...
Я хочу ...
ya khachu ...
check my email
проверить мой имэйл
praverit moi imeil
get online
подсоединиться к интернету
padsayedinitsa k internetu

Transport

What time does the ... leave?
В котором часу прибывает ...?
f katoram chasu pribyvaet ...?
What time does the ... arrive?
В котором часу отправляется ...?
f katoram chasu atpravlyaetsa ...?

bus
автобус
aftobus
fixed-route minibus
маршрутное такси
marshrutnaye taksi
train
поезд
poyezt
tram
трамвай
tramvay
trolleybus
троллейбус
tralleybus

When is the ... bus?
Когда будет ... автобус?
kagda budet ... aftobus?
first
первый
pervy
last
последний
pasledniy
next
следующий
sleduyushchiy

Are you free? (taxi)
Свободен?
svaboden?
Please put the meter on.
Включите пожалуйста счетчик.
vklyuchite pazhalsta schetchik
How much is it to ...?
Сколько стоит доехать до ...?
skol'ka stoit daekhat' do ...?
Please take me to ...
Отвезите меня, пожалуйста в ...
atvezite menya pazhalsta v ...

FOOD

breakfast
завтрак
zaftrak
lunch
обед
abed
dinner
ужин
uzhyn
snack
перекусить
peryekusit'
eat
есть/съесть
est'/s'yest'
drink
пить/выпить
pit'/vypit'

Can you recommend a ...
Не могли бы вы порекомендовать ...
Nye mogli bi vi parekamendavat' ...
bar/pub
бар/пивную
bar/pivnuyu

café
кафе
kafe
restaurant
ресторан
restaran

Is service/cover charge included in the bill?
Обслуживание включено в счет?
absluzhivanye vklucheno v schet?

For more detailed information on food and dining out, see pp15–18.

EMERGENCIES

Help!
На помощь!/Помогите!
na pomashch'!/pamagite!
I'm lost.
Я заблудился/заблудилась.
ya zabludilsya/zabludilas' (m/f)
I'm sick.
Я болен/больна.
ya bolen/bal'na (m/f)
Where's the police station?
Где милиция?
gdye militsiya?

Call ...!
Позвоните ...!
pazvanite ...!
the police
в милицию
v militsiyu
a doctor
доктору
doktoru
an ambulance
в скорую помощь
v skoruyu pomosch'

HEALTH

Where's the nearest ...?
Где ближайшая ...?
gde blizhaishaya ...?
chemist (night)
аптека (дежурная)
apteka (dezhurnaya)
dentist
зубной врач
zubnoy vrach
doctor
врач
vrach
hospital
больница
bal'nitsa

I need a doctor (who speaks English).
Мне нужен врач (англоговорящий).
mne nuzhen vrach (anglagavaryaschii)

Symptoms

I have (a) ...
У меня ...
u menya ...
diarrhoea
понос
panos
fever
температура
temperatura
headache
головная боль
galavnaya bol'
pain
боль
bol'
stomachache
болит желудок
balit zheludak

Glossary

aeroport – airport
apteka – pharmacy
avtobus – bus
avtovokzal – bus station
babushka – grandmother
banya – bathhouse
bilet – ticket
bulochnaya – bakery
bulvar – boulevard
dacha – country cottage, summer house
deklaratsiya – customs declaration
dom – house
duma – parliament
elektrichka – suburban train
etazh – floor (storey)
filial – annexe
gazetny kiosk – newsstand
gorod – city, town
grenki – bread fried in butter
gubernator – governor
ikra – caviar
kafe – café

karta – card
kasha – porridge
kassa – ticket office, cashier's desk
khachapuri – cheese pie
khleb – bread
khozyaystevennaya – hardware store
kniga – book
kolonnada – colonnade
kommunalki– communal flats
korpus – building within a building
koryushki – freshwater smelt
kruglosutochno – open 24 hours
kupe – 2nd class
kvartira – flat, apartment
kvas – juice distilled from fermented beets

lavra – most senior grade of Russian Orthodox monasteries

marshrutka – minibus that runs along a fixed route; diminutive form of *marshrutnoye taxi*
matryoshka – set of painted wooden dolls within dolls
mikrorayoni – Soviet housing estates, micro regions
morskoy vokzal – sea terminal
most – bridge
muzey – museum

naberezhnaya – embankment
novy – new

obed – lunch
oblast – area, region
ostrov – island

palekh – painted box
parilka – steam room
Paskha – Easter
perekhod – transfer
pereryv – break, recess
pereulok – lane, side street
pivo – beer
ploshchad – square
podyezd – entrance
polotentse – towel
priglasheniye – invitation
prospekt – avenue
prostinya – sheet

rechnoy vokzal – river terminal
reka – river
restoran – restaurant
Rozhdestvo – Christmas
rynok – market

samizdat – underground literary manuscript
sanitarny den – literally 'sanitary day'; the monthly day on which establishments shut down for cleaning (these days vary and often occur with little forewarning)
shosse – road
smetana – sour cream
smol – tar
sobor – cathedral
stary – old
stolovaya – canteen, cafeteria

taksfon karta – phone card
tapki – sandals
tapochki – slippers
teatr – theatre
teatralnaya kassa – general theatre box office
tekhnichesky pereryf – technical break
troika – horse-drawn sleigh
tserkov – church
tusovka – in crowd

ulitsa – street
uzhin – dinner

veniki – birch branches
voda – water
vokzal – station

yevroremont – Western standard

zal – hall, room
zavtrak – breakfast
zheton – token (for metro etc)

Behind the Scenes

THE LONELY PLANET STORY

The story begins with a classic travel adventure: Tony and Maureen Wheeler's 1972 journey across Europe and Asia to Australia. There was no useful information about the overland trail then, so Tony and Maureen published the first Lonely Planet guidebook to meet a growing need.

From a kitchen table, Lonely Planet has grown to become the largest independent travel publisher in the world, with offices in Melbourne (Australia), Oakland (USA) and London (UK). Today Lonely Planet guidebooks cover the globe. There is an ever-growing list of books and information in a variety of media. Some things haven't changed. The main aim is still to make it possible for adventurous travellers to get out there – to explore and better understand the world.

At Lonely Planet we believe travellers can make a positive contribution to the countries they visit – if they respect their host communities and spend their money wisely. Every year 5% of company profit is donated to charities around the world.

THIS BOOK

This 4th edition of *St Petersburg* was researched and written by Tom Masters. The 3rd edition was written by Steve Kokker and the 1st and 2nd editions by Nick Selby. The guide was commissioned in Lonely Planet's London office, and produced in Melbourne. The project team included:

Commissioning Editors Fiona Christie & Imogen Franks
Coordinating Editor Sasha Baskett
Coordinating Cartographers Tony Fankhauser & Valentina Kremenchutskaya
Coordinating Layout Designer Margaret Jung
Assisting Editors & Proofreaders David Andrew, Sarah Bailey, Miriam Cannell, Kate Daly & Kate McLeod
Assisting Layout Designers Indra Kilfoyle & Laura Jane
Cover Designer Kristin Guthrie
Cover Artwork Yukiyoshi Kamimura
Managing Cartographer Mark Griffiths
Managing Editors Bruce Evans & Yvonne Byron
Freelance Layout Manager Kate McDonald
Mapping Development Paul Piaia
Project Manager Fabrice Rocher
Language Content Coordinator Quentin Frayne

Thanks to Sally Darmody, Ryan Evans, Mark Germanchis & Adriana Mammarella

Cover photographs by Lonely Planet Images: The Hermitage Building or Winter Palace in St Petersburg, by a part-frozen river, on a winter's afternoon, Steve Kokker (top); Women folk dancing in costume, Georgi Shablovsky (bottom); Chesma Church, Jonathan Smith (back).

Internal photographs by Jonathan Smith/Lonely Planet Images except for the following: p132 (#2), p138 (#1), p199 John S King; p138 (#3) Martin Moos; p195 Simon Richmond; p138 (#2), p190 Georgi S Shablovsky; p138 (#4) Alain Tomasini. All images are the copyright of the photographers unless otherwise indicated. Many of the images in this guide are available for licensing from Lonely Planet Images: www.lonelyplanet images.com.

THANKS

TOM MASTERS

First of all thanks to the two friends who first showed me St Petersburg: Leila Rejali and Volodya Dubilei. So much has changed since those wonderful few days a decade ago (for a start, I no longer prefer Moscow) but I'll never forget.

My perceptions and enjoyment of the city have been hugely influenced by a number of other people. Thanks first of all to Barnaby Thompson who gave me a job at the *St Petersburg Times* in 2000, which allowed me to make the city home for a while. Of course, thanks to my other colleagues at the paper, especially Simon Patterson who has shared more vodka and *shashlyk* with me around dives in the city than either of us would care to remember; to Galina Stolyarova for her tireless help and advice and to the inimitable Tom Rymer for his unusual take on city life. Others I owe a debt of gratitude to for good times include Andrei Cherepkov, Dmitry Dzhafarov, Dmitry Makarov, Marc de Mauny, Valera Katsuba, Tima Zaitsev, Artyom Lavrov, Yulia 'zhaba' Tarasova, Misha Krasanov, Des and Dima, Olga Makarova and Ismail Mamedov.

Specifically for this book, extra thanks to Steve and Nick for an excellent first three editions to work from, Imogen Franks and Fiona Christie at Lonely Planet London, and the production team in Melbourne.

Also to those who read and commented on my drafts and to those with whom I've had countless nights out in the city – Zeeba Sadiq (the Grafinya), Chris Courtney, Gray Jordan, Gabriel Gatehouse, Mike Christie, Alex Tampokopolous, Mima Garland, Gilly Argyle and my parents.

OUR READERS

Many thanks to the travellers who used the last edition and wrote to us with helpful hints, useful advice and interesting anecdotes:

Mark Allen, Chris Bendick, Nick Berry, Mark Brandt, Betty Ann Buss, Silvia Canavero, Yvonne Clark, Bradley Coates, Terry Collins, Marcel De Vroed, Janet Denye, Andy Diamond, Stephan Dorrenberg, Ian Douglas, V Downes, Mark Dudman, Mario Falzon, Eli Feiman, Tommaso Ferigo, Robert Freer, Julien & Florence Fuchs, Tim Gabelko, Karin Gallagher, Sebastian Giessmann, Rutger Graas,

Kate Hammond, Paul Hannon, Anna Harmala, Vernon Henderson, Lisa & Rune Henriksen, Marcel Huibers, Alex Ions, Hans W Joel, Dr Christopher Johnson, Alice Jones, Lisa Jones, Helene Karsen, Teja Klobucar, Tobias Kochsiek, Karin Kuhm, Rebecca Lange, Dr Andreas Langenohl, Lee Leatham, P A Macaitlem, Neil & Anna McLaughlin, Bob Moll, Shane Monks, Tony Monolakis, Tara Murphy, Paige & Gabriel Newby, Sara Normington, Markus Friebe Nuremberg, Monica Oancea, Shannon O'Loughlin, Lars Pardo, Julia Parfitt, Christina Paul, Sven Peters, Joseph Placek, Ortrun Poettering, Pam Poole, Aase Popper, Jan Raes, Karen & John Reilly, Susan Renkert, Chris Riede, Peter Robinson, Patti Ryan, David Salas, Richard Salveter, Rachel Savidge, Robert Schwandt, Craig & Mel Scutchings, Joshua Sharkey, Laura Sheahen, Pavlina Simkova, Juuk Slager, Per Stenius, Timo Stewart, Sandy Tarpinian, Jon Turpin, Leander Van Delden, Anne Warburton, Liz & Todd Werner, Alyson Witts, Jennie Wright

SEND US YOUR FEEDBACK

We love to hear from travellers – your comments keep us on our toes and help make our books better. Our well-travelled team reads every word on what you loved or loathed about this book. Although we cannot reply individually to postal submissions, we always guarantee that your feedback goes straight to the appropriate authors, in time for the next edition. Each person who sends us information is thanked in the next edition – and the most useful submissions are rewarded with a free book.

To send us your updates – and find out about Lonely Planet events, newsletters and travel news – visit our award-winning website: www.lonelyplanet.com/feedback

Note: We may edit, reproduce and incorporate your comments in Lonely Planet products such as guidebooks, websites and digital products, so let us know if you don't want your comments reproduced or your name acknowledged. For a copy of our privacy policy visit www.lonelyplanet.com/privacy.

Notes

Index

See also separate indexes for Eating (p233), Shopping (p234) and Sleeping (p234).

000 map pages
000 photographs

Index

000 map pages
000 photographs

EATING

SHOPPING

SLEEPING

000 map pages
000 photographs

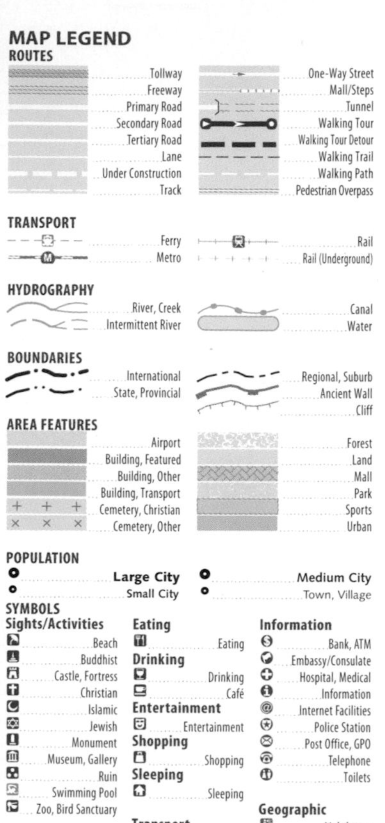

MAP LEGEND
ROUTES
Tollway
Freeway
Primary Road
Secondary Road
Tertiary Road
Lane
Under Construction
Track
One-Way Street
Mall/Steps
Tunnel
Walking Tour
Walking Tour Detour
Walking Trail
Walking Path
Pedestrian Overpass
TRANSPORT
Ferry
Metro
Rail
Rail (Underground)
HYDROGRAPHY
River, Creek
Intermittent River
Canal
Water
BOUNDARIES
International
State, Provincial
Regional, Suburb
Ancient Wall
Cliff
AREA FEATURES
Airport
Building, Featured
Building, Other
Building, Transport
Cemetery, Christian
Cemetery, Other
Forest
Land
Mall
Park
Sports
Urban
POPULATION
Large City
Small City
Medium City
Town, Village
SYMBOLS
Sights/Activities
Beach
Buddhist
Castle, Fortress
Christian
Islamic
Jewish
Monument
Museum, Gallery
Ruin
Swimming Pool
Zoo, Bird Sanctuary
Other
Other Site
Eating
Eating
Drinking
Drinking
Café
Entertainment
Entertainment
Shopping
Shopping
Sleeping
Sleeping
Transport
Airport, Airfield
Bus Station
Parking Area
Information
Bank, ATM
Embassy/Consulate
Hospital, Medical
Information
Internet Facilities
Police Station
Post Office, GPO
Telephone
Toilets
Geographic
Lighthouse
Lookout
River Flow

Map Section

AROUND ST PETERSBURG

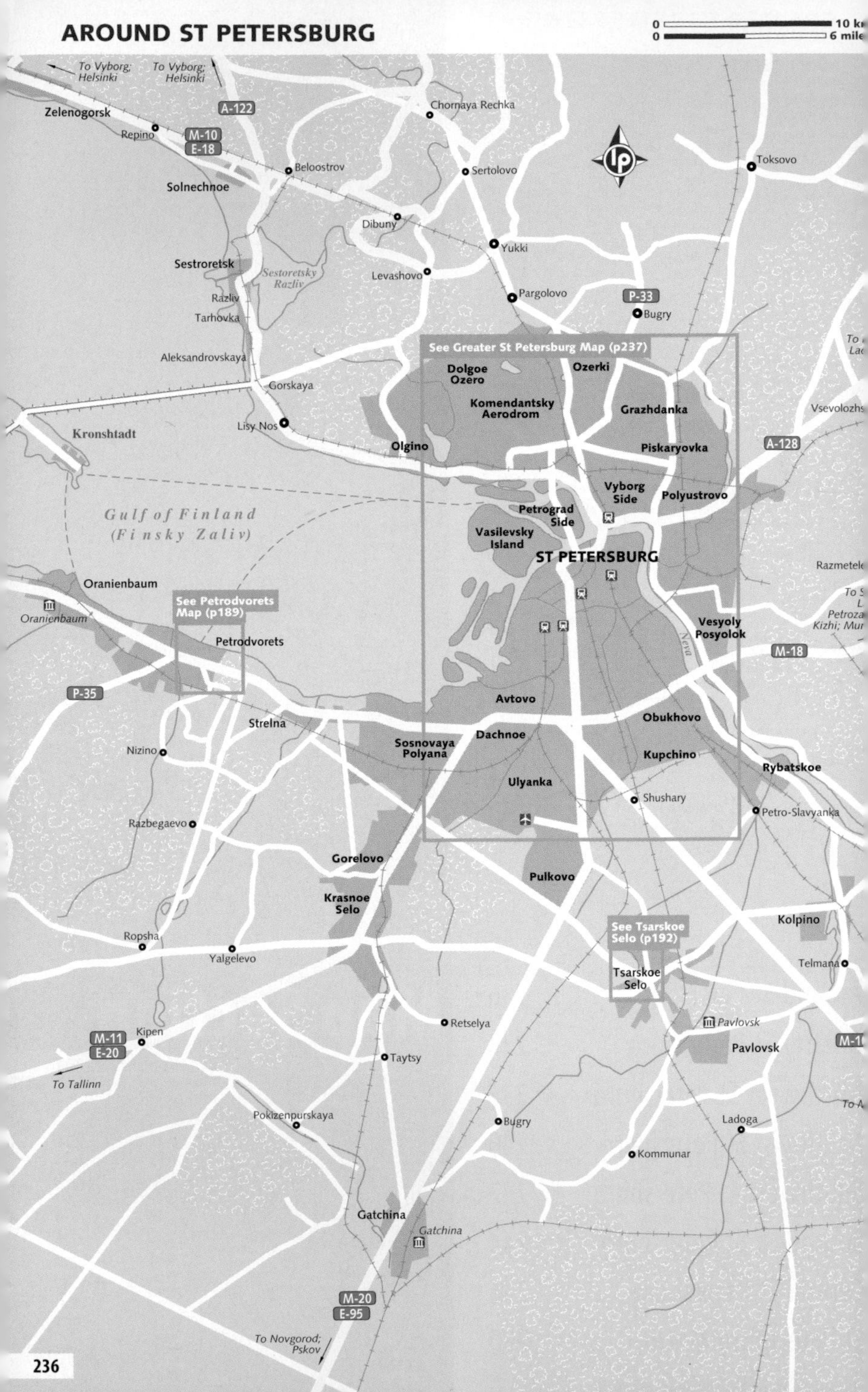

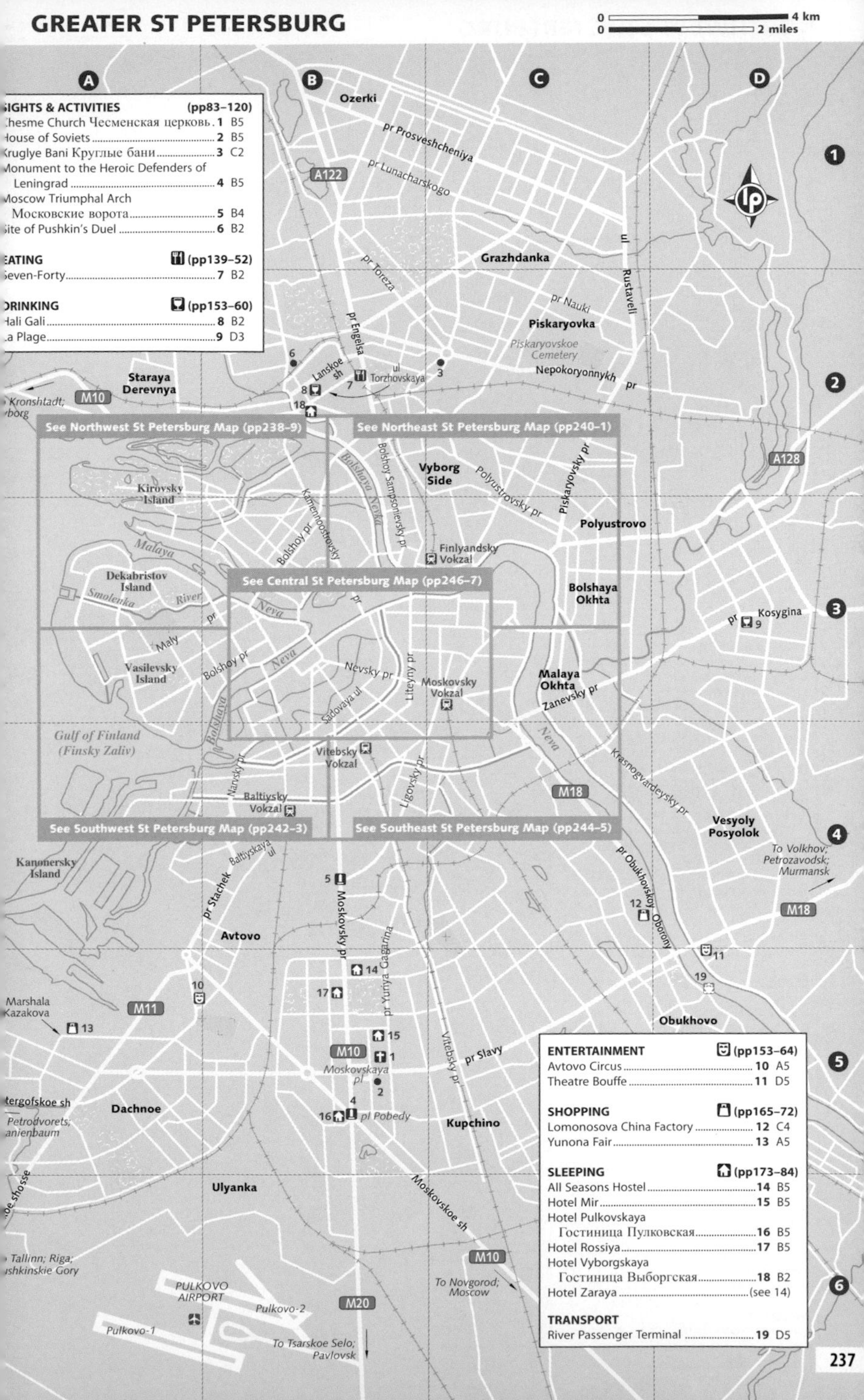

GREATER ST PETERSBURG
0 4 km
0 2 miles
A
B
C
D
1
2
3
4
5
6
IGHTS & ACTIVITIES (pp83–120)
hesme Church Чесменская церковь 1 B5
ouse of Soviets 2 B5
ruglye Bani Круглые бани 3 C2
onument to the Heroic Defenders of Leningrad 4 B5
oscow Triumphal Arch Московские ворота 5 B4
ite of Pushkin's Duel 6 B2
ATING (pp139–52)
even-Forty 7 B2
RINKING (pp153–60)
ali Gali 8 B2
a Plage 9 D3
ENTERTAINMENT (pp153–64)
Avtovo Circus 10 A5
Theatre Bouffe 11 D5
SHOPPING (pp165–72)
Lomonosova China Factory 12 C4
Yunona Fair 13 A5
SLEEPING (pp173–84)
All Seasons Hostel 14 B5
Hotel Mir 15 B5
Hotel Pulkovskaya Гостиница Пулковская 16 B5
Hotel Rossiya 17 B5
Hotel Vyborgskaya Гостиница Выборгская 18 B2
Hotel Zaraya (see 14)
TRANSPORT
River Passenger Terminal 19 D5
See Northwest St Petersburg Map (pp238–9)
See Northeast St Petersburg Map (pp240–1)
See Central St Petersburg Map (pp246–7)
See Southwest St Petersburg Map (pp242–3)
See Southeast St Petersburg Map (pp244–5)
Ozerki
pr Prosveshcheniya
pr Lunacharskogo
A122
Grazhdanka
ul Rustaveli
pr Toreza
pr Nauki
pr Engelsa
Piskaryovka
Piskaryovskoe Cemetery
Lanskoe sh
ul Torzhovskaya
Nepokoryonnykh pr
Staraya Derevnya
M10
Kronshtadt;
A128
Kirovsky Island
Bolshaya Nevka
Bolshoy Sampsonievsky pr
Vyborg Side
Polyustrovsky pr
Piskaryovsky pr
Kamennoostrovsky pr
Bolshoy pr
Polyustrovo
Finlyandsky Vokzal
Malaya Neva
Dekabristov Island
Smolenka River
Bolshaya Okhta
pr Kosygina
Maly pr
Vasilevsky Island
Bolshoy pr
Neva
Nevsky pr
Liteyny pr
Moskovsky Vokzal
Sadovaya ul
Malaya Okhta
Zanevsky pr
Bolshaya Neva
Gulf of Finland (Finsky Zaliv)
Vitebsky Vokzal
Narvsky pr
Ligovsky pr
Krasnogvardeysky pr
M18
Baltiysky Vokzal
Vesyoly Posyolok
To Volkhov; Petrozavodsk; Murmansk
Kanonersky Island
Baltiyskaya ul
pr Obukhovsky Oborony
pr Stachek
Moskovsky pr
Avtovo
pr Yuriya Gagarina
Marshala Kazakova
M11
Obukhovo
Vitebsky pr
pr Slavy
Moskovskaya pl
pl Pobedy
Dachnoe
Kupchino
Petrodvorets; Oranienbaum
Ulyanka
Moskovskoe sh
Tallinn; Riga; Pushkinskie Gory
To Novgorod; Moscow
PULKOVO AIRPORT
Pulkovo-2
Pulkovo-1
M20
To Tsarskoe Selo; Pavlovsk

NORTHWEST ST PETERSBURG

A
B
C
D
1
2
3
4
5
6
To Kronshtadt; Vyborg; Helsinki
ul Savushkina
Primorsky pr
Park 300-letiya Sankt Peterburga
3-y Elagin most
Bolshaya Nevka
31
3-y Yuzhny pr
Srednyaya Nevka
Rowing Canal
nab Martynova
Severnaya Doroga
Kemskaya ul
FINSKY ZALIV
Kirov Stadium
KRESTOVSK
Seaside Park of Victory (Primorsky Park Pobedy)
21
Yuzhnaya al
Yuzhnaya Doroga
Krestovsk
Malaya Nevka
Bol Petrovsky most
ul Savinoy
Petrovskaya kosa
Petrovskaya p
Admiralsky pr
Korablestroiteley ul
Uralskaya ul
Uralskaya
DEKABRISTOV
Nalichnaya ul
pr KIMa
per Dekabristov
Zheleznovodskaya
per Kahovskogo
pl Baltiyskih Yung
Zheleznozavods kaya ul
per Dekabristov
Novosmolenskaya nab
Primorskaya
ul Odoevskogo
Novosmolenskaya nab
Kams
ul Nahimova
SIGHTS & ACTIVITIES (pp83–120)
Amusement Park Аттракционы 1 H5
Buddhist Temple Буддисткий дацан 2 D1
Church of St John the Baptist Церковь Иоанна Предтечи 3 G1
Kamennoostrovsky Palace Каменноостровский дворец 4 H1
Kirov Museum Музей С М Кирова 5 H4
Kitchen Building Кухонный корпус 6 E1
Peter's Tree Дуб Петра I 7 F2
Planetarium Планетарий 8 H5
Polovtsev House Дача Половцова 9 F1
St Petersburg Zoo 10 H5
Sigmund Freud Museum of Dreams Музей Сновидений Сигмунда Фрейда 11 G5
Sphinx Monuments Сфинксы 12 G2
Stables Конюшенный корпус 13 E1
Toy Museum 14 G3
Yelagin Palace Елагинский дворец 15 E2
Yelizarov Museum 16 G3
EATING (pp139–52)
Byblos 17 F6
Ivanhoe Иванхое 18 G4
Kafe Tbilisi Кафе Тбилиси 19 H4
Na Zdorovye На Здоровье 20 G5
Russkaya Rybalka 21 C3
Staraya Derevnya 22 E1
U Tyoshi na Blinakh 23 H4
ENTERTAINMENT (pp153–64)
Jam Hall Na Petrogradskoy 24 H3
SHOPPING (pp165–72)
Staraya Kniga Старая Книга 25 G5
Sytny Market Сытный маркет 26 H4
SLEEPING (pp173–84)
Hotel Eurasia 27 H4
Leningrad Palace of Youth 28 G3
Prestige Hotel 29 F6
SPB Vergaz Hotel 30 F6
TRANSPORT
Boat Rental Stand Прокат лодок 31 D1
See Southwest St Petersburg Map (pp242–3)

0 1 km
0 0.5 miles
E
F
G
H
1
2
3
4
5
6
Dibunovskaya ul
ul Pokrusheva
Serebryakov per
ul Oskalenko
Shishmarevsky per
ul Akademika Shimanskogo
Chyornaya Rechka
To Hotel Vyborgskaya (250m)
nab Chyornoy Rechki
Primorsky pr
Ushakovsky most
nab Adm Ushakova
nab r Bolshoy Nevki
nab r Sredney Nevki
Bolshaya al
Letnyaya al
Glavnaya al
Kirov Park
YELAGIN
KAMENNY
Teatralnaya al
Polevaya al
2-ya Beryozovaya al
1-ya Beryozovaya al
1-y Elagin most
Bokovaya al
nab r Maloy Nevki
Kamennoostrovsky most
Lopushinsky Gardens
ul Akademika Pavlova
2-y Elagin most
Zapadnaya al
nab r Krestovki
Deputatskaya ul
Esperova ul
Olgina ul
Krestovsky Ostrov
Maly Krestovsky most
Malaya Nevka
Vyazemsky Gardens
Vyazemsky per
Kamennoostrovsky pr
ul Graftio
ul Chapygina
Prozhektornaya ul
Eletinskaya ul
Konstantinovsky pr
Grebnaya ul
Deputatskaya ul
pr Dinamo
Pesochnaya nab
ul Grota
Morskoy pr
ul Professora Popova
Dalya ul
Karpovsky per
Silin most
Karpovsky most
Krestovsky pr
Petrogradskaya ul
Barochnaya ul
nab r Karpovki
Karpovka
Geslerovsky most
ul Literatov
pr Medikov
See pp240–1
Dinamo Stadium
Sportivnaya ul
Vyazovaya ul
Petropavlovsky most
Krestovsky most
PETROGRAD SIDE
Ordinarnaya ul
Spartak Stadium
Levashovsky pr
Vsevoloda Vishnevskogo ul
Petrogradskaya
pl Lva Tolstogo
Lazersky most
nab Admirala Lazareva
Reznaya ul
Barochnaya ul
Lodeynopolskaya ul
Pudozhskaya ul
Plutalova ul
Barmaleeva ul
Polozova ul
ul Lenina
Maly pr
Podrezova ul
Podkovyrova ul
Bolshoy pr
Kamennoostrovsky pr
ul Malaya Zelenina
ul Bol Zelenina
Novoladozhskaya ul
Pionerskaya ul
Chkalovsky pr
Gatchinskaya ul
Lahtinskaya ul
PETROVSKY
Korpusnaya ul
Oranienbaumskaya ul
ul Lenina
Bol Raznochinnaya ul
Chkalovskaya
ul Shamsheva
Matveevsky per
Kronverkskaya ul
Zhdanovskaya ul
ul Krasnogo Kursanta
Ropshinskaya ul
Kolpinskaya ul
Malaya Pushkarskaya ul
Pushkarsky per
Petrovsky pr
Remeslennaya ul
Petrovsky per
Mal Raznochinnaya ul
Rybatskaya ul
Shyrokaya ul
Baltika Stadium
Bol Pushkarskaya ul
ul Voskova
Sytninskaya ul
Sytninskaya pl
Gimnazich per
Maly pr
Monchegorskaya ul
Sablinskaya ul
Petrovsky Park
nab r Zhdanovki
Zhdanovskaya ul
Pionerskaya ul
Vvedenskaya ul
ul Markina
Kronverksky pr
SERNY
Oftsersky per
Maly pr
Bolshoy pr
Lizy Chaykinoy
ul Blagoeva
MALAYA NEVA
See Central St Petersburg Map (pp246–7)
Sportivnaya
Odoevskogo
Sportivnaya
pr Dobrolyubova
Kronverkskaya nab
Bolshoy pr
Kronverksky pr
nab Makarova
PETROGRADSKY
nab r Smolenki
Mytninskaya nab
2-ya i 3-ya linii
4-ya i 5-ya linii
Maly pr
Birzhevoy most
nab Makarova
12-13 linii
10-11 linii
8-9 linii
6-7 linii
Syezdovskaya & 1-ya linii
Sredny pr
Vasilevsky
Vasileostrovskaya
See Southwest St Petersburg Map (pp242–3)

NORTHEAST ST PETERSBURG

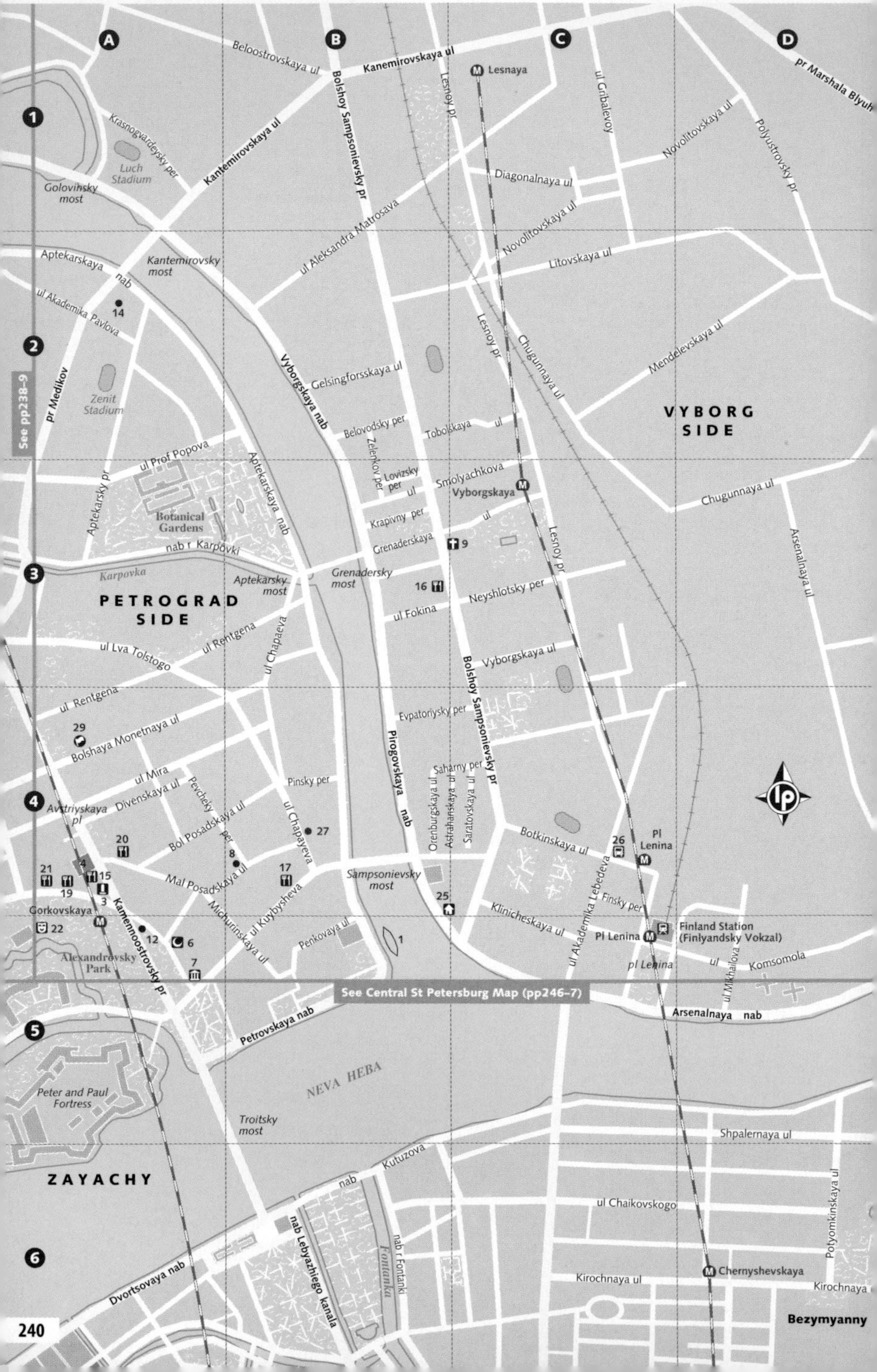

A B C D
1 2 3 4 5 6

Beloostrovskaya ul
Kanemirovskaya ul
Lesnaya
Bolshoy Sampsonievsky pr
Lesnoy pr
ul Gribalevoy
pr Marshala Blyuh
Krasnogvardeysky per
Luch Stadium
Kantemirovskaya ul
Novolitovskaya ul
Polyustrovsky pr
Golovinsky most
Diagonalnaya ul
ul Aleksandra Matrosova
Novolitovskaya ul
Aptekarskaya nab
Kantemirovsky most
Litovskaya ul
ul Akademika Pavlova
14
Lesnoy pr
Chugunnaya ul
Mendelevskaya ul
pr Medikov
Zenit Stadium
Vyborgskaya nab
Gelsingforsskaya ul
VYBORG SIDE
See pp238–9
Belovodsky per
Tobolskaya ul
ul Prof Popova
Zelenkov per
Lovizsky per
ul Smolyachkova
Aptekarsky pr
Aptekarskaya nab
Vyborgskaya
Chugunnaya ul
Botanical Gardens
Krapivny per
ul
Grenaderskaya
9
Arsenalnaya ul
nab r Karpovki
Karpovka
Aptekarsky most
Grenadersky most
16
Lesnoy pr
PETROGRAD SIDE
Neyshlotsky per
ul Fokina
ul Rentgena
ul Lva Tolstogo
ul Chapaeva
Vyborgskaya ul
Bolshoy Sampsonievsky pr
ul Rentgena
Evpatoriysky per
29
Bolshaya Monetnaya ul
Pirogovskaya nab
ul Mira
Saharny per
Pinsky per
Divenskaya ul
Pevcheky per
Orenburgskaya ul
Astrahanskaya ul
Saratovskaya ul
Avstriyskaya pl
Bol Posadskaya ul
ul Chapayeva
27
Botkinskaya ul
26
Pl Lenina
20
17
8
21
19
4
15
3
Mal Posadskaya ul
Sampsonievsky most
Gorkovskaya
Kamennoostrovsky pr
Michurinskaya ul
ul Kuybysheva
25
Finsky per
ul Akademika Lebedeva
22
12
6
Penkovaya ul
1
Klinicheskaya ul
Pl Lenina
Finland Station (Finlyandsky Vokzal)
Alexandrovsky Park
7
pl Lenina
ul Mikhailova
ul Komsomola
See Central St Petersburg Map (pp246–7)
Petrovskaya nab
Arsenalnaya nab
NEVA HEBA
Peter and Paul Fortress
Troitsky most
Shpalernaya ul
ZAYACHY
Kutuzova nab
ul Chaikovskogo
Potyomkinskaya ul
nab Lebyazhiego kanala
Fontanka
nab r Fontanki
Dvortsovaya nab
Chernyshevskaya
Kirochnaya ul
Kirochnaya
Bezymyanny

See Southeast St Petersburg Map (pp244–5)

SOUTHWEST ST PETERSBURG

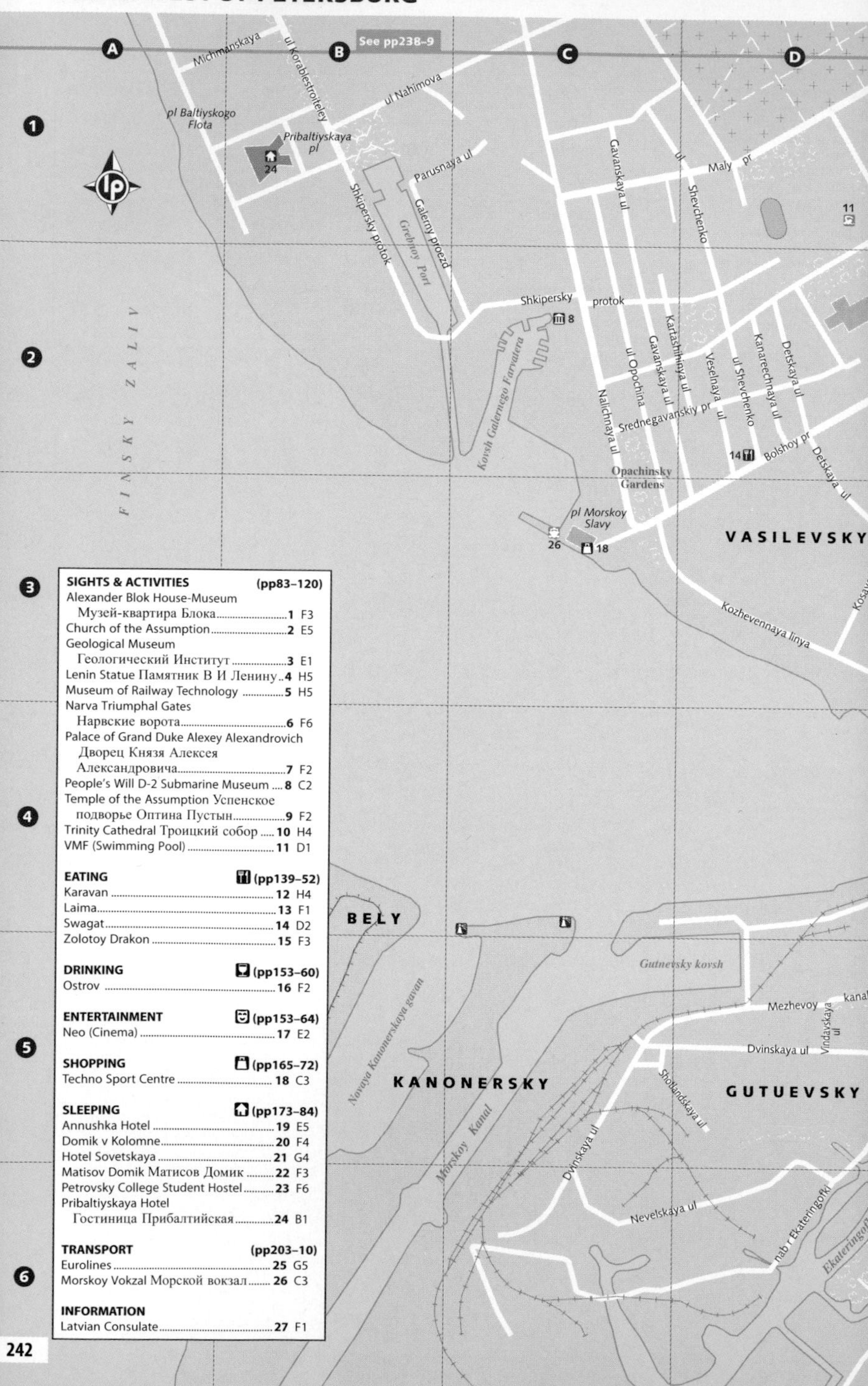

See pp238–9
A
B
C
D
1
2
3
4
5
6
Michmanskaya
ul Korablestroiteley
ul Nahimova
pl Baltiyskogo Flota
Pribaltiyskaya pl
Parusnaya ul
Shkipersky protok
Galerny proezd
Grebnoy Port
Gavanskaya ul
ul Shevchenko
Maly pr
Shkipersky protok
Kovsh Galernego Farvatera
Kartashihina ul
Gavanskaya ul
ul Opochina
Nalichnaya ul
Veselnaya ul
ul Shevchenko
Kanareechnaya ul
Detskaya ul
Srednegavanskiy pr
Bolshoy pr
Detskaya ul
Opachinsky Gardens
pl Morskoy Slavy
VASILEVSKY
Kosaya
Kozhevennaya linya
FINSKY ZALIV
BELY
Gutnevsky kovsh
Mezhevoy kanal
Vindavskaya ul
Dvinskaya ul
Novaya Kanonerskaya gavan
KANONERSKY
GUTUEVSKY
Sholiandskaya ul
Morskoy Kanal
Dvinskaya ul
Nevelskaya ul
nab r Ekateringofki
Ekateringofka
SIGHTS & ACTIVITIES (pp83–120)
Alexander Blok House-Museum Музей-квартира Блока 1 F3
Church of the Assumption 2 E5
Geological Museum Геологический Институт 3 E1
Lenin Statue Памятник В И Ленину 4 H5
Museum of Railway Technology 5 H5
Narva Triumphal Gates Нарвские ворота 6 F6
Palace of Grand Duke Alexey Alexandrovich Дворец Князя Алексея Александровича 7 F2
People's Will D-2 Submarine Museum 8 C2
Temple of the Assumption Успенское подворье Оптина Пустын 9 F2
Trinity Cathedral Троицкий собор 10 H4
VMF (Swimming Pool) 11 D1
EATING (pp139–52)
Karavan 12 H4
Laima 13 F1
Swagat 14 D2
Zolotoy Drakon 15 F3
DRINKING (pp153–60)
Ostrov 16 F2
ENTERTAINMENT (pp153–64)
Neo (Cinema) 17 E2
SHOPPING (pp165–72)
Techno Sport Centre 18 C3
SLEEPING (pp173–84)
Annushka Hotel 19 E5
Domik v Kolomne 20 F4
Hotel Sovetskaya 21 G4
Matisov Domik Матисов Домик 22 F3
Petrovsky College Student Hostel 23 F6
Pribaltiyskaya Hotel Гостиница Прибалтийская 24 B1
TRANSPORT (pp203–10)
Eurolines 25 G5
Morskoy Vokzal Морской вокзал 26 C3
INFORMATION
Latvian Consulate 27 F1

0 1 km
0 0.5 miles
See pp238–9
Vasileostrovskaya
Vasilevsky
NOVOADMIRATELSKY
Novaya Gollandiya
Kazansky
Kolomensky
MATISOV
Pokrovsky
BOLSHAYA NEVA
Bolshaya Neva
Moyka
Fontanka
Pryazhki
See Central St Petersburg Map (pp246–7)
See pp244–5
Sredny pr
Bolshoy pr
nab Leytenanta Shmidta
Universitetskaya nab
Admiralteyskaya nab
Angliyskaya nab
Dvortsovy most
most Leytenanta Shmidta
Izmaylovsky most
Izmaylovsky Gardens
Polsky Gardens
Park Yekateringoff
ul Truda
ul Dekabristov
pr Rimskogo-Korsakova
Sadovaya ul
Gorokhovaya ul
Voznesensky pr
Lermontovsky pr
nab reki Moyki
nab reki Fontanki
pr Moskvinoy
Rizhsky pr
Kurlyandskaya ul
nab Obvodnogo kanala
Staropetergophskiy pr
Narvsky pr
pr Stachek
Baltiyskaya
Baltic Station (Baltiysky Vokzal)
Narvskaya
Mitrofanevskoe shosse
1 Krasnoarmeyskaya ul
13 Krasnoarmeyskaya ul
8 Krasnoarmeyskaya ul
9 Krasnoarmeyskaya ul
10 Krasnoarmeyskaya ul
11 Krasnoarmeyskaya ul
12 Krasnoarmeyskaya ul

SOUTHEAST ST PETERSBURG

A
B
C
D
1
2
3
4
5
6
Bezymyanny
nab reki Moyki
Moyka
Fontanka
Sadovaya ul
Liteyny pr
ul Nekrasova
ul Vosstaniya
ul Zhukovskogo
Nevsky Pr
Gostiny Dvor
Nevsky pr
Ligovsky pr
6-ya Sovetskaya
5-ya Sovetskaya
4-ya Sovetskaya
3-ya Sovetskaya
2-ya Sovetskaya ul
Gorokhovaya ul
Griboedova Canal
nab reki Fontanki
Mayakovskaya
Pl Vosstaniya
Moscow Station
(Moskovsky Vokzal)
Spassky
Dostoevskaya
Vladimirskaya
Sadovaya
Sennaya Pl
Moskovsky pr
Zagorodny pr
Gorokhovaya ul
See Central St Petersburg Map (pp246–7)
Pushkinskaya
Vitebskaya pl
25
Vitebsk Station
(Vitebsky Vokzal)
Podezdnoy per
Pionerskaya pl
ul Marata
Zvenigorodskaya ul
Borovaya
ul Konstantina Zaslonova
8
13
Ligovsky Pr
Transportny per
ul Chernyakhovskogo
29
Romenskaya ul
27
ul Pechatnika Grigorieva
Voronezhskaya ul
ul Tyushina
Pavlogradsky per
Dnepropetrovskaya ul
9
Tekhnologichesky Institut
1 Krasnoarmeyskaya ul
26
ul Vvedenskogo kanala
Ruzovskaya ul
Mozhayskaya ul
Vereyskaya ul
Podolskaya ul
Serpukhovskaya ul
Bronnitskaya ul
Klimsky pr
Malodetskoselsky pr
17
Olimpia
28
See pp242–3
nab Obvodnogo kanala
Maslyany per
Ribinskaya ul
Borovaya ul
23
11
Prilukskaya ul
Kurskaya ul
Tambovskaya ul
24
19
21
Dnepropetrovskaya ul
Rasstannaya ul
Frunzenskaya
Zaozyernaya ul
Smolenskaya ul
Moskovsky pr
ul Krasutskogo
Kievskaya ul
ul Bulaysкogo
Chernigovskaya ul
Ligovsky pr

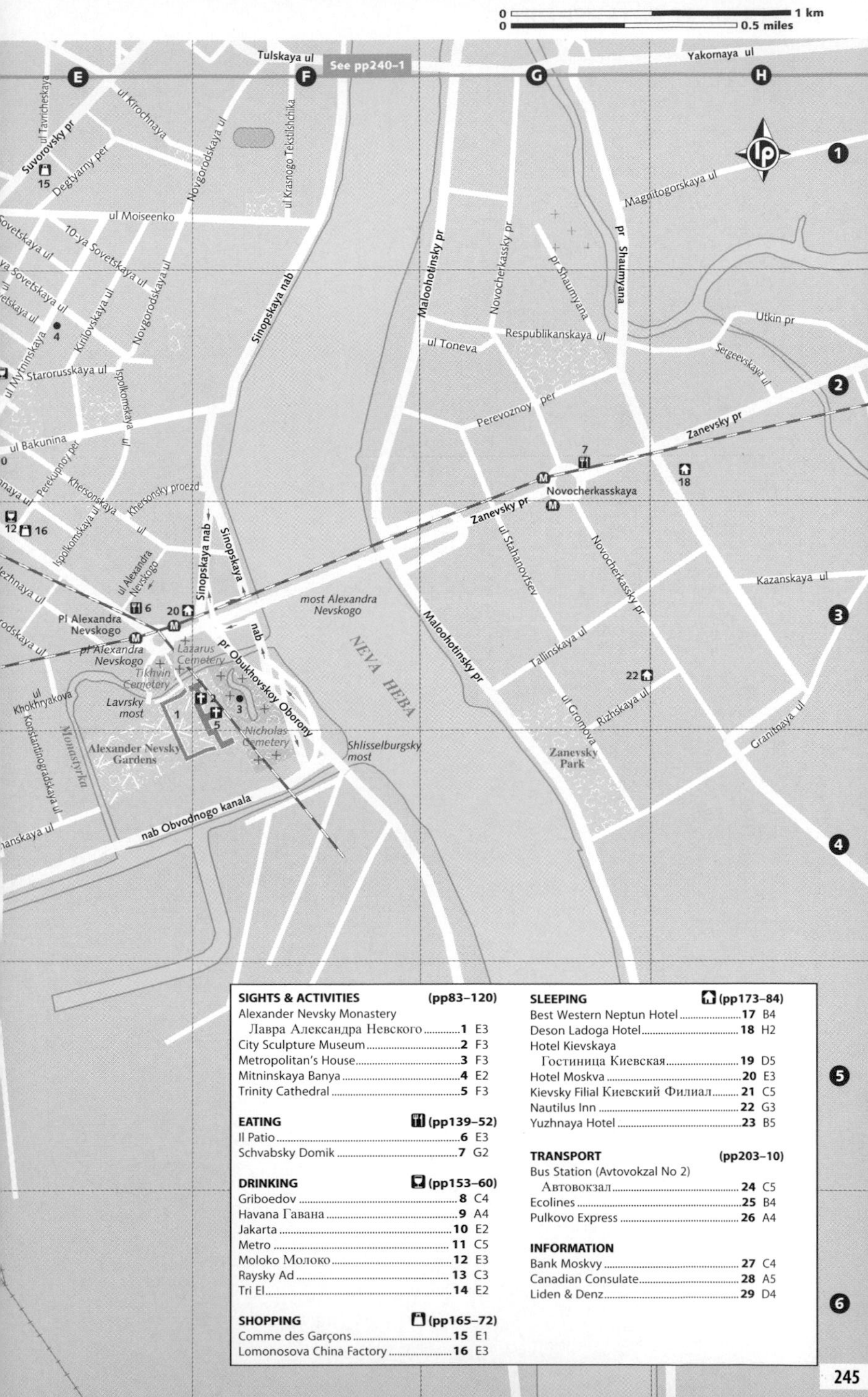
0 1 km
0 0.5 miles
Tulskaya ul
See pp240–1
Yakornaya ul
E
F
G
H
1
2
3
4
5
6
ul Tavricheskaya
Suvorovsky pr
ul Krochnaya
Degtyarny per
15
Novgorodskaya ul
ul Krasnogo Tekstilshchika
ul Moiseenko
10-ya Sovetskaya ul
Magnitogorskaya ul
pr Shaumyana
pr Shaumyana
Novocherkassky pr
Maloohotinsky pr
Sinopskaya nab
Kirilovskaya ul
Novgorodskaya ul
4
Utkin pr
Respublikanskaya ul
ul Toneva
Sergeevskaya ul
ul Mytninskaya
Starorusskaya ul
Ispolkomskaya ul
Perevoznoy per
Zanevsky pr
ul Bakunina
Perekupnoy per
7
18
Novocherkasskaya
Khersonskaya ul
Khersonsky proezd
Zanevsky pr
12
16
Ispolkomskaya ul
Sinopskaya nab
Sinopskaya nab
ul Stahanovtsev
Novocherkassky pr
Kazanskaya ul
ul Alexandra Nevskogo
6
20
most Alexandra Nevskogo
Pl Alexandra Nevskogo
pl Alexandra Nevskogo
Lazarus Cemetery
pr Obukhovskoy Oborony
NEVA
НЕВА
Maloohotinsky pr
Tallinskaya ul
Tikhvin Cemetery
22
ul Khokhryakova
Lavrsky most
1
2
3
5
ul Gromova
Rizhskaya ul
Granitnaya ul
Monastyrka
Alexander Nevsky Gardens
Nicholas Cemetery
Shlisselburgsky most
Zanevsky Park
ul Konstantinogradskaya
nab Obvodnogo kanala
SIGHTS & ACTIVITIES (pp83–120)
Alexander Nevsky Monastery Лавра Александра Невского 1 E3
City Sculpture Museum 2 F3
Metropolitan's House 3 F3
Mitninskaya Banya 4 E2
Trinity Cathedral 5 F3
EATING (pp139–52)
Il Patio 6 E3
Schvabsky Domik 7 G2
DRINKING (pp153–60)
Griboedov 8 C4
Havana Гавана 9 A4
Jakarta 10 E2
Metro 11 C5
Moloko Молоко 12 E3
Raysky Ad 13 C3
Tri El 14 E2
SHOPPING (pp165–72)
Comme des Garçons 15 E1
Lomonosova China Factory 16 E3
SLEEPING (pp173–84)
Best Western Neptun Hotel 17 B4
Deson Ladoga Hotel 18 H2
Hotel Kievskaya Гостиница Киевская 19 D5
Hotel Moskva 20 E3
Kievsky Filial Киевский Филиал 21 C5
Nautilus Inn 22 G3
Yuzhnaya Hotel 23 B5
TRANSPORT (pp203–10)
Bus Station (Avtovokzal No 2) Автовокзал 24 C5
Ecolines 25 B4
Pulkovo Express 26 A4
INFORMATION
Bank Moskvy 27 C4
Canadian Consulate 28 A5
Liden & Denz 29 D4

CENTRAL ST PETERSBURG

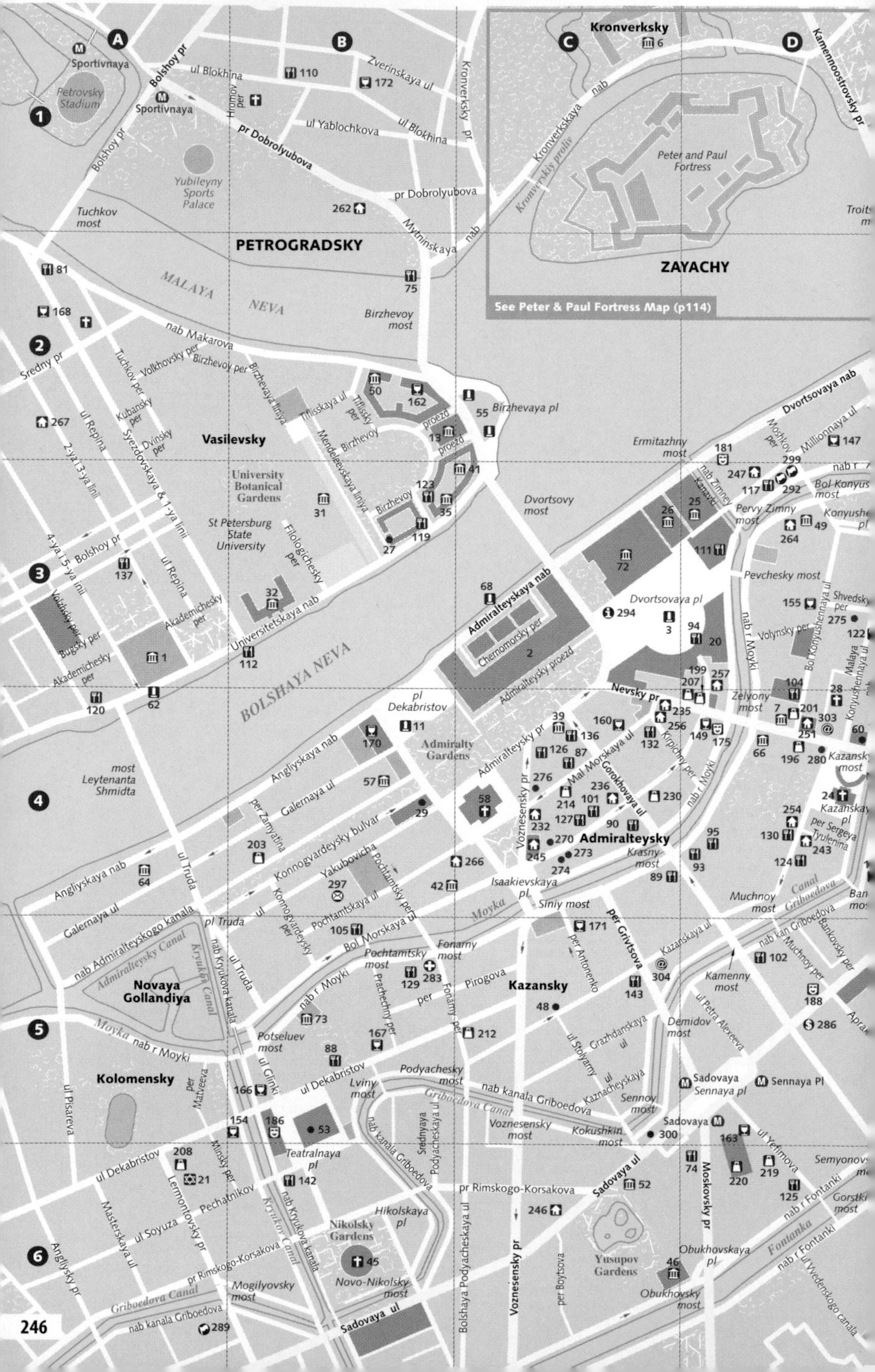

A
B
C
D
1
2
3
4
5
6

Kronverksky
Sportivnaya
Petrovsky Stadium
Bolshoy pr
ul Blokhina
Zverinskaya ul
Kronverksky pr
Kamennoostrovsky pr
Hromov per
Sportivnaya
ul Yablochkova
pr Dobrolyubova
Yubileyny Sports Palace
Tuchkov most
Mytninskaya nab
Kronverkskaya nab
Kronverksky proliv
Peter and Paul Fortress
Troitsky most
PETROGRADSKY
ZAYACHY
MALAYA NEVA
Birzhevoy most
See Peter & Paul Fortress Map (p114)
nab Makarova
Sredny pr
Tuchkov per
Volkhovsky per
Birzhevoy per
Birzhevaya liniya
Tifliskaya ul
Tifilisky per
Birzhevoy proezd
Birzhevaya pl
Kubansky per
Dvinsky per
Syezdovskaya & 1-ya linii
ul Repina
2-ya i 3-ya linii
Vasilevsky
University Botanical Gardens
St Petersburg State University
Mendeleevskaya liniya
Filologichesky per
Dvortsovy most
Dvortsovaya nab
Ermitazhny most
Moshkov per
Millionnaya ul
nab Zimney Kanavki
Bol Konyushennaya most
Pervy Zimny most
Konyushennaya pl
Pevchesky most
4-ya i 5-ya linii
Bolshoy pr
Volzhsky per
Bugsky per
Akademichesky per
Universitetskaya nab
Admiralteyskaya nab
Chernomorsky per
Admiralteysky proezd
Dvortsovaya pl
nab r Moyki
Volynsky per
Shvedsky per
Bol Konyushennaya ul
Malaya Konyushennaya ul
BOLSHAYA NEVA
Nevsky pr
Zelyony most
pl Dekabristov
Admiralty Gardens
Angliyskaya nab
Admiralteysky pr
Mal Morskaya ul
Gorokhovaya ul
Kirpichny per
Kazansky most
Kazanskaya pl
per Sergeya Tyulenina
most Leytenanta Shmidta
Galernaya ul
per Zamyatina
Konnogvardeysky bulvar
Voznesensky pr
Admiralteysky
Krasny most
ul Truda
Yakubovicha
Pochtamtsky per
Isaakievskaya pl
Siniy most
Moyka
Canal Griboedova
Muchnoy most
Bankovsky most
Angliyskaya nab
Galernaya ul
Konnogvardeysky per
Pochtamtskaya ul
pl Truda
nab Admiralteyskogo kanala
Admiralteysky Canal
Kryukov Canal
nab Kryukova kanala
Bol Morskaya ul
Pochtamtsky most
Fonarny most
per Antonenko
per Grivtsova
Kazanskaya ul
nab kan Griboedova
Bankovsky per
Muchnoy per
Novaya Gollandiya
nab r Moyki
Prachechny per
Pirogova per
Kazansky
Kamenny most
Apraksin
Moyka
Potseluev most
Fonarny per
Demidov most
ul Petra Alexeeva
Grazhdanskaya ul
ul Stolyarny
Kaznacheyskaya ul
Kolomensky
ul Glinki
ul Dekabristov
per Matveeva
Lviny most
Podyachesky most
nab kanala Griboedova
Sennoy most
Sadovaya
Sennaya pl
Sennaya Pl
ul Pisareva
Griboedova Canal
Voznesensky most
Kokushkin most
Sadovaya
ul Yefimova
Semyonovsky most
ul Dekabristov
Minsky per
Teatralnaya pl
Srednyaya Podyacheskaya ul
pr Rimskogo-Korsakova
Sadovaya ul
Moskovsky pr
nab r Fontanki
Gorstkin most
Masterskaya ul
ul Soyuza Pechatnikov
Lermontovsky pr
Nikolsky Gardens
Hikolskaya pl
Angliysky pr
pr Rimskogo-Korsakova
Novo-Nikolsky most
Bolshaya Podyacheskaya ul
Voznesensky pr
per Boytsova
Yusupov Gardens
Obukhovskaya pl
Fontanka
nab r Fontanki
ul Vvedenskogo canala
Mogilyovsky most
Griboedova Canal
nab kanala Griboedova
Sadovaya ul
Obukhovsky most

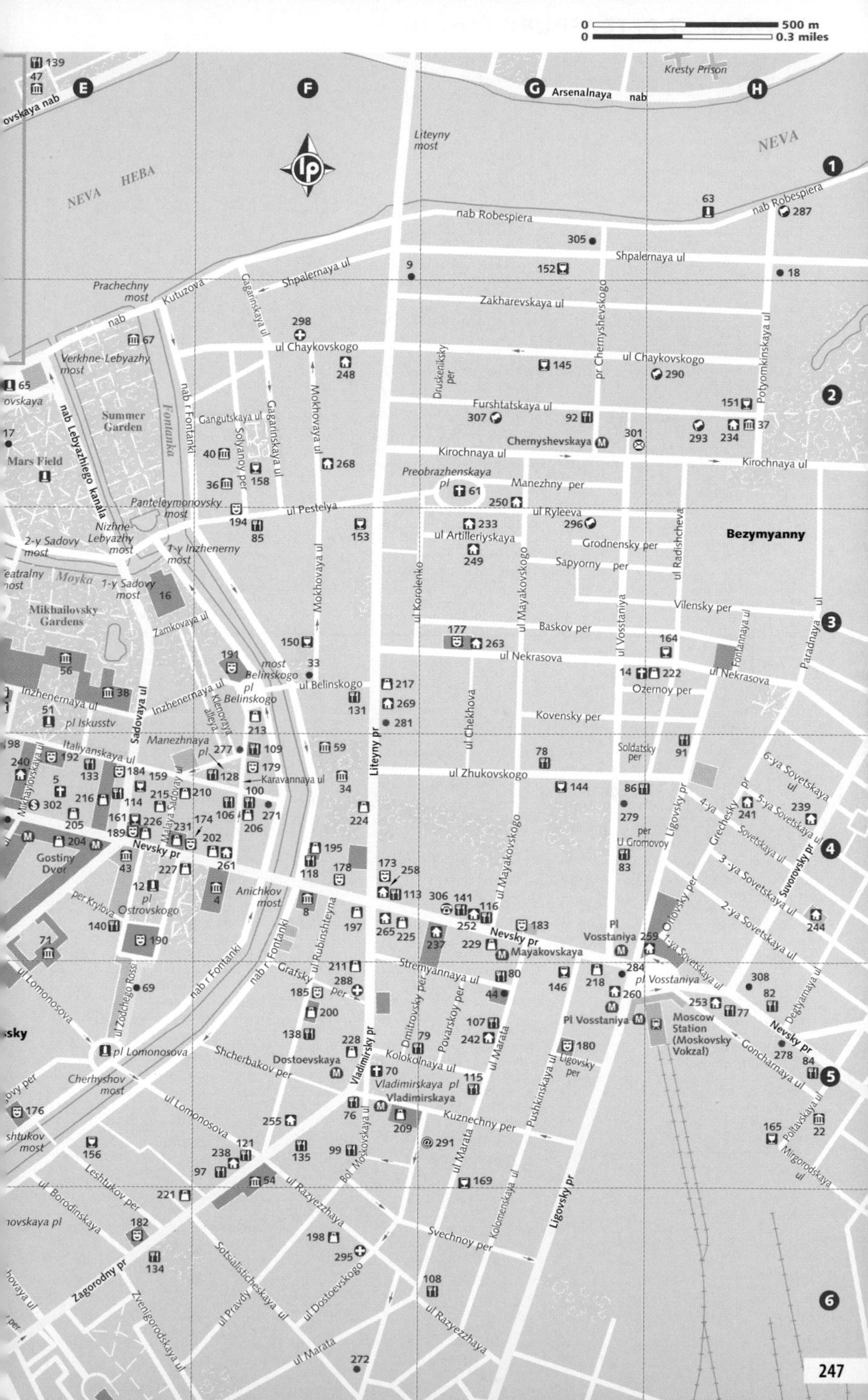

0 500 m
0 0.3 miles
Kresty Prison
Arsenalnaya nab
NEVA
NEVA
Liteyny most
nab Robespiera
Shpalernaya ul
Zakharevskaya ul
ul Chaykovskogo
Furshtatskaya ul
Kirochnaya ul
Chernyshevskaya
Preobrazhenskaya pl
Manezhny per
ul Pestelya
ul Ryleeva
ul Artilleriyskaya
Grodnensky per
Sapyorny per
Bezymyanny
Vilensky per
Baskov per
ul Nekrasova
Ozernoy per
Kovensky per
Soldatsky per
ul Zhukovskogo
Summer Garden
Mars Field
Mikhailovsky Gardens
Fontanka
Moyka
Nevsky pr
Gostiny Dvor
Anichkov most
Liteyny pr
Vladimirsky pr
Dostoevskaya
Vladimirskaya
Mayakovskaya
Pl Vosstaniya
Moscow Station (Moskovsky Vokzal)
Ligovsky pr
Suvorovsky pr
Zagorodny pr
ul Lomonosova
pl Lomonosova
Kuznechny per
Svechnoy per
ul Marata
ul Razyezzhaya

CENTRAL ST PETERSBURG (pp246–7)

SIGHTS & ACTIVITIES (pp83–120)

Academy of Arts Museum Музей Академия художеств **1** A3
Admiralty Адмиралтейство **2** C3
Alexander Column Александровская колонна **3** C3
Anichkov Palace Аничков дворец **4** F4
Armenian Church of St Catherine **5** E4
Artillery Museum **6** C1
Association of Free Artists Gallery **7** D4
Beloselsky-Belozersky Palace Дворец Белосельских-Белозерских **8** F4
Bolshoy Dom (Former KGB Headquarters) ГУВД Большой дом **9** F1
Brodsky House-Museum Музей-квартира Бродского **10** E3
Bronze Horseman Медный всадник **11** B4
Catherine the Great Statue **12** E4
Central Naval Museum (Old Stock Exchange) Центральный военно-морской музей **13** B2
Church of St John of Kronshtadt **14** G3
Church on Spilled Blood Храм Спас на Крови **15** E3
Engineers' Castle Инженерный замок **16** E3
Eternal Flame Вечный огонь **17** E2
Floral Exhibition Hall Выставочный зал **18** H1
Former Town Duma **19** E4
General Staff Building Здание главного штаба **20** D3
Grand Choral Synagogue Синагога **21** A6
GUVD Museum Музей ГУВД **22** H5
Kazachie Bani **23** E6
Kazan Cathedral Казанский собор **24** D4
Large Hermitage Большой Эрмитаж **25** D3
Little Hermitage Малый Эрмитаж **26** C3
Lomonosov Statue Памятник Ломоносову **27** B3
Lutheran Church **28** D4
Manege Central Exhibition Hall Манеж центральный выставочный зал **29** B4
Marble Palace **30** D2
Mendeleev Museum Музей Менделеева **31** B3
Menshikov Palace Дворец Меншикова **32** B3
Monolit **33** F3
Museum of Anna Akhmatova in the Fountain House Музей-квартира Анны Ахматовой **34** F4
Museum of Anthropology & Ethnography (Kunstkamera) Музей антропологии и этнографии **35** B3
Museum of Decorative & Applied Arts Музей прикладного искусства Штиглова **36** F2
Museum of Erotica **37** H2
Museum of Ethnography Музей этнографии **38** E3
Museum of Political History Annexe **39** C4
Museum of the Defence & Blockade of Leningrad Мемориальный Музей обороны и блокады Ленинграда **40** F2
Museum of Theatrical & Musical Arts Шереметьевский дворец (see 59)
Museum of Zoology Зоологический музей **41** C3
Nabokov Museum **42** B4
National Library of Russia Российская Национальная Библиотека **43** E4
Nevskie Bani **44** G5
Nikolsky Cathedral Никольский собор **45** B6
Old Yusupov Palace Юсуповский дворец **46** C6
Peter's Cabin Домик Петра Великого **47** E1
Planet Fitness **48** C5
Pushkin Flat-Museum Музей-квартира АС Пушкина **49** D3
Pushkin House (Institute of Russian Literature) Институт русской литературы (Пушкинский дом) **50** B2
Pushkin Statue **51** E3
Railway Museum **52** C6
Rimsky-Korsakov Conservatory Консерватория Римского-Корсакова **53** B5
Rimsky-Korsakov Flat-Museum Музей-квартира Римского-Корсакова **54** F5
Rostral Columns Ростральные колонны **55** C2
Russian Museum Русский музей **56** E3
Russian Vodka Museum **57** B4
St Isaac's Cathedral Исаакиевский собор **58** C4
Sheremetyev Palace **59** F4
Singer Building **60** D4
Spaso-Preobrazhensky Cathederal Спасо-Преображенский собор **61** G2
Sphinx Monuments Сфинксы **62** A4
Sphinx Monuments Сфинксы **63** H1
State Museum of the History of St Petersburg Музей истории Санкт-Петербурга **64** A4
Statue of Suvorov **65** E2
Stroganov Palace **66** D4
Summer Palace Летний дворец **67** E2
Tsar-Carpenter Statue **68** C3
Twelve Colleges (see 31)
Vaganova School of Choreography Хореографическое училище имени Вагановой **69** E5
Vladimirsky Cathedral **70** F5
Vorontsov Palace Воронцовский дворец **71** E4
Winter Palace Зимний дворец **72** C3
Yusupov Palace Юсуповский дворец **73** B5

EATING (pp139–52)

Adzhika Кафе Аджика **74** D6
Aquarel **75** B2
Bistro Ochag **76** F5
Bistrot Garçon **77** H5
Blin Donalt's **78** G4
Bliny Domik Блины домик **79** G5
Borsalino (see 232)
Cat **80** G5
Chardash **81** A2
Chaynaya Lozhka **82** H5
Chaynaya Lozhka **83** G4
Che **84** H5
Chornaya Koshka, Bely Kot **85** F3
Congo **86** G4
DaVinci **87** C4
Dvoryanskoye Gnezdo Дворянское Гнездо **88** B5
Fasol **89** C4
FX **90** C4
Gauranga **91** H4
Gin No Taki **92** G2
Harbin **93** D4
Hermitage Restaurant **94** D3
Herzen Institute Canteen **95** D4
Il Patio **96** E4
Imbir **97** F5
Kalinka Malinka **98** E4
Kashmir **99** F5
Kavkaz **100** F4
Khristofor Христофор **101** C4
Kilikia **102** D5
Kristoff (see 255)
Kyoto **103** D5
La Strada **104** D4
Landskrona (see 237)
Le Paris **105** B5
Mama Roma **106** F4
Marius Pub **107** G5
Matrosskaya Tishina Матросская Тишина **108** G6
Milano **109** F4
Nash Piter **110** B1
NEP **111** D3
New Island **112** B3
Nyam Nyam **113** F4
Onegin **114** E4
Orient Express **115** G5
Planeta Sushi **116** G4
Pogreba Monakha **117** D3
Propaganda **118** F4
Restoran **119** B3
Russian Vodka Museum Traktir (see 57)
Russky Kitsch **120** A4
Shinok **121** F5
Shyolk **122** D3
Staraya Tamozhnya Старая таможня **123** B3
Sukawati **124** D4
Sumeto **125** D6
Tandoor **126** C4
Taverna Oliva **127** C4
Teremok **128** F4
The Idiot **129** B5
Tinkoff **130** D4
Tolstiy Frayer (II) **131** F3
Tolstiy Frayer **132** C4
Tri **133** E4
Troitsky Most **134** E6
U Tyoshi Na Blinakh У Тёщи на Блинах **135** F5
Udachny Vystrel **136** C4
Ustrichny Bar **137** A3
Vanil **138** F5
Yakitoriya **139** E1
Yakitoriya **140** E4
Yolki Palki **141** G4
Za Stsenoy **142** B6
Zov Ilyicha **143** C5

DRINKING (pp153–60)

All Star Café **144** G4
Café Rico **145** G2

CENTRAL ST PETERSBURG (pp246–7)

ST PETERSBURG METRO

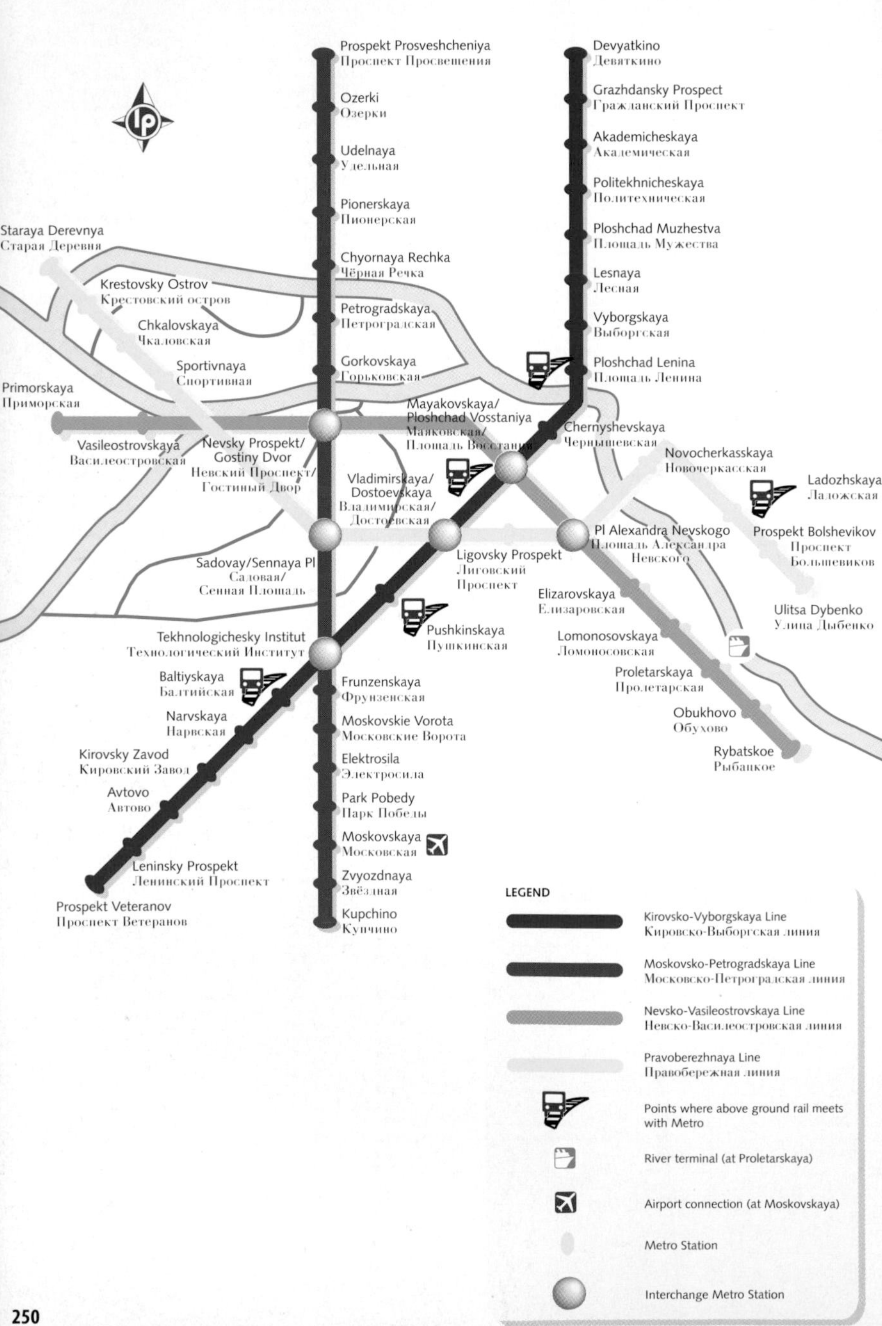
Prospekt Prosveshcheniya
Проспект Просвещения
Ozerki
Озерки
Udelnaya
Удельная
Pionerskaya
Пионерская
Chyornaya Rechka
Чёрная Речка
Petrogradskaya
Петроградская
Gorkovskaya
Горьковская
Devyatkino
Девяткино
Grazhdansky Prospect
Гражданский Проспект
Akademicheskaya
Академическая
Politekhnicheskaya
Политехническая
Ploshchad Muzhestva
Площадь Мужества
Lesnaya
Лесная
Vyborgskaya
Выборгская
Ploshchad Lenina
Площадь Ленина
Staraya Derevnya
Старая Деревня
Krestovsky Ostrov
Крестовский остров
Chkalovskaya
Чкаловская
Sportivnaya
Спортивная
Primorskaya
Приморская
Vasileostrovskaya
Василеостровская
Nevsky Prospekt/
Gostiny Dvor
Невский Проспект/
Гостиный Двор
Mayakovskaya/
Ploshchad Vosstaniya
Маяковская/
Площадь Восстания
Chernyshevskaya
Чернышевская
Novocherkasskaya
Новочеркасская
Ladozhskaya
Ладожская
Vladimirskaya/
Dostoevskaya
Владимирская/
Достоевская
Pl Alexandra Nevskogo
Площадь Александра
Невского
Prospekt Bolshevikov
Проспект
Большевиков
Sadovay/Sennaya Pl
Садовая/
Сенная Площадь
Ligovsky Prospekt
Лиговский
Проспект
Elizarovskaya
Елизаровская
Ulitsa Dybenko
Улица Дыбенко
Pushkinskaya
Пушкинская
Lomonosovskaya
Ломоносовская
Tekhnologichesky Institut
Технологический Институт
Proletarskaya
Пролетарская
Baltiyskaya
Балтийская
Frunzenskaya
Фрунзенская
Obukhovo
Обухово
Narvskaya
Нарвская
Moskovskie Vorota
Московские Ворота
Rybatskoe
Рыбацкое
Kirovsky Zavod
Кировский Завод
Elektrosila
Электросила
Avtovo
Автово
Park Pobedy
Парк Победы
Moskovskaya
Московская
Leninsky Prospekt
Ленинский Проспект
Zvyozdnaya
Звёздная
Prospekt Veteranov
Проспект Ветеранов
Kupchino
Купчино
LEGEND
Kirovsko-Vyborgskaya Line
Кировско-Выборгская линия
Moskovsko-Petrogradskaya Line
Московско-Петроградская линия
Nevsko-Vasileostrovskaya Line
Невско-Василеостровская линия
Pravoberezhnaya Line
Правобережная линия
Points where above ground rail meets with Metro
River terminal (at Proletarskaya)
Airport connection (at Moskovskaya)
Metro Station
Interchange Metro Station